Andrew Gayed

QUEER WORLD MAKING

CONTEMPORARY MIDDLE EASTERN DIASPORIC ART

University of Washington Press Seattle

Queer World Making was supported by a grant from the McLellan Endowment, established through the generosity of Martha McCleary McLellan and Mary McLellan Williams.

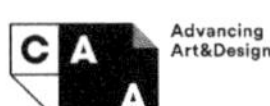

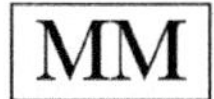

Publication of this book has also been aided by a grant from the Millard Meiss Publication Fund of CAA.

Design by Mindy Basinger Hill

Composed in Minion Pro, ITC Avant Garde Gothic Pro, ITC Avant Garde Gothic W1G

28 27 26 25 24 5 4 3 2 1

Printed and bound in the United States of America

UNIVERSITY OF WASHINGTON PRESS *uwapress.uw.edu*

LIBRARY OF CONGRESS CONTROL NUMBER: 2023951268

ISBN 9780295752297 (paperback)
ISBN 9780295752303 (ebook)

∞ This paper meets the requirements of ANSI/NISO Z39.48-1992 (Permanence of Paper).

Dedicated to those
of you who have been made
to feel lesser for living
your true authentic selves.
I see you, you are important,
and this book is for us.

Also dedicated
to my chosen family
for lifting me up,
being there for me,
and continually being
a positive part
of my life.

CONTENTS

ILLUSTRATIONS

Color plates follow page 154.

I would like to thank the Social Sciences and Humanities Research Council for supporting my graduate research and awarding me the Joseph-Armand Bombardier Canada Graduate Scholarship for both my masters and doctoral studies. I would also like to acknowledge the generous funding from various departments at Carleton University and York University, including the School of Art, Media, Performance, and Design; the York Centre for Asian Research; the Nathanson Centre on Transnational Human Rights; and the Faculty of Graduate Studies. It is through their generous support that I was funded to present my doctoral research at conferences before Canadian audiences as well as internationally at the University of Oxford, Harvard University, University of California Berkeley, the British Museum, St. Petersburg State University, and the Salzburg International Academy of Fine Arts in an effort to develop these ideas.

Thank you to the adjudication committee at York University for awarding me the distinguished Provost Dissertation Scholarship for an outstanding doctoral project, and to the provincial adjudication committee for awarding me the Ontario Graduate Scholarship for this research. Notably, the School of Art, Media, Performance, and Design, as well as the incredible faculty within the Visual Art department, truly encouraged me to develop and grow this research to its highest potential, and I am grateful to them for supporting me and believing in my work.

A special thank-you to the two members of my PhD cohort, Siobhan Angus and Vanessa Nicholas, who were foundational to my success in the program. Thank you for reading more drafts of my dissertation than I can count and for your endless support, generosity, and love that helped get us through to the finish line. I would also like to thank Dr. Danielle Blab for her kindness and generosity in editing my doctoral dissertation and for her friendship over the years.

Chapter 7 of this book is a revised version of an article within the *Routledge Handbook on Middle Eastern Diasporas*, edited by Dalia Abdelhady and Ramy Aly (New York: Routledge, 2022). A revised version of chapter 5 appeared in *Unsettling Canadian Art History*, edited by Erin Morton (Montreal: McGill-Queen's University Press, 2022). I am grateful to these editors for their feedback and to Routledge and McGill-Queen's University Press for publishing this earlier research and supporting my scholarship.

It is important that I thank my many wonderful students who contributed to my research, learning, and growth. I especially want to thank the OCAD University graduate students from my master's class in Transnational Queer Theory. Graduate students like Veronica Waechter, Paulete Poitras, Sujeet Sennik, and Samuel McGuire were a major inspiration in finishing this book, and our weekly seminars became a generative space to develop and expand these ideas together. I would also like to thank my undergraduate research assistant Kelly Xu and my graduate research assistant Kyrie Robinson, who helped me immensely when I was in the final stages of writing this book.

Foremost, I would like to thank my incredible supervisory committee, Dr. Hong Kal, Dr. Amar Wahab, and Dr. Ming Tiampo. Through their mentorship, they devoted their time to fostering my research and helped me grow as a scholar and researcher. Collectively, they so generously supported my project and worked enthusiastically with me to encourage and develop this research, guiding me to get the most out of my graduate degrees. I would like to thank them for believing in me and for providing close mentorship along this journey. I am incredibly grateful to Dr. Ming Tiampo and Dr. Amar Wahab for seeing potential in me and investing their time and energy even after I had graduated to guide me through the academic job market. Your mentorship provided some of the most valuable experiences of my life, and your dedication gave me the confidence to continue. My success is your success, and I could not have done any of this without your guidance.

Also, a thank-you to Dr. Jessica Mace for being the chair of my doctoral defense committee, and a thank-you to Dr. Zulfikar Hirji for being the outside member on my defense committee. I would like to express my appreciation to my external reader, Dr. Gayatri Gopinath from New York University's Center for the Study of Gender and Sexuality, for her support during the defense of my thesis. I owe Dr. Gopinath a debt of gratitude for believing in me and my research from an early stage, and for continuing her mentorship during my postdoctoral appointment at New York University's Center for the Study of Gender and Sexuality, where I finished a final chapter of this book. Thank you, Dr. Gopinath, for taking the time to meet me when I was only starting my doctoral research; thank you for seeing the value in my work and for mentoring me through the next stages of my journey after I graduated from the PhD program. I am grateful to have had the opportunity to learn from you and grow with you by my side. Your investment in me meant the world.

I would lastly like to acknowledge my loving partner, Mathieu Bélanger, for providing support and encouragement throughout the entire journey from when we first met during our undergraduate degrees, throughout graduate school, and during this book project. Your patience, love, and humor enabled me to complete this research, and you pushed me to always do my best. Your love for me has been a driving force in my life, and when at times it felt like I was abandoned and untethered in this world, I always found my grounding in you. You are the source of my strength, and I would not have the compassion and empathy to do this work without your constant love and support. You challenge me every day and encourage me to grow into my best self. You helped teach me what chosen family meant, and you always encouraged me to live my true authentic self. I am so grateful to have you as my best friend and to be on this journey together. We have achieved many milestones while developing this research; my dreams came true with you by my side, and the publication of this book will be just one of many more milestones to come.

It is by the generosity of these individuals that my research was made possible, and I am truly grateful to have been supported so encouragingly throughout the tenure of my graduate research at Carleton University, York University, and New York University, which has ultimately led to my appointment as a faculty member at the Ontario College of Art and Design University (OCADU).

AUTOTHEORY
A QUEER FEMINIST PRACTICE

> Autotheory has emerged as a term to describe the practices of engaging with theory, life, and art from the perspective of one's lived experiences; an emergent term, it is very much in the zeitgeist of contemporary feminist and queer feminist cultural production today. While the term "autotheory" circulates specifically in relation to third-wave and fourth-wave feminist texts, such as American writer Maggie Nelson's *The Argonauts* and American filmmaker and art writer Chris Kraus's *I Love Dick*, theorizing from the first person is well established within the genealogies of feminist practice.
>
> LAUREN FOURNIER, "Sick Women, Sad Girls, and Selfie Theory"

For the purpose of this book, I feel it important to be forthcoming with my own subject position and my connection to the research. Raised as a Coptic Orthodox Christian, I unfortunately always knew that my sexuality would never be reconciled with my cultural background and with my religious upbringing. Born in Toronto from parents who immigrated to Canada from Egypt, I identify as a first-generation Egyptian Canadian. While I tried hiding my sexuality from my family and the community for a number of years, it became clear that the articulation of both my Arabness and my sexuality was nonnormative and nonconforming. Praying the gay away was a common occurrence in my household even if it was not always named, and this lifelong internalization of shame, fear, and guilt took many forms. I would regularly wake up to priests in my home waiting to pray for me and explain the damnation of the gays; I was chased around the house I grew up in with holy water on more than one occasion; I would secretly be given holy water, oil, and blessings as though my soul needed curing and an exorcism; and violent family interventions where I was locked in a car with a family member outlining each passage of the Bible that condemns homosexuality became common events I encountered when visiting my family even after I moved away for university. After the worst fears of my parents were confirmed and I was pushed out of the closet, a cycle of emotional abuse began to be more prevalent and defined our future relationship.

In the summer of 2013, I was outed by social media (Twitter), the one place

I felt where I had the liberty to be open and follow queer organizations and human rights campaigns from around the world. This is where my father found out my association with queerness and confirmed what had been unspoken and ignored in my family for many years. In fact, when I was blatantly asked by my father that day if I was gay, I responded by telling my parents that they should not ask questions they were not ready to hear the answers to. This was followed by yelling and tears from both my parents, and I felt immediately unsafe, as I was only visiting my family for the weekend at the time while I was away for school. I was left to gather whatever personal possessions I could quickly find and throw them in my suitcase, and I hurriedly left the house even without my shoes as I needed to find my way from the suburbs to downtown Toronto in order to catch an overnight bus back to Ottawa, where I was living for school. Briskly walking through the streets alone in a panic, I realized my worst fears had come true. I wandered the streets of my suburb walking great distances as I tried to make sense of the situation, phoning everyone I could as I tried going through the backup plans I already had in place if I was ever found out and put in an unsafe situation while visiting my family. I remember sitting in a children's playground at my old elementary school, feeling the coarse sand between my toes as I sat there, not knowing how I was supposed to move forward alone. Unfortunately, in this time of urgency, none of these contingency plans seemed to work, but I was eventually able to get myself to downtown Toronto's bus terminal, which I felt was my only safe haven at the time. That overnight bus ride back to Ottawa was a painful one, and I remember being ashamed and embarrassed by my disheveled appearance and the dirtiness of my feet. I cried continuously as I left Toronto sitting at the back of the bus trying to be unnoticed, but I felt like I was finally going to be okay. When I arrived in Ottawa in the middle of the night, I was greeted by my boyfriend, Mathieu, and one of my closest friends, Leah, who were both there to give me a hug as soon as I got off the bus and make me feel loved again. We stayed up all night in friendship, laughter, and love, and it was at this moment that I truly understood what chosen family meant. Even though I was disowned by my parents that night, I felt the love and warmth of my family by the selected people I chose to have in my life.

After this event, it became clear that I was no longer a part of my family unit, and my parents would do things to make this clear, like send me my old mail but violently cross out my last name from the envelopes. My parents emptied our joint bank account while I was in undergrad to try and financially blackmail me into submission, and thus began their more tactical strategies to try to bring me to homelessness and dropping out of school if it meant returning to them and no longer being gay. I had to survive since this moment, and a trauma response kicked in to urgently prevent their wishes from coming true. I was continuously being told that there was no room for me in this world as I am, and in that moment I chose life and strived to make room for myself, vowing not to let my family and community silence me. In spite of them, I worked several jobs just to afford tuition, I was able to maintain my rent because of my loving partner who I lived with at the time, and I got myself through undergrad with honors in order to make it to graduate school with enough funding to sustain myself. These were all things my biological family did not want to be possible without them, especially since I did these things while living my true authentic self, and they still resent the success I have based on the openly gay life I live.

When I was thrown out and disowned by my family unit, this was followed by being abandoned by my cultural community, losing most of the friends I had grown up with. The common theme that reoccurred was that I was disgracing the family and that my parents had immigrated to Canada for a better life for their children, one they did not see in my queer identity. Blinded by homophobia, my immediate and extended family disowned me, and I was no longer a part of their family unit in any way. I then became excommunicated by my cultural community, with my friends from the Coptic church community no longer associating with me. Members of the church would send anonymous hate mail to me and my family, chastising them for my existence. While these harmful acts of violence were meant to tell me that there was no room for me within my cultural community or even within my culture in general, it was difficult finding solace in a queer community that saw me only as a victim of a "barbaric" Arab upbringing. I was surrounded by coming out stories that sounded nothing like mine, and I felt isolation from both my family who disowned me, my cultural community who abandoned me, and a queer community who wanted to accept me but didn't quite understand my experiences.

In a continual process of being outed and coming out, it felt as though in one fell swoop I had lost not just my family and cultural community but my overall connection to my culture as well. It felt difficult accessing my culture from a basic place of language when I had fewer people around me to speak Arabic with; eating my cultural food became more of a challenge when I could not simply phone my mother for her recipe; and my connection to Egypt, what was always considered our homeland by my immigrant parents, became even more obscured. The violence I experienced during this rupture manifested itself on a deeply emotional level not only for the abandonment I experienced by those closest to me but also by the implications that my cultural identity as an Egyptian was being held hostage by my family and my community, contingent upon my heterosexuality. This feeling of contingency, and that I was being obstructed from even accessing my cultural identity to some degree, led to a fraught search for cultural heritage outside of just my family and lineage. The emotional blackmail I experienced from my family and friends made it very clear to me that their message was "Egyptians don't behave like this," and that if I were gay, I couldn't be a good or "real" Egyptian. The void left behind from my culture within my day-to-day, culinary, linguistic, and community experiences created its own sort of trauma, where I internalized what it was to be less Egyptian than those I grew up with. My journey to discover what my Egyptian cultural background can look like with my queerness has been fraught with emotional abuse by those around me in an effort to demonstrate that their love for me was always conditional on my heterosexuality, and that there were limits to the love my parents, brother, cousins, aunts, uncles, and friends had for me if I were gay. To this day, this trauma still haunts me, and the emotional abuse inflicted by those closest to me created a psychological isolation that was part of their tactic they hoped would change my queerness. Not only was I isolated physically from friends and a community I had grown up with, but I was also emotionally isolated by the cultural gatekeepers of my Egyptian identity. These calculated moves by my family and community to make me feel alone in an effort to break me led to a lifelong search for reconciling where I feel safe and how I can incorporate Arabic speakers and Egyptian culture within these spaces of safety.

On this journey of self-acceptance and discovery, I completed a bachelor of fine arts degree in visual arts with a minor in women's and gender studies.

As an artist, I always produced work that was autobiographical and about the homosexual experience in the Middle East. I did not know it at the time, but this flourished into my master's degree in art history, where I also looked at how political art is being used by the Middle Eastern diaspora in North America by artists (like myself) to cope with issues of sexuality and trauma. My PhD in art history and visual culture was another part of my healing process; like all of the schooling I have done up until this point, it helped me not only to research and understand my situation better but also to contribute to the scholarship in an effort to fill in the gaps where my diasporic experience is not accounted for. This became an incredibly powerful tool for me in that it helped me to know that I am not alone in my experience and allowed me to actively educate and voice my story in ways that are beneficial to myself and others.

Because of my own subject position, I see the importance of art's dialogical potential to open, foster, and make accessible the knowledge surrounding marginalized subjects. Coming to terms with my own subject position, a queer diasporic person of color, was a conflicting task, caught between a stringent cultural practice and being socialized in a largely Eurocentric environment. The aim of my work is not only to advance research on global history by introducing new methods for the intersectional study of sexuality and visual culture, but I also strive to introduce an interdisciplinary theorization to Middle Eastern contemporary art with diaspora theory in order to help better understand the human rights issues surrounding sexual identity and cultural production.

Stuart Hall is joined by many scholars who believe in the production of identity as an always-changing process and never-ending performance. Theorists such as Jacques Derrida, Judith Butler, Gilles Deleuze, José Esteban Muñoz, and others have developed ways of articulating the changing production of one's identity and self-identification. From Butler's performativity to Muñoz's disidentification, all of these theorists seek to deconstruct how dominant ideology negotiates minority culture and shapes the identities of the social group Gayatri Spivak refers to as the "subaltern."[1] Using my own subaltern voice, this book is informed by my experiences, and my research provides a means of consolidating, integrating, and more rigorously conceiving the ways in which queer diasporic bodies are understood. By informing this scholarship through my own subject position, it seeks to increase our understanding of queer diasporic experiences by expanding our knowledge of visual art production and the lens through which we analyze the experiences of queer subjects of color.

As a writing practice, I employ "autotheory" as a way of activating theoretical discourse that does not account for my lived experience as a self-conscious way of engaging with theory alongside lived experience. The term "autotheory" emerged in the early part of the twenty-first century to describe works of literature, writing, and criticism that integrate autobiography with theory and philosophy in ways that are direct and self-aware.[2] According to theorist Lauren Fournier, "Artists turn to autotheory both for its troubling of dominant epistemologies and approaches to philosophizing and theorizing and for its capacity to make space for new ways of theorizing and understanding their lives."[3] As a feminist practice that is used often by queer and BIPOC (black, Indigenous, and people of color) cultural production, such as Sarah Ahmed's queer feminist affect theory, I use this practice of theorizing from the first person that was well established within genealogies of feminism. Autotheory can be traced back to early feminist conceptual art, video art, performance, and body art, as well as interdisciplinary writings by women of color like Audre Lorde, Gloria E. Anzaldúa, Sylvia Wynter, and bell hooks.

In this prologue I find it useful to directly incorporate my personal experiences within theoretical writing, and this is a way of acknowledging my subject position as I approach this research. From there, my subject position becomes an important vantage point that allows me to read existing scholarship and work through new ideas from a unique lens that is rooted in my experiences as a queer Egyptian person of color living within the diaspora. This is an effort to displace a masculinist conception of unbiased theoretical studies in which the researcher is far removed from their research subject to instead question how research would change if we decolonized the way we understand bias. What was once commonplace for studying other cultures and ethnographies as objective science, the feminist practice of autotheory shows the impact that writing from the inside can have on the knowledges we produce.

QUEER WORLD MAKING

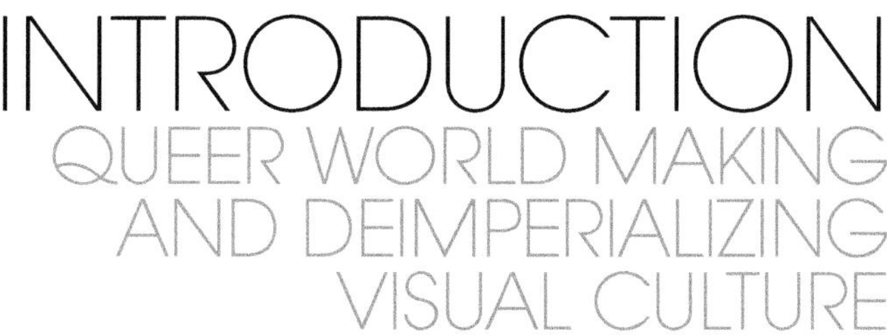

INTRODUCTION
QUEER WORLD MAKING AND DEIMPERIALIZING VISUAL CULTURE

> Perhaps instead of thinking of identity as an already accomplished fact . . .
> we should think, instead, of identity as a "production" which is never complete,
> always in process, and always constituted within, not outside, representation.
> STUART HALL, "Cultural Identity and Diaspora"

The past three decades have seen a new wave of Western scholars interested in representations of sexuality in the Arab and Muslim worlds. Generally, authors on Middle Eastern sexualities contend that the West created a discourse around sexuality that the Middle East never had,[1] leading to imperialist ideologies in the name of sexual tolerance or *homocolonialism*. Sociologist Momin Rahman defines homocolonialism as "the deployment of LGBTIQ rights and visibility to stigmatize non-Western cultures and conversely reassert the supremacy of the Western nations and civilization."[2] Specifically, Rahman characterizes "Western exceptionalism as the primary political idea that is triangulated through the process of 'homocolonialism' that institutes the opposition of Muslim cultures and sexuality politics by deploying LGBTIQ rights and visibility to punish non-Western cultures, and conversely reassert the supremacy of the 'home' Western nations and civilization."[3] This is seen in the work of political theorist Joseph Massad, who coined the term the "Gay International," which seeks to export Western models of homosexuality into places where it had not previously existed. Massad defines the Gay International as the missionary universalization of Western gay rights with an "orientalist impulse, borrowed from predominant representations of the Arab and Muslim worlds in the United States and Europe, [that] continues to guide all branches of the human rights community."[4] What results is the erasure of local forms of sexual identity scripts in the Middle East, at least according to his argument, as queerness replicates itself in the region through Western norms. As a push against colonial forces and imperialism, homosexuality in the Middle East was historically made into an illegal identity category—one that, many argue, did not exist prior to increased contact with Western explorers and travelers.[5] The travelogues that consist of books and manuscripts written by travelers from Europe to the Ottoman Middle East provide instances of external vantage points that compare intimate sexual scripts between the West and the Other. As an apparatus from which Orientalism spread, these travelogues used homosociality in the Middle East as a sign of perverted morality and "stood for the Orient's passivity, laziness, cowardice, and submission."[6] It is important to understand how the emergence of the Gay International coincided with that of Western gay sexuality studies. These issues are all at the forefront in the study of Islamicate sexualities.[7] Following Marshall Hodgson's definition of the *Islamicate* rather than the less precise terms *Arab*, *Middle Eastern*, or *Islamic*,[8] I use the notion of Islamicate sexualities referring not directly to the religion of Islam itself but to the social and cultural complexities historically associated with Islam and Muslims and inclusive of non-Muslims living within the regions of the world that share imperial and colonial histories.

Diasporic artists provide a rich platform to investigate the relationship of both colonial trauma and displacement within Middle Eastern communities in North America and how the conception of homeland complicates a transnational sexual identity.[9] There is an incompatibility between how diasporic subjects are socialized to become queer subjects in the West and the conflicting, often contradictory, values and understandings of their own sexual desires from a cultural perspective. I will problematize this lens from a critical race perspective, illustrating that the process of colonization and the immense struggle that Islamicate sexual discourses faced in the age of modernization still reverberates and affects multigenerational subjects in the diaspora. Studying the cultural production of the queer diaspora is fruitful in investigating the ways we can complicate the reductive narrative that characterizes Middle Eastern cultures as sexually oppressive and intolerant and Western cultures as sexually liberated and accepting.[10] Instead, we ought to examine a negotiation of diasporic sexuality by incorporating different sociological strategies to help self-identification categories be less dichotomous. To do so, in this book I study the existing literature on Middle

Eastern diasporic communities and bring queer identity within theoretical discussions around diaspora as a framework of analysis.

This book investigates Middle Eastern diasporic artists in North America who are creating political work engaging with queer identity.[11] I use the contrapuntal study of contemporary art in relation to historical archives in order to better explore contact zones as a way of discussing queer identity.[12] Queer identity is studied in relation to contemporary art being produced by the Middle Eastern diaspora, and my research contributes to the growing scholarship on postcolonial queer theory, Middle Eastern contemporary art, and diaspora studies.[13] Examining the contemporary works of artists Jamil Hellu, Ebrin Bagheri, 2Fik (Toufique), Alireza Shojaian, Laurence Rasti, and Nilbar Güreş in relation to historical photographic archives of colonial encounter in the Middle East, I explore the concept of multiple modernisms and their relationship to displacement, trauma, and Arab sexualities/masculinities/femininities within a postcolonial and anti-imperialist framework.

Born into the Syrian diaspora, San Francisco artist Jamil Hellu illustrates the friction between Arab ethnicity and American gay identity through his practice and considers the conflicts that emerge at the intersection of Middle Eastern heritage and queerness. Ebrin Bagheri is an Iranian Canadian artist whose ink-and-paper drawings evoke histories of premodern same-sex desires in Iranian culture, complicating ideals of Persian gender performativity within the diaspora. Montreal-based 2Fik is a multidisciplinary artist who uses his own diasporic identity as a subject in his work to explore the dichotomies of his Moroccan Canadian culture and his lived experience as a queer Arab. Alireza Shojaian is an Iranian artist who began his career in Tehran. He later moved to Beirut, where he explored queerness in his art with less censorship, and has been based in Paris since 2019. As an artist, he aims to challenge societal norms of gender and sexuality to make space for nonheteronormative masculine identities by reflecting on the queer history of West Asia and putting it into contemporary context through his lived experience. Laurence Rasti is an Iranian Swiss visual artist who photographs queer Iranian refugees in Turkey. The work of Nilbar Güreş, a diasporic Turkish visual artist living and working in Vienna, sheds light on the immense violence and trauma that queer and trans subjects face in both the Middle East and the diaspora.

The close study and comparative analyses of these artists add crucial discourses to transcultural art history and allow for diasporic Middle Eastern contemporary art to foster a more nuanced canon highlighting the geographical relevance of the Middle East in the art production of the diaspora in Canada, the United States, and Europe.[14] My research emphasizes themes of transnationalism, cultural exchange, and the political artwork that is associated with diasporic communities, paying particular attention to the ways in which transnationalism intersects with culturally specific histories of same-sex desire and sexual identification.[15] I examine the cultural production of these artists in order to explore non-Western ways of being queer that are informed by diaspora consciousness, a sociological and psychological component to diaspora studies.[16] Each chapter of this book contributes to a better understanding of diaspora consciousness and the impact it has on both art production and queer diasporic subjectivity. The ways in which queer diasporic subjects are socialized to be both queer and racialized in Western settings can be incommensurable with the often contradictory values and understandings of their own sexual desires in a culturally appropriate way. Ultimately, I argue throughout this book that colonialism did not fully extinguish the local gender discourses and codes of same-sex desire that existed in the Middle East for centuries. Instead, my contention is that the premodern sexual scripts and codes of desire still exist today and that the study of diasporic homosexualities is a valuable link to connect a colonial moment to a diasporic present.

As Gayatri Gopinath writes in her first book, *Impossible Desires*, "queer diaspora" is a reading practice and a hermeneutic. Evoking Stuart Hall's articulation of "the past" as characterizing a conservative diasporic imaginary, Gopinath writes about queer desire in an effort to reorient the backward-looking glance of diaspora. To Gopinath, "rather than evoking an imaginary homeland frozen in an idyllic moment outside history, what is remembered through queer diasporic desire and the queer diasporic body is a past time and place riven with contradictions and the violences of multiple uprootings, displacements, and exiles."[17] Building on the important work of queer theorists Gayatri Gopinath, David Eng, and Martin Manalansan, this book centers on diasporic contemporary art as case studies because queer diasporic cultural forms and practices point to submerged histories of racist and colonialist violence that continue to resonate in the present. As part of this collective project of decentering whiteness and dominant Euro-American paradigms by theorizing sexuality both locally and transnationally, I build on Gopinath's articulation of a queer diasporic framework. This queer diasporic framework is in contradistinction to the globalization of a "gay" identity that replicates a colonial narrative of development and progress that judges all "other" sexual practices against a normative model of Euro-American sexual identity.[18]

A goal of this line of inquiry into diaspora consciousness is to illustrate how the study of visual culture contributes to queer theory and transnationalism by illustrating the fact that premodern Islamicate sexual scripts are not fully colonized and live on in multigenerational subjects of the diaspora. As will be clarified throughout the chapters of this book, the process of colonization and the immense struggle Islamicate sexual discourses faced in the age of modernization still reverberates and affects multigenerational subjects in the diaspora.[19] The study of visual culture (both the historical archival records and the contemporary art of living artists) shows how remnants of these sexual scripts continue to affect the consciousness of the diaspora and how they are socialized as queer citizens. The double bind that the queer diasporic subject often faces can be linked to these aftereffects and tensions, and the study of visual art and culture helps illustrate the specific ways in which these sexual scripts are both manifested and negotiated by non-Western subjects in the West.[20]

Throughout the chapters of this book, I will outline the changes to local gender norms imposed by European travelers in the Middle East. The diaspora has a privileged position in my study because some of these changes are so recent. For instance, changes to the Arabic language, including different sexual-linguistic codes, happened as late as the 1950s, directly affecting generations of people who are still living firsthand effects of these changes.[21] This act of imperialism was achieved by removing local understandings of homosocial desire—something that existed as a nonissue, something that was not seen as an identity and did not need a name or categorization—and replacing them with specific Arabic words created by Europeans that reflected Western sexual practices. This implicates the queer diaspora in insidious ways, for the former generations in the mid-twentieth century were socialized with these new disavowals of unmodern homosociality and the simultaneous demonization of Western homosexuality.[22] The next generation and those within the diaspora have been left with a homosocial history that is still steeped within their own cultural traditions but now with the contradictory disavowal of homosexual subjectivity. In order to challenge the concept of stable or fixed identities, postcolonial theorist Homi K. Bhabha argues that cultural hybridity results from various forms of colonization and leads to cultural collisions and interchanges. In the attempt to assert colonial power and create civilized subjects, he says, "The trace of what is disavowed is not repressed but repeated as something different—a mutation, a hybrid."[23] This hybrid subject, or the contemporary queer diaspora, contradicts both the attempt to fix and control indigenous cultures and the illusion of cultural authenticity or purity. Here, the notion of the in-between is relevant, for the diasporic (in this case, also the queer diasporic) is then left with opposing views of Western and non-Western sexual practices, a tense historical framing of Arab-sexual discourses, all the while being measured by Western narratives of modernity, progress, and enlightened (Euro-American) sexual identity.

Is "Gay Identity" Universal?

Current literature engaging with Middle Eastern homosexuality is focused on issues of modernity, multiple modernities, and the West's claim to modernity.[24] Modernity as a time period signals social, political, and historic conditions at the end of the nineteenth and early twentieth centuries. Numerous scholars now question this imperial structure of power and examine how modernity can be used to colonize social and cultural practices in the name of Western advancement. Theorists such as Walter Mignolo, Irene Silverblatt, and Sonia Saldívar-Hull are just a few who question this new imperial structure of power and examine how modernity is used to colonize social and cultural practices in the name of Western advancement.[25] They argue that modernity was formed by European philosophers, academics, and politicians and that modernity involves the colonization of time and space in order to create a border in relation to a self-determining Other and its own European identity. In this way, Europeans colonized the world and built on the ideas of Western civilization and modernity as the endpoints of historical time, with Europe as the center of the world.[26] Mignolo also goes so far as to say that *coloniality* is constitutive of modernity and that "there is no modernity without coloniality."[27]

To illustrate the complexities of becoming a queer subject for the diasporic individual and the ways these experiences intersect with queer discourses in the Middle East, it is useful to return to Joseph Massad's theories that outline how "the Western gay agenda" has imposed a universalist, identitarian epistemology onto same-sex desire in the Arab world.[28] Through homocolonialism, incitement to discourse,[29] and what he terms the Gay International, Massad locates a Western exceptionalism that seeks to export Western models of homosexuality into places where it did not previously exist, effectively erasing local forms of sexual identity scripts. This creates a standardized *homosexuality* in places where same-sex desires have a more complex relationship with identity, nationalism, and social politics.[30] While Massad's work has been heavily critiqued by many—including Valerie Traub and Momin Rahman,[31] both concerned about the risk of the West "owning" gay identity and the implications of queer Arab subjects having no agency to identify themselves—this book charts how homocolonialism and its connection with modernity is undoubtedly a valuable framework for the study of the queer diaspora.[32] This historic record of desire is instrumental in locating contemporary notions of sexual discourse in the Middle East, the necessary cause-and-effect relationship that historic sexuality discourses have on contemporary understandings of sexuality, and how this history affects those currently living in the diaspora.

The problem lies in the imposition of a seemingly universal "gay" identity that is inherently Western and, according to Massad, inherently linked to colonialism and colonizing discourses. To Massad this means that because most non-Western civilizations, including Muslim Arab civilizations, have not subscribed historically to these binary categories of gender and sexuality, their imposition is producing harmful governing effects. Thus, Massad is emphasizing that the term *homosexual* is a genealogy of sexuality that is decidedly Euro-American.[33] This incitement to discourse, I argue, also exists in different ways for diasporic subjects due to the fact that the categories and binaries that they are forced to navigate, fit into, and circumvent are strikingly similar.

It is difficult to avoid the rhetoric of human rights when discussing a topic as divisive as homosexuality and same-sex desire in the Middle East. To illustrate why "human rights" is a contentious term often mobilized by imperialism, I turn to the two-volume anthology *Islam and Homosexuality*, edited by Samar Habib.[34] Habib uses the conceptual frame of human rights in order to address Massad's argument about the Gay International and homocolonial discourses of exporting Western homosexualities to the Middle East. She denies Massad's protest against the view that there is an authentic form of homosexual identity that is indigenous to the Arab world. Habib rejects Massad's assertion that coming out and visibility strategies are Western imports that are colonial impositions, labeling this line of thought as oppressive to Arab individuals who identify as gay and still live in the Middle East. Shifting away from Massad's "incitement to discourse" theory, Habib focuses on a human rights discourse in an attempt to universalize human security and a need to rid social oppression that is a "universally shared physiology."[35] This physiology is predicated on the assumption that everyone everywhere shares the same need for basic human rights and freedoms. She asserts that "this was precisely how the Islamic states reacted to the [Universal Declaration of Human Rights] which was seen as a culturally imperialist attempt to enforce one set of Rights."[36] This means that narrowly focused human rights agendas that privilege Western epistemologies are insidiously a part of an imperial incitement to discourse. In Habib's attempt to undermine Massad's denial of an indigenous homosexuality in the Arab world, I worry that she is repackaging the incitement to discourse within a new, universal human rights framework. I worry that if human rights that are not rooted in postcolonial thinking become the predominant discussion around gay rights in the Middle East, a universalization (of both human rights and homosexuality) becomes inevitable, thus further committing a homocolonialism that continues to erase local understandings of gender and sexuality.

Here, Habib is making, at its root, the same argument of colonial discourse that Massad makes. What Massad calls the homocolonial Gay International Habib argues is the exportation of human rights in the name of colonialism.[37] I posit that the question then becomes whether this exportation of human rights can happen in a way that allows for hybridity and the productive translation of these Western models, giving room for critique and transgressive research that challenges binaries, accessing "hidden histories by negation (Munoz, 1996) by emphasizing instability and the disruptive (Krahultik, 2006), and by using deconstructive practices."[38] Where Habib truly differs from Massad is in her argument of cultural specificity and respect of self-identification. Specifically, she argues, "The critiques of culturally insensitive approaches to sexual practices in the Arab world have overlooked their own insensitivity to the very real struggles of homosexual people in the Arab world (regardless of whether such a term is universally identified with, these individuals are in the least aware of their inherent difference and exclusion from the socially sanctified sexual currencies of marriage and children)."[39]

In this vein of thought, the lived experience of homosexual-identifying subjects in the Middle East is more of a priority than how they came to label themselves. Habib sees risks in demarcating all homosexual identities in the Middle East as colonial legacies of Western sexual discourses and rejects Massad's theoretical premise by refusing his argument that "your sexual preference or identification is not really your own, it is a Western construct, you do not really exist."[40] To this end, Massad is also emphasizing that the term *homosexual* is a genealogy of sexuality that is decidedly Euro-American, and the adoption of human rights discourse globally is the adoption of a specifically Western gay identity.

Other scholars have made similar human rights arguments, such as Brian Whitaker in his book *Unspeakable Love: Gay and Lesbian Life in the Middle East*. While outlining key issues in Middle Eastern sexuality studies through interviews and firsthand accounts, Whitaker takes a similar human rights stance that dichotomizes sexuality discourses into Western categories of identification and that of the Other. This othering of sexual discourses that do not resemble discourses of Western homosexuality is one of the pitfalls that this universalist human rights methodology creates. In this way, further research is integral to breaking up the hegemony of human rights discourses that are based on universal terms while simultaneously speaking to local ways of expressing queer desire in the Middle East that are also articulated by the diaspora in North America and Europe.

It is important to contextualize arguments of decolonization as it pertains to homosexual tolerance and liberation in the Middle East. The arguments thus far presented take issue with the historical upset of Middle Eastern sexualities by an intolerant Western colonialism. This imperialist pressure impacted the local sexual discourses that were more fluid and not identity-based, forcing a Western binary gender-identity model of heteronormativity onto the so-called Other in the Middle East. At the time of this colonial impact, homosexuality was also illegal in the Global North, and homosexuality being outlawed and prohibited in the Middle East was a measure taken to replicate the formula of Western modernity. This is precisely the role that modernity and modernism has within my project, for the parameters of contemporary gender identity and desire are heavily influenced by historical discourses of sexual liberation. In fact, homosexuality was criminalized and illegal in the West until very recently,[41] so in efforts to emulate modern civilization, most countries in the Middle East, Africa, and Asia followed suit and made homosexuality into an illegal identity, when just before the turn of the century it was not even seen as an identity at all in Islamicate contexts. After nations in the Global North started decriminalizing homosexuality, the goalposts of modernity moved and homosexual liberation became inextricably tied to being a modern nation.[42] Homosexuality and gay liberation are thus used as a newly changed endpoint of Western modernity, excluding the Middle East from ever reaching progress as defined by the Global North. The hostility that queer people feel in the Middle East today is tied to this colonial history and is an aftereffect of Western imperialism changing local sexual discourses. While homosexuality is currently restricted and criminalized in Middle Eastern societies but is relatively protected in certain Western cultures, contemporary discourses of sexual liberation need to be attentive to these histories of imperial violence at the risk of replicating the same coloniality that led to gay criminalization in the first place. The only way to correct the historical colonialism that caused irreparable damage for sexual discourses in the Middle East is a human rights advocacy that does not focus on protecting people's sexuality today in a monolithic version of queerness that is manufactured in and exported from the Global North. Echoing Massad's claims, this suggests that human rights discourses that seek to replicate Western queer models of identity will only be a recurring act of imperial control over sexual discourses in the Middle East.

Queering Locally

What does it mean to queer locally? As the case studies within this book will illustrate, kinship affiliation and embodiment become reimagined as contemporary diasporic artists like Hellu, 2Fik, Bagheri, Shojaian, Rasti, and Güreş insist on remembering and reinventing historical ways of being. Such reimagining is an integral relationship to the colonial archive, as it provides a way of using the past in order to imagine a different present. This is part of what it means to "queer locally." *Queering locally* incorporates temporal and geographic flexibility, and the flux and flow of historical moments across multiple geographies allows for colonial archives to speak to one another in productive and meaningful ways. By developing the framework of queering locally alongside an Islamicate methodology, this intervention allows for the tracing of same-sex desire and gender fluidity within Egypt and North Africa in order to assess beauty standards in Persia and gender roles within the Ottoman Empire, all through the purviews of contemporary Syrian, Iranian, Moroccan, and Turkish art. To "queer locally" does not imply micro studies of specific locales or limited geographic studies of only one place. In fact, quite the opposite is true. While such micro studies are relevant and necessary, an important facet of queering locally is the local-to-local connection that is created through joint analysis. This local-to-local methodological approach relates to an inter-Arab referencing system that will be elaborated upon further in this introduction, and each chapter of this book does this local-to-local work in theorizing different Islamicate regions in relation to one another. Therefore, one queers locally by broadening their geographic scope in order to avoid the colonial pitfalls of area studies and to better account for transnational connections between different geographic spheres.

In the various chapters of this book, I approach the terms *local*, *regional*, *transnational*, and *global* in different ways. As art historian Alpesh Patel argues, the incorporation of queer theory and feminist critique into the growing literature that explores art history in the context of the "transnational," "global," "world," and "diaspora" has been sorely lacking.[43] In approaching the *local*, I look at the culturally specific ways in which the diaspora articulate their sexuality within North America. This is particularly true in the ways I explore the "local" within ideas of queering locally. While the use of the term *regional* has similar connotations, in this case it refers to the interconnectedness of the Islamicate histories of same-sex desire and is closely linked to historical colonialism in the Middle East and is not tied to one specific locale. In this book I employ a *transnationally local* lens of study. The term *transnationalism* is used to describe the rearticulation of culture across rigid national boundaries and dislodging "diaspora from adherence to a conventional nationalist ideology."[44] The term *global* is used more within the context of themes like global art histories, and "on the most general level, we need it as a catchword that allows us to discuss seemingly different pasts in one frame, and to look into connections that earlier paradigms rendered invisible. On a very specific level, it helps us address the emergence of truly global structures."[45] Scholars Françoise Lionnet and Shu-mei Shih argue that the theorists of transnationalism who argue for a borderless world vis-à-vis outdated notions of globalization are the perpetuators of reifying binary North/South and dominant/resistant modes of culture.[46] Instead, they are for a "cultural transversalism [that] includes minor cultural articulations in productive relationship with the major (in all its possible shapes, forms and kinds), as well as minor-to-minor networks that circumvent the major altogether."[47] To elaborate on their argument, I find the writing of historian Sebastian Conrad illustrative. Conrad argues that, generally speaking, a global history agenda and an interest in specific locales are not mutually exclusive. He uses the term "glocalization" to suggest that global processes that were experienced in and constituted by local contexts point to the vexed relationship between the global and the local. Ultimately, Conrad suggests that "an exclusive focus on macro-perspectives is therefore not sufficient—and neither is a language of specificity and contingency alone."[48] Together, the decolonial logics that I employ in using these terms signals the necessary reshaping of the landscapes of knowledge and to "rescue history from container thinking."[49]

For these reasons, I begin to develop the theory of queering locally as a methodological tool to write a horizontal queer history instead of a more traditional vertical one imbued with hierarchies of value. In this case, culturally specific art historical narratives are situated in relation to other local sexual discourses in accordance with the horizontal paradigm. This method is applied to illustrate how the power dynamics that place homogeneous

Western histories at the center are flawed. Methodologically, this shifts dynamics in the relationship between the center and the periphery. I wish to advance a horizontal art history of the Middle East that veers away from the "geographico-hierarchical" paradigm of Eurocentric modern history and to instead contribute to the development of a transnational art history that works horizontally and in unison with a transnational queer theory. This will take place through the south-south comparisons of artists from different diasporic backgrounds throughout the book, and the contrapuntal study of visual art and queer theory to revision a history of sexuality that looks back in time to better understand the sexual discourses existing today that govern and affect contemporary queer subjects. Such an approach is a strategic use of interdisciplinary research and what Shu-mei Shih calls "relational comparison"; it relies on horizontal methods and historiographies of decentering, decanonizing, and localizing to combine and create new analytics and histories between different disciplines. I propose queering locally as both a method of deimperializing the study of queer theory and a way of providing a horizontal approach to art historical analysis.

To illustrate the dimensions of queering locally and the ways in which it is a framework that reimagines geography, I locate the terminology within the wider scope of queer literature. In her article "Queer Visual Excavations," feminist theorist Gayatri Gopinath coins the term "queer regions," which she uses "to name the particularities of gender and sexual logics in spaces that exist in a tangential relation to the nation as it is hegemonically defined, even as these spaces are constituted through complex regional, national, and global processes."[50] To Gopinath, queer visual aesthetic practices can destabilize nation-centric versions of area studies that are too limited by one geographic region, demonstrating the value in linking multiple geographic regions as a form of analysis.[51] Influenced by this methodology, queering locally displaces area studies through queer theory and applies a transtemporal exploration of the archive to better understand the current moment. It is important to question how these sexual logics connect historic colonialism with the contemporary diaspora. By portraying alternative modes of desire, embodiment, kinship, and affiliation, artists Jamil Hellu, Ebrin Bagheri, 2Fik, Alireza Shojaian, Laurence Rasti, and Nilbar Güreş insist on remembering and reviving historic ways of being in order to imagine a different present. Connecting the history of same-sex desire across multiple Islamicate regions allows for a translocal queer reading of contemporary art and the representation of desire within the diaspora. In this way, this book is not about comparative diasporas or fixating on Bagheri's Iranian heritage and contrasting his experience to 2Fik's Moroccan identity, for example; instead it is about linking diasporas and diasporic histories to highlight the important connections and divergences that existed and may have been extinguished during colonial expansion and imperial encounter. To use Gopinath's language, this research takes a transtemporal queer gaze on diasporic artists and the archives of colonial European photography and the art historical canon.

I locate my usage of *queering locally* and the ways I connect different and seemingly unrelated locales of the Islamicate as being complementary to Gopinath's second book, titled *Unruly Visions: The Aesthetic Practices of Queer Diaspora*, and builds on her rubric of the "aesthetic practices of the queer diaspora" and her theories of "queer regions." A focus on the region or the local is, quite often, a turn to the autobiographical and is inextricably tied to the project of narrating the self while deconstructing an essentialist logic of identity, place, and belonging.[52] I expand on Gopinath's framework of "queer regions" and develop the notion of queering locally as a way of describing how queer diasporic artists of color articulate a non-Western same-sex desire in the West. In these ways, I build on Gopinath's use of queer regions that allows her to make connections between regions that seemingly do not belong together, primarily through my intellectual use of the term *Islamicate*, elaborated on in chapter 2. In clarifying her use of the term *region* and her attempt to shift the focus of diaspora studies away from the nation, Gopinath states the following: "If you think about the typical ways in which diaspora has been formulated, it's always in relation to the nation. The nation becomes the constant and inevitable reference point for diaspora. The nation is that which diasporic subjects leave, that they return to or long to return to. So what I'm saying is that in fact thinking not so much about diaspora–nation but diaspora–region allows for all kinds of different social and political formations to become apparent that are in fact occluded within nationalist narratives."[53]

Demonstrative of what studying minor transnationalisms looks like, I am inspired by this theorization of diaspora and have followed the same method of inquiry in resisting thinking through the nation as a way of imagining a new cartography. Instead, I have shifted focus away from the subnational—smaller subsect of the national—characteristics of queer regions that are always linked to a failed or unmodern nationalism in order to emphasize the colonial implications of queer theory within minor-to-minor and south-south transregional analysis. In this way, queering locally goes beyond transnational analysis in that "transnationalism" still connects locales between nationalisms, and nation-state identities remain unquestioned and central to transnational theory. Rather, queering locally provides a framework for connecting locales through imperial and colonial ties and uses the archives to excavate the sexual discourses connecting different locales without the rigid, and often unproductive, parameters of the nation-state. Queering locally, then, is another strategy to discuss geographic specificities without being tied to the borders and limits of nation-states. This is part of an inter-referencing system that builds on postcolonial work within cultural studies like Kuan-Hsing Chen's book *Asia as Method*, and the theories of Françoise Lionnet and Shu-mei Shih on minor transnationalisms.[54] Queering locally is complementary to Gopinath's "queer regions" in its queer optic, or the south-south relationality. Where the terms converge is the site of their analysis. While a queer region is the subnational place that is conducive to understanding gender and sexuality formations in relation to the nation,[55] Gopinath writes of the aesthetic practices of the queer diaspora as being those that emerge from an artwork and its aesthetics. In this way, queering locally is a complementary theory that helps analyze what the aesthetic practices of the queer diaspora looks like in that it offers the potential of imagining a queer present that is intertwined in the complexities of multiple geographic spheres, temporalities, and histories. This means that my usage of *queering locally* is less concerned about national and subnational identities and instead focuses on how queer otherness is visualized, depicted, and actualized by diasporic queer subjects of color in North America and Europe. This theory works within Gopinath's framework of the aesthetic practices of the queer diaspora, and queering locally gives language to how art from the diaspora can simultaneously express the artist's own experience of queer identity and also highlight how they reference different geographies and histories in order to complicate linear identity narratives.

As Gopinath elaborates on her choice of terminology, she explains that the region is both a subnational and supranational space, and queering the ways in which we think about different regions produces alternative cartographies.[56] What a concept like queering locally provides is another framework that follows a rubric similar to that of "queer regions" and contributes to understanding the aesthetic practices of the queer diaspora from multiple angles. The main differentiation between my own theoretical framework and Gopinath's is that queering locally allows me to center the visual content from an art historical perspective, being attuned to the ways in which aesthetic practices of queer otherness are articulated in a bottom-up analysis. Therefore, queering locally is a part of many differing but converging strategies that work together as a framework that contributes to better understanding the art production of queer diasporic subjects in the West and how queerness is visualized.

Conceptually, the Islamicate, transnationalism, and diaspora are connected insofar that *Islamicate diaspora* might be a useful terminology to theorize diaspora even further removed from a singular nation-state and envision diaspora theory through a more interconnected lens. Within formations of diaspora, the Islamicate holds new possibilities for conceptualizing the ways diasporic subjects are identified in relation to a singular nation-state and offers another framework to discuss diasporic entanglements with nation and empire. Conceptualizing an "Islamicate diaspora" prioritizes connecting diaspora to more than simply one "host nation" in the ways it offers a new way of envisioning a more complex understanding of cultural circulation, heritage formation, and community outside of colonial nation-state definitions that ignore imperial histories and legacies.

Taking these links even a step further, to think queerly about the Islamicate diaspora introduces another layer of compounded identities within a transnational context, showing us what queering locally can look like. The comparative analysis of multiple regions that seem unconnected is a vital part of this logic, extending the ideas Gayatri Gopinath writes about when defining queer regions. Rather than focus on specific regions in the Global South to create south-south relationality, however, queering locally studies minor transnationalisms by centering diasporas in the simultaneous conception of homeland and nation. In this way, queerness in Egypt, for instance, is being studied as being historically contingent within the region but also affected by and directly impacting queer Egyptians in the diaspora. Queering locally is about bringing the study of queer regions in close proximity to queer diasporas, putting nation and homeland in direct conversation with each other in ways that bridge gaps, build solidarities, and create a history connecting queer people within the nation and the diaspora who are defined by nationalism but are physically outside of national borders. There is a great deal of privilege that comes with writing, studying, producing, making, and living in the diaspora. However, it is important that diasporic queerness does not stagnate on this privilege, and the violence that a queer diasporic person of color might experience should not be overshadowed by this privilege. In the diaspora, this allows for the racism, homophobia, and violence from both a white supremacist society and a homophobic cultural community to go unchecked, and violence from family or the cultural community becomes steeped in racist logics of assumed homophobia in the homeland.

As the diaspora is stuck between racism and homophobia while living with relative privilege in the Global North, there is still an immense vulnerability because of these nationalist tensions that leads to parents disowning their children at higher rates compared to nonracialized queer experiences as well as the increased suicide rates that follow being a vulnerable queer youth in North America or Europe. Queering locally, then, is meant to be a way out of this binary logic of "homophobic homeland" versus "privileged diaspora." Instead, it is about bringing locally relevant nationalist discourse into the experiences of the queer diaspora as a way of discussing nation, homeland, and diaspora within the same impulse. It is a way to bridge solidarities between queerness inside and outside of nation, and this book aims to historicize and contextualize homophobia in the Global North and South in an effort to focus on queer experiences globally rather than only on the violence that queer people face. For instance, queering locally would require us to examine a queer Egyptian's experience in North America not only as diasporic and part of specific immigrant discourses wrapped up in white settler nationalisms in Canada and the United States, but it would also require us to historicize, conceive of, and integrate the history of sexuality and queer desire in Egypt as being a major driving force to how this diasporic Egyptian experiences their queerness, even if they have never lived in Egypt.

This impulse to bring the local into the diaspora is the precise aim of queering locally, for it not only allows for an objective study of how gender and sexual discourses developed in Egypt over time, to continue with this one example, but it also allows for a better understanding of how these Egyptian sexual discourses either developed differently in the diaspora or stagnated completely. The way that nations in the Middle East have been developing a gendered and sexual discourse within their own postcolonial contexts after European control is something that should not be taken for granted in the diaspora, even if relative freedom and safety exist for queers living in some of these regions. When the sexual and gender discourses that are held on to within the diaspora are not a part of this continual change that is happening inside the nation, the nationalism shaping queer experiences in the diaspora can look even more stagnant when cultural identity becomes an unchangeable force when growing up in a racist and hostile diasporic environment. This is not to say that queer people in the Middle East can now live in relative safety because of this progression of gender discourses that has happened over the decades since imperialism ended in the region, far from it. Rather, the unique ways that queer people in the region have found ways to live, prosper, and flourish, even with great difficulty, are something that is not seen or acknowledged within diasporic imaginaries of queerness. Instead, there is a generational thinking that has helped maintain the gender discourses in the region as unchanging, since it is a part of a nationalism and cultural identity that is the most important distinction between "us" and "them" within immigrant mentalities. Thinking of queering locally in this way allows us to study sexuality and queerness outside of racism and homophobia and allows for these logics to be studied both independently from nation while simultaneously affording us the comparative analysis of queer experiences in a transnational sphere.

Queering locally is an intellectual effort to avoid describing gay life using linear narratives of progress, "gauging improvements in the rise of 'tolerant' attitudes and the growth of Western-style gay identities, gay friendly spaces, and lesbian, gay, bisexual and transgender (LGBT) organizations."[57] These Orientalist logics occur on multiple levels, which, sociologist Ghassan Moussawi calls "fractal Orientalisms." Orientalism relies on irreconcilable binaries and differences between the West and the Middle East to explain the region, cities, and peoples of the Middle East, and Moussawi suggests that Orientalisms within the Middle East provide a circular and repetitive form of this racist logic that has been both imposed and internalized. Building on what Edward Said describes as traditional Orientalism, or the historical discursive misrepresentations of the Middle East that tend to paint it as homogenous and backward, Moussawi argues for disrupting linear narratives of progress and modernity through his evocation of fractals, which is a never-ending pattern that replicates itself endlessly, and fractals are self-similar even on different scales. According to Moussawi, "Unlike Orientalism, which does not account for the multiple scales by which binaries are produced and circulated, fractal Orientalism shows how the same binaries simultaneously operate on global, regional, and local scales."[58] According to Moussawi, since fractal Orientalism simultaneously operates on multiple scales and a fractal takes the same shape as the whole, we can choose to focus on one level or a scale of the fractal and still get a narrative that seems complete. Rather than take for granted that Orientalism produces a single binary of East-West, thinking in this way allows for a zooming in and out to capture the multiple layers in which Orientalism operates.[59] Moussawi developed this analytic lens because, as he argues, "current representations (including scholarly work) on gender and sexuality in the Middle East rely on binaries and a flattened understanding of culture as a site of difference."[60]

I am interested in extending his thinking about Orientalism operating on different scales to the queer diaspora. If Orientalism operates, replicates itself, and continually informs its own logic "concurrently at the transnational, regional, national, and city levels,"[61] then bringing this logic to a diasporic experience of Orientalism can offer another level of racial thinking. In particular, when using the lens of fractal Orientalism to better understand the experiences of the queer diaspora, the racism experienced in places like North America and Europe produce an Orientalism that the diaspora faces simultaneously at national, transnational, even regional levels. Particularly when sexuality is used as a compounding factor of difference for a racialized queer diasporic subject, the mathematic term of the fractal, which describes the repetition of detailed geometric shapes, becomes a metaphor for the racial logics that surround and overwhelm diasporic subjects in an intricate web of Orientalism and racism that surrounds them on many levels and scales. Corresponding to sociologist Vrushali Patil's framework of webbed connectivities, "The goal is to move the starting point of analysis from an assumption of nation-states as ahistorical containers to nation-states as historically consolidated sites within cross-border networks of relations," a methodological tactic she calls 'thinking sideways.'[62] As a theoretical lens, fractal Orientalism and thinking sideways are helpful to think through ideas of queering locally, for they contribute methods to assess racism and homophobia concurrently at the transnational, regional, national, and community levels. In fact, following cultural theorist Arjun Appadurai, one can also say that local experiences are to be considered within a larger, global economic, social, and cultural network, because "locality is itself a historical product . . . subject to the dynamics of the global."[63] This logic is helpful, for it provides us with a multiscale model that allows methods like queering locally to illustrate how transnational discourses of national and sexual exceptionalism operate simultaneously within diaspora and homeland in both converging and unique ways.

Cultural Production of the Queer Diaspora

The texts that examine same-sex desire in relation to transnational and diasporic experiences often rely on visual culture as a central theme of their arguments. Often located outside the discipline of art history, these theorists hinge their arguments on films, representation in magazines, and images of popular culture to help support their claims and provide sociological evidence for their arguments. This need for queer theorists and critical race theorists to use visual production as case studies is itself evidence of the strong connection that lies between sexual desire, diasporic subjectivity, and modes of visual and cultural expression. Such limited work within the academy has been done surrounding this entanglement of transnationalism and queer theory so that visual culture provides theorists with another language to articulate the complexities of this triangulation of identity.[64]

Situating this queer theory and visual art analysis within the literature of diaspora studies, I find useful frameworks for the conceptual interrogation of terms like *nationalism*, *diaspora*, and *belonging*. In her book *Arab America: Gender, Cultural Politics, and Activism*, critical race theorist Nadine

Naber analyzes the varied concepts of Arabness within middle-class Arab American families and within Arab and Muslim anti-imperialist social movements. Naber interrogates the dichotomies that ensnare Arab communities as they clamor for a sense of safety and belonging in the United States. When addressing nationalism in the context of the Middle Eastern diaspora in North America, I use Naber's framework, which argues that "conventional nationalisms rely on a patrilinear heteronormative reproductive logic that maintains community boundaries through the ideal of heterosexual marriage and reproduction."[65] The artwork produced by diasporic subjects entangled by these dichotomies is immensely important in helping the viewer better understand how the artist navigates and belongs to various community identifications. In Naber's view on articulating Arabness in the United States, the diaspora has been shaped by an assemblage of different visions of how Arabs survive in North America.[66] This means that oftentimes the racism and cultural differences Arab families experience in the West can lead to an intensification of nationalism and a reification of some sort of "authentic" cultural heritage. For diasporic subjects, this means that differences and dichotomies are heightened, and notions of what it means to be Arab in North America are radically different from being Arab in the Middle East. This often is related to the ways in which nationalism, nationhood, and essentialist versions of Arabness become stuck in time and oriented toward past memories for families of migration who have settled in a new land. While nations in the Middle East are fundamentally changing and developing over time, the diasporic experience of nationhood could mean holding on to an unchanged version of what national identity looks like and an unmoving conception of what it means to be Arab. Articulations of Arabness, then, are grounded in Arab traditions and sensibilities about family, selfhood, and ways of being in the world but are also hybrid and historically contingent.[67]

If ideas of Arab national identity remain static, stuck in time, and unmoving in the diaspora, how does this affect conceptions of gender and sexuality for those living outside the Middle East? Importantly, Naber says that for the Middle Eastern diaspora in the United States, gender and sexuality are among the most powerful symbols for consolidating an imagined difference between Arabs and Americans. In understanding the power of gender and sexuality in forming citizens and shaping their articulations of nation-ness, queer theory and transnational theory can never be discussed as exclusionary from each other. What is important is the analysis of the artwork the queer diaspora produces, the cultural signs and visual materials its artists create that help them work through their articulations of Arabness in North America, and their belonging to gendered cultural practices and traditions. Just as the nation relies on gender and sexuality to form its citizens, shape their belonging, and govern their participation in a national identity, so too does identification or disidentification with a nation rely on visual culture as a tool, method, and language to form queer subjects.

Cultural theorist Mehdi Semati has mapped how "Brown" became used as an identity category within Islamophobic race politics. Semati argues that Brown, once the signifier of exoticism, has come to embody the menacing Other in today's geopolitical imagination, in a context where September 11 provided the horizon to recast (global) sociopolitical antagonisms in "cultural" terms.[68] In this argument, Brown also becomes an identity category in its own right. The critique and study of this racist imagination have been central to the work of postcolonial and antiracist theorists like Paola Bacchetta (2002), Tina Campt (2007), Inderpal Grewal (2006), and Caren Kaplan (2002), to name a few. These feminist theorists argue that the production of a new racial category exposes arbitrary racial constructions that are emerging globally. "Anyone who looks like a Muslim" becomes a target of racism, including Muslims, Arabs, Sikhs, and any other people with olive or Brown skin.[69] The same processes of racialization are happening in Canada, according to sociologist and critical race theorist Sherene Razack, who maps the racial structure of Canadian citizenship. Razack shows the importance of examining the production of a new Other at the forefront of all racial critiques of nationalism, belonging, and inclusion. She notably uses the terminology of "Muslim-looking" for the racist nature of the discourses confusing what is Muslim Arab with what is Arab (both Muslim and non-Muslim), as a part of the resurgence of an old Orientalism that "provides the scaffold for the making of an empire dominated by the United States and the white nations who are its allies."[70] Methodologically, in a post 9/11 context, the terminology used by these thinkers is crucial for understanding the reduction and creation of "Brown" as an identity category and provides a more specific grammar to locate the Islamophobic rhetoric within this process of racialization. Razack's use of "Muslim-looking" and Semati's deconstruction of the Brown subject are only two examples that are part of a larger network of racialization in which Brown identity is effective in locating the intersections of Arabs, Muslims, and Middle Easterners and how these bodies can be "cast out," as Razack puts it, from national identity and legal sanctions.

As Benedict Anderson's formative text *Imagined Communities* has argued, nation, nationality, and nationalism have all proved notoriously difficult to define, let alone to analyze. He argues that *nationality*, *nation-ness*, and *nationalism* are cultural artifacts that require interrogation, especially their coming into being and the ways their meanings have changed over time.[71] Extending Anderson's argument, what would happen to our interrogations when postcolonial queer subjects who have traditionally been excluded or written in the margins of nationalism are recontextualized within the historic events that help create nationalisms? As Anderson identifies nation-ness and nationalism as being imagined, limited, and sovereign,[72] it is his idea of the nation being imagined as a community that helps inform issues of representation and belonging both in the field of visual culture more broadly and issues of representation within visual arts. Cultural studies theorists from the 1980s and 1990s, such as Paul Gilroy and Stuart Hall, provide a concept of diaspora that moves away from its traditional orientation toward homeland, exile, or return and instead lives within a diasporic subjectivity that exists through, not despite, cultural difference. My research is indebted to the theories of hybridity, like those of Homi Bhabha, as being a concept of identity and embrace of diaspora for its potential to displace nationalist projects and rigid hierarchies of relation between nation and migration.[73]

Anthropologist Ramy Aly speaks to this point directly in his book *Becoming Arab in London*, through an ethnographic exploration of gender, race, and class practices among the Arab diaspora in the United Kingdom. Aly traces behavior in cultural spaces (such as shisha cafés, Arab clubs, and culturally traditional restaurants) as ways of performing "Arabness." Aly uncovers narratives of living in the diaspora and the codes of sociability that make/create British Arab men and women. In examining the aesthetic trends of Arab youth living in London, Aly notes, "Fashions and aesthetic orientation in the Arab world and the Arab diaspora seem to flow in opposite directions. While middle-class Arab lifestyle magazines in the Middle East abound with images of Arabs in the latest Western fashions and interiors as testament to their inclusion in (a European) modernity, Arabs in London draw on folkloric Arab past to make the same kind of self-validating visual statements about themselves within the context of multicultural London."[74]

Aly's central argument—that there is theoretical proximity in the process of being "raced" and "gendered"—is hinged on the analysis of visual culture as an *expression* of the diasporas' subjectification. In examining the aesthetic practices of the queer diaspora within this book, I find it useful to think about this contradictory flow of cultural authenticity and interrogate how these ideas are manifested by artists and depicted in visual art.

Within the same body of literature, sociologist Momin Rahman's book *Homosexualities, Muslim Cultures, and Modernity* critiques the erroneously assumed mutual exclusivity between queer and Middle Eastern or Asian cultures.[75] Rahman aims to illuminate the intersections and complexities of current binaries within Muslim communities and families, gay communities and culture, and wider Western political culture and discourses. Rahman argues that we must accept that the Muslim experience of sexual diversity politics is significantly different from the Western one and that this reality undermines any assumption that the processes of Muslim modernization would inevitably lead to the same outcomes around sexuality as those experienced in the West. In other words, Middle Eastern homosexuality will never look the same as Western homosexuality. He posits that the queer Muslim is intersectional and challenges the monolithic, monocultural versions of queer Western identity politics and the positioning of queer politics. Here, the very existence of queer diasporic Muslims destabilizes Western queer discourse. It is this assertion of the Muslim queer subject lying outside of normative Western queer politics that points to issues of genuine difference and incompatibility. I contend that these ideas are steeped in issues of colonialism and imperialism and the remnants of precolonized sexual scripts that make the Islamicate queer subject an outlier. In these performances and failures, belongings and exclusions, recognitions and disidentifications, this postcolonial queer subject articulates nation-ness in complex ways, and the visual culture they produce informs this process.

The study of transnationalism contributes greatly to our understanding of diasporic visual culture, particularly in conjunction with queer theory. In this triangulation, we can assess the complexity of homeland relations, how one belongs to a nation-state, how national identity is expected to be performed, and the repercussions of failing to perform nationalism correctly. According to gender studies theorist Evren Savcı, "These diametrically opposed treatments of neoliberalism and Islam in queer studies are symptomatic of a key epistemic problem in the field—that of reading non-normatively gendered and sexualized subjects elsewhere through the paradigm of anthropological difference."[76] These issues call for a discussion of modernity from a critical transnational and diasporic perspective, and sociologists Paola Bacchetta, Sunaina Maira, and Howard Winant bridge these gaps in their writing about global raciality. According to them, "Race, racialization, and racism—today largely recognized as socially and historically 'constructed'—remain deeply intertwined with modernity, imperialism, colonialism, and decoloniality. Different racist practices emerged from multiple forms of colonialism—including administrative and economic colonialism, settler colonialism, and deterritorialized forms of empire."[77] These concerns show the importance of better illustrating the ways in which the postcolonial queer subject articulates nation-ness in complex ways and how the visual culture they produce informs this process. All of these cultural and social texts come together in the examination of community and in the different ways the diaspora forms this sense of community and complex articulations of Arabness through visual art production.

Building on critiques of the Eurocentric writing of history, this research explores Middle Eastern homosexuality and focuses on contact zones to explore issues of modernity, multiple modernisms, and the West's claim to modernity. I consider Arab homosexualities in terms of desire and alternative masculinities and femininities rather than Western notions of visibility and coming out; these narratives are not necessarily conducive to understanding how queer Arabs living in the West experience their sexuality. Discussing modernity from a critical transnational and diasporic perspective is vital to dismantling "historically constructed (and presently sustained) asymmetrical global power structures [to work beyond] the false binaries of Islam/modernity, and Islam/West."[78]

Part 1 of this book is largely theory driven and is meant to be a foundation for discussing artworks. In part 2, the analysis of visual artworks by Jamil Hellu in chapter 4, "An Alternative History of Sexuality: Diaspora Consciousness and the Queer Diasporic Lens"; Ebrin Bagheri in chapter 5,

"Queering Archives of Photography: Linking a Colonial History to a Diasporic Present"; 2Fik in chapter 6, "Coming Out *à l'Orientale*: Diasporic Art and Colonial Wounds"; and Alireza Shojaian, Laurence Rasti, and Nilbar Güreş in chapter 7, "Historicizing Homophobia: Contesting the Double Binds of Homonationalism and Homocolonialism," all work to investigate the codification of Middle Eastern masculinity, femininity, and gender norms through a visual language and destabilize homocolonial discourses of Western modernity in a discussion rooted in sociological ideas of gender, nationalism, and sexuality, and the triangulation of identity and oppression that could arise at their intersection.[79] These diasporic artists provide a rich platform to investigate the relationship between colonial trauma, racism, and displacement within diasporic communities in North America and Europe and how the conception of homeland complicates a transnational sexual identity. I investigate whether we can reach a narrative of Western and non-Western modernity that functions beyond assumptions of sexual oppression (in the Middle East) versus sexual acceptance (in the Global North), and examine a negotiation of diasporic sexuality by incorporating different sociological strategies to help self-identification categories be less dichotomous. Within this binary, transnationalism offers a queer critique aimed at the deployment of LGBTQ rights globally to justify imperial wars and Islamophobia, and within this framework, transnational and diaspora theory unsettles the authentic-versus-colonial binary that often underlies queer theory scholarship focusing on the region.

Scope, Parameters, and Limits of Research

The study of how homocolonialism exists within and functions through visual culture is necessary. I contend that visual culture is a primary vehicle for homocolonial discourses (whether through historical homo-Orientalist paintings, homoerotic archival photography, or more recent propagandistic and racist visual imagery), and the connection between homocolonialism, Orientalism, and the imperialist production of visual culture is necessary. This includes how homocolonial and homoerotic Orientalist discourses are embedded within the history of photography and other Orientalist art forms, not simply a fringe narrative of the field. The history of photography is so closely related to the Middle East and the representation of Arab people that an intersectional study of European encounters in the Middle East must take place between the history of visual culture, the study of empire, and the history of sexuality.[80]

Current literature on Middle Eastern homosexuality is largely historic in scope and focuses on the study of premodern sexual desire based on European travel journals, Arab-Islamic literature and poetry, and archival visual material from periods of "high imperialism." Early canonical writing about sex and gender were written in a context of high imperialism "amidst the 'Scramble for Africa,' imperial expansion and consolidation of older imperial actors such as Britain and France, and the entrance of new formal colonial actors such as Germany and the United States."[81] Racial sexual othering mattered for the different racial and colonial projects emerging in the period, but these historic records are important even for contemporary scholars of sexuality, as they map a shift in sexual discourses in the Middle East, discourses that are closely related to colonialism and increased contact with the West. Early fifteenth-to-nineteenth-century premodern archival records from the Middle East are the center of interpretation for most contemporary scholars on the subject in order to piece together different sexual scripts within a given geographic and temporal period. Using such archival records, authors locate the production of Arab sexual discourse by illustrating both the official gender norms condoned by the state (such as those governed by medical, legal, and religious writing) and the unofficial, often radically different ways sexual desire was manifested and understood in society (through visual arts in addition to literature and poetry).[82] Methodologically, this book focuses on visual analyses of contemporary artwork and finds their resonances with the archival studies of eighteenth- and nineteenth-century premodern Arab same-sex desire. Extensive archival research already exists, and my research uses these studies as a base to inform my analysis.

The parameters of my study are not geographically based; rather, contemporary artists were chosen based on the artworks they produced and their wider artistic practice. In using terminology like *Islamicate* as a way of encompassing broader geographic regions in the Middle East, I do not delimit this book to the study of only Islamic art, Arab artists, or the common conflation of the two. Instead, it encompasses artists who produce visual art pertaining to gender and sexual identity, and their artworks are the site of analysis. Diasporic artists living in North America were selected not based on the location of their origin but based on their artwork, thus contributing to a better understanding of homoerotic visual culture in the Middle East. From there, the historic archival studies of gender and sexuality done by other scholars informs the patterns, similarities, and histories of colonialism and the resemblances of contact zones in different regions. This means that while 2Fik, for instance, is a Moroccan artist, this book does not lay claim to studying Morocco or Maghrebi visual art. Rather, 2Fik's artwork speaks to the wider history of art production in the Middle Eastern diaspora, with the analysis of gender and sexuality being at the forefront. This book not only advances research by introducing new dimensions to issues of visual representation through homocolonial discourses, but it also introduces an interdisciplinary theorization to diasporic Middle Eastern contemporary art that will help us to better understand the human rights issues surrounding sexual identity and resistance art production.

The examination of contemporary artists alongside these historic studies contributes to the growing literature on gender discourse and premodern Islamicate sexual desire. These historic archives are necessary starting points, for they help investigate the modernist production of heterosexuality through the screen of gender and its reconceptualization of the gender norms prior to increased contact with Europe in the sixteenth century. Using these archival materials, I will contribute to the mapping of homoerotic figures in premodern Persia, much of the Ottoman Empire, and other Islamicate regions by linking their histories to colonialism and sites of European encounter. This historic record of desire is instrumental in locating contemporary notions of sexual discourse in the Middle East, the causal relationship that historic sexuality discourses have on contemporary understandings of sexuality, and how this history affects those currently living in the diaspora.

Book Structure: Histories of Art, Sexuality, and Colonialism

To develop these concerns, this research is informed by methods of global art histories, notions of "worlding," and the praxis of postcolonial theories.

This book charts this journey in two parts with seven main chapters. Part 1 lays the groundwork for methodological, theoretical, and philosophical issues within art historical research on the Middle East and the study of diasporic art. Part 2 is where the majority of queer artists are discussed, and where queer visual art is explored in detail. Opening with a foundational discussion of antiracist methods and strategies to think through both art history and queer theory, chapter 1, "Thinking Decolonially: Horizontal Methods to Queer Theory and Art History," investigates what decolonizing the study and writing of art history can look like.

Chapter 2, "Trauma and the Single Narrative: Reading Arab Art and Photography," investigates the major methodological issues faced in the making of Arab art and photography and their relationship to understanding how conflict is photographed. I investigate the intersection of Middle Eastern art histories and their relationship to colonialism as a way of discussing new challenges in the study of contemporary art and photography. Focusing on the ubiquitous single narrative of war and trauma that is associated with the Middle East, I explore racial issues that hinder the full reading of Middle Eastern photography. Using Middle Eastern contemporary art as the focus of my analysis, I examine how viewers of Arab photography are conditioned to expect certain narratives or visual imagery. This in turn affects the making of art itself, as Arab artists are conditioned to produce photography that is aesthetically similar to pervasive trauma and war photography in order to be viable in the international art market. In examining such pressing methodological concerns about the process of both producing and interpreting Arab photography, I aim to investigate the relationship between abundant trauma photographs of popular culture and their impact on the production of photographic art in the Middle East. This chapter brings into play Middle Eastern photography research and postcolonial studies by exploring the place of race and colonialism in terms of the recording and writing of art histories. Bridging links between the technology of media saturation plaguing the Middle East and the photography being produced by Arab artists, my analysis provides reflection and new perspectives on methodological approaches that are attentive to both the process of creating Middle Eastern art and that of interpreting photography in transnational contexts.

Ultimately, chapter 2 outlines the dangers of the single narrative, the history of focusing on the racialized artist's biography within art history, and how this ultimately leads to what I call the *single-narrative biography*, a lens of analysis that limits and reduces the full understanding of art produced by artists of color.[83] I contend that before we read queer images, we need to understand the dimensions and the ways viewers read trauma. Queer analysis disrupts the single-narrative biography in interesting ways, for it opens up new ways of being, imagines Arab futurity in powerful dialogues with queer futurity, and complicates how trauma is represented.[84] Queer identities are often left outside of this single-narrative biography, which reinforces the binaries of queer identity being rejected in the Middle East and is a marker of modernity and progress that is associated with Western artists. While queer identity is increasingly becoming part of the single-narrative biography for racialized artists, we must bring visibility to the ways historical analysis can limit the reading of full, nuanced lives and the multiplicities of experiences within Arab art production.

Chapter 3, "Islamicate as Method: Minor Transnationalisms and Worlding Art History," is about the methodologies used within my research and provides language and frameworks in order to theorize the complex ways in which geography influences the study of Islamic art. This chapter investigates transnationalism within global narratives of "worlding" and finds praxis for this method of inquiry within art historical research and museum exhibitions. While studies of globalization and diaspora have challenged the authority of nation-state identities and rigid cultural categorization, art histories are still written through center-periphery models that maintain Euro-American exceptionalism. How can we engage with intercultural and transnational encounters and write productive global art histories in order to dismantle the center-periphery binary that maintains such colonial structures? Globalizing and decentering histories can be more integrative and can meaningfully incorporate the histories of multiple locales in order to examine how they converse and engage with one another in terms of their own relationships to power and representation. I examine these issues by introducing what I contend is a useful art historical framework, the Islamicate, as a case study to reassess seemingly fixed nation-state borders and to reconsider the mobility of art history. I use the notion of the Islamicate to critique epistemologies of knowledge production and dissemination within museums; it is meant to be one instance where "worlding" art history can be put into praxis, and methodologies of global art histories can be theorized in a more practical application of exhibition making and art historical research. This chapter provides an important methodology that is used throughout the book, as it explains in depth the ways in which terms such as *Islamic, Middle Eastern,* and *Arab* are used within this research and the reasons why it is important to reimagine geographic borders when conducting such interdisciplinary and postcolonial research.

In part 2 the focus is on a handful of individual artists, beginning with a visual analysis of Syrian American artist Jamil Hellu. Chapter 4, "An Alternative History of Sexuality: Diaspora Consciousness and the Queer Diasporic Lens," acts as a literature review that provides historical context to colonial discourses within the history of sexuality in the Middle East. This chapter demonstrates the ways in which Michel Foucault's *History of Sexuality* created a pitfall for scholars of Middle Eastern sexual discourses; it also seeks alternative methodologies of postcolonial and antiracist research in gender studies. These issues involve Foucault's relegation of premodern Islamicate homosociality and same-sex desire as being a distant historical phenomenon, the minimization of colonial power within the analysis of premodern sexual discourses, and the reductive distinction made between sexual identities (West) and sexual acts (East), all of which work to flatten entire complex networks of desire and homosocial cultural attitudes. What is needed, I contend, is an alternative history of sexuality, one with a more complex understanding of colonial discourses and their influences and impact on gender, sexuality, and all cultural and legal texts governing Islamicate bodies. Importantly, the analysis within this chapter is meant to challenge the Eurocentrism of dominant queer theory and gay scholarship by focusing on alternative sexual discourses that are not reducible to hegemonic Euro-American notions of gay identity.

Chapter 5, "Queering Archives of Photography: Linking a Colonial History to a Diasporic Present," historicizes same-sex desire in the Middle East, across North Africa, and the regions formerly a part of the Ottoman Empire to better investigate Middle Eastern contemporary art and its relationship to gender colonial discourses that had an impact on same-sex desire. I begin by historicizing European and colonial encounters in the Middle East at the turn of the nineteenth century, illustrating the effect Victorian sensibilities had on premodern homosociality and same-sex desire in the Middle East. This history of changing sexual discourse is later illustrated through European colonial photographs in the Middle East that depict homoeroticism, primarily focusing on European travelers who photographed local young men. I analyze the aesthetics of these photographic archives in relation to contemporary drawings by Iranian artist Ebrin Bagheri as a way of investigating the modernist production of heterosexuality and the erasure of local gender norms. In analyzing the art of a queer diasporic subject, I focus on how Bagheri's contemporary drawings bring together traces of premodern same-sex desire in order to elucidate that the colonial remainders of the colonized local sexual scripts are still alive and deeply embedded within diaspora consciousness. My analysis of historic colonial encounters in relation to contemporary diasporic art becomes another logic used to challenge area studies scholarship, which remains too nation-centric; simultaneously, it challenges the homogeneity of "global gay identity" by addressing how colonial encounters have been transformed and negotiated in local sites.

As a way of exploring themes of historical and colonial modernity in more detail, chapter 6, "Coming Out *à l'Orientale*: Diasporic Art and Colonial Wounds," analyzes the work of Moroccan artist 2Fik (Toufique). Using performance and photography as his primary modes of art production, 2Fik invents multifaceted characters that transform and translate different aspects of his cultural and sexual identity, performing each character in complex narratives within his photography. His performance art becomes an integral and inseparable part of his photography, for these characters provide a level of depth in investigating the process of cultural transformation that allows him to navigate geographic borders, geopolitics, and decolonial aesthetics. In this chapter, I analyze 2Fik's performative photography in order to illustrate the complexities of Islamicate sexualities within the diaspora. I use the visual art of 2Fik as a case study to investigate the historical links that contemporary queer diasporic identities have to modernity and Western imperialism. To do so, I begin by outlining different epistemologies of coming out as a way of showcasing the particularities of transnational queer identity and, in this case, *coming out à l'Orientale*. Next I turn to modern art to question the ways in which premodern Islamicate sexual scripts colonized by modernity might still exist within diasporic subjects today. Then I analyze the fictional characters that 2Fik has created within his artistic practice as a way of establishing tensions between different dichotomies within his own diasporic identity: East and West, traditional versus modern subjectivity, and transnationalism versus hybridity. Throughout this discussion I draw links between settler colonialism and its intersection with the queer diaspora. Issues of modernity and progress in Canada (as well as the Euro-American context) are intrinsically tied to queer rights, liberal tolerance, and how they uphold whiteness and naturalize settler colonialism. This discussion illustrates the various ways contemporary art can be used to queer kinship models and how queer identity can give nuances to theories of transnationalism and diaspora, especially the different ways sexuality is performed in transnational contexts. I contend that queer contemporary Arab artists can be seen as a necessary link that bridges art history and modernity to contemporary queer identity.

Chapter 7, "Historicizing Homophobia: Contesting the Double Binds of Homocolonialism and Homonationalism," offers an analysis of Middle Eastern diasporic conditions through a focus on queer diasporic art and identity, especially under the auspices of migration. By engaging with the visual art of Alireza Shojaian, Laurence Rasti, and Nilbar Güreş, the analysis sheds light on the immense violence and trauma that queer and trans subjects face in the Middle East and the diaspora. The argument contends that these artistic expressions and compositions from a broadly defined Islamicate queer diaspora offer disruptive readings of both homocolonialism and homonationalism. The artists in this chapter show us the places where culture and sexuality meet transnationally and the ways they articulate their own experiences and identities that better inform this process.

I conclude this book by creating praxis, links, and connections between critical race theory, gender analysis, and diaspora theory within museum studies and the writing of art history. While theories of diaspora consciousness are explored within each chapter, I conclude by focusing on the conscious and subconscious ways that the diaspora holds historical ways of being within their own queer subjectivity. Through these chapters I aim to address the following concerns: By reimagining geography, what does decolonizing the study and writing of art history look like? What does it mean to conduct research on the global contemporary—or art after modernism broadly speaking—with special attention to spatial problems on a large scale? How can macro studies of global art histories and world art studies be productively theorized alongside micro studies of specific locales? Where does the study of diaspora fit within world art studies? How might methods of entangled geographies—that is, locales connected historically by empire, imperialism, and colonialism—speak productively to themes of transnational connections and diaspora? Ultimately, how can geography be theorized and examined within contemporary art both regionally and globally while avoiding the rigid nation-state epistemologies of area studies? In such a way, global history is used as an analytic device, writing a history that traces specific interactions and patterns of exchange, centering periphery geographies and no longer theorizing them only in the limited purview of the nation-state. I contend that gender and sexuality are necessary to understanding the ways in which race and culture are visualized and depicted within art. Locating sexuality discourses at the center of our debates on visual culture creates a paradigm shift in which methodologies that are traditional to visual art and art history become displaced and histories of colonialism and imperialism can more productively be brought to the fore.

The overall goal of this book is to examine how the artworks of the aforementioned artists exemplify networks of communication that are different from the global-to-local homocolonial imposition of gay identity that is the focus of most contemporary literature on the topic. Arguing instead that Middle Eastern diasporic subjects create an alternative coming out narrative and identity script to the inscribed Western models, my aim is to point out the ways in which local instances of homosociality cite premodern sexuality scripts within contemporary Middle Eastern art and its diaspora and reject the Western queer identity narrative that becomes exclusionary in non-Western contexts. There is an incompatibility with how diasporic subjects are socialized to become queer subjects in the West and the conflicting, often contradictory, values and understandings of their own sexual desires from a cultural perspective. These selected artists provide significant examples of how local networks of identity are transmitted through visual language and how alternative sexuality scripts can be written.

PART ONE
DECOLONIAL METHODS

IMAGINING A HORIZONTAL ART HISTORY AND QUEER THEORY

ONE

THINKING DECOLONIALLY

HORIZONTAL METHODS TO QUEER THEORY AND ART HISTORY

Hans Belting explains that *world art* was initially coined as a colonial notion that was in use for collecting the art of "the others" as a different kind of art, an art that was evaluated by anthropologists rather than art critics:

> *World art* and *global art* today have very different meanings, ever since the notion *global art* came up around twenty years ago. *World art* is an old idea complementary to modernism. . . . It continues to signify art from all ages, the heritage of mankind. In fact, world art included art of every possible provenance while at the same time excluding it from Western mainstream art—a colonial distinction between art museums and ethnographic museums. *World art* is officially codified in international laws for the protection of cultural heritage and monuments. *Global art*, on the other hand, is recognized as the sudden and worldwide production of art that did not exist or did not garner attention until the late 1980s. By its own definition global art is contemporary and in spirit postcolonial; thus it is guided by the intention to replace the center and periphery scheme of a hegemonic modernity, and also claims freedom from the privilege of history.[1]

How, then, are *world art studies* and the more contemporary *global art history* implicated in a project of decoloniality, and how do they work to displace the center and periphery power dynamic that misrepresents a hegemonic Western modernity at the center of all histories? To do this work, it is important to lay the foundation of our understanding of colonialism, coloniality, decolonization, and imperialism. My theories and framework of colonial modernity are shaped by literary theorist Walter Mignolo and his important extrapolations on the complex matrix of power that has been created and controlled by Western powers during the Renaissance, colonially positioning Europe as the center of the world. In his latest study, *On Decoloniality*, Mignolo emphasizes the difficulty of defining terms like *colonialism*, for there are few sources elucidating the meaning of the word.[2] Turning to the *Stanford Encyclopedia of Philosophy*, *colonialism* is defined as a system of domination that involves the subjugation of one people to another, and *imperialism* is defined similarly as the political and economic control over a dependent territory.[3]

Mignolo, however, finds issue with the *Stanford Encyclopedia of Philosophy*'s writer defining *imperialism* as being almost exactly the same as the etymological dictionary definition of *colonialism*. Helpfully, Mignolo suggests that we think "decolonially" instead and conceive of colonialism as the complement to imperialism. With this, Mignolo asserts that there is no imperialism without colonialism and that colonialism is constitutive of imperialism.[4] This exercise in decolonial thinking, and what I would call an anticolonial writing of history, lays bare the workings of Eurocentrism within art historical analysis and theories of diaspora and queerness. As a way of thinking *decolonially*, I use the terms *colonialism* and *imperialism* as being synonymous and constitutive of each other and do not signal a historic moment of colonialism per se.[5] With this said, the Middle East has had a long and vexed relationship with imperialism and being colonized by various countries at various times in history.[6] With the North American focus of this book, and with brief explorations of experiences of the queer diaspora in Europe, I center the understanding of Canada and the United States in a settler-colonial context, and I keep the critiques of scholars Eve Tuck and K. Wayne Yang in mind, as I wish to avoid the ways in which the "language of decolonization has been superficially adopted into education and other social sciences."[7] Foregrounding assertions that decolonization is not a metaphor, colonialism is a very real dimension of human history in the Middle East that has impacted the workings of indigenous, local ways of being through its colonial legacy. I refer to colonialism in my research not in the abstract nor as a singular historical event, for each history of colonialism in different regions has locally specific histories and contexts. However, in order to produce a more macro-level study of homocolonialism's impact on historic visual culture, contemporary art, and the contemporary Arab diaspora, focusing on specific nation-states does not provide a full picture of how gender and sexuality changed during periods of imperialism in the Middle East. This begs the question: How does one approach the history of colonialism and actively situate knowledge without looking at a specific nation-state unit? To explore this query, I use the term *colonialism* as a way of signaling the colonial matrix of power that is entwined with imperialism and imperial ways of being that centered European tradition as normative, modern, and superior to cultures and traditions in the Middle East.[8]

Decolonizing versus Deimperializing: The Canon of Arab Art

This chapter investigates what decolonizing the study and writing of art history can look like. According to sociologist Vrushali Patil, "While critiques of race, the transnational, and coloniality have gone a long way in correcting problematic approaches to the other, they have been less successful in transforming dominant approaches to the white, northern self."[9] In order for anticolonial research to exist as a central query of thought, rather than on the periphery engaging with dominant modes of representation and discourse, I propose centering deimperialization and not just decolonization within this work. In understanding that knowledge production is one of the major sites in which imperialism operates and exercises its power, deimperializing will be a milestone in how we decolonize the structural limits that currently condition knowledge production. To help unpack these terms, I turn to Kuan-Hsing Chen's book *Asia as Method: Toward Deimperialization*. I argue that the methods of inquiry developed by Chen could inform the study of Arab art within a broader scope of postcolonial and anticolonial art production. As Chen describes, "Decolonization is the attempt of the previously colonized to reflectively work out a historical relation with the former colonizer," involving the process of self-critique, self-rediscovery, and identity formation.[10] This decolonization of art history has been the primary focus for the majority of scholars of Arab art (e.g., Nada Shabout, Saleem Al-Bahloly, Kamal Boullata, Iftikhar Dadi, Liliane Karnouk, Omar Kholeif, and Saeb Eigner), and their important contributions give visibility to artistic creation, movements, and techniques that originated from or existed in the Middle East and Islamicate regions. While canon building and providing an overview of art from the Middle East that is defined by movements and linear history is not within the purview of my research, the histories that these scholars focus on in relation to larger art historical narratives has been instrumental in how I relate diasporic art to art from the MENASA region (Middle East, North Africa, South Asia). As literary scholars Françoise Lionnet and Shu-mei Shih argue, "More often than not, minority subjects identify themselves in opposition to a dominant discourse rather than vis-à-vis each other and other minority groups. We study the centre and the margin but rarely examine the relationships among different margins."[11] When the relationships among different margins are ignored, there is a risk of making invisible the complex networks of cultural thriving that exist external to colonial metropoles. In other words, what is at stake when we study the center and the margin, but rarely study the relationships between different margins, is the upholding of center-periphery power dynamics that favor Western narratives.

Deconstructing the Western canon of art acknowledges the possibility of creating more expanded notions of what constitutes "important" art while accepting responsibility for the privileged subject position of their histories and that of their art. Canons of art are actively established and reinforced through the questions or themes historians choose to focus on, the sites or artists they study, and the methods of inquiry they employ. While critics have defined the canon as expressions of universal standards of quality, the canon itself can function as a mechanism of oppression, a guardian of privilege, and a vehicle for exclusion through which structures of class, gender, and race are hidden. As art historian Anna Brzyski argues, "It is more than curious, therefore, that despite the extensive nature of the critiques of canonicity and their wide acceptance, mainstream art history continues to embrace canonical logic in its day to day operations, research, presentation of scholarship, pedagogy, and curatorial practice."[12] With this in mind, I wonder whether decolonization is enough to deconstruct the Western canon, which has become universalized, or whether peripheral histories remain addendums to a master narrative.[13] While decolonization is mainly the active work carried out by the colonized, *deimperialization* is work that must be performed by the colonizer first.[14] This includes the evaluation of the colonizer's relationship with its former colonies. Deimperialization, I argue, is the current roadblock affecting postcolonial and anticolonial scholars of the study of art history. As reflected in Brzyski's critique of the ongoing centrality of the Western canon, I contend that this self-reflection of the colonizer's writing of history has not yet taken place, as evidenced by the preservation of the Eurocentric art historical canon within the academy and within museums.[15]

Within this operation, the diasporic subject situates themselves between the decolonial and the deimperial. Decolonization is the priority and should drive diasporic research in order to further displace Eurocentrism within conceptions of art and culture; however, the diaspora first needs to be attentive to the deimperial work already taking place within colonial logics. Because the diaspora can sometimes write from a place of privilege, or can be situated in the Global North, the diasporic artist or scholar must be attuned to the reflexive work taking place by the colonizer or colonial institution that actively reflects on how racism, settler-colonialism, white supremacy, and imperial domination have shaped dominant discourse. From there, the diasporic subject can do meaningful decolonial work that reflects on the historical relation with the former colonizer, involving the processes of self-critique, self-rediscovery, and identity formation. While the diasporic subject stands within a complicated place in this dynamic as they operate on both sides of the antiracist project, this formula should be a way forward for any research that aims to destabilize Western hegemony over art, culture, canons, and discourse.

If the deimperialization is the active, reflective work done by the colonizer first, requiring the close evaluation of power and control held over former colonies, then decolonial work carried out by the racialized, diasporic, or postcolonial subject must necessarily come after. This decolonization happens by the formerly colonized to expand canons, illustrate the gaps that exist within colonial time and history, and fill in those gaps with artists, cultures, geographies, languages, and identities that were previously excluded due to colonial legacy and epistemic violence. Decolonial research is thus vital to remove an inherent Eurocentrism within disciplines, but the deimperial work done by the colonizer first is what creates room for engagement that will most productively contribute to a shift in the center-periphery dynamic that dictates Global North/South binaries and destabilizes Europe's place within that center.

For a burgeoning field of study like Arab art (broadly speaking), it is important to be critical of the fact that these secondary histories are forced to engage with the Western canon in order to prove their worth and validity. Periphery histories (in this case, Middle Eastern art histories) are constantly existing in relation to the dominant (and Western) canon in order to locate themselves within linear history, but unfortunately the dominant canon is not forced to engage with the periphery, thus reifying its position in the center.[16] An example is the exclusion of artists from Islamicate regions within key art history textbooks used in the majority of undergraduate survey classes. While some books like Helen Gardner's *Art through the Ages* have tried taking a more global approach to the study of art, wide-ranging gaps and exclusions continue to exist (for instance, the scholars of modern Arab art who are working with great rigor to include Arab histories within the dominant history of modern art movements).[17] Cultural theorists Peggy Levitt and Markella Rutherford write the following in their study of the most recent general knowledge art history publications:

> 306 modern artists were catalogued. Of these, 261 (85%) are Western and 45 (15%) are Non-Western. The Non-Western artists are from Asia, Africa, South America, and the Middle East. Disagreements among editors about the importance of individual Non-Western modern and contemporary artists remains high, with only 4 artists (9%) appearing in more than one textbook sampled for the period. In contrast, for Western artists, there is an even higher degree of editorial convergence, with 54% of artists included in this period appearing in more than one textbook. This means that Western modern artists are 7 times more likely than Non-Western modern artists to be recognized across multiple recent art history textbooks.[18]

Importantly, according to Levitt and Rutherford's data, world-famous New York–based Iranian artist Shirin Neshat appeared a total of three times in the published textbooks that comprise the art history pedagogical canon, and she was the only Islamicate visual artist to be included in these textbooks.[19]

What becomes clear is that in order to create legibility to art histories that fall outside of the linear history of the Western canon, Arab art movements are often compared to the modern and contemporary art as defined by and understood in the West. This creates incompatibilities and forces the history of Arab art to somehow mirror Western art movements in order to be legible and to be recognizable within the academy and as art worth studying within the already defined parameters of "good art." While the writing of this alternative history is important and necessary, the canon here remains intact because of the compulsory association the Global South needs to have with the Global North. As feminist art historian Aruna D'Souza states, "As art historians committed to a true reimagining of the field in which we work, we must be willing to attend to the ways in which art history is spoken differently. That is to say, we must be attendant to both the exportation of our discipline to other sites of art history as well as to the importation of methods emerging from the study of the non-Western or those areas marginalized by the discipline up to now to our analyses of Western art."[20]

What is lacking in the binary model of global versus the local is an awareness and recognition of the creative interventions that networks of minoritized cultures produce within and across national boundaries—that is, the micro-practices of transnationalism.[21] This is where the process of deimperialization is urgent within the study of art history in order to avoid an uncritical importation of minoritized culture. This deimperialization has the power to dismantle the absoluteness of the canon and open up alternatives for other histories to exist, engage with, and inform one another in a productive fashion. In this book I engage in such deimperialism to bring into dialogue the histories of same-sex desire in the Middle East with the study of diasporic art production, centering the processes of imperialism and how they have affected the ways in which gender and sexuality are depicted and actualized through history. This is a grand task but one that must be taken up in order for critiques of colonialism to be at the forefront of the writing of history and for postcolonial projects within art history to be spotlighted and engaged with productively.

Deimperializing the Study of Arab Art

Deimperialization can happen in different ways. In *Asia as Method* Chen suggests using other cities and countries within Asia as reference points to one another rather than the mandatory reference and comparison to the West. Changing the frame of reference from Western theoretical propositions to more locally relevant theoretical concerns can disassemble the Euro-American universalist contention that Stuart Hall calls "the West and the rest."[22] This allows for the possibility of an inter-Arab referencing system in which works of modern art from different regions in the Middle East would be compared to one another in a way that connects their shared histories of colonialism and imperialism, providing locally relevant contexts to better inform modern art production in the Middle East. Redefining the canon and history of modern Arab art is outside the purview of this book, but I use this inter-Arab method as a part of the decolonial methodology that informs my research and is theorized within my use of the term *Islamicate*. I expand on this method throughout the book to develop my emerging theory, *queering locally*, and I use a local-local framework that links different Islamicate histories, regions, and diasporas within a south-south relationality. This south-south relationality is the very thing that makes the inter-Arab referencing system a worthwhile framework, for it expands the possibilities of understanding periphery histories in a way that does not center Eurocentric understandings of art, geography, and sexuality. This inter-Arab method proves helpful in framing postcolonial tactics of representation with other nations' strategies of identity formation and independence. This way, Arab art takes on more powerful resonances that relate heavily to postcolonialism, national identity, and the construction of autonomous Arab subjectivity.

Just as modern Egyptian artists such as Mahmoud Mukhtar leading a neo-Pharaonism movement in the early 1900s, or similarly Ragheb Ayad and Muhammad Nagui being associated with the Egyptian Awakening (also known as Egypt's Renaissance or *Nahdat Misr*),[23] so too did modern artists in Syria, Lebanon, Iraq, Jordan, and Sudan revert to their historical roots for artistic inspiration as a way of forging a new cultural identity in the periods after colonialism. As art historian Nada Shabout deftly outlines, art societies, salons, and educational institutions were established during colonial occupation to support a new artistic tradition that moved away from traditional Islamic art that was regarded as craft, and structurally worked to legitimize the culture and lessons of the new (Western) colonial powers. As early as 1851, various Sociétés des Beaux-Arts were founded in Algiers, for instance, with membership restricted to artists of French origin. Museums were established to exhibit Orientalist art, and the École des Beaux-Arts was eventually opened by French authorities to prepare students for admission to similar schools in Paris. Arab artists, however, were generally excluded from this institutionalized and hierarchical structure that worked as an apparatus of colonial rule.[24] Thus, when the first generation of modernist Algerian painters appeared on the scene between 1914 and 1928, they were mainly self-taught artists who had made the transition to easel painting and whose work exhibited a strong Orientalist influence in both style and content.[25]

As other scholars have outlined, this process of decolonization is precisely what led to the birth of Arab modern art, and this decolonization continues to impact individual nations' self-discovery, returning to their roots, and self-fashioning of an artistic expression that is socially and locally relevant to the population.[26] This focus and rewriting of history is necessary, as it introduces new movements to the art historical canon and challenges previously accepted historical narratives. In this way, the aesthetic comparison of modern art from Syria to that of New York or Paris created a reductively linear narrative that proved unproductive. This forced linear narrative and point of comparison became a stumbling block that accuses and assumes the history of modern Arab art as being derivative, lacking, and years behind that of Western modern art. What prevented the admission of the integral role played by minority cultures during colonial rule is the politics of recognition and the oftentimes reductive adherence to a binary North/South, dominant/resistant model of culture.[27] Accordingly, Euro-American theory is simply unhelpful in our attempts to understand these conditions and practices born out of colonization and cultural subjugation. There is something wrong, and arguably violent, with the academy's frame of reference.[28] Developing Chen's idea of *Asia as method* for these purposes would require an open-ended imagination in localizing certain practices in relation to diasporic subjectivity. Throughout this book I implement decolonial methods like the *Islamicate*, *queering locally*, and *horizontal art histories* as a way of developing locally relevant ways of being, creating, and seeing within a transnational and global context.[29]

Modernizing Arabs: National Identity through Modern Art and Sexuality

Ultimately, at a time when modern art in the Middle East was defined by a period of self-discovery, patriotism, and nationalism following colonial encounters and liberation, a Western sexuality script became normalized. During this period of ascribing to modernity in all facets of society, the exacting terms of Victorian heterosexuality and queerness, the fixity of gender binaries, and the rigid codes governing masculinity and femininity became ingrained within modern Middle Eastern society. As other scholars have demonstrated the import of these sexual codes through colonialism, I would like to stress that these codes were normalized in the early twentieth century in the same temporal period of modernity and modernization in the Middle East. These new Victorian gender and sexual norms were a direct aftermath of imperialism and took place during a vital cultural moment of heritage formation and a rediscovery of Arab identity. The new identities—both sexual and national—forged during this period are a part of the Arab enlightenment (*Nahda*), a beginning of Arab modernity (*Hadatha*), and created the nucleus for the postcolonial modern art that quickly followed. In this way, modernity in the Middle East and the sexual identities that ensued cannot be understood as a universal narrative of progress and innovation and instead need to be understood as a Western ideological project imposed by colonialism that resulted in drastic changes in sexual identity, cultural production, and the very nationalism that forged a nation as modern.

Just as the modern artists in Egypt, Syria, Iraq, and Lebanon, among others, were faced with the impossible task of forging a new identity after their countries achieved independence, contemporary Arab artists working in the diaspora are demystifying the identities associated with homosocial and same-sex histories in the Middle East. While I am not arguing for conflating the modern and the contemporary decolonization as being the same, nor seeking to ignore the different aesthetic practices of both periods, I contend that linking the postcolonial and anti-imperial aspects of modern Arab art (a field currently being discovered, written about, and driving its way into the academy) to the political work of contemporary Arab artists in the diaspora has the potential to keep social histories and identity formation at the core of anti-canonical art production. In uncovering these histories and links, there emerges a larger network of cultural organization that the totalizing Western canon cannot choose to ignore. It is precisely this link that brings my study of contemporary art in such close proximity with modernity and the study of modern art. This process, I argue, will be a step in deimperializing the Western art historical canon and will bring histories of Western imperialism and colonialism into forced dialogue with postcolonial critiques and decolonizing practices.

Methodologically speaking, Arabs have been left out of the discourses of both art and the history of sexuality in very similar ways. Linking the studies of visual cultures to those of sexuality studies opens up new possibilities within postcolonial theory. Visual analyses of Arab artists and those focusing on issues of sexuality and same-sex desire illuminate the ways in which local instances of homosociality cite traditional sexuality scripts within contemporary Middle Eastern art and its diaspora while rejecting the Western queer identity narrative that becomes exclusionary in non-Western contexts. These visual forms provide significant examples of how local networks of identity are transmitted through visual language and how alternative sexuality scripts are written. In her book *Webbed Connectivities: The Imperial Sociology of Sex, Gender, and Sexuality*, Vrushali Patil suggests naming this exact problem. She suggests moving from the moniker "heterosexual matrix" to "racial-colonial heterosexual matrix" or "imperial heterosexual matrix." This shift in focus would resist whitewashing the history of sexuality by moving from concepts like "sexuality" to instead center on concepts of "racial-imperial sexuality" or "racial-colonial sexuality."[30] In this way, linking the problematic of contemporary Arab art and aesthetics to a broader history of politics and representation would help create discourse on art from the Middle East more broadly and, I contend, more productively.

While the scope of this project does not include reworking the very foundation of Arab art, its aesthetics, and its history, I am interested in how these histories affect the understanding of contemporary art from and relating to the Middle East. Racial biases within visual culture, as outlined in chapter 2,

"Trauma and the Single Narrative: Reading Arab Art and Photography," are not only problematic solely due to the poor contemporary representations of the Middle East in the media but are also multifariously informed by the ways these images are positioned within a wider history. Narratives of the Middle East being associated with a singular narrative of war/trauma and Arab art historically being inherently homophobic, unmodern, and deficient both have baggage in the very value that is associated with Middle Eastern history and Arab subjects today. This historic dismissal of value and worth plays a role in informing the essentialist associations of Arab art and conflict and with images that posit Arabs as being perpetually unable to reach modernity, productivity, and peace. As will be made clear in chapter 2, the narrative of war and trauma in relation to the Middle East is problematic because this relationship affects how all visual art from or about the region is understood. Notwithstanding the problematics of creating a spectacle of trauma in the Middle East that is seen only from a distance in the comfort zone, the legacy of trauma imagery from the conflict zone informs the ways in which Arab artists exist within wider visual culture today.

Horizontal Art Histories / Horizontal Queer Theories

A global-to-local method of analyzing gay or queer culture in the Middle East presupposes that "good" values from the Global North, like gay marriage and pride parades, trickle down and become adopted by the Global South. This vertical line of thinking presupposes a hierarchy of values and an order of principles that further creates center-periphery binaries. Art historian Piotr Piotrowski theorizes this vertical paradigm and reasons that "the center provides canons, hierarchy of values, and stylistic norms—it is the role of the periphery to adopt them in a process of reception."[31] While Piotrowski speaks of art historical models relating to dominance and canons, I contend that studying queer theory under his lens of dismantling the vertical discourses that create and order center-peripheries can allow us to more aptly bring into perspective the histories of sexualities left in the margins. In sketching the basic principles of what a horizontal art history looks like, Piotrowski says the following:

> A horizontal art history should begin with the deconstruction of vertical art history, that is, the history of Western art. A critical analysis should reveal the speaking subject: who speaks, on whose behalf, and for whom? This is not to cancel Western art history, but to call this type of narrative by its proper name, precisely as a "Western" narrative. In other words, I aim to separate two concepts which have usually been merged: the concept of Western modern art and the concept of universal art. Western art history can thus be relativized and placed next to other art historical narratives—in accordance with the horizontal paradigm. The consequence of such a move will be a reversal of the traditional view of the relationship between the art history of the margins and that of [Western] art history.[32]

In this vein of thought, horizontal queer theories would function in a similar fashion. A horizontal queer theory should deconstruct the supposed authenticity and assumed stability of Western gay identity. In this interdisciplinary study of art history, queer theory, and critical race theory, asking these same questions (who speaks, on whose behalf, and for whom) reveals the power dynamics at play in the history of sexuality while simultaneously interrogating racial and gender discourses within the history of representation. Removing universality from Western theories and tenets seems to be the primary goal of Piotrowski, and other scholars have also sought to provincialize Europe in the same way.[33]

The value of such horizontal methods within this book is its interdisciplinarity and potential to dismantle multiple sites of authenticity that relativize Western theory simultaneously in multiple disciplines. I inform these ideas with scholarship on the creolization of theory, a way of producing knowledge that encourages us to see historical, social, political, and cultural issues as forming part of a creolized system of knowledge.[34] I employ horizontal methods to queer theory while focusing on diasporic Middle Eastern artists in North America by deconstructing the universality of what it means to be both diasporic and queer, and I use horizontal methods to art history where I decenter the traditional Western narrative. This methodology plays a role in relativizing canonical understandings of art production and instead places queer diasporic art production in relation to the wider discipline of art history. Even though I do not write about Middle Eastern artists still living in the Middle East in this book, I localize knowledge without looking at local discourses in the Middle East or specific nation-state units by historically locating how queer diasporic subjectivity is tied to being racialized subjects within North America. Therefore, this research is less concerned with micro discourses in specific locales and more on how diasporic artists explore the "local" in their artistic expressions by articulating aspects of their Islamicate cultural heritage in North America and Europe. This deep attention to historical ways of being plays a corollary relationship to the ways I explore queer diasporic imaginaries within North America and Europe and bring to the fore local understandings of queer subjectivities from uncovering histories of sexuality in the Middle East.

Shifting Methods: Queering Art History to Uncover Colonialism and Empire

The methodology I propose is important for the discipline because of the strategic and, I contend, necessary linking of the history of sexuality to that of art. This much-needed intervention will advance the study of colonialism and give it a seat at the table of art historical discourses; it will also clarify the manifestation and effects Western modernity had on the gender and sexual norms of not only the greater Ottoman Empire but today's Middle East and central Eurasia as well. The "queering" of art history to bring dialogue between visual culture studies and gay studies is not a new concept and has been theorized by art historians such as Amelia Jones, Richard Meyer, and Jennifer Doyle.[35] Catherine Lord and Richard Meyer's edited volume, *Art and Queer Culture*, one of the few comprehensive surveys dedicated to the rich visual legacy of art's relationship to queer culture, is a notable example for their project contributes to a canon of queer art.[36] In a noble effort to anthologize queer artists from around the world, Lord and Meyer attempted to destabilize the art historical canon by informing it with queer artists left outside the walls of representation. What is unfortunately not destabilized are the assumptions made about sexuality itself and the expectation that homosexualities and same-sex desires look the same everywhere in the world.

This assumption recreates a Euro-Americanization of queerness as the center and forces queer artists of color from the Global South to be, once again, restricted to the periphery. Queer artists of color located outside of normative conceptions of queer subjectivity become whitewashed, or Europeanized, into a gay history that is not culturally specific and ignores the complexities of queer relationalities that exist outside the Western paradigm.

It is here that I find value in changing our basic assumptions and research questions to focus on the history of colonialism with regard to the Middle Eastern diaspora and how they become queer subjects. I find it necessary to study a history of art that includes a history of sexuality within its disciplinary strictures and avoid studying *only* the history of art or *only* the history of sexuality, as though visual culture were not related to the depiction, creation, and formation of sexual ways of being. Creating interdisciplinary research that contributes to each respective field has the potential of uncovering colonial histories that were made invisible by the Eurocentric hangovers within each discipline, bypassing epistemologies that once left the colonial matrix of power and imperialism as irrelevant to the construction of dominant canons.

To help rectify the issues posed in this chapter, I have suggested that changing the starting point of our research—to be a history of visual cultures' engagement with colonialism and imperial domination in the Middle East rather than a singular history of art—will be a productive methodological shift. In doing so, anticolonial art production will shift to the core of the discussion, but the history of art, then, *must* contend with wider disciplinary concerns, including histories of gender and sexuality. This decentering of Western knowledges in an interdisciplinary fashion will help Arab art histories grow as a discipline while removing them from their silo of the academy. The history of colonialism in visual culture helps to bridge the necessary gaps between the history of representation and the impacts this has had on local populations. As scholars such as Ali Behdadi and Luke Gartlan are rewriting the history of photography to show how the Middle East has been part of the development of the photographic medium since its conception—rather than being a solely British or French phenomenon later taken up by the rest of the world—so too does the representation of gender and sexual discourses require close reevaluations. As photography was developing in the Middle East at the turn of the century, both by local practitioners and by Orientalist travelers, the women photographed in harem settings and the young boys dressed in flowers and nearly nude must be theorized as being a part of, and contributing to, the history of photography rather than solely being a part of the history of sexuality or vice versa. This is one of the disciplinary failings of the academy, the canons it upholds, and the structures it maintains. In separating the history of sexuality from the history of art, in this case photography, the application of photography as a tool used to colonize local sexual scripts in the Middle East is ignored, obscuring its role in being part of the Europeanizing mission of Western modernity. The necessary linking of the history of sexuality to the history of art is an urgent intervention that will help the study of colonialism be apparent in the inner working of art historical writing and the manifestation and effects Western modernity has had on the gender and sexual norms of Arab peoples. Here, I contend that changing our basic assumptions and research questions to focus on the histories of colonial encounters rather than the history of art from a strictly aesthetic sense or solely the history of sexuality will contribute to both fields while uncovering histories that were made invisible.

Recent studies linking the study of Arab sexualities and visual culture show that there is a need for this juncture; however, there is still much to be explored. Literary scholar Joseph Boone's study *Homoerotics of Orientalism*, for instance, maps out a history of homoerotic Orientalism—in literature, poetry, visual arts, travel journals—that includes contemporary hangovers of Orientalism. The study is noteworthy for its art historical focus, linking the history of representation contrapuntally in relation to sexual narratives in literary, legal, and religious texts. Boone locates the fissures in Orientalist representation, including positive depictions of the Orient within European artworks, homoerotic Occidentalism present within Middle Eastern artworks, and various instances of sexual diversity in both sets of works. Likewise, Ali Behdad and Luke Gartlan's edited collection, *Photography's Orientalism: New Essays on Colonial Representation*, explores similar themes. Gartlan's chapter in particular, "Dandies on the Pyramid," explores the medium's relationship to masculinity and examines the significance of outdoor photographs and photography itself as being productive and expressive of male bonding within the traveler-artist circle. He argues for the centrality of same-sex intimacy in the travels of Orientalist artists and photographers and insists that the photographic sessions facilitated the performance of homosocial desire for Europeans traveling to the Middle East. On an individual level, these two studies linking queer studies, postcolonial theory, and the study of visual culture offer a revisionist approach to Eurocentric writings of art history and the creation of the photographic medium. The contributions that studying histories of the visual culture of sexuality will make to postcolonial theory and vice versa is seen in the fissures and ruptures created in the normative historiography of both the history of art and the history of sexuality.

Diaspora and transnational identity have posed many issues when it comes to imagining geography within global contemporary art practice.[37] This discussion is urgent, as it accounts for the lived conditions of globalization and migration and points to the disciplinary limits of art history. These limits posed by area studies make it difficult to adequately consider the right questions and to generate answers that help explain the realities of a networked and globalized world. However, in order for diaspora and the queer diaspora to be adequately addressed within art history, queer theory, and museum studies, the very limits of knowledge production need to be reimagined. In imagining the issues posed by geographic borders, this research grapples with the disciplinary limits of art history that were inherited from area studies, suggesting that diasporic artists and their cultural production illustrate the incompatibility of colonial definitions of borders, nation-states, and identities.[38] It is when geographies and borders are reimagined that the migration and movement of people can be developed productively and fully within art historical frameworks and in relation to the gendered and sexual identities embodied by diasporic subjectivity.

As an intellectual shift away from colonial ideologies that define and limit the borders of nationalisms, in this book I use the term *Islamicate* as a methodology of global art histories. I explain in chapter 3, "Islamicate as Method: Minor Transnationalisms and Worlding Art History," that the term *Islamicate*, as defined by Marshall Hodgson, refers not directly to the religion of Islam itself but also to the social and cultural complexities historically associated with Islam, including non-Muslims living within the same regions. While the limitations of the terms *Middle East*, *Arab*, and *Islamic* will become apparent in chapter 3, I use *Islamicate* as a conceptual movement away from area studies and for its power to displace nineteenth-century universalizing

European ideas that distinguished, demarcated, and made distinctions between the world's cultures.[39] Through an interdisciplinary queer theory lens, I bring regions of the Middle East, North Africa, and Asia together in this study that would be left outside of academic paradigms regarding the "Middle East" as a stable geographically contained location, and I illustrate how diaspora and nation-state identities hinder the very ways in which complex cultural identification is articulated and understood. Only by keeping imperialism at the forefront of the study of sexualities can we situate how premodern Islamicate sexual scripts have resisted complete colonization and continue to exist today and in the diaspora.

TWO

TRAUMA AND THE SINGLE NARRATIVE

READING ARAB ART AND PHOTOGRAPHY

In this chapter I outline the dangers of the single narrative, the tradition of focusing on the artist's biography within art history, and how this ultimately leads to what I call the *single-narrative biography*, a lens of analysis that limits and reduces the full understanding of art produced by artists of color. A critique of the single-narrative biography is done by exploring documentary photography, its aesthetics, and its impact on Arab photography more broadly. I investigate the major methodological issues faced in the making of Arab art and photography and their relationship to understanding the ways in which conflict is photographed. Focusing on the ubiquitous single narrative of war and trauma that is associated with the Middle East, I investigate racial issues that hinder the full reading of Middle Eastern art and photography. Throughout this chapter, I explore the single narrative using Middle Eastern contemporary art as the focus of my analysis in order to discuss how viewers of Arab photography are conditioned to expect certain narratives or visual imagery. This association between conflict and the Middle East affects the making of art itself, as Arab artists are conditioned to produce photography that is aesthetically similar to pervasive trauma and war photography in order to be viable in the international art market. In examining such pressing methodological concerns about the process of both producing and interpreting Arab art and photography, I investigate the relationship between abundant trauma photographs in popular culture and their impact on the production of contemporary art in the Middle East.

What does trauma and the ways audiences interpret images have to do with queer desire in the Middle East, and how does this effect the interpretation of queer imagery? I contend that before we read queer images, we need to shift our understanding of the dimensions and the ways in which viewers interpret trauma through visual imagery. Queer analysis disrupts the single-narrative biography in interesting ways, for it opens up new manners of being, imagines Arab futurity in powerful dialogues with queer futurity, and complicates how trauma is represented. Queer identities are often left outside of this single-narrative biography, which reinforces the binaries of queer identity being rejected in the Middle East and is a marker of modernity and progress that is associated only with Western artists. While queer identity is increasingly becoming a facet of the single-narrative biography for artists of color, it is important to make visible how traditional visual and historical analysis can limit the reading of full, nuanced lives and the multiplicities of experiences within Arab art production.

In order to answer these difficult questions, this chapter begins by historicizing photography in the Middle East and foregrounds the rocky power dynamics associated with the medium since its creation. I will examine what it means to "picture the Middle East," and discuss how the ubiquity of trauma imagery influences the aesthetics of photography itself. I will then turn to issues of methodology and examine the ways art history is written and show how this too impacts both art production and the types of imagery that are even allowed to be pictured and photographed. Lastly, I will discuss the Arab subject and their artistic aesthetics as a way of opening up the discussion on how documentary photography impacts the aesthetics of contemporary photography. Not only is this relevant to Arab artists, but it also affects the global consumption of imagery and how the West consumes photographic trauma. Today it is accepted as truth that photographers can photograph whatever they choose, and to a large extent that statement is accurate. However, the ways artists produce photography and the ways they *choose* to document a reality are all part of a wider system of historical value and conditioned ways of seeing the world.

Before locating the queerness of an image, I must lay the foundations and understand how viewers interpret visual imagery from and about the Middle East. What does it mean to document the world in which we live? Why do we document, who is this documentation for, and how are audiences meant to interpret documentary photography? Since photography easily circulates in a groundless and seemingly context-free environment, what representational strategies have been developed by artists to make sense of political strife and conflict? Ultimately, how is trauma pictured and how do audiences and viewers of photography interpret cultural difference? These questions are relevant when examining Wafaa Bilal's 2010 artwork *3rdi* (figure 2.1). In this work, the Iraqi artist had a camera surgically implanted and attached to the back of his head, where it remained for one year. Capturing one image per minute of his daily life, all of the photographs were live-streamed to a global audience on its own website (still accessible today), acting as a sort of photographic archive.[1] This documenting, archiving, and sharing of Bilal's personal life can be linked to the power of photography as a medium and its use as a meaningful tool for Arab artists. Photography's link to politics and surveillance might be clear from the artwork's description, but the use of photography instead of another artistic medium is best illustrated in relation to Bilal's personal history. Born in Iraq in 1966, Bilal has experienced trauma that is undeniably marked by imperial wars within his homeland. In 2005 American forces killed his brother Haji in Iraq, and his father subsequently died from the resulting grief of losing his son. Bilal spent time in refugee camps in Kuwait and Saudi Arabia before relocating to the United States, where he currently lives. In an interview with art historian Anthony Downey, Bilal expresses a sense of regret that he was unable to record those journeys through all of their chaos and uncertainty:

> During my journey from Iraq to Saudi Arabia, on to Kuwait and then the U.S., I left many people and places behind. The images I have of this journey are inevitably ephemeral, held as they are in my own memory. Many times while I was in transit and chaos the images failed to fully register, I did not have the time to absorb them. Now, in hindsight, I wish I could have recorded these images so that I could look back on them, to have them serve as a reminder and record of all the places I was forced to leave behind and may never see again.[2]

In this artwork, Bilal not only documents his life, but also he captures images that he himself does not see (figure 2.2). With the camera on the

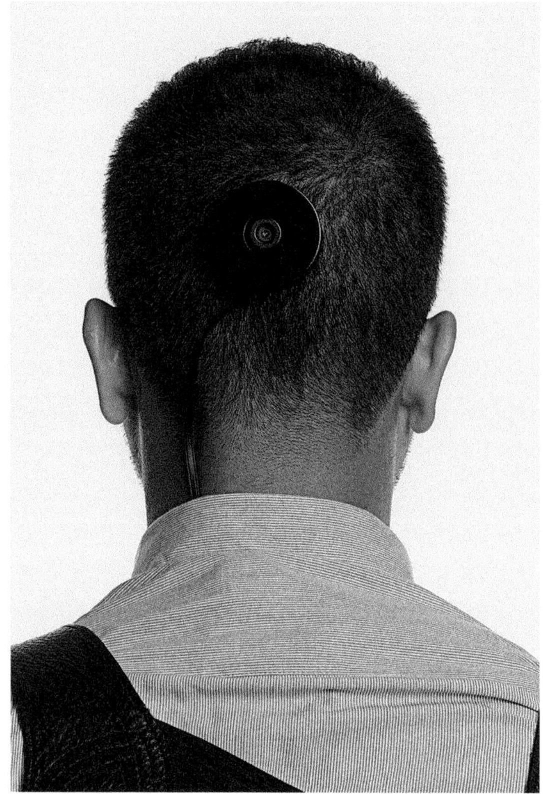

2.1. Wafaa Bilal, *3rdi*. Surgically implanted camera (2010). Courtesy of the artist. See also plate 1.

back of his head, he not only has little control over the image itself, but he is picturing a fleeting reality that is always in the past and continuously behind him. This photographic documentation and the lack of privacy that ensues cannot be removed from notions of surveillance, and these images being publicly broadcasted on the internet speaks to the racialization of the Brown body, and in this case the refugee body, as always being watched. It is through the medium's pervasiveness, accessibility, and circulation that the line is blurred between being watched and being on display, a powerful utilization of photography to speak to the entanglement a racialized subject might feel. In analyzing the mass media visual culture of trauma and conflict that pervades the Middle East, how, then, can artists produce images in relation to culture that is not solely interpreted through trauma? According to Bilal, it was when his brother was killed at a U.S. checkpoint in Iraq that

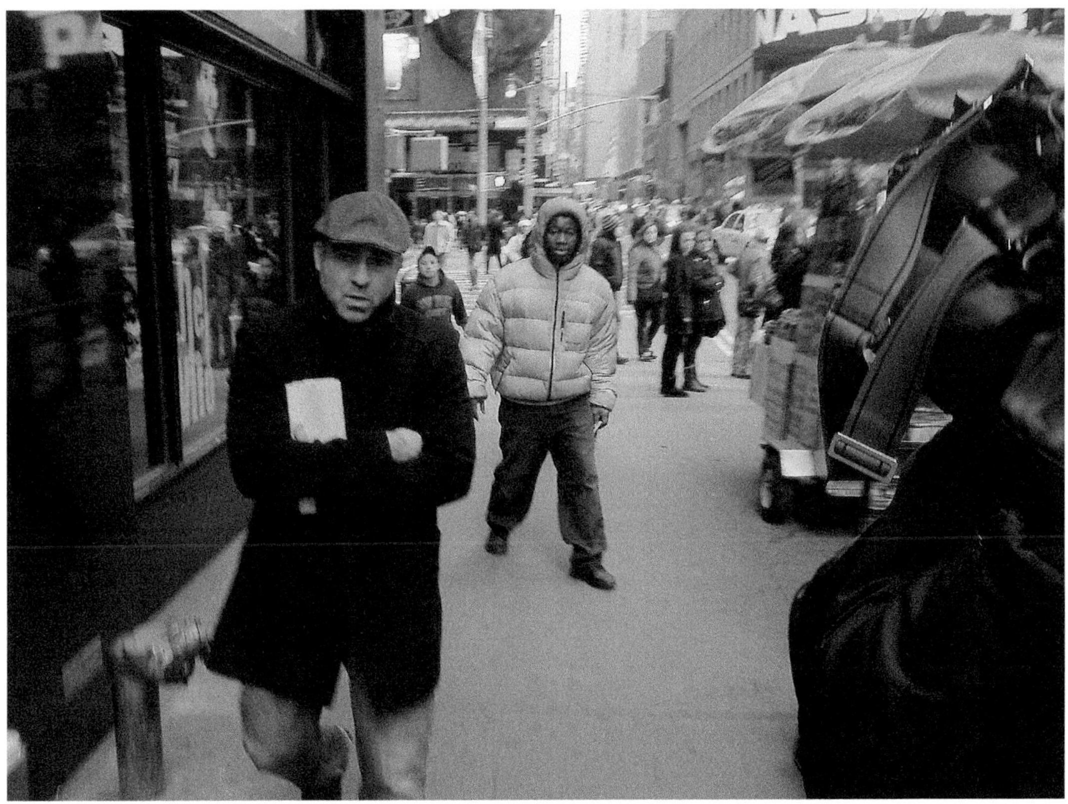

2.2. Wafaa Bilal, *3rdi*. Photograph from surgically implanted camera (2010). Courtesy of the artist.

he decided to use his art as a way of confronting those in the comfort zone with the realities of life in a conflict zone.[3] Now, with Bilal working in New York, what does it mean to interpret an artwork like *3rdi* in relation to documentary photography as a way to understand the political use of new media in the Middle East?

Audiences and viewers of Middle Eastern art are forced into negotiating the images of popular culture, the news, and the overall pervasiveness of photography depicting the Middle East negatively in order to decipher how they attribute meaning to an artwork. It is through this process of visualization that I aim to disassemble Euro-American universalist art history—or "the West and the rest"—and I hope to speak to the ways in which conflicts are pictured and imaged. Bridging links between the technology of media saturation plaguing the Middle East and the photography being produced by Arab artists, this analysis provides reflection and new perspectives on methodological approaches that are attentive to both the process of creating Middle Eastern contemporary art and the process of interpreting photography in transnational contexts.

Historicizing Exclusion and Representation

The history of art, the canon, and the methodologies of history writing shape how viewers interpret and assign value to an artwork. So too does the history of photography shape Arab artists' use of the medium. It is important to conceptualize the history of photography in relation to the Middle East to obtain a greater understanding of the context in which contemporary artists are using photography in their practice. How has the history of photography in the Middle East shaped the current use of the medium by Arab artists? Does the impact that photographic technologies had in the Middle East resonate with the way contemporary Arab artists use photography today? With photography and new media being prevalent and widespread in North Africa and the Middle East, can the current moment of art production be traced to historical exclusion from the history of photography? One must question the intersection of Middle Eastern art histories and their relationship to imperialism as a way of discussing new challenges within the study of contemporary art and photography.

The history of photography is traditionally understood as emerging in two competing forms in 1839: in France, Louis-Jacques-Mandé Daguerre invented the daguerreotype, and in England, Henry Fox Talbot invented calotype negatives. Since the invention of the medium, Arabs have never had control over their photographic representation, at least not within dominant art history.[4] The study of photography in the Middle East is not traditionally focused on local indigenous photographers in the region but rather historiographies of European photographers traveling to the Middle East on imperialist adventures during a period of colonial expansion.[5] Photography was accepted as something that travelers brought from Europe, and these travelers held the power of producing both an image and a narrative.

As historians Ali Behdad and Luke Gartlin argue, a crucial link between the history of photography and Europe's knowledge about the Middle East has existed since the invention of photography.[6] In fact, both France and England published photography manuals about the value of using photography in the Middle East due to the abundant sunshine in the region, which was needed for early photography techniques that required longer exposure times.[7] In subsequent decades, many European photographers, with the support of various governmental institutions, traveled to the Middle East to amass portfolios of Egyptian antiquity, sites of the holy lands, and the exotic Other, making the region one of the principal training grounds for the early practice of photography.[8] The dominant historical canon understands photography as a Western import into Eastern lands, and photography was a tool for Europeans to photograph and capture the Other within an image. According to photo scholars Issam Nassar, Stephen Sheehi, and Salim Tamari, recent scholarship is provincializing European photography and dispelling the conception of photographic practice as a European import and, therefore, indigenous and foreign photographies as two discrete practices.[9] While it is true that an emerging history of photography in Southwest Asia, North Africa, and the Middle East is freeing us of the assumptions that come with a hegemonic Eurocentric history of photography, tellingly, all of these European photographers and photography studios still define the imagery and historical narrative of photography in the Middle East.

In his detailed study of Middle Eastern portrait photography, *The Arab Imago: A Social History of Portrait Photography, 1860–1910*, Stephen Sheehi suggests that trying to locate the differences between a Middle Eastern and and a European master narrative of photography only reinscribes the binaries of the dominant historical narrative of European modernity. Rather than ask how Arab photography is different from Western photography and enforce a binary that is neither productive nor accurate, I look at the function of photography and the power of being photographed. Important here is the use of photography to create narrative, and in the historical instance above, the narrative was an Orientalist one to be disseminated across Europe. The challenge becomes how we can analyze the image while not burdening the interpretation and reading of the image by a Western exceptionalism that created the very aesthetic rules that govern what an Arab looks like within the photographic frame. It is vital to learn how to read images by keeping

Orientalism's asymmetries of power at the forefront of the discussion and assess the Western exceptionalism that produced the aesthetics of photography in the Middle East as being a part of the subject matter itself.[10]

The clear divide between the abundance of European photographers in the Middle East and the absence of the study of local photographers practicing photography there only enforces and makes possible the universalizing tropes of Orientalism and now pervasive trauma photography in the Middle East.[11] According to Ariella Azoulay, the photograph has always been a "product of encounter—even a violent one—between a photographer, and a photographed subject, and a camera, an encounter whose involuntary traces in the photograph transform the latter into a document that is not the creation of an individual and can never belong to any one person or narrative exclusively."[12] Therefore, the history of photography illustrates how Arabs have historically been photographed and is in keeping with the current trend in visual culture to depict the Middle East in troubling ways. In other words, within such media imagery, Arabs themselves are not in control of their own representation within the frame of the photograph. The authority of photography, and the power dynamics associated with who is photographed versus who takes the picture, is a part of a Western exceptionalism that maintains a Eurocentric master narrative that disenfranchises Arabs from proprietorship of the universalizing power of photography.

Picturing the Middle East

In terms of contemporary photography, art from the Middle East has undergone a global shift and is actively becoming a major part of the international art market and art historical narrative.[13] Yet, even with the establishment of art institutions and strong university programs to enhance art education in the Middle East, the former director of Art Dubai, Myrna Ayad, points to the skepticism and hesitation of the broader art world to take Middle Eastern art seriously:

> As an arts writer, I've heard the uninformed allegations countless times: the Middle Eastern art scene is a bubble; its art arena is five minutes old; there is no institutional interest or acquisition. And the worst: "It

is art inspired by conflict"—a sweeping statement that seeks to equate one aspect of the region, i.e. politics, to its art. For me, that last one had always been the zinger, laced with parochialism. As were headlines or exhibitions that used the terms "veil," "unveiled," "women artists from the Middle East," and other sensationalist synonyms.[14]

The narrow-mindedness Ayad speaks of, which equates and reduces an entire region to conflict, is the issue at hand. Arab artists are at an impasse when they consider their practice, participation in the international art market, and the writing of art history. Like other artists working outside of the West, Arab artists are forced to represent their cultural heritage within their artwork and visually describe their nationality and political surroundings. The problem, therefore, is not the artists' representation of their cultural, religious, or national identity, but the essentialized readings, interpretations, and sometimes representations of these artworks. The West expects this of Arab artists, both implicitly and explicitly, through art exhibitions and the study of art: implicitly in the curation of Middle Eastern art exhibitions in the West revolving around singular and reductive narratives, and explicitly in the exclusion of Arab artists from the dominant canon of art history.

The single narrative—that is, the essentialist focus on one aspect of a region that comes to define all ideas associated with a culture—is a major hurdle for Arab artists to overcome, as the compulsory association with war and trauma creates an impossible cycle of art production and art consumption that traps art of the Middle East and hinders complex readings of visual art. As theorist Susan Sontag argues in *Regarding the Pain of Others*, the moment of death is the most celebrated and reproduced war photograph.[15] Visual media on Arab subjects has been curated in the news to be a singular story of trauma, war, and conflict, and the news has strongly influenced the visual imagery that is associated with the region (figure 2.3). With photography being a medium that holds an assumed truth (a truth that Sontag critiques), I argue that the sheer association of "Arab" and "art" or "photography" instills a compulsory association with images of war-torn cities reduced to rubble, riots in the streets as citizens overthrow dictatorships, and the ruthless policing of Arab women in religious clothing. Is it coincidental that these general examples likely garner *specific* images of

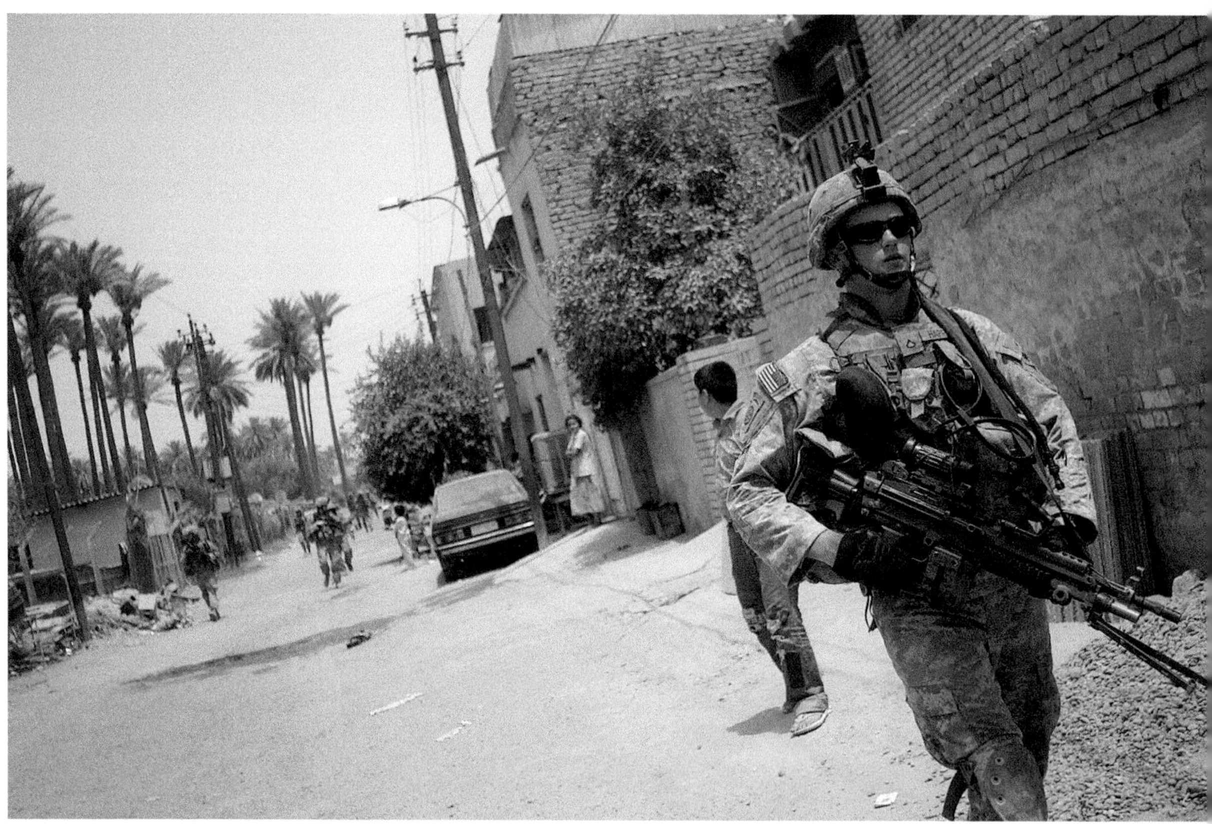

2.3. The Iraqi locals of Al Suleikh come out of their homes to see Paratroopers of 1st Platoon, Alpha Battery, 2nd Battalion, 319th Airborne Field Artillery Regiment, 82nd Airborne Division, as they conduct dismounted patrol. Photo by Sgt. Jeffrey Alexander (June 20, 2007).

Syrian children running around the rubble of decimated towns, scenes of Iraqi citizens toppling the statue of Saddam Hussein, and images of the Taliban riding in the back of trucks, rifles in hand, policing the streets of Afghanistan? These inherent associations with trauma, representation, and the expectation of suffering haunt and plague Arab and Middle Eastern artists producing contemporary art.

Indeed, there are suspicions and skepticism regarding the capacity of visual images to adequately and ethically redeem traumatic events without violating the integrity of victims and survivors. However, there are also discussions on the different effects of visualized depictions of suffering. For example, Ann Kaplan discusses different ways of representing traumas.

She distinguishes different (though blended) kinds of representations that generate different emotional responses to images of catastrophe. These differing kinds of representations include images that make the spectator overly aroused, such as disturbing images of atrocities; the images that generate "empty empathy," which lack any context, knowledge, or perspective of the victim; and the images that allow "ethical witnessing," which involve a stance that may transform how the viewer understands the structure of injustice and perhaps make them feel obligated to take responsibility for preventing future occurrences.[16] Because of these distinctions, I believe it is counterproductive to evaluate the artworks that represent trauma as being the same as media imagery depicting violence; instead, the economies of visual representation, Orientalism, and cultural essentialism should be the target of analysis here. The relationships that these different depictions of trauma have with one another and the ways in which they operate within a larger system of cultural production are what affect the very reading and understanding of art itself, and it is the relationship between trauma, cultural representation, and visual art production that requires further probing.

While Ariella Azoulay's views on photography differ from that of Sontag's, Azoulay's writing about the phantom picture helps us to understand how and why these images are reproduced and remembered. To Azoulay, a phantom picture is one that does not really exist but is a mental picture that has been planted and created by external sources, such as through stories or visual depictions. Phantom pictures, unlike photographs, have no single, individual author and allow for viewers to negotiate and determine how they attribute meaning to a photograph. It is the moment when a viewer gives meaning to a photograph that is always tainted by the phantom image. To illustrate what a phantom image looks like, Azoulay recalls memories of her childhood that have been planted by her mother and how she accepts these memories and images as truth. For Azoulay, an Israeli living in occupied territories at the time, these memories and planted pictures include scenes of threat that the author asserts are often associated with a particular place. Examining the ways trauma and racism are normalized through the screen of memory, she recalls images of Arab markets in Palestine and places like the stairwell in her childhood home as being sites of danger. Reflecting on the process of how these memories were planted, Azoulay writes:

> My mother wouldn't allow me to go to the beach on Fridays. That's the day the Arabs go. "They go with their clothes on," she muttered. Ever since, I've carried around in my head an image of Arabs half-submerged in the middle of the sea, struggling to get up, with the weight of their wet clothes pulling them down. While I remember this image as if it were a photograph I actually saw, I know it was planted in my brain, courtesy of my mother's tongue as she tried to embody her warnings.[17]

Azoulay argues that each one of us carries with them an album of these planted pictures, and I assert that this contributes to viewers' understanding and reception of images from and of the Middle East. Here, the images planted from memory, by stories and by visual media, are a part of what plagues Arab artists. These planted images lead to the expectation of trauma, the aesthetic of photojournalism, and the medium of street photography when viewing artworks by Arab artists. These expectations can be subliminal and unintentional but are a part of this album of planted memories that everyone carries. Media images and visual narratives that become normalized and accepted as truth inform these associations. The viewer makes this subconscious connection when experiencing artworks by Arab artists or photographs with Arab content, mediating how the artwork is understood and received.

The differentiation between the image and the photograph is where Azoulay disagrees with Sontag. What Azoulay distinguishes as a phantom image (and being different from a photograph) is what Sontag amalgamates together as the unrelenting visual imagery that bombards the viewer on a daily basis. In *Regarding the Pain of Others*, Sontag claims that a photograph's meaning is based on the viewer's interpretation and that it falsely represents truth because images are first filtered through image takers. Sontag explains that a picture's meaning is derived through a synthesis of artifice, context, and experience.[18] Importantly, the viewer's prior experience and the context of the viewing all contribute to the meaning of a photograph. Azoulay argues that the phantom image leads to the creation of the image itself, even if this phantom image is not really a photograph. But for Sontag, the issues lie within the ruse of picturing truth and the camera's falsehood as representing objective reality. Therefore, the media saturation portraying trauma in the Middle

East is a purposeful representation strategy that shapes our conception of truth and meaning. For the Arab artist, it is important to understand the impact of these phantom images and how they condition the reception of the artwork by the viewer while simultaneously conditioning the way Arab artists are expected to produce art.

Why Photography?

The artistic use of contemporary photography, a medium that many Arab artists increasingly choose, must be examined within this same paradigm of power and representation. The history of the medium itself and its common use in wider visual culture, to a certain degree, shapes the artwork Middle Eastern artists are producing. Art historian Salwa Mikdadi argues that new media and video art is more transportable than other mediums, and its portability has benefited artists living with restrictions.[19] This includes artists who have limited mobility between countries as well as artists who must pass checkpoints within national walls. The choice of photography and digital media installations have likewise proven to be suitable mediums for the political and social nature of Arab art, as illustrated through Wafaa Bilal's artwork *3rdi*, discussed at the start of this chapter. Therefore, with photography and digital media being suitable both practically and conceptually for works by Arab artists, how the West consumes and interprets Arab art needs to be better connected to the transnational potential of visual media. The phantom images that condition the Western audience's expectations and assumptions, and the subconscious associations of war and trauma, should be read in conjunction with the medium itself and how photography is used in the making of Arab contemporary art. Whether or not the singular narrative and the association of war and trauma is mostly affecting Arab artists working with photography, rather than painting or sculpture, would speak to the medium itself and its use in the broader circulation of images within visual culture. The problematics of representation must be examined in more detail, for there is a clear relationship between photography and new media being a practical and suitable trend in the making of Arab contemporary art, the consumption of these war images in the news and media outlets, and the reception of Arab art in the West. These causalities and dynamics of power and representation are therefore closely related to the function and use of photography as a medium and as an artistic tool of creation. In this way, the work of Middle Eastern artists is informed by—but never reducible to—a history of representation that has presented Middle Eastern contexts in troubling ways and continues to do so.

As the edited volume *Uncommon Grounds: New Media and Critical Practices in North Africa and the Middle East* elucidates, these issues are not local, nor do they pertain only to the Middle East. Art historian Anthony Downey argues that "this is an international rather than provincial concern, inasmuch as there remains the ever-present interpretive danger that visual culture from the region is legitimized through the media-friendly symbolism of conflict."[20] This speaks to the tactic of the media to bombard viewers with images of conflict in the Middle East, and the curated visual material that becomes circulated is therefore rooted in Orientalist ambitions of determining the Middle East as worthy of attention only in relation to lack of modernity, nonprogressiveness, and extremism. When contemporary artists are using photography and new media to respond to political events, one must dissect the language that the artist uses in relation to the language of wider visual culture and interrogate the relationship between the two. That is to say, the rhetoric of conflict and the spectacle of trauma need to be discussed in relation to an aesthetic ambition that seeks to explore "the often inconsistent relationship of the subject to history."[21]

Artist Larissa Sansour uses photography both purposefully and politically. In her oeuvre, Sansour produces videos and photographs fusing futuristic aesthetics with issues surrounding Palestinian identity and Israeli occupation. In response to the Israeli-Palestinian conflict and unsuccessful attempts at peace, she addresses displacement in her art by creating fictional spaces for Palestinians to settle. Sansour explains that her choice of medium is important, and it is her tool in depicting Palestinian consciousness and the experience of displacement through tropes such as humor and science fiction.[22] Also important to her practice, and most relevant to this analysis, is her use of high-budget film and expensive high-production photographs to create science fiction motifs. She produces these narratives and costly visuals consciously because, as she indicates, there is an expectation that as a Palestinian artist she would be producing low-budget documentary photographs that resemble amateur war photography. In this instance, the baggage of representation has a powerful control over the narratives that are being told and how they are permitted to be told.

These practical issues of visualizing, picturing, and documenting are central to how aesthetics are theorized. Part of the baggage of representation outlined thus far relates to the writing and recording of Arab art histories. Art historian Nada Shabout argues that the Middle East lacks formal art criticism and instead relies on Western models for the writing of art history that do not start with the work of art. Rather than provide an analysis of the visual elements first, the critic starts with the artist's biography. If an Arab artist's identity is the only way to attribute meaning to their artwork, we cannot escape the lack of objective criticism for Arab artists.[23]

The use of the artist's biography started with the Italian Renaissance and sixteenth-century Italian painter, writer, and historian Giorgio Vasari. Vasari is commonly thought of as the first art historian, and his book *Lives of the Most Excellent Painters, Sculptors, and Architects* is considered the ideological foundation of art historical writing. He focuses on the artist as genius and contends that the biography of the artist is the most important aspect in understanding their work and art practice.[24] While the concept of "artist as genius" is heavily critiqued in modern scholarship as being masculinist and exclusionary,[25] it still haunts the writing of art history whenever the starting point of analysis is the artist's biography. What started with Vasari anthologizing the lives of living artists during the Italian Renaissance turned into a biographical approach to recording history that quickly cemented itself and developed into the primary mode of art writing. While initially affecting how Europeans wrote about other European art, this method of analysis became the primary vehicle for art historical writing in the West and, most importantly, about art outside the West. For non-Western artists, I contend the focus of the artist's biography slowly shifts the discussion from "artist as genius" to one of "artist as different." The biographical information of the Arab artist is used as a marker of differentiation from a Western norm, a difference that informs and is reinforced by the analysis of the artwork itself.

The Arab Subject and Their Aesthetics

The construction of Arab visual culture is a point of concern. Art critic Nat Muller reinforces that presenting the generic image of the Middle East as "bad news" to Western audiences forces artists into a rocky power dynamic where they play into expected perceptions or representations.[26] When addressing international audiences, artists from the region are expected to somehow personify both the historic and the national—an impossible task seemingly reserved only for racialized and Arab artists, and not expected of Western artists. Muller insists that "if we want to lay out conditions of focusing on a contemporary practice, we have to look further and beyond the identitarian markers of ethnicity, politics and geography . . . and let the art first and foremost speak for itself—or in other words, let the socio-political and historical undercurrents speak from the art, rather than the other way around."[27]

Scholar Dina Ramadan calls this entanglement of representation, authenticity, and identity the "objectification of the artist."[28] This occurs when non-Western artists are stripped of their individuality and are expected to act as a mouthpiece for "the collective"—Arab, Muslim, Other—as well as having to represent both "modernity" and "authenticity," while maintaining a balance in order to avoid accusation of imitating the West or being too folkloric. The question, then, remains, When evaluating the production of meaning in an artwork, can aesthetics be the starting point of analysis before considering the sphere of the historical and political?[29] The binary idea of aesthetics and politics is a modernist paradigm, and the debate that criticizes the separation of aesthetics and politics is not my argument. Binary thinking between politics and aesthetics is simply not helpful, and these logics should not be separated from one another. But even with the ideological linking of aesthetics and politics, the aesthetics of the artwork, particularly art produced by Arab subjects, are one of the last things to be evaluated. Aesthetics are given less importance than the biography of the artist, their national identity, and their geographic location. The politics and the aesthetics should always be in conversation with each other; however, the artwork of the Arab artist is overshadowed by the politics of their national identity. Indeed, Kaplan argues for "the need for scholars in psychology and the media to learn more about the interactions among a traumatic image, its source, genre and placement, and psychological response in an era of global proliferation of images and related cultural emotions. Journalism, advertisements, television, movies, the internet, political and religious propaganda and other sorts of appeals enlist the power of images to move their audiences in ways prior to, or under the radar of, cognition. Emotions produced in these ways may be called 'Public Feelings.'"[30] These "public feelings" are indeed related to aesthetics, as they account for the psychological response viewers have when witnessing Arab art and their relationship to the emotions produced when bombarded with trauma imagery that proliferates the news and media. This relationship between trauma, aesthetics, and Orientalism is one that needs to be returned to, revisited, and re-explored in as many ways as possible until Arab artists are no longer ghettoized within exhibitions, in the writing of art history, and within the international art market overall.

Because of this dilemma, art historian Saleem Al-Bahloly argues for approaching aesthetic forms differently. He sees the necessity to stop understanding aesthetics in relation to the artist but instead in relation to the world event or experience in which the artist is responding to. He calls this the de-subjectivizing of artistic creation and the displacing of the artist.[31] As a way of escaping the shadows of representation that follow Arab bodies and Arab artists, he argues that viewers should not pose questions of aesthetics to a single artist nor even compare one artwork to another. Instead, viewers should pose the question of aesthetics in relation to the world—time, an event, an experience, a problem—and examine the ways in which aesthetics are performed by an artwork in relation to its political surroundings. This is an important argument, for it seeks to rectify the issues previously outlined plaguing discourses of art and the Middle East.

Can reevaluating methods of formal analysis within art history be a solution? As a way of illustrating what de-subjectivizing the artist may look like, I turn to figure 2.4. In this photograph, a woman stands in an empty room that is void of furniture except for a seemingly uncomfortable plastic chair and a glass table supporting a single coffee cup that has spilled on its side. In the center of the room, the subject waters a luscious green olive tree that is jutting out of the floor, cracking through the ground, and its vibrant greenery provides the only color inside the home as it is reflected on the mirrored floor. The watering can in the subject's hands, however, seems to be sprouting roots rather than water, such that the figure is providing the roots of the olive tree in order for it to survive in a different environment. The large windows remain permanently shut and display a view of a desert, the top of a brick wall, and a watchtower that stands at the height of the window. In the distance, the viewer sees a crowded village scene that is bathed in sunlight, breaking the darkness and reflecting color onto the roof of a recognizable building, the Dome of the Rock (or the great Mosque of Jerusalem.) With this one identifying feature, the aesthetics of the photograph, the composition of the scene, and the subject matter itself begin to take shape. In understanding that the town bathed in sunlight is Jerusalem, the viewer understands that the scene takes place in Palestine. More specifically, the watchtower does not just become any panopticon or lookout and is instead connected to the apartheid walls of Palestinian territories occupied by Israel. Being at the same height as the apartment windows, the watchtower that houses soldiers of the Israeli Defense Forces implies that the civilian is always under watch and, more importantly, always enclosed by its walls. The subject of this picture is nurturing the olive tree, which, from its size, must be hundreds of years old, signaling a long historic relationship between Palestinian culture and the olive trees that grow on this land. An important symbol of Palestinian heritage and culture, the figure providing the roots of the olive tree in order for it to survive the trauma of migration poetically speaks to the forced relocation and migration that many Palestinians experience. The Palestinian woman nurturing her own heritage, the tremendous emotional trauma experienced by being constantly watched and policed, and the isolation that results from being separated and partitioned within her own country—these are all features of the artwork that speak from the image itself, not elements that are deduced or assumed from the artist's national identity. This science fiction, highly edited (and therefore expensive production value) photograph was created by Palestinian artist Larissa Sansour and is part of a photo series called *Nation Estate* from 2012. Through this visual analysis, Sansour's subject position did not inform our reading; rather, the true and lived experience of apartheid and colonial trauma as expressed by the artist was fully realized and, most importantly, not biased by imperial assumptions or expectations in relation to the artists' own Arab identity.

To Al-Bahloly, the study of aesthetics must take the artist out of the equation

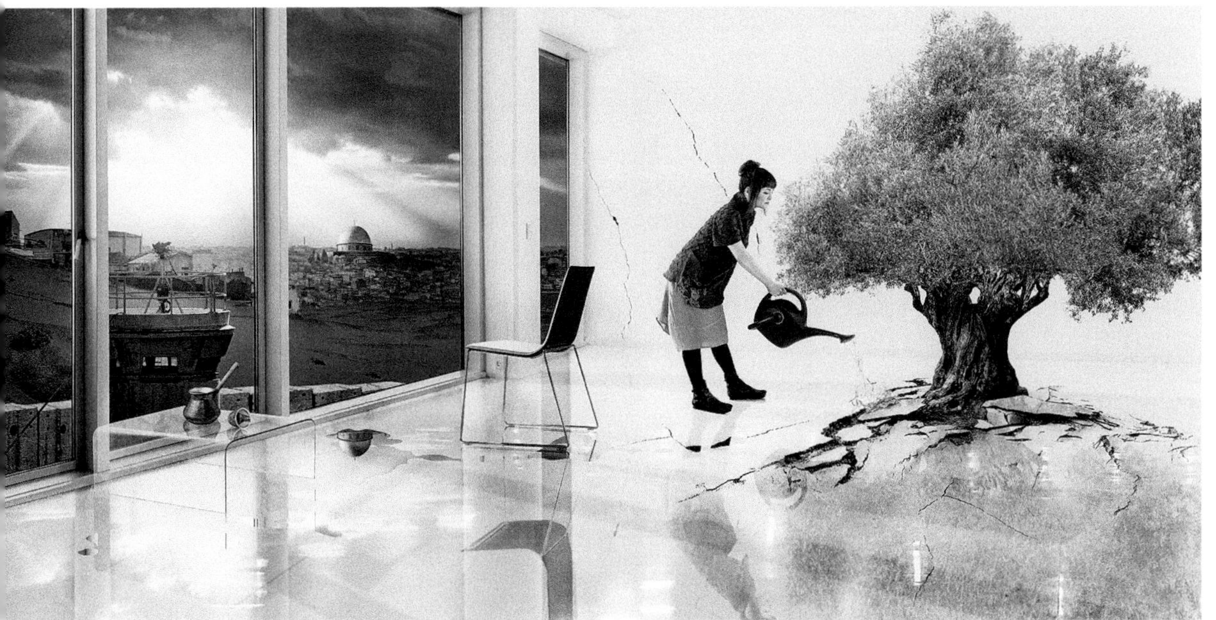

2.4. Larissa Sansour, from *Nation Estate* photo series, *Olive Tree*, C-print, 75 × 150cm, (2012). Courtesy of the artist. See also plate 2.

and let the sociopolitical and historical undercurrents speak *from* the art rather than inform the art itself. This provides a way to enhance the description of the aesthetics of the artwork, giving a different relationship to art and politics and the ways that art can provide aesthetic forms through which political issues are articulated. Therefore, rather than use an artist's birthplace (Palestine, for instance) to dictate the assumed content of the work (mandatorily being about apartheid and war), the artwork itself speaks for the nuanced lived condition of the artist's experience. This is noteworthy, as it alters the demand of the Arab artist of having to produce art about a singular narrative in order to be intelligible to the global art market and shifts the focus to the aesthetics and visual language of the artwork to open up the understandings of the political struggle to which the artwork relates.

Again, Ann Kaplan's theory of *empty empathy* is useful in discussing problems of such images that represent disasters as spectacles and the themes that are expected in exhibitions by Arab artists. Using Martin Hoffman's definition of empathy as "the involvement of psychological processes that make a person have feelings that are more congruent with another's situation than with his own situation,"[32] Kaplan says that empathy can have positive social aspects. However, "empty" empathy does not result in positive social behavior, and this has to do with the current ways audiences view images of catastrophe in excess. Kaplan argues that viewing too many images in succession can diminish a viewer's emotional response; thus the empathy from the images dissipates and "each catastrophe image cancels out or interferes with the impact of the prior image."[33] Next is the risk of "fleeting" empathy, which, Kaplan argues, is caused by the "array of separate images of suffering without any context or background knowledge, focusing on the pain of individuals whom we see at a distance and who are strange to us [so] cannot elicit more than a fleeting empathy. There is no socio-political context for actually putting ourselves in the situation of those suffering from catastrophe."[34]

Due to the different and varying ranges of empathy that viewers feel when witnessing Arab art and imagery, when the artist's single-narrative biography is the dominant starting point of analysis, the artist's identity informs the reading of the artwork rather than having the aesthetics of the artwork itself inform the experience of the artist.[35] The reason why this Western method of writing history is problematic for Arab artists can be traced back to the beginning of this chapter—the inherent associations made by viewers of Arab art and the trauma imagery inherently associated with Arab photography. We are left in a catch-22 situation, an endless cycle that produces the very Arab art it conditions. The artist's Arabness will always inform the art they produce, and in Sansour's case, for example, the artist's Palestinian-ness will be the sole marker for viewers to interpret the work of art. This results in a cycle of singular narratives in which the viewer comes to expect only a certain artwork or narrative of the Arab artist. As illustrated by historian Sheyma Buali, viewers have become accustomed to the digitized, highly spectacular images of emotive events in the Middle East (figure 2.5).[36] This singular narrative flattens the complex experiences of Arab artists to being only a dominant story of war, trauma, and conflict. This means that an Arab artist whose work does not reflect the photographs informed by these phantom images will be left outside of dominant expectations. These dominant expectations are important because they dictate the type of exhibitions that museums organize, and they inform the types of artworks that are acquired

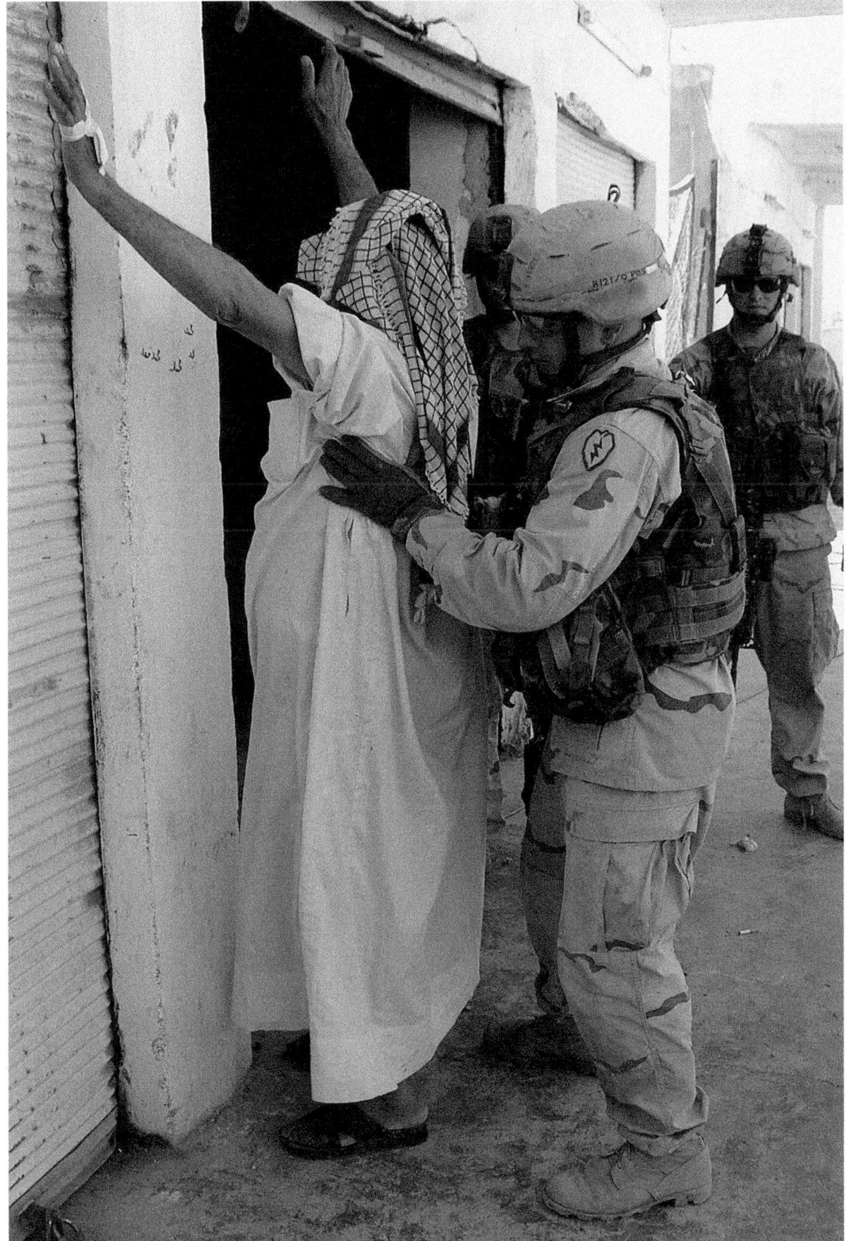

2.5. Staff Sergeant Jesse Wyant, a squad leader with Co. B, TF 1-27 Inf., searches an Iraqi man in Hawija during Operation Wolfhound Power. Photo by Sgt. Sean Kimmons (November 13, 2004).

within permanent collections.[37] Problematically, both the collection and exhibiting of homogenizing singular narratives are misconstrued as being art representative of the region, and the cycle thus continues. Viewers of such exhibitions subsequently expect to see a particular kind of art or representation that mirrors the dominant visual culture in the Middle East, and the dominant aesthetics of what Arab art looks like gradually starts to cement itself within exhibitions, permanent collections, and audience expectations. Slowly, the phantom image is reified and another album of phantom images is made.

Does Race Always Matter? Horizontal Art Histories and the Problem-Centered Approach

The questions asked within this analysis pose specific challenges concerning theoretical approaches for examining contemporary art production and methodological questions about the writing of art history. We must consider that the implications of an artist being conditioned to produce artwork that looks "Arab," are similar in aesthetics to trauma photography or, even if not aesthetically similar, are at least informed by war and conflict photography. What does this line of inquiry say about the agency of contemporary artists in the Middle East? In arguing that Eurocentric image production has conditioned the market for Arab art and the very ways in which art in the Middle East is made, is the artist's agency underestimated? Or can subversion happen at different levels that inform or speak to the art market and writing of art history? Thus far, I have illustrated how the aesthetics of an artwork, particularly art produced by Arab subjects, are one of the last things to be evaluated within art criticism. Aesthetics are given less importance than the single-narrative biography of the artist, their national identity, and, most often, their geographic location, creating bias in the very reading of their artwork.[38] I argue for taking the subject (artist) out of the visual analysis (or at least from the beginning of a visual analysis) in order to deemphasize their national identity as a way to understand aesthetics in relation to the world event or experience in which the artist is responding to, as opposed to in relation to the artist themselves.[39]

With this said, the identity of the artist is an important discussion in places such as North America, where racialized artists fight to be represented ethically. For example, in the 2017 Whitney Biennial, nonracialized artists producing work about race became a central concern.[40] Can the race and identity of the artist be the primary mode of visual analysis in some contexts and not in others? Is there a way to negotiate between Arab artists being ghettoized and biased within art historical narratives and other artists of color producing art that is meant to be analyzed under the purview of racial identity? In the case of the Whitney Biennial, American artist Dana Schutz painted the work *Open Casket* (2016), a haunting portrait of the gruesomely disfigured corpse of Emmett Till, a Black fourteen-year-old boy murdered by a Mississippi lynch mob in 1955 after a white woman falsely accused him of whistling at her. The fact that Schutz is a Caucasian artist who produced a painting showing Black suffering and African American trauma is what led to the controversy. The white identity of the artist is integral to the politics of the situation, yet in the case of Arab artists it is their racial identity that makes the politics of their work disappear behind preconceived notions informed by Orientalism. This discussion opens up, perhaps, a reconceptualization of aesthetics that is better informed by the power dynamics involved in the racialization of the artist, viewer, and cultural production.

The question, then, remains: When evaluating the production of meaning in an artwork, can aesthetics be the starting point of analysis before considering the sphere of the historical and political? In order to look further and beyond the identitarian markers of ethnicity, politics, and geography, can the sociopolitical and historical undercurrents speak from the art itself? If so, does this work in all contexts, or are some postcolonial contexts in need of the identitarian markers of ethnicity more than others (such as Indigenous artists in Canada or Black and Latinx artists in the United States), and are the aesthetics of these artworks more productively read through such politics?[41]

To answer these important questions, we must identify that the differences between a North American–Arab comparison lie within the differences between vertical and horizontal art histories. Art historian Piotr Piotrowski defines vertical art histories as being when "the arts from other peripheral regions . . . are presented as fragments of the global or universal art history established in the West, which reveals . . . [a] West-centric approach to art history, and the dominance of the premises of modernist art geography in general."[42] He argues that this type of vertical narrative implies a hierarchy—often between East and West, modern and unmodern, good and bad—and that a universality becomes established based on the center rather than the periphery. Instead, Piotrowski argues for a horizontal art history:

> A horizontal art history should begin with the deconstruction of vertical art history, that is, the history of Western art. A critical analysis should reveal the speaking subject: who speaks, on whose behalf, and for whom? This is not to cancel Western art history, but to call this type of narrative by its proper name, precisely as a "Western" narrative. In other words, I aim to separate two concepts which have usually been merged: the concept of Western modern art and the concept of universal art. Western art history can thus be relativized and placed next to other art historical narratives—in accordance with the horizontal paradigm. The consequence of such a move will be a reversal of the traditional view of the relationship between the art history of the margins and that of [Western] art history.[43]

This approach to decenter Western art history locates the source of power within art production and history writing and asks these questions: Who speaks, on whose behalf, and for whom? A horizontal art history in this context would not be a one-to-one comparison of art produced by Arab artists and art produced by Black artists in North America, for this would replicate vertical art histories and increase the risk of reinforcing center-periphery dynamics. Such a top-down approach would carry with it value judgments of Arab modernity and Western superiority, especially when art centers like New York become the epicenter of analysis. Instead, a horizontal art history in this scenario would be more conducive to evaluating the place of race and racialization within art analysis.

To illustrate what this horizontal approach to art history looks like, I turn to comparative historiography as a field of study. Methodologically speaking, it may not be a productive task to analyze the racism that Arabs experience as being the same as the racism that other people of color experience in North America or Europe. I do not believe a one-to-one comparative approach would be helpful here. So too it is problematic to even think of racism or racial experience as being constant and stable, for even the racism Arabs experience in Canada is different from that experienced in Europe, Asia, or Africa, for instance, and fluctuates according to local and global events. How can an analytical approach to the study of visual art be developed both thoughtfully in the global connections involved while simultaneously being attentive to the local intricacies of specific histories? Historian Hannes Siegrist writes, "Today, in the age of methodical pluralism and a certain degree of de-disciplining of science (or shifting and blurring of traditional disciplinary boundaries), attention must be focused on problems which need to be detected, analyzed and resolved together."[44] He argues that the focus is being shifted from a "method-centered" to a "problem-centered" approach, and I find this problem-centered approach to be most useful within the study of Arab art and transnationalism.

In focusing on the problems within art historical research, the methods we use can be adapted to better solve the specific issues that have been raised from the onset of research. This would change research questions and their assumptions, create new art historical knowledge focused on identifying the problems within visual analyses that are impacted by issues of race, and develop new ways of dealing with these concerns rather than use the same traditional methods that may have left these questions unanswered or even unexplored. While the dilemma seems clear—that race is relevant and centered in some contexts and should be decentered in other contexts—it is the site of comparison that needs shifting. Rather than the comparative geographic and historical study between North America and the Middle East, the site of study should be different (and horizontal) racial quandaries within the history of art and the art market. This would mean asking the aforementioned questions—who speaks, on whose behalf, and for whom—laterally in a way that does not compare traumas but rather evaluates their points of convergence and separation. In this way, "there is an urgent need for scientific methods and modes of interpretation which are able to detect, evaluate and represent the general and the particular, what connects and what separates."[45] When cultural transfer, interculturality, transnationalization, globalization, and localization are evaluated horizontally within the context of the racialized North American artist or the Arab artist, the racial dimensions of their experiences and their impact within the history of art produces new methods of analysis.

A horizontal art history in this way would remove the value judgments imbued within a vertical ranking of world cultures and instead shift our orientation toward a more equitable view of cultural transfer and global exchange. Borrowing from queer theory the method of assemblages, art historical assemblages would make junctures and comparisons in interesting ways. Queer theorist Jasbir Puar's writing on assemblage theory claims that intersectionality may not always be enough for understanding how age, gender, ability, and race interact to create privileges in some spaces and disadvantages in other spaces. I like to use the metaphor of the birdcage to explain intersectionality, where each individual metal strand represents a facet of identity, such as gender and race, and each looks independent until we look at the top of the birdcage and see the metal rods all come together and meet at one spot, creating the oppression of the cage. However, seeing each of these factors coming together to create the oppression one faces in this way does not fully take into account when only two of these facets of identity converge at one time nor the times when these convergences of certain facets create privileges or oppression dependent on context.

This is where assemblage theory becomes helpful, for if we map these parts of our identities three-dimensionally, and spiraling through space in all directions, we can imagine contexts where some of these aspects of our identities intersect, some do not, and some intersect with other aspects of our identities while not intersecting with others. Rather than the stability of the metal rods of the birdcage, we are left with a constellation of strings that twist, curve, bend, and spiral in all directions, with individual points of identity converging in some places but not in others. This is an important contribution to thinking of race, culture, and sexuality horizontally instead of vertically—meaning, if different world cultures were mapped horizontally and on a horizontal axis like a bar graph, nonlinear lines would emanate from the graph in all directions and would represent global power, imperial struggle, colonial domination, Orientalism, racism, classism, and sexism to show interesting convergences between different art histories while also illuminating privileges in the ways certain lines do not intersect with other points on the graph. While further analysis illustrating what this intellectual task looks like is outside the scope of this book, I have sketched out what a horizontal art history that is intersectional at its core can look like, and I employ these logics throughout the book as I bring queer theory and critical race theory together in the study of art and culture. Within this study, this means that by firmly including and reflecting on the dimensions of difference and exchange, future research that is attentive to social and cultural historical comparison will be productive in the interdisciplinary study of art, race, class, gender, and culture.

Reading Queer Diasporic Images

This discussion becomes an important critique of what I call the "single-narrative biography"—that is, the way in which work by Arab artists is invariably seen through the lens of war and trauma—and individual biography rather than the work being approached first through its aesthetics. The difficulty in this critique is how trauma, war, and personal biography are indeed central to much of the work under discussion. For instance, this chapter begins with the work of Wafaa Bilal, where the biographical (the death of his brother) is crucial to understanding Bilal's entry into art in the first place. This means that as critics we can and must engage with the biographical and with histories of loss and trauma that, as I have noted, are indeed intrinsic to much of the work, without enacting the Orientalist and reductionist reading of the work that he rightly critiques. In other words, this discussion is modeling for us a mode of engaging with the biographical without enacting a single narrative. As Gayatri Gopinath notes, "The aesthetic practices of the queer diaspora are archival practices that excavate and memorialize the minor histories (personal, familial, collective, regional) that stand outside of official nation-centered narratives" that foreground the personal and biographical.[46] In fact, later within her own study, Gopinath goes on to explain that to study queer diasporic experiences more locally and within regions is quite often a turn to the personal or autobiographical, often inextricably linked to the project of narrating the self even in an attempt to deconstruct an essentialist logic of identity, place, and belonging.[47] There is an undeniable centrality of the personal and the autobiographical in the project of queering visual representation and the project of reading visual images transnationally. It becomes clear that we must be explicit in our usage of the artist's biography in an effort not to ghettoize the reading of their work; rather, we must mobilize the autobiographical in crucial ways that contribute to an alternative personal, aesthetic, and artistic genealogy.

As mentioned at the onset of this chapter, I contend that before we read queer images, we need to understand the dimensions and how viewers read trauma. When queer identity is intertwined with the single-narrative biography of Arab artists, the result is a clichéd expectation of queer failure, queer trauma, and Arab homophobia. Queer identities are either left outside of this single-narrative biography, or they are central to it. Both cases reinforce the binaries of queer identity being rejected in the unmodern Middle East, contrasted with the freedom of sexual and artistic expression seen in Western artists. It is the inherent association with trauma and queerness that compounds the racial logics of the single-narrative biography to once again limit the reading of full, nuanced lives and the multiplicities of experiences within Arab art production. As the subsequent chapters of this book will explore, the single-narrative biography can truly be dismantled productively when queer embodiment is visualized in complicated ways and in relation to other facets of subject formation. This means that trauma is never the driving force in reading the artworks within this book; rather, the assemblage of queer and racial diasporic identities is articulated through visual analysis. Colonial trauma, imperial violence, and historical suffering are not assumed truths based on the ethnic or national identity of the artist; instead, these dimensions are developed out of a nuanced analysis that uses horizontal writing of both art history and queer theory as an exercise in relational comparison being its driving force. The problematics discussed within this chapter are necessary to inform both racialized and queer trauma in order to work beyond the single-narrative biography into a more thoughtful historical analysis. It is important to identify that reading queer trauma is linked to the single-narrative biography in the association that queer Middle Eastern identity has to compulsory queer failure and Orientalist ideas of savage unprogressiveness.

Likewise, these theories inform how we read diasporic images. While Middle Eastern suffering was the broad subject of this chapter, most artists and institutions analyzed were either diasporic or currently located in the West. Reading diasporic images is absolutely a component of this logic, and diasporic artists face the same issues with their artwork not despite the single-narrative biography but because of it. The refugee experience of artist Wafaa Bilal and the diasporic experience analyzed in the artwork of Larissa Sansour are absolutely tied to issues of an assumed singular Arab experience that limit the full reading of their nuanced artwork. Diasporic art in particular is interwoven with the racial dimensions of Arab art more broadly. This is due in part to the binary structure of progress and civilization that is rooted in Orientalism and Western modernity: a center-periphery or us-and-them binary that structurally disempowers the Middle East and is a barrier that the diaspora also faces in North America and Europe.

Ultimately, this chapter contends that the single-narrative biography is the real culprit of creating a clichéd identity and leading to reductive understandings of the art produced by people of color. The problematics addressed here are that artworks by Arab artists are still read through the single-narrative biography, and that is the predominant lens from which Arab art histories are written. The situation for Arab artists is not necessarily different in North America from that of the Black, Latinx, and racialized artists they work alongside. The main issue is that the single-narrative biography that reduces the artwork of people of color to being about only a select handful of themes is what stifles the full reading of postcolonial art. There are particularities that the Arab artist faces in a post-9/11 context, so essentialism has manifested itself in a very visible way affecting the reading of Arab art. Because of this, it is important to separate the artist from the expectation of certain modes of artistic production based on cultural heritage and personal identity. The critique of the artist "biography" may not be the real issue here, for biography is central to identity and identity is central to these concerns; the culprit is the *single-narrative biography* when it creates only limited expressions of complicated experiences.

This reconceptualization of not just the historical narratives being told but the focus of why certain narratives are told is a way of escaping these shadows of representation that follow Arab bodies and contemporary Arab artists. While such a project is historic in nature, reworking the very foundation of Arab art, its aesthetics, and its history, both within the Middle East and in dominant art history, will be productive in informing the ways in which contemporary Arab art is understood. The issues of representation as outlined in this analysis does not start its problematic solely with the poor depiction of the Middle East in the media but is multifariously informed by how these images are positioned within a wider history. Both narratives of the Middle East being associated with "bad news," or Arab art as being unmodern and deficient have baggage in the very value that is associated with Middle Eastern history and Arab subjects. This historic dismissal of value and worth, as reflected in Myrna Ayad's quote at the start of this analysis, plays a role in informing the inherent associations between Arab art and conflict and with images that posit Arabs as being perpetually unable to reach modernity, productivity, and peace.

This chapter has analyzed dilemmas in interpreting and understanding the visual art produced in the Middle East and by the Arab diaspora. But what if the issues are more systemic than the artworks produced and the ways audiences interpret them? What if the very structures that exhibit, analyze, and theorize artworks by people of color are not fully accounting for the complex realities of a networked and globalized world? In the next chapter, I take a more macro approach to this discussion and analyze notions of "worlding" and how methodologies within global art histories can evolve to include complex racial dimensions of nationalism, colonialism, and nation-states. As I introduce the *Islamicate* in more detail, the primary method used within this book, it is important to build on the ideas of horizontal art history mentioned here in order to disassemble center-periphery epistemologies that define the canon. Later, in chapter 4, "An Alternative History of Sexuality," these horizontal approaches to art history are coupled with horizontal queer theory, thus creating a praxis. As a whole, these first four chapters not only lay the foundation for the entire framework of the book but also foreground various postcolonial and antiracist methods and strategies for analyzing the art production of the queer Middle Eastern diaspora.

THREE

ISLAMICATE AS METHOD

MINOR TRANSNATIONALISMS AND WORLDING ART HISTORY

Current theorizations of modern art reveal the dominance of colonial and imperial epistemological structures within art history: the exclusion of multiple sites of modernity and the entrenchment of binaries that relegate non-Western aesthetic languages as offshoots to dominant Western art movements.[1] While studies of globalization and diaspora have challenged the authority of nation-state identities and rigid cultural categorization, art histories are still written through center-periphery models that maintain Euro-American exceptionalism. How, then, can global art histories be written in a way that productively dismantles the center-periphery binary that maintains such colonial structures?[2] Art history as a discipline is currently undergoing a radical transformation that accounts for transnational connections in the global art world and challenges Eurocentric historiographies currently in place.[3] As art historian Ming Tiampo argues, "Articulating a World Art History is one of the most urgent issues facing art historians today, in both the academy and the museum. However, most attempts face a double bind: ambitious global narratives lack specificity and historical rigor, while precise micro-histories neglect range and the conceptual importance of rethinking larger art historical narratives."[4]

For any such global narrative to take place, art historians and critics are first faced with unpacking and identifying the baggage associated with the Western canon and the pitfalls associated with the entire system of cultural appraisal. The canon, defined as a body of works traditionally considered to be the most significant and, therefore, the most worthy of study, has lately been theorized as a mechanism of oppression, a guardian of privilege, and a vehicle for exclusion.[5] As art historian Anna Brzyski states in the introduction of the edited book *Partisan Canons*, art history has been structurally committed to the idea of tradition.[6] Brzyski and her fellow contributors question where canons are formed, by whom, and how they are maintained, illuminating that, until recently, such questions had largely been ignored and accepted as unproblematic. Within art history, this attention to global systems works side by side with the development of "world art studies." As Kitty Zijlmans and Wilfried van Damme argue, it is through a combined global and multidisciplinary approach that world art studies are creating a new framework in the study of art.[7] Art historian John Onians first introduced the concept of world art studies in 1996. He suggested that this new field of study be not only global in orientation but also multidisciplinary in approach.[8] Within the mapping of world art studies, postcolonial theory can be a useful approach, which is particularly concerned with the impact of colonialism and its aftermath on art and culture.[9]

To problematize and advance the ways in which art historical narratives risk flattening colonial histories, this chapter is informed by the approaches of comparative transnationalisms, notions of "worlding,"[10] and the limits of current art historical models. I aim to address the following concerns: What does decolonizing the study and writing of art history look like? How can anticolonial research be spotlighted rather than exist as peripheral engagements with dominant (and Eurocentric) modes of representation and discourse? Understanding that knowledge production is one of the major sites in which imperialism operates and exercises its power, how can we decolonize the structural limits that currently condition knowledge production? I argue that to globalize art history is not simply to mention or pay lip service to other locales within the history of art. Globalizing and decentering histories need to be more integrative and should incorporate fully the histories of multiple locales in order to examine how they speak to and engage with each other in terms of their own relationships to power and representation.

I introduce the *Islamicate* as a method of global art histories that is a useful museological and art historical framework to critique epistemologies of knowledge production and dissemination within museums. As a case study and potential methodology, the Islamicate brings together global narratives and world art studies and is meant to be one instance where world art history as a theoretical and disciplinary shift can be put into praxis, and global studies of art history can then be theorized in its application within both the academy and the museum. The concept of the Islamicate is a primary method used throughout this book and provides a complex framework for linking various areas around Africa, the Middle East, parts of Asia, and, notably, the Arab diaspora in North America and Europe—areas that would otherwise be excluded from traditional ideas of what territories constitute Arab lands. Overall, the Islamicate is a core concept within this book, but it is only one of many possible answers to some of the larger methodological problems facing global art histories. This is a case study rooted in practice, and it has immediate practical implications for the museum and for the academy.[11]

The Islamicate: Shifting Representation

In 1974 historian Marshall G. S. Hodgson published *The Venture of Islam: Conscience and History in a World Civilization* and coined the term "Islamicate" as a way of opening up the borders posed by modern scholarship, which is also found in current museum structures, both institutionally and thematically within exhibitions. First, Hodgson identifies the issue in using the terms "Islam" and "Islamic" in unspecific ways. He argues that it has become common in modern scholarship to use the terms "Islam" and "Islamic" too casually, signifying both the religion itself and the overall society and culture historically associated with the religion. Hodgson stresses that "one can speak of 'Islamic literature,' of 'Islamic art,' of 'Islamic philosophy,' even of 'Islamic despotism,' but in such a sequence one is speaking less and less of something that expresses Islam as a faith."[12]

Underlying museum structures are colonial epistemologies of knowledge that are predicated on suppressive colonial borders and Eurocentric imperial connections to culture, and this leads to museum departments being structured around geopolitical borders. Exhibition themes that result from such structures often lead to overarching representation of the "Arab Islamic World."[13] For this reason, I turn to Hodgson's terminology of the *Islamicate* as a way of reimagining the parameters in which art from these areas of the world is theorized, organized, and exhibited. Hodgson writes:

> For this, I have used the adjective "Islamicate." I thus restrict the term "Islam" to the *religion* of the Muslims, not using that term for the far more general phenomena, the society of Islamdom and its Islamicate cultural traditions. . . . The adjective "Islamic," correspondingly, must be restricted to "of or pertaining to" Islam *in the proper, the religious, sense*, and of this it will be harder to persuade some. When I speak of "Islamic literature" I am referring only to more or less "religious" literature, not to secular wine songs, just as when one speaks of Christian literature one does not refer to all the literature produced in Christendom. When I speak of "Islamic art" I imply some sort of distinction between the architecture of mosques on the one hand, and the miniatures illustrating a medical handbook on the other—even though there is admittedly no sharp boundary between.[14]

I propose a reading into the Islamicate that can foster new meanings not only to "Islamic art" but also to art from other regions of the world that share colonial histories and are linked intermittently in various ways.[15] The "Islamicate" therefore refers not directly to the religion of Islam itself but to the social and cultural complexities historically associated with Islam and Muslims and is inclusive of non-Muslims living within the same region.[16] This means that the Islamicate is not confined to describing the art of Islamic culture, Islamic people, or even Islam itself. It is necessarily inclusive of a number of populations who are not Muslim and the many layers of cultural and historical contributions over the centuries, particularly from Christians and Jews.

I assert that the Islamicate as a framework can serve as a way of criticizing and restructuring the current museum model that focuses on nation-state identities, and it provides a useful example of how world art studies can be implemented institutionally. In productively dissolving the borders that hold rich cultural histories between rigidly defined temporal boundaries, we can create interesting dialogues in exhibitions that could be supported structurally at museums' level of organization and their organization of culture. These semantics are not trivial, and as critical race theorist Rinaldo

Walcott argues, "The politics of naming, in a very specific way, is central to the governmentality of heritage as it frames exactly how one officially belongs to the nation."[17] This methodology provides a way to further our understandings of colonial histories and the ways in which nation-states can be reimagined and recontextualized in postcolonial ways. Therefore, as a case study, the Islamicate acts as a common thread that can help pose instances of clarification, mediation, and sometimes complication.[18] In thinking of the Islamicate as a curatorial and museological tool, one needs to ask, How would current exhibitions on the Middle East change if they were Islamicate in intention? What different narratives could be told if the Islamicate were the central mode or organization? How would thematic exhibitions, then, change if the Islamicate were institutionalized within museum departments and official mandates?

Curator of the Sharjah Biennial in the United Arab Emirates and president of the Sharjah Art Foundation (SAF), Sheikha Hoor Al-Qasimi has experienced struggles similar to the politics of naming while curating art from the Middle East. In an interview with the *Globe and Mail*, Al-Qasimi says, "A lot of [Western] institutions visit and scout and do research and find interesting work. . . . But there's this problem with packaging artists into one geographical definition. . . . Is it Middle East to what? Or is it Middle East, not Africa? Or if you are Middle East, are you including other countries like Turkey and Iran? Or if you're looking Arab-wide, then you have to include North Africa because that's also Arab. Then Sudan is also Arab."[19]

Sheikha Hoor Al-Qasimi suggests that thematic representations that incorporate many geographic regions might be most productive.[20] Al-Qasimi's statement above is indicative of the barriers that might prohibit such thematic exhibitions from taking place, especially when institutional models still seek to package artists into one geographical definition. In fact, the need for more specific language becomes clear when analyzing the terminology the Sharjah Art Museum uses. "Arab Art" is used to describe their collection rather than terms like "Islamic" or "Middle Eastern," thus allowing for possibilities (and a museological framework) to include art that is not bound by Islam per se. Being one of the rare instances in which a museum actively uses the tactical designation of "Arab Art" to define its collection, this illustrates the consideration of these issues and gives the museum the opportunity to exhibit artists from the Gulf regions while also including artists from around the Middle East and North Africa. This is in line with scholars redefining the very limits of such terminology, as art historian Nada Shabout outlines in her edited volume *New Vision: Arab Contemporary Art in the 21st Century*. Shabout distinguishes between "Arab Art" and "Islamic Art," stating that "Arab Art . . . I loosely define as adhering to an aesthetic formula that is modern and distinct from that of Islamic Art, and that embraces a plurality of experiments and visions united by a conscious negotiation of cultural elements."[21] For Shabout, the difference between Arab and Islamic art lies in modernity and the aesthetics associated with modern art rather than a more historic Islamic art tradition.

While this is a step in the right direction, the terminology of "Arab" or "Middle Eastern" can still fall short when compared to using the more inclusive "Islamicate." This is because the geopolitical designations of using the "Middle East" or the cultural designations of using "Arab" would fail as measures of adequate "worlding" and also lack in providing the lateral connections needed within global art histories. This is because of the flattening that happens through a reductive terminology that aims to homogenize distinct cultures and groups of people into an easily identifiable category. Aside from the Sharjah Art Museum and its specific collections, when it comes to broader theoretical concerns, neither "Arab" nor "Middle Eastern" would be inclusive of predominantly Muslim regions like Turkey or Iran in West Asia, or Pakistan and Bangladesh in South Asia. The value of bringing these regions into dialogue is clear and is reflected in the coinage of the MENASA region (Middle East, North Africa, South Asia) in cultural studies. Here, the Islamicate would provide a framework where the MENASA and diaspora could be engaged with productively and possibly account for more geographic spheres that this ever-extending acronym might benefit from.[22] Rather than be a reductive term that flattens distinct cultures and ethnic groups within regions, a term like *Islamicate* specifically highlights the connections *between* regions and across borders to add specificity to the complex intercultural relations within colonially defined regions, like the Middle East.

Arguably, the majority of "Islamic art" collections in the West are too broadly labeled and often exhibit nonreligious Middle Eastern or Arab art, including Christian art from those regions. According to Kitty Zijlmans and

Wilfried van Damme, world art studies as a discipline calls for scholarly attention to the interculturalization within the arts. This refers to the artistic influences that are exerted by one culture or tradition onto another, or the mutual artistic cross-fertilization that takes place between two or more sites of study.[23] Traditionally, the concept of interculturalization, or transculturation, has had a legacy of encompassing only one-way traffic of cultural encounter that has become attached to initial concepts of acculturation. With the mislabeled "Islamic art" collections hindering these connections, the Islamicate transcends nation-state and arbitrary colonial borders to better elucidate a potentially two-way process of cultural exchanges, in this case specifically artistic exchanges, and the complex histories that can arise at these intersections. Scholars of global art histories, such as Steven Nelson, Reiko Tomii, Iftikhar Dadi, Sonal Khullar, and even world literature scholar Pheng Cheah, have also articulated the need for these issues of geography to be addressed, some fearing that such strong geographic anchors have the potential to disallow a broader art history based in materials and practices.[24]

To foreground the need for such methodology, it is important to stress that museum exhibitions are sites of knowledge production. Unfortunately, museum structures themselves can limit the ways cultural exchanges are displayed and curated. Museums are frequently organized into colonial, region-specific departments, such as Asian, Islamic Middle East, South and Southeast Asian, or Near East.[25] The epistemologies underlying these separations materialize at the thematic level of exhibition curating. Colonial borders are maintained and complex histories are dissolved, flattened, or ignored, and countries then vie for representation and inclusion. An instance of contention would be deciding whether to include Iranian art in an exhibition of Arab art or works from Turkish artists. The same is true for the difficult decision to include Indian art alongside Chinese art, which share a continent but have vastly different geocultural traditions. For instance, which department could fit a nation like Kurdistan within its geographic-based structure? With colonial borders separating Kurdistan and making it part of Iran, Turkey, Syria, and Iraq, how can the art and history of Kurdistan exist both within a department of a museum and thematically within exhibitions? When asking such questions, departmental structures in museums become an unspecific way of grouping and organizing cultures, bound by colonial categories and nation-state borders that limit their representation and lateral connections. It is through these lateral connections that, I argue, postcolonial narratives can take place, and links of colonial histories and pasts are then created in a productive fashion that reveal how boundaries and borders are maintained. These questions outline the problems and gaps within current museum models and demonstrate the need to explore the practical application of different museological approaches that bring postcolonial inquiry and critical race theory in further dialogue with museum studies.

It is important to question the very politics of naming and identification, for the sheer inclusion of such histories within the history of art is a newer development. The study of the visual arts from cultures with an oral tradition, rather than a textual tradition like in Africa, Southeast Asia, Oceania, and the Americas, was at first left mainly to cultural anthropologists. It is during the second half of the twentieth century that art historians increasingly examined these art forms. Art historians "doing fieldwork" adopted the methods and approaches of anthropologists to a large extent, and their work tended not to be published in mainstream art history journals.[26] Because of this struggle, it is vital that frameworks like the Islamicate be adopted in museum models institutionally and not only at the thematic discretion of individual curators, for the risk is too high to fall back within the boundaries already drawn in the sand by the disciplinary and institutional structures historically upheld and currently in place.[27]

Lateral Connections: Local-to-Local

The case study examined in this section illustrates how the Islamicate reinforces and provides a solid example for the disciplinary shift in global art histories. It does so in its facilitation of lateral connections between locales and its complication of the questions of geography within art history. These lateral, local-to-local connections not only wrest art history away from nationalist frameworks, but they also have the potential of eclipsing Eurocentrism.

In his chapter of *Art History: In the Wake of the Global Turn*, art historian Steven Nelson writes about a conference panel at the Clark Art Institute in November 2011 dedicated to these pressing issues. He explains how panelists of this conference on the "global turn" of art history asked whether current geographic categories — Africa, Eastern Europe, West Asia — still held meaning.[28] The scholars of the roundtable wondered whether there were other kinds of formations that would enhance and push forward art historical inquiry. They asked how one might theorize geography, what would be the role of art and art history (academic as well as curatorial practice) in doing such work, and whether we had the tools to describe what is going on in the world in terms of globalization, transnationalism, and cultural hybridity.[29] In fact, the conference and its working groups seemed dedicated to discussing a new order of shifting away from geographic boundaries within the study of art history and how this method of inquiry could be feasible. To this day, scholars of global art histories are still grappling with the same concerns. It is through these issues and positioning of my research that I consider the case study of the Islamicate to be a demonstrable exercise in pushing the limits and boundaries of these questions and concerns.

In terms of methods, it is imperative to explore the praxis of rethinking art history in a global context while still paying rigorous attention to the local. A risk of global theorizations is the rise of an uncritical world art history and its effect on both comparative work and research that focuses on the local. It is with these concerns in mind that the Islamicate is applied as an art historical model both attentively and self-reflexively. For instance, art historian Reiko Tomii values making connections and finding resonances between artists from different geographic regions around the world. As she locates similarities between Japanese artists and non-Japanese artists, she impressively links the artists' local practices to the global narrative and illuminates the fundamentally "similar yet dissimilar" characteristics of their work.[30] Therefore, to quantify the uses of such global measures and their querying of geographic boundaries within art history, it is important to discuss the complications of the local within this globalization in order to avoid a reduction of theoretical concerns.

As a way of rethinking an exhibition strategy by incorporating the Islamicate, I focus on the exhibition *Embellished Reality: Indian Painted Photographs* held at the Royal Ontario Museum (ROM) in Toronto, Canada, in 2012. The exhibition, curated by Deepali Dewan, explored a transcultural history of photography. The exhibition catalogue explains that the methods of hand-painted photography were "introduced in the latter half of the nineteenth century, at a time when the world was seemingly getting smaller through ever-increasing trade, travel, and tourism, [and] painted photographs gave colour to black-and-white images of a changing world and new ways of being."[31] As the exhibition traces the evolution of painted photographs in India from the 1860s to the 2000s, the catalogue "explores photographic history in India and in Europe to show how Indian painted photographs fit into both local and transcultural practices of photographic manipulation."[32] While India is not officially a Muslim-majority country, the history of Islamic art within the Mogul Empire, for instance, brings Islam and Indian culture in close proximity to each other and they are therefore historically enmeshed.

I question, with a transcultural historiography of photography being an objective of the show, what types of histories could have been brought to the fore if hand-painted photography were examined within other "similar yet dissimilar" locales as well. Take, for instance, hand-painted photography in Egypt. The Middle East played a critical role in the development of photography both as a new technology and as an art form. Many European photographers traveled to the Middle East to amass portfolios of Egyptian antiquity, sites of holy lands, and the exotic Other, making the region one of the principal training grounds for the early practice of photography.[33] But what could the development of the photographic medium in a site such as Egypt offer to the development of photography in India? With Egypt first colonized by the French in 1798 and later enduring British occupation in 1882, colonialism and its interlocutors could be seen as a powerful link between the vastly different regions. While India has had a longer and more vexed relationship with colonization, being imperially under Dutch, Danish, French, British, and Portuguese rules, India was under British rule when photography was invented and developed. Therefore, the technological development of photography during these same periods could help outline another historiography: one of photography's involvements with colonial expansion and capitalism. If there had been a small component of the exhibition or catalogue to discuss hand-painted photography in Egypt, interesting ruptures would have occurred within traditional histories and understandings of photography. The relationship between hand-painted photography in India and Egypt, and the capitalism that closely followed the colonial European travelers seeking such photographs, I contend, could have created new dimensions of studies within this history of photography.

Philosopher Gayatri Chakravorty Spivak coined the term "comparison in extremis" as referring to a comparative analysis that focuses on situations of extreme violence as a way of revealing underlying structures of power.[34] In fact, Spivak coined this term in an explicit critique of comparative studies (which is a major discourse in the discipline of area studies) in order to foster a close reading that is enabled by the deep knowledge of language, culture, and history. Therefore, comparison in extremis is a form of comparison that teases out, stresses, or performs differences (including epistemological differences), and the theory emerges from a context of unacknowledged suffering and the invisibility of subaltern identities.[35] Using the comparison of colonial histories between Egypt and India as an example, the Islamicate therefore fosters this close reading, and the comparison in extremis illustrates how European travelers purchased hand-painted photographs of the pyramids and of local populations in Cairo that fed into a highly Orientalized vision of the Middle East. These, then, have strong connections to the history of image making in India and their own colonial ties to the British Empire and perhaps influence how they informed and cited each other. To take this analysis further, this form of art historical analysis is part of what postcolonial literary theorist Shu-mei Shih termed "comparison as relation." According to Shih, "Comparison as relation means setting into motion historical relationalities between entities brought together for comparison, and bringing into relation terms that have traditionally been pushed apart from each other due to certain interests, such as the European exceptionalism that undergirds Eurocentrism. The excavation of these relationalities is what I consider to be the ethical practice of comparison, where the workings of power are not concealed but necessarily revealed. Power, after all, is a form of relation."[36] The above analysis demonstrates how shifting historical comparisons can be an act of deimperialization; photography's involvements with colonial expansion and capitalism is only one example where a worlding methodology like the Islamicate poses great potential to unlearning a Eurocentrism that has limited the scope of cultural studies from certain regions.

Zijlmans and van Damme have asserted that there are three fundamental topics that warrant attention once we start looking at the visual arts across time and place: the first concern is the origins of art, the second topic is intercultural comparison, and the third is the cross-fertilization of artistic tradition between cultures.[37] As illustrated through this exhibition, the Islamicate provides a way of operationalizing world art studies, as it becomes a methodology to address each one of these concerns. The capitalist function of photography comes to the fore and provides a fuller picture of hand-painted photography and its origins. The intercultural comparison between Egypt and India, however controversial, opens up a range of fundamental questions concerning the place and role of visual arts within the history of colonialism. Finally, the cross-fertilization that occurs because of colonial expansion and the very transportability of photographs leads to discussions about artistic exchanges between cultures and removes the invention and development of photography from its often-Eurocentric bubble. Therefore, the strategic inclusion of different but closely related locales illustrates a history of hand-painted photography that then becomes deeply enmeshed in issues of capitalism, imperialism, and colonialism. Literary theorist Walter Mignolo advocates for a decolonial methodology of comparison that focuses on the colonial matrix of power that shapes the production of knowledge, and the Islamicate does just that.[38] The exhibition's aim of developing a more robust transcultural history of photography would have been well supported by globalizing methodologies like the Islamicate, and a more global art historical narrative could have been developed through the study of hand-painted photographs in Egypt.

It is important to note that I do not wish to remove the study of a specific locale, nor do I wish to homogenize or group together all histories and temporalities. As scholars Rita Felski and Susan Stanford Friedman question how constructive comparison, or relational thinking, can be used productively to rethink history in postcolonial and global contexts, they find value in exploring new special modes of analysis based on networks, interrelations, and circulations.[39] I do contend that an exhibition of painted photography in India, like that of Dewan's, has great value. However, asking these important questions tests the types of knowledge that can be expanded upon and produced when the geography-based structures of museums are seen as hindering rather than fostering lateral connections.

To achieve what I advocate for, the conceptual framework of the exhibition in question would not need to be changed from exhibiting Indian hand-painted photographs to being an exhibition of Indian *and* Egyptian hand-painted photographs. I think that the inclusion of another locale such as Cairo can happen productively in an exhibition that is solely about Indian photography, for instance. Such inclusions may happen as ruptures throughout an exhibition, incorporated as a part of exhibition texts, and used within public programming. As historian Sebastian Conrad argues in his book *What Is Global History?* global and world historians cannot simply focus on the links and connections. Instead, Conrad explains how "connections need to be embedded in processes of structural transformation."[40] His concept of integration goes beyond connectedness and stresses that global history is not a history of globalization. Rather, it focuses on not only the degree to which world regions were integrated into global systems but also the relative material, cultural, and political impacts of their relationships to global structures. Therefore, studies and exhibitions of specific locales should certainly still exist, but imagining the complexity of that narrative when structured in relation to the colonial and imperial history of another locale could add dimensions to an art history that would have gotten buried through more traditional curatorial practices and art historical writing that is built along limited geographic boundaries. Through this integration of global systems, new art historical accounts become uncovered and complicate the Eurocentric canon that has been complicit in excluding such narratives from traditional historiography.

Deproblematizing the Islamicate

Oppositional views against more globalized narratives and decentered approaches to the history of art are worried about the disciplinary implications of disrupting the status quo. As scholars have argued, it is this exact worry that keeps the center-periphery dynamic within the discipline.[41] With the West's political and economic power being greatly undermined within art history, a common avoidance of these global narratives insists on the inescapability of the Eurocentrism of art history. As art historian Aruna D'Souza points out, with this mentality, Eurocentrism becomes a policing structure, a maintenance strategy that reproduces its perimeter by insisting that one cannot participate in art history meaningfully without simply contributing to its ideological boundaries that are inherently Eurocentric.[42] It is because of the too readily dismissed ideas of decentering and decanonizing that I find it necessary to deproblematize a methodology like the Islamicate. In thinking through the limitations of such ideas throughout this analysis, I contend that other theories that work with concepts of global art histories will be better equipped to develop and build on one another and create an incontestable argument for other postcolonial frameworks.

This analysis has outlined the pitfalls of thematic exhibitions when museum departments are organized too rigidly around geographic and often colonial borders. It becomes clear that an uncritical global system of cultural organization is not the answer and has the potential to reinforce the Eurocentrism present within art historical canons and traditional historiographies. In returning to museums and their either nonspecific or too narrowly geographic categories, I wonder where the Islamicate would fit between these two oppositional museum structures. Would the Islamicate function as another geographic category alongside Asian art, Indian art, and African art? Could the Islamicate function productively alongside—or, alternately, instead of—these geography-based structures as a way of providing possibility and flexibility for the cultures that do not fit so neatly within constructed colonial borders? I have outlined the problems and gaps within the current museum and art historical models and have determined that future scholarship needs to explore the practical application of other critical museological approaches that bring critical race theory and postcolonialism in further dialogue with museum studies.

Within this book, the Islamicate methodology allows for Syrian American artist Jamil Hellu to be analyzed alongside diasporic artists from different national identities, like Iranian Canadian artist Ebrin Bagheri, Moroccan Canadian artist 2Fik, Iranian Swiss artist Laurence Rasti, Turkish artist Nilbar Güreş, and exiled Iranian artist Alireza Shojaian. Within formations of diaspora, the Islamicate holds new possibilities for conceptualizing the ways in which diasporic subjects are identified in relation to a singular nation-state and offers another framework to discuss diasporic entanglements with nation and empire. This is because the Islamicate is connected to notions of transnationalism and diaspora in how it offers a new way of envisioning a more complex understanding of cultural circulation, heritage formation, and community outside of colonial nation-state definitions that ignore imperial histories and legacies. The Islamicate is also a noteworthy methodology when developed through an interdisciplinary queer theory lens, as I bring regions of the Middle East, North Africa, and Asia together in this study that would be left outside of academic paradigms regarding the "Middle East" as a stable geographic location. This framework decenters the nation-state as being foundational to identity formation and brings together artists from these seemingly disparate nationalisms in order to illustrate how diaspora and nation-state identities hinder the ways in which complex cultural identifications are articulated and understood. Thus, the Islamicate is used within this book as a way of keeping imperialism at the forefront of the study of sexualities in order to situate how premodern Islamicate sexual scripts have resisted complete colonization and continue to exist in the Middle Eastern diaspora within North America and Europe.

In this chapter I have laid the foundation of theorizing the Islamicate as a method to examine global art history, and I have explained in depth the inadequacies of current language and epistemologies for studying cultural production in the Middle East. The Islamicate provides a valuable framework for my research that allows me to link various geographies that are technically outside the Middle East but are otherwise connected in important ways. As will be made clear in the next chapter, this method is important for the study of gender and sexuality in the Middle East, as contact zones effectively changed gender discourses all across North Africa, West Asia, the Middle East, and the areas governed by the former Ottoman Empire. In order to adequately discuss these widely varying colonial histories in different geographic locations that are all undeniably tied to empire, the Islamicate is a useful concept for theorizing these concerns in a productive way. For these reasons, the Islamicate is not only the primary case study within this chapter, but it is also the primary method used throughout this book to bring theoretical proximity to regions that would otherwise fall outside the purview of traditional understandings of what constitutes the Middle East or the Arab world. Locating these leftovers from area studies that prevent a full understanding of imperial dimensions within cultural formation, this case study implemented the problem-centered approach mentioned earlier in chapter 2. As the Islamicate and this problem-centered-approach forms a larger framework for my research project, it is also an example of horizontal art histories being implemented through praxis in order to mitigate the ways in which center-periphery dynamics are formed.

Rather than articulating Arabness outside of imperial history and under the purview of Orientalist stigma, it is important that this book reconceptualizes Arabness from different diasporic perspectives in order to help delineate historic narratives of migration and cultural identity. Conceptualizing an Arabness outside of imperialism is part of the postcolonial predicament in the Middle East, and seeing the intertwined histories of different Arab nations through diasporic perspectives of place and belonging helps to envision Arab identity outside of Orientalism and instead as connected to a larger network of people, language, culture, and territory. The Islamicate as a decolonial method allows us to work through empire and imperialism in the way we conceive of and separate distinct cultures from different Arab regions throughout Asia, Africa, and the Middle East, and including diaspora in this expansive view is noteworthy. To use the term *Islamicate diasporas* would indicate a referencing of different Arab, Middle Eastern, African, and Asian identities as being both distinct culturally but also intertwined through empire, language, and traditions. "Islamicate diasporas" as a terminology gives coalition in instances where it can be helpful to work through issues of imperialism and ideas of nation-states that can pose roadblocks in postcolonial and anticolonial thinking, and such an idea can connect people who have been culturally demarcated by colonial borders in the region that were imposed by Europe.

PART TWO
QUEER DIASPORIC WORLD MAKING
VISUALIZING PLACE, RACE, AND SELF

FOUR

AN ALTERNATIVE HISTORY OF SEXUALITY

DIASPORA CONSCIOUSNESS AND THE QUEER DIASPORIC LENS

After establishing the Islamicate as a productive methodology and an example of world art studies, how can the history of sexuality be studied in a similarly postcolonial and decentered way? The fight to represent local experiences and histories of sexualities in the Middle East is a continuing challenge, partly due to the Eurocentric foundation on which the history of sexuality studies is built. Part of this issue comes from the mandatory starting point in addressing the history of sexuality within the academy, the canon of which includes Michel Foucault's influential book series, *The History of Sexuality*. It is my contention that this series, while a valuable contribution to the field, does not adequately address the history of colonial violence that the Western world committed on gender and sexuality in Islamicate regions. Therefore, it is important to examine the various sexualities and forms of desire that are excluded from Eurocentric histories of sexuality and contribute to non-Western ways of being as peripheral. In this chapter I demonstrate how Foucault's *History of Sexuality* neglects to recognize not only the various ways gender and sexuality in the Middle East are understood but also the blind spots of racialized discourses created in this void.

In order to study a history of same-sex desire that decenters Western epistemologies, I propose shifting the methodological approach to studying the history of coloniality rather than primarily centering history on a static and hegemonic concept like "sexuality." Methodologically speaking, starting with the history of sexuality as a point of analysis predetermines that there is a stable sexuality and universal sexual discourse available. As this chapter demonstrates, sexuality as an identity marker simply did not exist in premodern Islamicate regions. Non-Western sexual discourses that exist outside of such stable identity models—identity models of sexuality that are arguably Western constructs—start to unravel within this narrative. The danger in using hegemonic sexuality structures as the starting point of analysis is that, slowly, the study of sexuality reifies itself as one primarily understood and accepted in the Global North and insidiously cementing the West's imperial association with queer tolerance and progress. In keeping hegemonic concepts of sexuality as a methodological framework, working outside the Western model of sexual discourse is nearly impossible, and binary thinking between East and West becomes even more ingrained. In changing the assumptions about what sexuality means and looks like in other cultures—an act of worlding—other stories are uncovered and un-othered. As a way of providing a critical literature review outlining the history of Islamicate sexualities, this chapter starts by outlining why it is important to decolonize and deconstruct Foucault's *History of Sexuality*, a key text for the study of sexuality in academia. I propose a map of studies that I suggest are important to rethink methods, epistemologies, and understandings of alternative histories of sexuality in the Middle East and Islamicate cultures. Lastly, these ideas culminate in the analysis of Syrian American visual artist Jamil Hellu to illustrate how diaspora consciousness plays an integral role in ensuring that the premodern sexual scripts and codes of desire that were perceived to be colonized by Western epistemological ways of being queer still exist today.

In this chapter I find it necessary to dismantle the mechanisms of imperialism and the colonial structures that exclude these very histories from being a part of dominant discourse. While not diminishing the contributions Foucault and his successors made to the discipline, I argue that the parameters and limits of understanding Islamicate desire are unproductively predetermined when *The History of Sexuality* becomes the canon and starting point for disciplinary scholarship. In Foucault's own words, "The history of sexuality—that is, the history of what functioned in the nineteenth century as a specific field of truth—must first be written from the viewpoint of a history of discourses."[1] I propose doing just that, while also rejecting the very possibility of a stable sexuality and locating the structural and epistemological gaps that keep histories of Islamicate sexualities as periphery to the assumed universality that a stable "history of sexuality" holds. According to sociologist Vrushali Patil, "When it comes to theorizing on gender, sexuality, and sex, the global north is still the unnamed center and universal, while sites outside are the particular."[2]

In doing this work, I wish to continue the vein of inquiry that Ann Stoler initiates in her book *Race and the Education of Desire*, where she examines the role of colonialism within the study of sexuality and power. In critiquing the blind spot around colonialism in Foucault's history of sexuality, Stoler asserts that "the discursive management of the sexual practices of colonizer and colonized was fundamental to the colonial order of things."[3] Stoler goes on to suggest a wider imperial context that resituates racial thinking in the making of European bourgeois sexual identity.[4] In an effort to build on Stoler's thinking, this analysis is meant to contribute to a decolonial way of reading global histories of sexualities by researching how "certain colonial prefigurings contest and force a reconceptualizing of Foucault's sexual history of the Occident and, more generally, a rethinking of the historiographic conventions that have bracketed histories of 'the West.'"[5] Indeed, this chapter aims to correct "the ways in which our basic theoretical apparatus for thinking gender, sexuality, and sex is based on imperial histories and contemporary neocolonial and neoimperial processes are invisible."[6]

Colonial Modernity and Islamicate Desire

Current literature engaging with Middle Eastern homosexuality is focused on issues of modernity, multiple modernities, and the West's claim to modernity. Modernity as a time period signals social, political, and historic conditions at the end of the nineteenth and early twentieth-centuries. Ultimately, the literature on Arab sexualities contends that the West created a discourse around sexuality that the Middle East never had, resulting in homocolonialism (which I will discuss at length later in this chapter)—imperialist ideologies in the name of sexual tolerance. As a push against colonial forces and imperialism, homosexuality in the Middle East was then made into an illegal identity category, an identity category that many argue did not exist prior to this increased contact with Western explorers and travelers.[7]

Scholars such as Walter Mignolo, Irene Silverblatt, and Sonia Saldivar-Hull are just a few who question this new imperial structure of power and examine how modernity is used to colonize social and cultural practices in the name of Western advancement. They argue that modernity was formed by European philosophers, academics, and politicians and that modernity involves the colonization of time and space in order to create a border in relation to a self-determining Other and its own European identity. In this way, Europeans colonized the world and built on the ideas of Western civilization and modernity as the endpoints of historical time, with Europe as the center of the world.[8] Mignolo also goes as far as to say that coloniality is constitutive of modernity and that "there is no modernity without coloniality."[9]

The disregard of colonial power within Foucault's analysis of premodern sexual discourses and the reductive distinction made between sexual identities (West) and sexual acts (East) in his binary development of the *ars erotica* and *scientia sexualis* work to flatten entire complex networks of desire and homosocial cultural attitudes. What I pay attention to is an alternative history of sexuality that centers coloniality to expand on Foucault's *History of Sexuality*. This method complicates the understanding of colonial discourses and their influences and impacts on gender, sexuality, and all cultural and legal texts governing Islamicate bodies.[10]

To outline the foundation of Islamicate sexuality studies, I start by examining anthropological accounts of sexuality in the Arab world, a genre of scholarship that accounts for some of the earlier inquiries on the topic. Providing anthropological theories of the sexuality and gender norms of other cultures, their archives cannot be ignored, as they "add greatly to current Western discourses about sexuality."[11] For this reason, Stephen O. Murray and Will Roscoe's collection from 1997, *Islamic Homosexualities*, remains an important one. Moving beyond earlier and classically Orientalist writings by journalists and imperial travelers such as Arno Schmitt and Jehoeda Sofer's *Sexuality and Eroticism among Males in Moslem Societies* (1992),[12] Murray and Roscoe's various contributions draw more specifically on contemporary ideas in sexuality studies and give heavy emphasis to Islamic historiography. Outlining how status-differentiated homosexual patterns and age-differentiated sexual patterns were permitted, common, and transmitted through art and poetry within Islamic societies,[13] Murray concludes that his hypothesized model of the trans-Islamic "sexuality" is not distinguished between "homosexual" and "heterosexual" but between the sexual acts of being an active or passive sexual partner with someone of the same sex.[14] Overlooking the fact that local instances of homosociality existed in its own right,[15] Roscoe explains that although Egypt and Southwest Asia (including Persia) lacked institutionalized age-differentiated same-sex patterns, these areas were Hellenized during Alexander's conquests and exposed to Greek sexual patterns.[16] While it is important to trace transmission of sexual practices within this history of sexuality, it becomes an assumed truth that Egyptian, Syrian, Phoenician, and other North African cultures were exposed to homosexuality only as an import from Greek and Roman traditions, thus making their indigenous traditions presumably heterosexual.

Arguing that homocolonialism and the Gay International are responsible in part for the Western import of "gay" identity into the Middle East,[17] Joseph Massad is quite critical of Murray and Roscoe's collection and posits that their writing is indicative of their limited knowledge of Muslim societies.[18] Furthermore, Massad also finds that Murray and Roscoe's book has language-based errors and mistakes when translating from Arabic, and he holds that the issue becomes a fight to represent the so-called real Arab or Muslim position on male-male sexuality.[19]

Discourses of Power: Silencing and Colonial Change

Developing and expanding on the literature on Islamicate sexualities, this section focuses on the intersections of colonialism and sexual discourses to illustrate how imperialism changed how gender is expressed and sexualities were understood in Islamicate regions. Examining the various silencing practices that were introduced in the Ottoman Empire by colonial travelers, this section illustrates the Western pressures leading to the censorship of Ottoman homoerotic cultural practices. This suppression of local sexual scripts culminated in the drastic shift in local language, changing cultural traditions, and impacts to the gender presentation of Ottoman men and women. These radical changes in local norms were a direct result of Victorian sexual discourses that European travelers imposed on local populations, and it becomes clear that the history of colonialism is so deeply entangled with the history of Islamicate sexual desire that separating the two becomes an unproductive task.

Like Murray and Roscoe's work, much contemporary literature on premodern sexuality in the Middle East still relies heavily on Islamic historiography. Khaled El-Rouayheb's study *Before Homosexuality in the Arab-Islamic World, 1500–1800* pieces together archival sources from the Arab-speaking parts of the Ottoman Empire in the centuries immediately preceding the beginnings of modernization and Westernization in the nineteenth century. Less anthropological and based more on cultural and legal archives, the central contention of El-Rouayheb's work is that premodern Arab-Islamic culture lacked the concept of "homosexuality" that is understood in the Anglo-Euro-American sense as being an identity category. Rather, instances of homosocial and homoerotic behavior were commonly depicted in literature and openly written about in poetry and stories at the time. This openly accepted homoerotic behavior is then contrasted with later travel journals of European travelers who visited the Ottoman Empire, noting their astonishment and disgust that local men openly flaunted their relations with other men and adolescent boys.[20]

Noteworthy is El-Rouayheb's vehement assertion that Islamic law indeed prohibited sexual intercourse between men,[21] so to say that homosexuality existed as unproblematic is false. He notes, however, the overwhelmingly numerous amounts of biographical accounts, poetic anthologies, and literary writings (especially fiction, poetry, and drama) that are openly dedicated to same-sex relations, like poems of a man's passion for a teenage boy. El-Rouayheb criticizes modern historians for presuming these instances to be manifestations of "homosexuality" and urges more temporally and locally specific readings of these same-sex relations. In fact, he rigorously avoids labeling any of his findings as being indicative of homosexual tolerance at the risk of making sweeping generalizations about sexual practices in premodern Arab-Islamic civilizations. While this caution is needed, El-Rouayheb does little to compare these popular and numerous instances of same-sex infatuations with the encroachment of Western values and ideas on the region in the nineteenth century. In fact, it is not until his conclusion that modernity and coloniality are mentioned. Caught between the contradictions of anal intercourse between men being illegal under Islamic law and the noble and respected men who publicly expressed same-sex desire, El-Rouayheb affirms: "The profuseness of homoerotic poetry and anecdotes in Arab-Islamic literature may be seen as an indication that 'in practice' homosexuality was nevertheless indulged or tolerated in Arab-Islamic societies. Yet, as stated at the outset of this study, such an interpretation seems to simplify a more complex picture."[22]

In trying to avoid the sweeping generalizations of homosexual tolerance in the Arab-Islamic world, El-Rouayheb's findings seem to minimize the invisibility of homosexuality as a social issue prior to increased European contact. As historian Dror Ze'evi explicitly mentions in his study of the Ottoman Middle East of the sixteenth to twentieth centuries—the same time frame as El-Rouayheb's study—major conflicts about the permissibility of same-sex relations simply did not exist. Though legally frowned upon, same-sex desires were taken to be part of life, and their illegality was usually ignored until modernization (and Westernization) led to a previously invisible accepted norm to suddenly become an object for observation and comparison with Victorian cultural norms.[23] As seen in the understandable reluctance of El-Rouayheb to label the premodern Ottoman Middle East as being tolerant of same-sex desire, there is a historical tension in having these examples be construed as the existence and acceptance of homosexuality, which is inherently a modern concept. Thus, the evidence suggests that homosexuality did not exist in premodern Arab-Islamic civilizations, and instead same-sex desire was simply a non-categorized facet of everyday life that was legally condemned but otherwise openly tolerated within society.

Foucault traces the repression of sexuality of the bourgeoisie in the Victorian era and claims that on the subject of sex, silence became the rule.[24] The histories of change at the turn of the century show that the mechanisms of silence that Foucault writes about need to be extended beyond the power of Victorian rule over Victorian people and instead linked accordingly to the silencing practices that were introduced by European travelers to publicly shame the homoerotic practices present in the Ottoman Middle East. Dror Ze'evi's study *Producing Desire* successfully maps out the progress of Western sexuality colonizing the local traditions of homosocial desire in the Ottoman Middle East. Underlying all historicity in his study is the supposition that there was a great loss at the turn of the century, and local sexual scripts were erased but not replaced with new ones, leaving a silence and void in the discourse of Ottoman sexuality. Following Foucault's theory of silence on the subject of sex within Victorian puritanical society, such silences in the Middle East are evident in the imposed censorship on homosocial customs and traditions, expurgatory and suppressive practices in publishing literature, and in the public shame caused by the European travel journals in the nineteenth-century Ottoman Empire. Since these Victorian travelers deemed homosociality as not modern, there became an adversity toward all forms of "homosexuality" that became typical of the second half of the twentieth century.[25] Examples of imposed censoring include a new edition of *The Arabian Nights* published in Cairo in 1930, and although it followed the older editions of 1835 and 1890, this new version omitted the few stories that included pederastic love affairs that were same-sex in nature. Likewise, two years later, in 1932, a heavily expurgated version of the *Diwan* of Abu Nuwas was published in Cairo, but unlike the earlier 1898 and 1905 editions, it abandoned the traditional thematic organization of poetry in order to exclude a section for love poetry of male youths (*ghazal al-mudhakkar*).[26] As Ze'evi elaborates on modernity's stronghold on local sexual discourses in the premodern Ottoman Empire:

> Thus began the journey to suppress established sexual discourses, silence them, and replace them with others. None of the discursive scripts . . . — medicine, law, Sufi literature, dream interpretation, shadow theatre — were spared. As we have seen, they all either disappeared in the late nineteenth century or were transformed into almost sterile genres in which sex and sexuality are seldom discussed, and even then always obliquely. . . . The sense of embarrassment felt toward the old sexual discourse could not, in and of itself, produce a new one. As familiar sexual scripts collapsed under the onslaught of the travelogue, no new ones came to take their place. The Ottoman and Arab lands experienced unprecedented transformation: sexual discourse moves out of the textual sphere and into the arena of male and female intimate circles, while a curtain of silence descended on the sexual stage.[27]

This profound loss and silencing of Arab-Islamic homosocial desire, as outlined by Ze'evi, can be traced mechanically within language as well. This silence was achieved by removing local understandings of homosocial desire—something that existed as a nonissue, something that did not need a name or categorization—and replacing them with specific Arabic words created by Europeans that reflected Western sexual practices. Joseph Massad outlines the following:

> The Arabic word for sex, *jins*, appeared sometime in the early twentieth century[,] carrying with it not only its new meanings of biological sex and national origin but also its old meanings of type and kind and ethnolinguistic origin, among others. The word in the sense of type and kind has existed in Arabic since time immemorial and is derived from the Greek genus. As late as 1870, its connotation of sex had not yet come into usage. An unspecific word for sexuality, *jinsiyyah*—which also means nationality and citizenship—was coined in the 1950s by translators of the works of Freud.[28]

More recently Mutaʿ al-Safadi, Arabic translator of Michel Foucault's *History of Sexuality*, has introduced the more specific scholarly term, *jinsaniyyah*.[29] Important here is the legacy this linguistic coloniality has on the current Middle Eastern discourse of sexuality. European expressions of sexual deviance were adopted in Arabic in the mid-1950s, translating it literally as *al-shudhudh al-jinsi*, this derogatory terminology used to describe sexual paraphilia—the sexual arousal to atypical objects or individuals—became a coinage now commonly used in the media and in polite company to refer to the Western concept of homosexuality.[30] While not as derogatory as the commonly used terminology of *khawal* or *lutiyy*, in modern Egyptian slang these terms mean deviant, pervert, and faggot, and few options were available to describe same-sex relations in Arabic outside of these negative associations and limited terms. These changes in the Arabic language that normalize European concepts that define and govern gender and sexuality are significant emblems of the power Victorians had over the Ottomans and other Islamicate cultures. This power stems from European control over modernity and the Middle East's desire to be included within the tenets of being a modern region. These examples clearly illustrate the immense power colonialism had on the linguistic discourse on sexuality and the long-term effects that changing, altering, erasing, and replacing the language of sexuality has on a civilization and its future generations. Foucault expressly states, "If sex is repressed, that is, condemned to prohibition, nonexistence, and silence, then the mere fact that one is speaking about it has the appearance of a deliberate transgression. A person who holds forth in such language places himself to a certain extent outside the reach of power; he upsets established law; he somehow anticipates the coming freedom."[31]

Here, we see the immense influence that European travelers, European translators, European psychoanalysts, and European psychologists had in shaping the linguistic terms of homosexuality in Arabic. They were the true holders of power who created the very mechanisms of repression that did not formerly exist, and in creating the very rules of sexual conduct and modern sexual citizenship, Europeans impacted the heterosexualization of the Middle East. Such racialization of the sexual Other compared to the assumed heteronormative characteristics of Europeans is part of an imperial logic "where this heteronormativity is the cornerstone of the West's bid for racial and cultural superiority, and indeed for the West's self-definition."[32] The new system that was created in the region at the turn of the twentieth century established Victorian puritanical sexual discourses as the established law and thus the gold standard of successful modernity.

Blind Spots of the *Ars Erotica* and *Scientia Sexualis*

According to Foucault, "Historically, there have been two great procedures for producing the truth of sex. On the one hand, the societies—and they are numerous: China, Japan, India, Rome, the Arabo-Moslem societies—which endowed themselves with an *ars erotica*. In the erotic art, truth is drawn from pleasure itself, understood as a practice and accumulated as experience; pleasure is not considered in relation to an absolute law of the permitted and the forbidden."[33]

The knowledge passed on by the *ars erotica* is a knowledge of sensual pleasure, limiting the sexual discourses in Eastern civilizations as being concerned only with sexual acts. Determining that erotic art, or the *ars erotica*, exists in cultures as purely "pleasure" and outside the rule of social regulation is counterfactual to the historical nuances of *how* same-sex desire existed under the rule of Islamic law and was widely permitted within religious, social, and political contexts. The *ars erotica* both undermines and ignores the very social conditions that created limits and boundaries for same-sex desire and the social apparatuses that govern how same-sex love was permitted to exist in premodern Islamicate societies. Assuming a Western audience as his universal reader,[34] Foucault continues to state, "On the face of it at least, our civilization possesses no *ars erotica*. In return, it is undoubtedly the only civilization to practice a *scientia sexualis*; or rather, the only civilization to have developed over the centuries procedures for telling the truth of sex which are geared to a form of knowledge-power."[35] Determining that European civilization is the only civilization to develop rules governing sex and a science of sexuality undermines the complex systems of governance in premodern Islamicate societies and the ways in which official and unofficial social codes also had an imbued power dynamic between sexual truth and its citizens. This science of sexuality is an important facet to colonial discourses because of how Victorian laws governing sex became the only acceptable true rule of law for governing sexual desire. In Foucault's own words, "sexuality" is "the correlative of that slowly developed discursive practice which constitutes the *scientia sexualis*. The essential features of this sexuality are not the expression of a representation that is more or less distorted by ideology, or of a misunderstanding caused by taboos; they correspond to the functional requirements of a discourse that must produce its truth."[36] In theorizing the binaries that exist between Eastern and Western modes of sexual discourses, Foucault presents the West's *scientia sexualis* as being a more advanced process of the East's *ars erotica*, the former being imbued with scientific sexual truth and the latter being a variable version of sexual discourse tainted by local ideology. Thus, in Foucault's own words, the conflict is between the "*scientia sexualis* versus *ars erotica*, no doubt. But it should be noted that the *ars erotica* did not disappear altogether from Western civilization; nor has it always been absent from the movement by which one sought to produce a science of sexuality."[37] Here, the *ars erotica* is always a minor component to the more advanced *scientia sexualis*, but ultimately the erotic arts fail to have a science of sexuality as part of its discourse.

To avoid the way "Foucault haunts studies of sexualities of 'other places and other times,'" to use Afsenah Najmabadi's words,[38] Joseph Boone's *Homoerotics of Orientalism* anthologizes many of the themes discussed by the aforementioned scholars using a fluctuation between contemporary homoeroticism and historical same-sex desire as a way to avoid dichotomizing cultures.[39] This back-and-forth is necessary to Boone's methodological approach, for he argues that the critic needs to be prepared to encounter diversities that do not always fall into a neat bifurcation between, for instance, premodern erotic practices and "modern" sexual identities or types.[40] To avoid such dichotomization, Boone outright rejects a Foucauldian "history of sexuality," for it imbues a predetermined starting point for sexual discourse. Rather, Boone argues for the *necessity to work backward* as a way of avoiding predetermined claims about sexual identities (West) and sexual acts (East), a binary assumption that obscures the actual interplay of practices and identity throughout Islamicate history to the beginning of the twentieth century. Boone finds this distinction paramount in Foucault's concept of *ars erotica* and *scientia sexualis*, which has since been "accepted as axiomatic in studies of sexuality and queer theory."[41] It is clear that Foucault's constructed binaries between East and West leaves same-sex desire in Islamicate cultures widely misrepresented, and as Valerie Traub argues, this Orientalizing distinction is historically inaccurate.[42] According to Boone, Foucault distinguishes the sexual economies of East/West in such broad terms to conveniently "establish [the] pre-modern/modern periodization" that supports his argument about the West's evolution of a disciplinary regime of modern sexual types, while the East remains locked in a timeless *ars erotica*.[43] In referring to such dualistic and reductive distinctions, I echo that there is a clear sense of a thriving but not always welcome homoerotic subculture that coexisted with other subcultures in a multilayered social order whose constituencies often included overlapping members.[44] The many challenges this binary distinction creates is articulated by Najmabadi as she states that Foucault's "bold proposal that the homosexual as a type did not exist before it was invented in nineteenth-century Europe was critical to the ensuing rich work on the history of sexualities. . . . Crossing from eros to sex seems to make everyone screech to a halt. Most would agree that we could talk about same-sex acts but not about homosexuality as a concept that defined particular notions of erotic desire, which we now associate with the Foucauldian 'homosexual as a human type.'"[45]

To better illustrate the gaps and weaknesses within Foucault's *ars erotica* and the *scientia sexualis* theory, I turn again to Dror Ze'evi's examination of the Islamic legal system and literature on morality. Interestingly, Ze'evi introduces medicine and its ancillary disciplines—shadow theater, travel journals, and dream interpretations—into his study, allowing for the examination of different sexual scripts. These wide-ranging archival sources allow Ze'evi to examine a larger system of sexual desire that helps to illustrate how the average Ottoman subject lived with homosociality in their daily life. Taking, for instance, traditional dream interpretation manuals, although they were later banned and replaced with European psychoanalysis, they were widely popular and used in much of the premodern Middle East and North Africa. Representing an important layer of sexual consciousness, and considered to be scientific knowledge in many parts of the premodern world, such manuals evolved from ancient Greek origins and continued to proliferate through translations and contributions in many Islamicate societies.[46] The psychosexual connotations within these manuals, Ze'evi claims, can be extended to offer a glimpse of sexual discourse beyond the purview of only the Ottoman Empire.[47] These other sources also highlight the production of sexual discourse by illustrating both the *official* scripts being offered (like those governed by medical, legal, and religious writing) and the *unofficial*, often radically different ways sexual desire was manifested and understood in society (through the visual artistry of shadow theater, in addition to literature and poems).

This history of both official and unofficial sexual scripts of same-sex desire within the Ottoman Middle East is important because of Foucault's limiting and reductive development of the *ars erotica* and the *scientia sexualis* to discuss the economies of sex in premodern periods. Foucault writing about ancient Greece rather than the much more recent instances of homoerotic desire in Ottoman Empire is noteworthy, for it predetermines a starting point of same-sex desire as being located within Western civilization. Also interesting is the conflation of artistry (in this case, specific European ideas of artist workshops) and pederasty. As Foucault writes, "The relationship to the master who holds the secrets is of paramount importance; only he, working alone, can transmit this art in an esoteric manner. . . . The effects of this masterful art . . . are said to transfigure the one fortunate enough to receive its privileges: an absolute mastery of the body, a singular bliss, obliviousness to time and limits, the elixir of life, the exile of death and its threats."[48] For Foucault to assume that all homosocial relations happening between older men and younger adolescent boys happened in the realm of erotic art production flattens the complex histories of pederasty and mentorship that El-Rouayheb, Ze'evi, and other historians rigorously detail. The *ars erotica* also flattens histories of non-Western desires, for it ignores the many other ways homoerotic desire was embedded in premodern discourses in areas of the Middle East. This includes dream interpretations, legal writing, poetry, shadow plays, oral histories, and their connection to the common public. How the general population lived with homoerotic discourse as a nonissue is something that the *ars erotica* cannot account for, reducing complex premodern networks of homosocial desire in the Arab-Islamic world to mere visual accounts of pleasure and sexual acts.

The travelogues that consist of books and manuscripts written by travelers from Europe to the Ottoman Middle East provide instances of external vantage points that compare intimate sexual scripts between the West and the Other.[49] As an apparatus from which Orientalism spread, these travelogues used homosociality in the Middle East as a sign of perverted morality and "stood for the Orient's passivity, laziness, cowardice, and submission."[50] Convincingly proving the overall impact these travelogues had on the Ottoman Middle East once circulated, Ze'evi uses John Gagnon's and Jeffery Weeks's notions of "sexual scripts" to drive his theory.[51] Distinct from El-Rouayheb, Ze'evi asserts an internal and external blueprint for sexual actions, helping to govern desire. Through these scripts, it is possible to map out instances of normalcy, deviance, and where homosocial desires fit within this spectrum.[52] In terms of influencing the ways in which homosociality became unmodern and depraved, European travel had a profound impact because these travelogues were translated from their respective Anglo-European languages into Arabic and local languages and then circulated. This act of imperial violence, which was meant solely to shame local populations for deviating from Victorian sexual discourses, had far-reaching implications that reverberate in the Middle East to this day.

In keeping with this historiography of colonial discourse, Afsaneh Najmabadi's book *Women with Mustaches and Men without Beards* provides a detailed account of normative gender scripts being rewritten by narratives of

Western modernity and the change in signifiers of femininity and masculinity in nineteenth-century Iran. Rather than strictly focusing on homocolonial discourses that revolve around sexualities, Najmabadi's study adds crucial gender discourse to the notion of gender colonialism and the assimilation of local gender scripts after the nineteenth century in Iran. While El-Rouayheb and Dror Ze'evi investigate the partial convergence of European modernist productions of homosexuality as a vice with Islamic jurisprudential discourse on *liwāt* (sodomy), Najmabadi's study takes a different approach. She investigates the modernist production of heterosexuality through the screen of gender along with its reconceptualization from the gender norms prior to increased contact with Europe in the sixteenth century. Using visual art, written stories, and national archives, Najmabadi maps out homoerotic figures in premodern Persia (not unlike the beardless adolescent youths featured in El-Rouhayeb and Ze'evi's study of the Ottoman Empire) and the morphing of these figures and their aesthetic from something of sexual desire to something of social abjection. In doing so, gender norms changed to be more in line with the Europeanization and heterosexualization of the modernist project, as did the physical appearance of these genders.

This homocolonialism is paramount in the anxiety surrounding men with shaved beards. While an *amrad* was once a beardless adolescent and highly desired object of beauty in premodern Iran, the word later became a term for describing beardless Europeans, illustrating the complex relationship between desire, sexuality, and colonialism. What was once a standard of beauty, Persian women's upper-lip hair was likewise shamed as unmodern and manly by European travelers. Prior to this, the soft fuzz was attributed only to young boys and youth, not men, and was seen as a desired beauty standard before a boy develops a full beard. This resulted in facial hair becoming highly politicized and the development of Persian men with European mustaches instead of beards. While insidious, Najmabadi's study illustrates that becoming modern required one's modernity to be legible for the already modern, and Iran's modernity had to be recognizable by the Europeans (a pattern repeated in many non-Western sites).[53] The examples here document the process of looking European. Commonly critiqued by Najmabadi, Massad, and other scholars, Murray and Roscoe's previously mentioned book, *Islamic Homosexualities*, is one instance where same-sex practices as signs of premodernity are often reduced to homosexuality being a consequence of gender segregation and ignore the inner workings of colonialism and its role in actively changing local discourses on sexuality and gender. This homosexuality as a type of frustrated heterosexuality is a common pitfall of contemporary scholarship and creates a modernist disavowal of male and female homoeroticism as always something located in the past, always already resolved and overcome.[54]

Part of the problem outlined within this chapter has to do with Foucault's relegation of premodern Islamicate homosociality and same-sex desire as a distant historical phenomenon, framing complex same-sex relations as only a part of pederasty akin to that of ancient Greece.[55] As this book aims to demonstrate, my contention is that the premodern sexual scripts and codes of desire still exist today and that the study of diasporic homosexualities is a valuable link to connect a colonial moment to a diasporic present.[56] It is the existence of these premodern sexual scripts, which are assumed to be historic and long extinguished, that, I argue, creates tensions for the queer diasporic subject. These historical tensions that are at odds with contemporary queer subjectivity contribute to diasporic non-belonging within the Western gay imaginary, for they exemplify modes of same-sex desires and histories that veer away from Western conceptions of linear gay identity.

The first wave of scholarship on the sexualities of the Arab or Muslim world (which Murray and Roscoe's book would fall into) has been relatively colonial and rather othering. Because of this, I find great value in the later generation of postcolonial scholarship, as it is more reflective of the lived experience of Arab and queer subjects. Subsequent chapters of this book will consider more contemporary postcolonial issues focusing on themes of diaspora and contemporary queer transnational subjects in order to provide a much-needed continuation of the aforementioned histories. I outline this schism in scholarship intentionally to account for the difference in subject position and Arab-Muslim narratives in a post-9/11 context. This context separates all scholarship quite naturally, as it shifts narratives of homo-Orientalism to one of terrorism and identity categories viewed within the lens of homonationalism and human security.[57] Therefore, this book's incorporated analysis of the Arab homosexual subject post-9/11 within the historical study of gender and sexuality is necessary to advance the field.

Thus far, I have provided a comprehensive overview of the history of sexuality in the Middle East and in Islamicate cultures. What becomes clear is how deeply entangled the history of sexuality is with the history of colonialism and how imperial discourses have had a profound impact on the gender and sexual discourses in the Middle East to this day. Valuable scholarship exists chronicling the historiography of these entanglements and the changing sexual discourses over time in Islamicate regions, as well as focusing primarily on the diaspora and current lived experiences of transnational sexual discourses.[58] What seems to be lacking in this scholarship is the connection of the historic changes that took place over the course of modernity in the Middle East and how these changes have created a direct causal effect on the current understanding of queerness in the Arab world. There is an unintentional schism within the academy between modern and premodern histories of sexualities. The reality is that premodern sexual scripts in the Middle East, Islamicate cultures, and in the diaspora are still very much connected to the imperial powers that changed them over the course of modernization, and this is directly linked to diasporic subjects today.[59] I find it relevant to dismantle the very canon of queer theory and sexuality studies that contributes to totalizing versions of homosexuality and results in violent erasures, disavowals, and incompatibilities between the Middle East and homosexuality. It is because of this that I aim to further develop historical accounts of homosociality in the Middle East with the lived experiences of the queer diaspora today. It is through this direct one-to-one relationality that much value can be garnered in assessing current sexual discourses as being a result of colonial intervention and the direct consequences of imperialism.

Diaspora Consciousness: Visualizing Homocolonialism

How do these histories affect the queer Middle Eastern diaspora today? Because of the powerful links between visual cultural and diasporic subjectivity, I contend that queer diasporic artists play a role in keeping alive the link between the colonial past and the contemporary present, even at a subconscious level.[60] Whether or not this trait of diasporic artists is distinguishable from contemporary artists based in the Middle East today is beyond the scope of this one analysis, as diaspora consciousness is a key component as to why past histories can be embedded within diasporic imaginings of self, desire, and being.[61] More specifically, linking contemporary diasporic art to a colonial moment examines processes and practices that contribute to the formation of diaspora consciousness. "Diaspora consciousness" has been understood as a strong and enduring group consciousness of the homeland in which feelings of solidarity are more or less shared by the members of a diasporic collectivity in a host country or a new setting.[62] I contend that diaspora consciousness is an integral component to embedding colonial histories, trauma, and loss within diasporic experiences today, weaving traditional ways of understanding gender, sexuality, and the self with contemporary ways of being. Here I argue that beyond this definition, which seems well suited to capture some of the more historically prevalent experiences of diaspora, there are nuances and permutations in the present that might also constitute diaspora consciousness.

One such site of diaspora consciousness is the art of queer diasporic Middle Eastern subjects, where colonial histories, trauma, and loss are embedded within expressions of everyday queer diasporic experiences. Paul Gilroy argues that "identity provides a way of understanding the interplay between our subjective experience of the world and the cultural and historical settings in which that fragile subjectivity is formed."[63] There are productive links between diasporic consciousness on the one hand and identity on the other. However, as Gilroy cautions, identity is not simply that which is shared; rather "it is always particular, as much about difference as about shared belonging."[64] It is this interplay of sameness and difference that I find underpins the queer Arab diaspora's search for belonging. Historically, their same-sex desires have been marked by derision after the advent of Western modernity in the Middle East, and within North America there is a heightened sense of difference between "us" and "them"—that is, the assimilation process that marks a "good immigrant." As Sherene Razack notes, a common trope is "the story of the unassimilable, fatally pre-modern Muslim community encountering an advanced civilization."[65] This Orientalist trope is something that arguably enforces the strict binary that has been manufactured between same-sex desire and being Arab, a dichotomy felt both in the Middle East and in the diaspora. This theory linking diaspora consciousness to queer art production builds on James Clifford's theories on diasporic futures: "Diaspora consciousness is thus constituted both negatively and positively. It is constituted negatively by experiences of discrimination and exclusion. . . . Diaspora consciousness is produced positively through identification with world-historical cultural/political forces, such as 'Africa' or 'China.' The process may not be as much about being African or Chinese, as about being American or British, or wherever one has settled, differently."[66]

The powerful histories of coloniality and imperial power outlined in this chapter demonstrate how homosexuality in the Middle East was defined, criminalized, and outlawed at the turn of the twentieth century. These historic measures of change are not insular, and they affect the ways in which gender and sexuality are currently defined and understood in the Middle East and its diaspora.

While the interplays of race and sexual desire are not new, looking at these sites within the context of queer diasporic art is noteworthy. Artist Jamil Hellu is a San Francisco–based visual artist whose work revolves around representations of identity and exploring transnational interpretations of queer sexuality. Born and raised in Brazil with a Syrian father and a Paraguayan mother, Hellu uses photography, video, performance, and mixed-media art installations to create contrasting metaphors about the politics of cultural identities and the fluidity of sexuality. As Hellu says in an interview, "My father's family is from Syria, originally from a town called Mashta al-Helu, from which I bear my last name. Looking for ways to voice my despair over homophobia and violence in the Middle East, I started to produce works claiming my own Arab roots. My latest projects explore my identity as a gay man in relation to my Syrian heritage and Arab ethnicity."[67]

In his 2016 installation Be My Guest (figures 4.1 and 4.2), Hellu presents two refurbished antique chairs with a footrest positioned between them, creating an intimate seating area. The two chairs face each other at an angle and are flanked by white curtains featuring the same pattern on the furniture. The white fabric used in the furniture and curtains is adorned with figurative representations of Middle Eastern men engaging in various scenes of intimacy and undress (figures 4.3 and 4.4). Sometimes kissing, hugging, wrestling, and dancing, these representations of men are stamped repeatedly in black ink onto the white textile to create a repetitive design. In Be My Guest, Hellu cites the taboo of male homosexuality in both the Victorian-era empire and the Arab context that it colonized by using Victorian furniture as a metaphor for the cultural history of sexual repression in the Middle East.[68]

To be identified as Middle Eastern, the men are visibly hairy, play instruments that are popular in the Middle East, and wear clothing and headdress that are identifiably Middle Eastern. The tensions here between East and West, Arab and Victorian, modern and unmodern, Orientalism and Occidentalism, all work in complex ways with one another.[69] These scenes of homosexual intimacy and leisure were rendered invisible in the Middle East during the Victorian era.[70] By upholstering these tender and intimate depictions of Arab men onto the Victorian furniture, they now define the very surface that they cover. In this defiant act of colonizing the pristine white surface of the furniture with depictions of racialized same-sex intimacy, this installation ensures that these depictions are encrypted with the very Victorian discourses of sexual repression and knowledge production that sought to erase them. The power relations between the Victorian ruling class and the Middle East that were made invisible during imperializing missions of Western modernity are not only made visible in this artwork, but they are also inseparable from one another.

After nations in the Global North started decriminalizing homosexuality,

4.1. *left* Jamil Hellu, *Be My Guest* (2016). Installation: mirror, ottoman, 2 chairs, 2 pillows. Upholstered life-size furniture with textile pattern digitally printed on fabric.

4.2. *right* Jamil Hellu, *Be My Guest* detail, upholstered chair with textile pattern digitally printed on fabric.

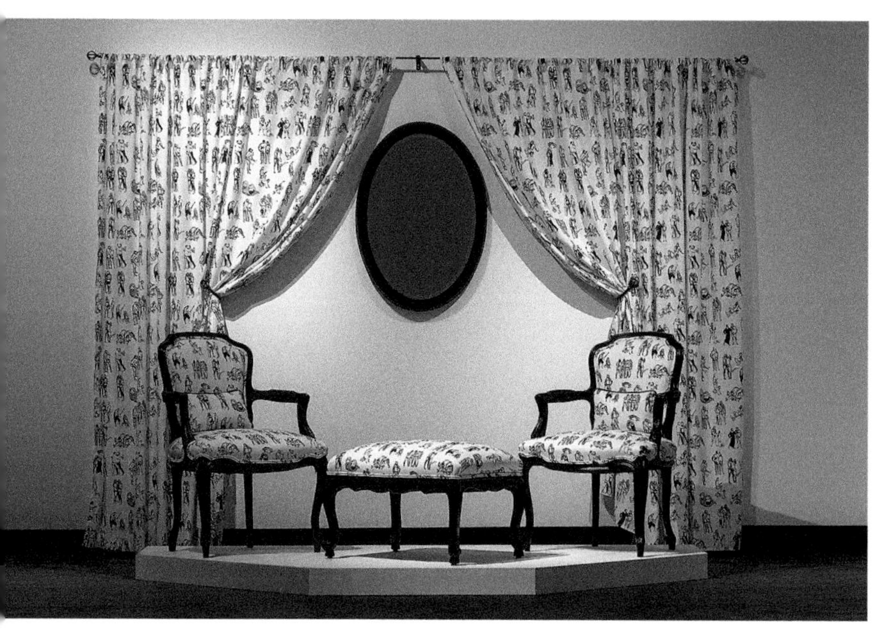

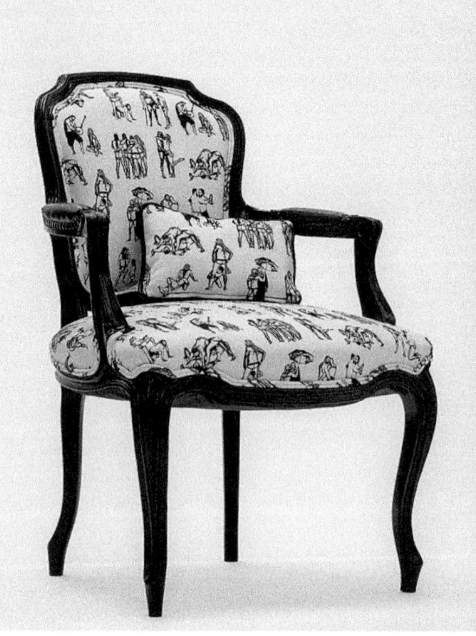

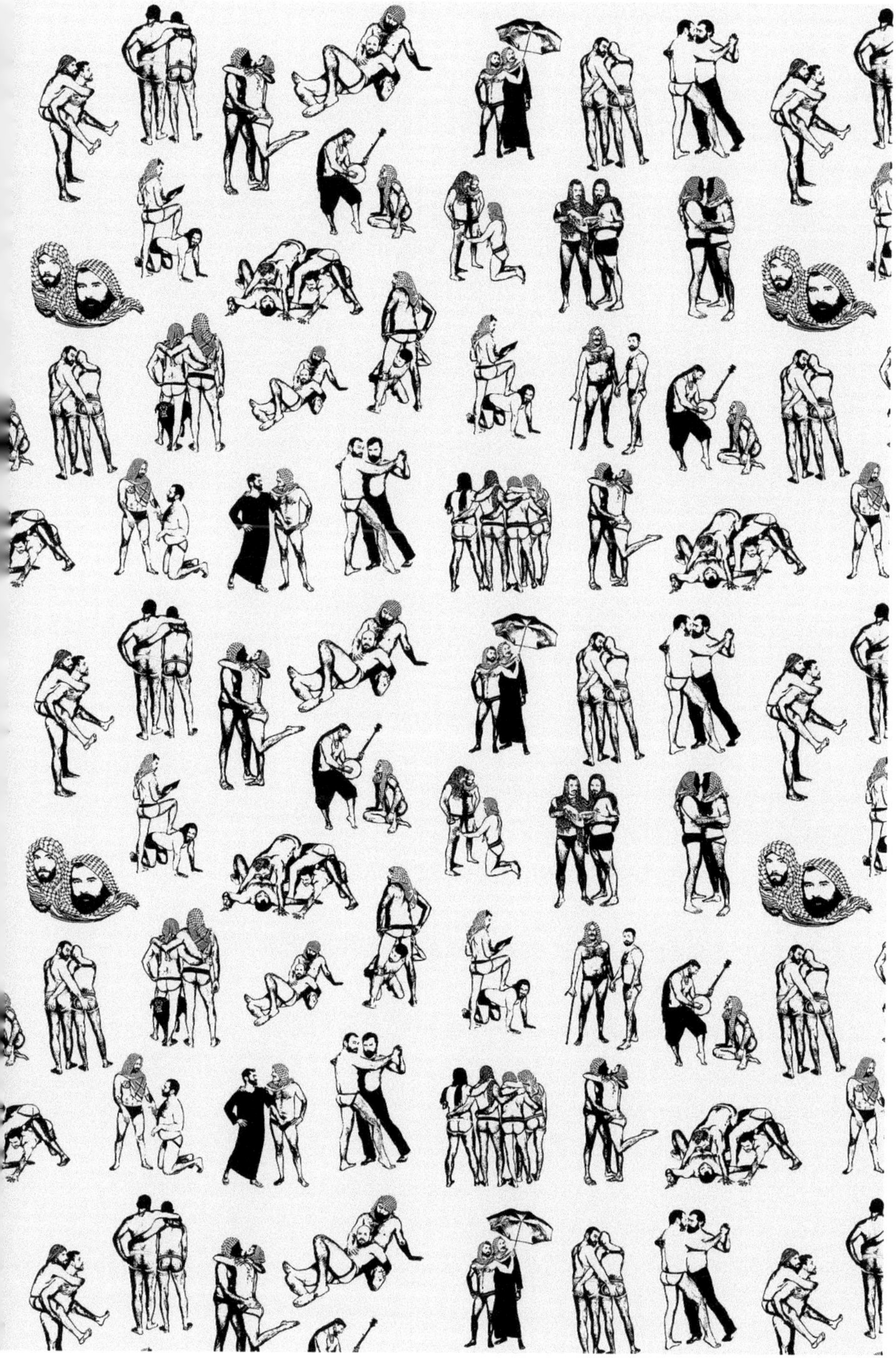

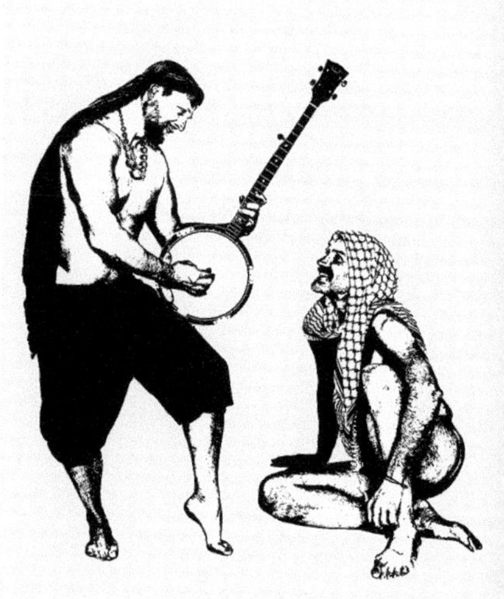

4.3. *left* Jamil Hellu, *Be My Guest*, detail of the fabric used to upholster the furniture, with a textile pattern digitally printed on fabric.

4.4. *right* Jamil Hellu, *Be My Guest*, detail from the textile pattern.

the goalposts of modernity moved and homosexual liberation became inextricably tied to being a modern nation.[71] Homosexuality and gay liberation are thus insidiously used as a newly changed endpoint of Western modernity, excluding the Middle East from ever reaching progress as defined by the Global North. As Hiram Pérez argues, "Neither gay liberation politics nor queer activism has ever fully reckoned with the tacit, if complex, participation of gay modernity in U.S. [and Euro-American] imperialist expansion."[72] The hostility that queer people feel in the Middle East today is in part tied to this colonial history. Thus, Hellu symbolically and visually traces the violence inflicted on homosexuals in the Middle East to the Victorian period while simultaneously linking this homocolonialism to the violence experienced by contemporary queer subjects today. This uncomfortable reminder seeks to critique and problematize the often heteronormative agendas of the West as the savior and defender of queer subjects in the Middle East.

Wanting to address the history of violence inflicted on homosexual discourse in the Middle East, Hellu traces this violence to a puritanical Victorian period while simultaneously linking this homocolonialism to the violence experienced by contemporary queer subjects. This artistic interrogation of coloniality deftly connects the historical moment in time when imperialism altered sexual discourses in the Middle East with the homophobic violence experienced by the contemporary diaspora. This link is paramount to my thesis, for the abject homophobia that has now been associated with the unmodern Middle East has visibly turned into a complex relationship with the Victorian rule of law governing sexual discourses, an import of colonialism, and erasing local intonations of same-sex intimacy at the turn of the twentieth century.

There is another dynamic tension present within the artwork: one between Western gayness and a more culturally relevant same-sex intimacy that has existed and still exists within Islamicate regions.[73] The Islamicate same-sex desire, facial hair, beauty standards, and conventions of homosociality that have permitted men to be intimate with one another (like traditional sporting activities, bathhouses, cafés, and shisha bars, to name a few) are put alongside markers of gay sex synonymous with the Global North, such as BDSM harnesses, jock straps, and sexual scenes that allude to cruising categories of gay male identification in the West, like being a *bear*, *otter*, or *cub*.[74] In this artwork, Jamil Hellu displays the many ways in which Arab men wear their traditional Middle Eastern headdress, using multiplicity and repetition as a visual strategy to illustrate the numerous variations of styles according to distinct nationalities.[75] In *Be My Guest*, Arab men wearing Palestinian *kiffaya* over their heads or the Saudi head-covering known as *ghutra* are engaging in the very tensions that their specific histories of gender, sexuality, and nationalism represent. Dressed as modern Arab men but engaging in sexual acts that have been made illegal and perverse, in part by Victorian-era travelers and their imperial apparatuses of Orientalism like travelogues circulating the Middle East, the historical tensions between acceptable and non-acceptable sexual behavior is made visible. These enmeshed historical entanglements are apparent through the frictions that emerge through the manufactured dichotomy of being Arab and being gay.

In creating a link between diaspora consciousness and sexual imperialism in the Middle East, artists like Hellu offer a "long overdue look at the way concepts of community and belonging are made across the diaspora, and produce insight into the possibilities for decolonising Arabness or rearticulating Arabness beyond Orientalism or reverse Orientalism."[76] The double bind of the queer Middle Eastern diaspora brings with it the racialization of their sexuality in the Global North, creating frictions with an imagined hegemonic gay community. Racial stigmatization of queerness in the Global North is echoed by Momin Rahman's assertion of the ostensibly Muslim queer subject lying outside of normative Western queer politics, pointing to issues of genuine difference and incompatibility.[77] This indicates that colonial trauma is deeply woven within diaspora consciousness and is reflected in the artwork created by the queer diasporic artists in North America looking to visualize and create complex representations of their own lived experiences. I assert that this diaspora consciousness can be a powerful driving tool in creating visual art, even at a subconscious level. Linking racial difference and the queer diaspora in the Americas to Western imperialism and colonialism, Hellu's artwork uses a complex homocolonial history to outline a coloniality that continues to inflict violence, isolation, and trauma to this day.

The question of temporality is key throughout this book, especially the way in which the artworks disrupt linear progress narratives within homocolonial framings of Arab sexualities. Scholarship on queer temporality, in particular José Esteban Muñoz, confirms that queer aesthetics map future social relations and that "queerness is essentially about the rejection of a here and now and an insistence on potentiality or concrete possibility for another world."[78] In reality, gay liberation campaigns rooted in Eurocentric ideas of queerness align only some people—namely, those who are white, gay, and living in the Global North—with a certain future. However, based on this logic, the location in which you arrive is linear and remains Eurocentric, for it does not speak to a future that accounts for hybridity, diaspora, and the racialization that impacts what an inclusive, liberatory queer futurity can really look like. Locating the Middle East within a queer futurity is an important task, for it creates room for racialization to factor in queer social relations. In *Cruising Utopia*, Muñoz finds it problematic that white privilege shapes the gay liberation movements that help imagine queer futurity and says, "There is something Black about waiting. And there is something queer, Latino, and transgender about waiting. Furthermore, there is something disabled, Indigenous, Asian, poor, and so forth about waiting. Those who wait are those of us who are out of time in at least two ways. We have been cast out of straight time's rhythm, and we have made worlds in our temporal and spatial configurations."[79]

This waiting that Muñoz writes about can also be seen in the progress narratives of modernity in the Middle East that becomes entangled in gay rights, keeping Arab queers in stasis, waiting in white straight time that fails to account for their localized reality. This notion of waiting is also important to queer people of color because it aligns their futurity as different from the futures of white queer subjects with relative privilege. When certain nations, peoples, and cultures are seen as "lacking modernity" or being a part of the "Global South," their temporality will be outside of the norm, and utopian queer futures rooted in progress would follow the same homocolonial tendencies associated with universalism. It is important that a queer futurity from the Global South, including racialized and diasporic subjects in the Global North, must align its goal outside of a Western sexual modernity narrative rooted in civilizational progress, because colonial logics cannot mend colonial harm.

In the examples shown of Hellu's artwork, a complex historical archive has been mined to create powerful resonances between an imperial past with a queer futurity that accounts for a diasporic present, and other artists may rely more heavily on their diasporic consciousness to create these links. As the visual analysis of Jamil Hellu's work illustrates, these colonial histories are articulated by visual artists who are creating historically contingent representations of queer diasporic intimacy that specifically outline a historical coloniality they have never lived, yet which reverberates today.

FIVE

QUEERING ARCHIVES OF PHOTOGRAPHY

LINKING A COLONIAL HISTORY TO A DIASPORIC PRESENT

In the previous chapter, I outlined how queer diasporic artists articulate diaspora consciousness and illustrated it as having components of former, colonized, historic ways of understanding gender and sexual identity. This in turn helps support the argument that queer diasporic artists play a role in keeping alive links between the colonial past and the contemporary present, even at a subconscious level.[1] These links are being kept alive, and in some instances they are also being activated to decolonize Eurocentric histories of sexuality and more forgotten cultural histories within the Middle East, Africa, and Asia. In this chapter I will continue to develop facets of diaspora consciousness and present a history of homocolonialism in the Middle East that is firmly linked to current diasporic subjectivity in North America. To do so, I will introduce photography as an invaluable tool to imperial discourses in helping to shape gender and sexuality at a time of colonial contact in the Middle East. Then I will introduce the artwork of Iranian Canadian artist Ebrin Bagheri, connecting his contemporary drawings to the colonial photographic archives in an attempt to show the connectedness of visual imagery. The colonial dimensions of the photographic medium are undeniably relevant to the study of visual culture and the history of photography, and I will demonstrate that these colonial dimensions of representation shape the ways in which gender and sexuality in the Middle East are pictured, depicted, and illustrated today. These rich archives of colonial encounter hold seeds of same-sex desire and representation that, I argue, are firmly incorporated in the diaspora consciousness of queer subjects in North America. More importantly, in analyzing the artwork of Ebrin Bagheri, I emphasize how these links happen subconsciously, unintentionally, and sometimes unknowingly to the diasporic artists, firmly supporting the link between historical colonialism in the Middle East and how coloniality actively and subconsciously shapes the experiences of gender and sexuality in the contemporary diaspora.

Visualizing Intimacy in the Global South

Just as histories of colonialism cannot be separated from histories of art, the emergence of Western gay scholarship on sexuality coincides with the rise of Western scholars interested in representations of sexuality in the Arab and Muslim worlds.[2] As noted earlier, Arab scholar Joseph Massad critiques what he terms the "Gay International," a mission of homocolonialism and Western exceptionalism cloaked in discourses of human rights that seeks to export Western models of homosexuality into places where it did not previously exist, effectively erasing local scripts of sexual identity.[3] This needs to be examined in relation to Western exceptionalism and the dominant (Euro-American) discourse on gay identity in the Middle East, which contends that homosexuality is hated, foreign, and not tolerated.[4]

Yet, as this analysis of contemporary visual art and archival research will show, queerness finds a way to dwell and remain in these seemingly "inhospitable" places like the Middle East, North Africa, and Asia. It begs the question: Who defines queer hospitality? The answer, of course, is Western queerness and its unquestionable authenticity within its own discourse. As I discussed previously, this in turn is reified by canonical texts like Michel Foucault's *History of Sexuality* in the way they become axiomatic texts on all histories of sexuality across all geographic periods rather than being only a limited study on sexuality discourses in Western Europe.[5] In this chapter I avoid discussing queerness in terms of global to local and instead make historical connections to the contemporary diaspora in order to see how the local subject speaks to queerness. This method takes away global powers of "importing" notions of queerness where they did not previously exist and instead examines how same-sex desires exist freely and locally within populations in the Middle East and the diaspora. With scholars arguing that queer identity is an inherently Western construct,[6] what would an analysis of same-sex discourses of the Global South look like if we do not speak of queerness at all? In other words, how would the conversation on same-sex desire in the Middle East change if we unlearned our assumptions and instead studied local-to-local historiographies more productively? This method would also consider the contribution of a translocal approach to the study of homosexual discourse in the Middle East and the relationship queerness has had with colonial histories of imperial expansion.[7] While I attempt to address some of these concerns in this chapter and in my overall research project, these questions are important to challenge Gay International discourses and to avoid a reproduction of colonial and imperial logics under a harmful universalist framework of human rights, gay liberation, and sexual freedoms that only mirror a Euro-American model.

The particular history of photography in the Middle East had an impact on the photographs that were taken, the power relationships between the photographer and the photographed subject, and the value given to contributions made by local populations to the nascent medium in the mid-nineteenth century. In establishing the importance between the history of photography in the Middle East and the power of representation, how do photographic and colonial encounters impact art production in the current diaspora? Do these imperial pasts have a direct correlation with how subjects in the diaspora conceive and visualize their own identities? Notably, where does eroticism lie within an image, and how do we read queerness in an image?[8] To work through these questions, I turn to visual analysis and examine the artwork of Iranian Canadian artist Ebrin Bagheri. Born in 1983, Bagheri is currently living and working in Toronto, Canada. Working primarily in drawing and painting, he has been exploring issues pertinent to Iranian culture and identity. Particularly, he uses portraiture to explore themes of masculinity and gender. In these portraits, Bagheri alludes to historical notions of premodern desire and alternative gender norms. Greatly invested in Persian literature and poetry, his large-scale drawings echo Persian miniature paintings in their details and intricacy. Using these poetic and literary tropes in conjunction with elements of Persian visual culture, Bagheri's work complicates notions of Persian culture, contemporary Iranian identity, and the conflicting themes of gender and sexuality that might arise at their intersection.

In his 2015 artwork *Untitled* (figure 5.1) from his *Eastern Desires* series (2014–2017), Bagheri uses delicate drawing techniques coupled with immense detail to depict scenes of Iranian men that fluctuate between contemporary subjects and Iran prior to the Industrial Revolution. These intimate scenes, at times evocative of *hammam* or bathhouse settings, are coupled with visual motifs reminiscent of Qajar dynasty Persian paintings that point to a masculinity unlike traditional depictions of Iranian men.[9] Later series of works like *Someone Who Is Like No-One* (2017) take similar historical references and delicate drawing techniques, coupled with jarring visual tropes that look out of place. Such tropes include bloodied hands like in *Untitled [I]* (2017; figure 5.2) or figures with red noses seen in *Untitled [II]* (2017; figure 5.3) that add a dimension of abnormalities within the characters. These tropes can be interpreted as being linked to themes of illness, disease, quarantine, and, in the case of the clown-like red nose, even a trickster element to imply that these are figures that fall outside of normative social acceptance. This theme of not-belonging is extended in the artist's use of traditional notions of hiding and in various critiques of the binaries between private/public culture and visibility/invisibility. Using these different strategies, precolonial and colonial discourses of sexuality are examined as part of the context of Bagheri's art, and this lens helps us to understand queer diasporic art production in relation to a colonial legacy and the complex agency of diasporic artists.

I find it important to question the language used to title the series and whether or not this language is a type of self-Orientalizing. If so, does this language speak to Bagheri's distance from his Iranian culture by being in the diaspora, heightening his need for cultural authenticity? In "The Powerful Art of Qajar Photography," Ali Behdad defines Orientalism within aesthetic discourse as being "not 'natural' or 'objective' representations. Rather, they reproduced, and consequently reinforced, certain Orientalist stereotypes about the Middle East—its 'backward' people, and 'exotic' cultures—stereotypes that provided the ideological rationale for colonizing the Middle East in this period."[10] Specifically, in his article on Orientalism and self-Orientalizing in nineteenth-century Iran, Behdad concludes that Qajar photographers used visual tropes that imitate Orientalist European painters and photographers who were prevalent in the region in order to create an image of Iran's dynastic power while maintaining a mimetic relation with the ways

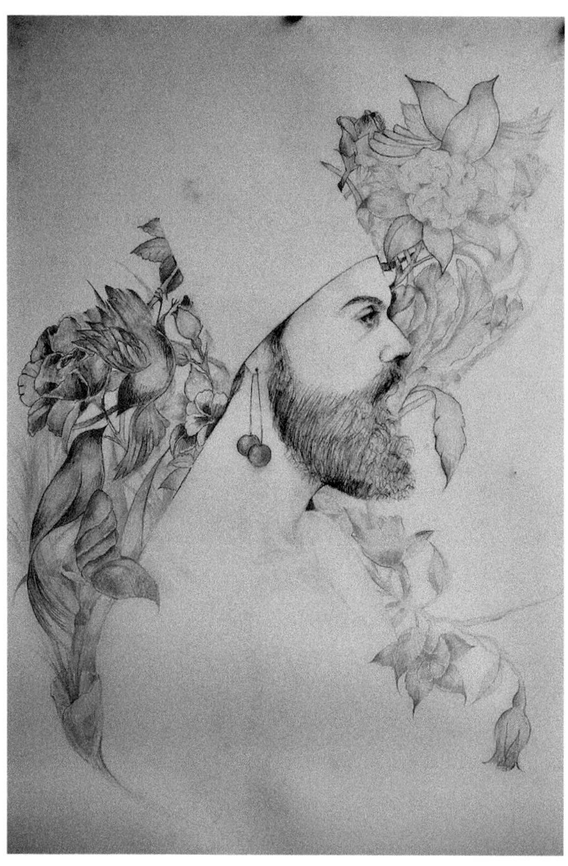

5.1. Ebrin Bagheri, *Untitled*, from *Eastern Desires* series (2015). Pencil crayon and ballpoint pen on paper. Courtesy of the artist.

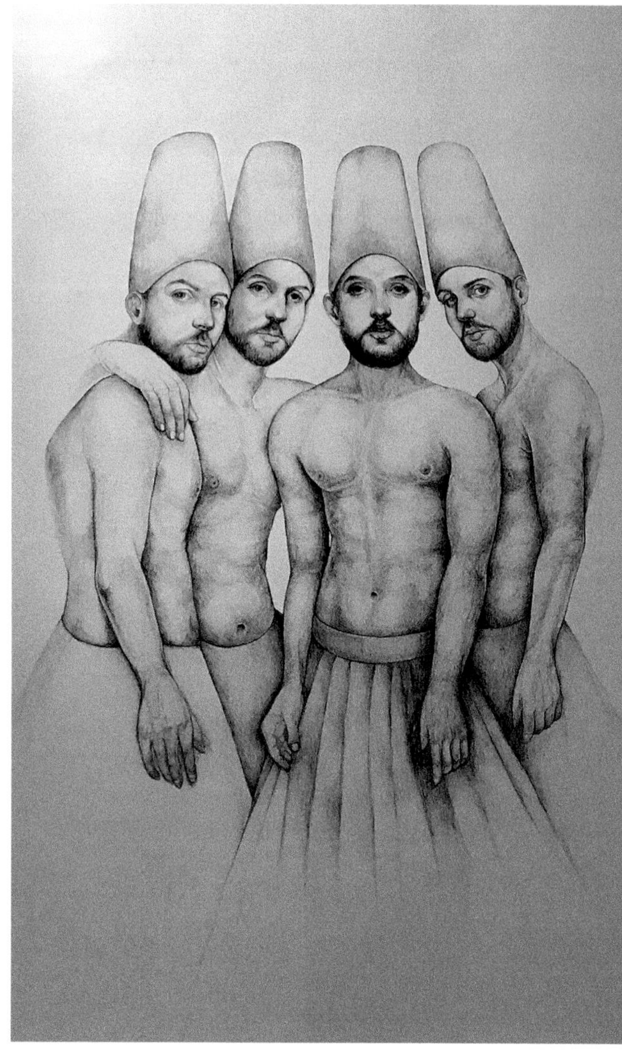

5.2. Ebrin Bagheri, *Untitled [I]*, from *Someone Who Is Like No-One* series (2016). Pencil crayon and ballpoint pen on paper. Courtesy of the artist.

Europeans exoticized the Middle East.[11] In thinking through these themes, I contend that Bagheri using tropes such as foreignness, exoticism, and otherness can be done productively and strategically in order to add critical discourse to sex and gender. The historicity that is analyzed within this chapter is an example of how Orientalist tropes are a part of a wider system of cultural and visual elements that are entangled within a web of imperial and colonial contact.

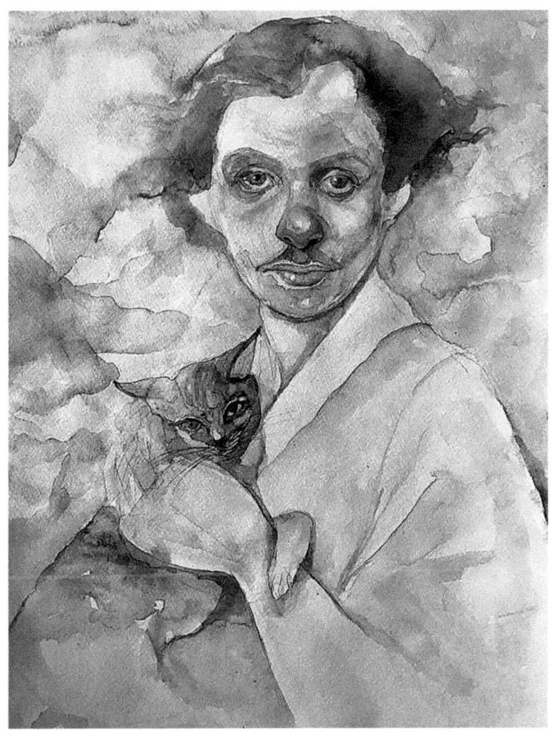

5.3. Ebrin Bagheri, *Untitled [II]*, from *Someone Who Is Like No-One* series (2016). Watercolor paint and ballpoint pen on paper. Courtesy of the artist. See also plate 4.

Because of this, it is not whether Bagheri's language/tropes are self-Orientalizing; rather, I am more concerned with the links and connections between his visual imagery, histories of sexuality, and histories of colonialism, all of which include Orientalism as a primary component within the asymmetries of power. Because of this, "Orientalism, therefore, should not be viewed as a unilateral artistic, intellectual, and political force, but instead as a particular system of ideas, aesthetic expressions, and intellectual practices that was internalized by 'Orientals.'"[12] Following this logic, I argue that Bagheri's work is in some measure also responding to and is critically resonant with Canadian Islamophobia, racism, and homo-Orientalism. This response to racism and Orientalism can be seen in Bagheri naming his series historically Orientalist terms such as *Eastern Desires*, and he critiques the isolation and othering that can be felt by the queer Iranian diaspora in his series *People You May Know*. He does so by utilizing tropes from Orientalism but does not replicate the stereotypes that provided the ideological rationale for colonizing the Middle East. Instead, Bagheri uses his artistic agency to employ the aesthetic traditions that are undeniably shared between Orientalist art and traditional Iranian art to better create links between diasporic identity and powerful conceptualizations of homeland that still dictate transnational discourse.

Histories of (Colonial) Photography in the Middle East

A crucial link between the history of photography and Europe's knowledge about the Middle East has existed since the invention of the daguerreotype in 1839.[13] When Louis-Jacques-Mandé Daguerre introduced his invention to the Chambre des députés in France, politician, mathematician, and physicist Dominique François Arago commented on "the extraordinary advantages that could have been derived from so exact and rapid a means of reproduction during the expedition to Egypt" and recommended that the Institut d'Egypte be equipped immediately with the new visual technology.[14] In subsequent decades, many European photographers followed Arago's suggestion, and with the support of various governmental institutions, photographers traveled to the Middle East to amass portfolios of Egyptian antiquity and the sites of the holy lands, making the region one of the principal training grounds for the early practice of photography, in part due to the abundance of natural sunlight.[15] This link between photography and the Middle East is likewise seen in Daguerre's British counterpart, William Henry Fox Talbot, who invented the salted paper and calotype photographic processes. In 1846 Talbot published a pamphlet titled "The Talbotype Applied to Hieroglyphics," which was distributed among archeologists and Orientalist scholars.[16]

The dominant historiography understands photography as a Western import into Eastern lands. This assumed and maintained Eurocentrism has to do with the widely accepted belief that French artist Louis-Jacques-Mandé Daguerre invented the daguerreotype process of photography. The history of Daguerre and his contemporary British rival, Henry Fox Talbot, is well documented, but they were only two figures in a much broader exploration of light, lenses, and light-sensitive substances in the period. Take, for example, tenth-century Iraqi mathematician and scientist Abu Ali Al-Hasan Ibn Al-Haytham. Known simply as Ibn al-Haytham, his name was later Latinized into Alhazen. He was foundational to the history of photography for his *Book on Optics* (written in 1021). Ibn al-Haytham used the camera obscura to experiment with understandings of vision, optics, and light during the Islamic Golden Age (a period of cultural, economic, and scientific flourishing in the history of Islam, traditionally dated from the eighth century to the fourteenth century). When his groundbreaking *Book on Optics* was translated into Latin and other languages, his ideas influenced European scholars during the European Renaissance and their photographic technologies hundreds of years later. The impossibility of writing one linear history of photography becomes apparent through his interventions, as Al-Haytham was instrumental in early thinking of photography, yet he is seldom, if ever, included within the master narrative. Historians of photography have generally assigned only marginal importance to the Middle East in the works of the many European photographers in the nineteenth century and even less importance to the various traditions of indigenous photography that emerged in the region soon after the introduction of the daguerreotype in 1839.[17] Currently, the study of photography in the Middle East does not focus on indigenous photography but rather on historiographies of European photographers traveling to the Middle East on imperialist adventures during a period of colonial expansion.[18] These European photographers and photo studios that dominated the history of Middle Eastern photography include Le Gray, Du Camp, Salzmann, Tancrède Dumas, Francis Frith, Felice Beato, Emile Béchard, Hippolyte Arnoux, and Alexandre Leroux; as well as Maison Bonfils, Maison Lehnert and Landrock, Maison Garrigues, Photoglob Zurich, and Underwood and Underwood.[19]

Tellingly, all of these photographers and photography studios still define the imagery and historical narrative of photography in the Middle East. Then, how does one study, interpret, and read the visual imagery of Middle Eastern photography from local photographers and artists? While fully answering this question is beyond the scope of this book, it is important to consider it when locating the power that photography had in colonial missions of imperialism in the Middle East and the gaps in knowledge created in its wake. In his detailed study of Middle Eastern portrait photography, *The Arab Imago: A Social History of Portrait Photography, 1860–1910*, historian Stephen Sheehi argues that asking how Middle Eastern photography is *really* different only reinscribes the binaries of the dominant historical narrative of Middle Eastern photography.[20] Cultural difference, and arguably Western exceptionalism, is maintained if photography from "Eastern lands" is distinct from the Western master image, and called derivative of the Western original. Rather than strictly analyzing the subject matter of the image itself, Orientalism's asymmetries of power should be read as part of the photographic image as much as the subject matter.[21] The clear divide between European photographers in the Middle East and local photographers in the Middle East is indicative of the Western exceptionalism that maintains this Eurocentric master narrative and disenfranchises Arabs from proprietorship of the universalizing power of photography.[22]

Photography in the Middle East can be used to excavate the image of gender, the changing sexual discourses within the archive, and the visualized homoeroticism of a local population. To push this further and illustrate a moment of *queering locally*, I argue that photography in the Middle East during colonial periods can also provide a useful link for understanding the contemporary diaspora's relationship to their own locally relevant—in Bagheri's case, Persian—history. Photography, then, acts as a tool that links these colonial histories to the contemporary moment, giving better insight into how those in the diaspora experience their sexuality. This removes the value judgments of modernity, progress, and social acceptance from the discussion and instead provides an analysis that is rooted in historical causality and seeks to find the cause-and-effect relationships between colonial histories in the Middle East and the current queer diaspora.[23]

Reading Loss in an Image

To understand the context in which the photographic archives exist, it is important to further outline the complex relationship between sexuality and colonialism. To do so, I find it productive not to discuss colonialism as only a minor component within the study of sexuality; instead, I contend that the history of colonialism is a valuable tool, and in some ways one of the most important tools, to access what a history of sexuality looks like. As feminist historian Afsaneh Najmabadi notes, "In the nineteenth century, homoeroticism and same-sex practices came to mark Iran as backward; heteronormalization of eros and sex became a condition of 'achieving modernity,' a project that called for heterosocialization of public space and a reconfiguration of family life."[24] This heteronormalization lies in the deep overlaps between colonialism, same-sex desire, and how visual culture was used within the imperial civilizing mission of Western modernity. Part of the heteronormalization that Najmabadi writes about is a direct result of European travelers in the Ottoman Empire who openly criticized and judged local traditions, inevitably leading to the censorship of homoerotic cultural practices. These silencing practices culminated in a drastic shift in language that resulted from Victorian sexual discourses being imposed on local conceptions of gender, sexuality, and physical presentation. Historians have documented the travel journals (also known as travelogues) of European travelers who visited regions of the Ottoman Empire, noting their astonishment and disgust with same-sex traditions whereby local men openly flaunted their relations with other men and adolescent boys. It should be noted that these travel journals were translated from their respective Anglo-European languages into Arabic and local languages to be circulated in order to cause shame and embarrassment, making the journals an irreparable act of repression and sexual imperialism.[25]

As Najmabadi notes, nineteenth-century Qajar sensibilities deemed that a beautiful face could belong to either a young male or a female with identical features. The assumed normalcy of the man/woman binary became a European imposition and negatively affected modes of maleness in nineteenth-century Iran that were distinct from manhood or masculinity. As Najmabadi asserts, "In early Qajar art, for instance, beauty was not distinguished by gender. By the end of the nineteenth century, however, a highly gender-differentiated portrayal of beauty emerged, along with a concept of love that assumed heterosexuality as natural."[26] As I examined in chapter 4, in *The History of Sexuality* Michel Foucault traces the repression of sexuality in the Victorian era of the bourgeoisie, claiming that on the subject of sex, silence became the rule.[27] The mechanisms of silence that Foucault writes about, however, need to be developed and linked according to the silencing practices that European travelers introduced to publicly shame the homoerotic practices present in Islamicate regions. Dror Ze'evi also contends that, likewise, in the Ottoman Empire there was a great loss at the turn of the century, and local sexual scripts were erased but not replaced with new ones, leaving a silence and void in the discourse of Ottoman sexuality. Such silences are evident in the imposed censorship in literature, expurgatory practices in publishing literature, and in the public shame caused by the European travel journals in the nineteenth-century Ottoman Empire.[28]

I argue that we can read this loss through the photographs of European Orientalists in the Middle East, like the Austro-Hungarian photographer

Rudolf Lehnert and his Swiss business partner Ernst Landrock. Lehnert was born in Bohemia in 1876, which was then part of the Austro-Hungarian Empire and now part of the Czech Republic. He first traveled to Tunis in 1904, where he met his friend and later business partner Ernst Landrock, and the pair established a photographic studio in Tunis and worked closely together for more than twenty years. They later established studios in Munich, Leipzig, and Cairo, publishing their photographs under the studio name Lehnert & Landrock.

In their 1910 photograph *Young Man, Loosely Dressed* (figure 5.4), a young, adolescent-looking local boy stands in front of the camera. His pose is a frontal portrait framing his shoulders, and he sits reclined within the scene, making his face and gaze the focus of the picture. Staring at the viewer, the boy has no facial hair, and dark, luscious hair peeks through the loosely wound turban covering his head. While not immediately clear, this photograph pictures the very loss outlined above, both in the subject of the young boy, and in the elements excluded from the scene, like facial hair. As many authors have marked the significance of facial hair and age in homoerotic literature and cultural traditions,[29] Najmabadi points out that "the growth of a full-grown beard marked adult manhood, [and] the adolescent male's transition from an object of desire to a desiring subject."[30] Facial hair was so important to aesthetics of beauty that an adult man who shaved his beard in premodern Persia was thought to be declaring his craving to be desired by other men, also known as *mukhannas*, which translates to mean an adult man desiring to be an object of desire for other adult men.[31] As explained in the eleventh-century Persian book of advice, *Qabusnamah*, etiquette and moral behavior that prohibited men from shaving their beards were related to this critical transition from one state to the next.[32] It should also be noted that "for a male adolescent, to be an object of desire of adult men was considered unavoidable, if not acceptable or cherished by all."[33] In the photograph taken by Lehnert and Landrock (figure 5.4), the subject is lacking most visible facial hair, making him an *amrad*, a young adolescent male who, according to the beauty standards of the premodern Persian culture, was an object of utmost desire. Therefore, the viewer is meant to assume that this boy does not yet have a beard and is still not marked by adult manhood. This implies that the young local boy photographed by Lehnert and Landrock would be an object of desire par excellence, yet the standards of beauty in Islamicate societies change rapidly over the course of the century when facial hair became a visible cultural difference between Europeans and local populations. In Qajar-period Iran, men's beards (and, later, women's mustaches) were a visual marker of difference between Europe and Iran. As Najmabadi argues, "This dilemma at every step was compounded by a sexual anxiety and fear: the European man, especially with his beardless face, looked to Iranian men's eyes, perilously like an *amradnuma*—an adult man making himself look like an amrad."[34] To further investigate this loss, I contend that we must look outside the frame of the photograph in order to engage with the content of the photograph itself.

To elucidate the colonial ramifications of a photograph such as Lehnert and Landrock's or the changing discourses of gender that are recorded, circulated, and therefore influenced by the medium of photography, I suggest we compare this photograph to a contemporary drawing by Bagheri. One might immediately recognize the Islamicate attributes to the figure but not necessarily the homoeroticism behind the drawing. In conducting a deep reading of the symbolic and stylistic elements, it becomes clear that this drawing speaks to the photography of Lehnert and Landrock in surprising yet harmonious ways. Bagheri's 2015 drawing *Untitled [II]* (figure 5.5) from his series *Eastern Desires* bears many resemblances to the aforementioned photograph, mirroring the focus of a young adolescent boy, the composition of the frontal portrait, and the soft drawing techniques echoing the fogginess of the photograph itself. In this drawing a young male of no more than twenty years of age stares longingly at the viewer. His head, covered in a turban that is slightly askew, makes visible to the viewer his long, luxurious locks of hair falling to the side. His long eyelashes, steady gaze, and wisps of faint facial hair accentuate his soft features. The figure is clothed in a tunic embellished with red cherries, mirroring the cherries adorning one of his earlobes like an earring. Similar to the young local boy in the European photograph, the youthful boy in Bagheri's drawing does not have a full beard and instead has a *khatt*, which is the mere hint of a mustache and marks the moment before the full growth of facial hair takes place.[35] It is at this time that an adolescent is considered most beautiful, but that hint of a mustache also heralds the beginning of the end of his status as an

5.4. Rudolf Lehnert and Ernst Landrock, *Young Man, Loosely Dressed* (1910). Gelatin print/glass-plate negative and hand-colored photogravure. Courtesy of the Ken and Jenny Jacobson Orientalist Photography Collection, Getty Research Institute, Los Angeles.

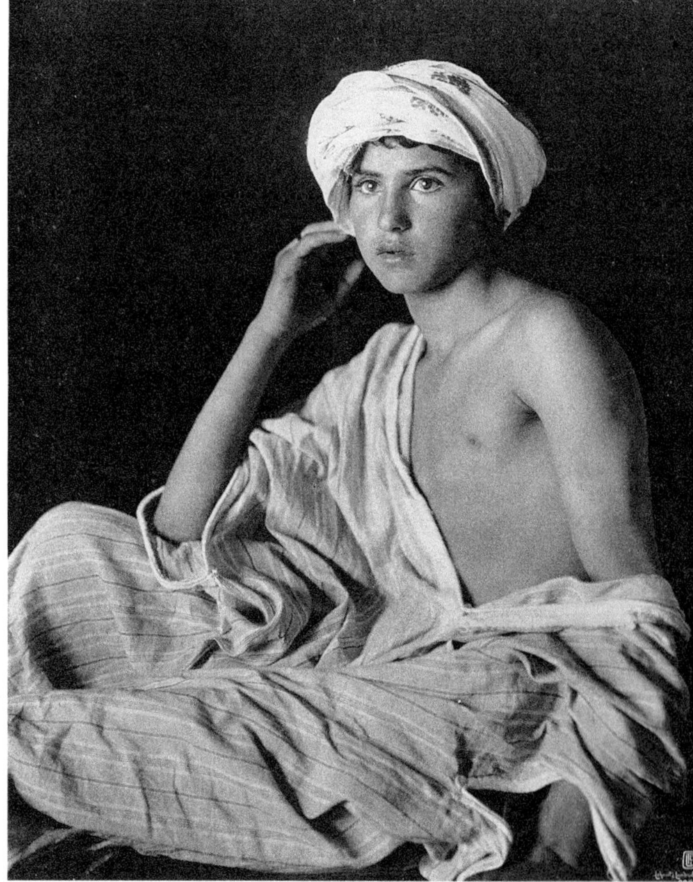

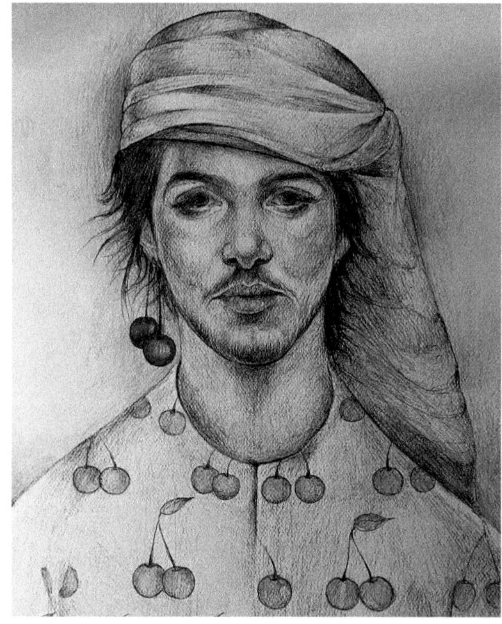

5.5. Ebrin Bagheri, *Untitled*, from *Eastern Desires* series (2015). Pencil crayon and ballpoint pen on paper. Courtesy of the artist. See also plate 3.

object of desire for adult men and his own movement into adult manhood. It has been noted that displaying abundant curls of hair was particularly associated with male sexual fantasy, fulfilling "adult male desire for music, wine, dance, homo/heterosex, or just plain voyeuristic pleasure."[36] Here, Bagheri captures the moment when this boy is still an amrad, a young adolescent male who, according to the beauty standards of the premodern Persian culture, was still an object of utmost desire.

The cherries juxtapose the perceived masculinity of the boy with their fragility and softness. Repeated over his tunic, they might speak to a delicateness and softness incongruent with normative depictions of masculinity, and his earring references another homosocial instance in Islamicate historiography. Both the loosely dressed boy with his tunic falling off his shoulder in Lehnert and Landrock's photograph (figure 5.4) and Bagheri's subject adorned with a rich, red cherry earring evoke the history of the dancing boys, or *köçek*, present in the Ottoman Empire. While Ze'evi analyzes these dancing boys for their gender-bending sexual fluidity, historian Joseph Boone relates that the dancing boys were an established norm throughout the Middle East and North Africa and performed in cafés, at court, in wedding processions, and even at religious festivals. These dancing boys were adorned with jewelry and were elaborately dressed, and numerous Orientalist photographs document the European fascination with these young boys.[37]

French photographers Hippolyte Délié and Émile Béchard are an Orientalist team who showed much fascination in producing photographs of the Middle East and the local population. Working in Egypt, French photographer Henri Béchard operated a studio in Cairo in the Ezbekiah Garden district, where he sold photographs of the region, as well as ethnographic photographs and Egyptian costume studies, to tourists.[38] French photographer Émile Béchard (assumed to be related to Henri) is best known for having presented at the Universal Exhibition of 1878 in Paris a set of photographs he took in Egypt; this earned him a gold medal. Émile Béchard formed a studio with Hippolyte Délié in their Ezbekiah studio in Cairo during the 1870s, then going by the moniker "Délié et Béchard."[39] The partnership was dissolved sometime after 1872 and both continued to work in Egypt as commercial photographers.[40]

The photograph *Au Jardin de l'Esbekieh (Cairo)* by Délié and Béchard (c. 1870; figure 5.6) is no exception to the homocolonial fetishism of local aesthetics of beauty and illustrates a young boy dancing. As mentioned above, known as a köçek and elaborately adorned with body jewelry and long, dangling earrings to accompany his long, flowing gown, the boy holds cymbals in each hand. The provenance of the photograph signals that the image was captured in Cairo, so this likely Egyptian boy shows us what the köçek looked like before they disappeared from public discourse. As historian Joseph Boone writes, instead of recognizing an androgynous ideal of beauty in the Middle East, European travelers tended to see what seemed like an unsettling class of effeminate traits combined with a dress that was neither male nor female.[41] In fact, the nineteenth-century British Orientalist William Ouseley, who served as ambassador in Persia, described the köçek as "wearing the complete dress of a woman, and imitating, with the most disgusting effeminacy, the looks and attitudes of the dancing girl."[42] The consequences of the value judgments imposed by European critiques led to the banning of the köçek from public performances in the mid-nineteenth century. These discourses of sexuality emerge within a dense web of religious, cultural, political, military, economic, and scientific connections with the Black, Brown, and non-European world. This is part of what sociologist Vrushali Patil calls an "interimperial conversation producing theorizations of nonnormative sexual praxis and subjectivity in the metropole . . . circulated by historic and contemporaneous imperial webbed connectivities."[43] This example indicates a degree to which Middle Eastern people were seeing their heritage negatively reflected back to them in Western writings, and they began to modify those cultural traditions that seemed to stand in the way of achieving Western modernity.[44] In Islamicate regions, homosexually suspect activities, as determined by Europeans, then became a cultural aspect seen as being part of a regressive past, and thus a homoerotic and homosocial tradition was extinguished.

The subject in Bagheri's drawing marks a moment before the banning of the köçek from public performances in the mid-nineteenth century, before European travelers' shaming the unabashed homoerotic culture of coffeehouses and public baths that were too lurid for their tastes, and before language was created to give derision to long-standing local traditions that were

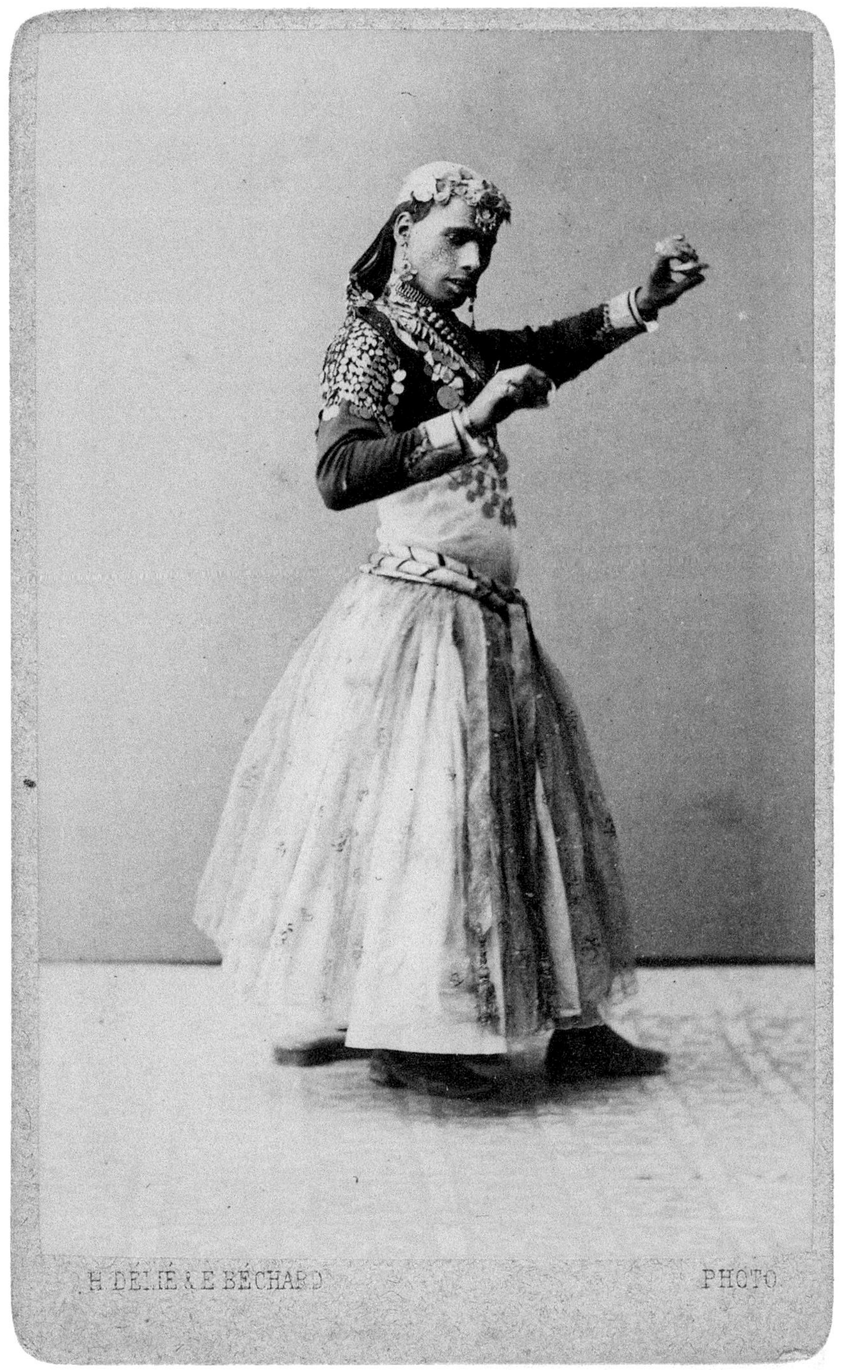

5.6. Henri Délié and Émile Béchard, *Au Jardin de l'Esbekieh (Cairo)* (1870s). Cartes-de-visite photograph. Courtesy of the Ken and Jenny Jacobson Orientalist Photography Collection, Getty Research Institute, Los Angeles.

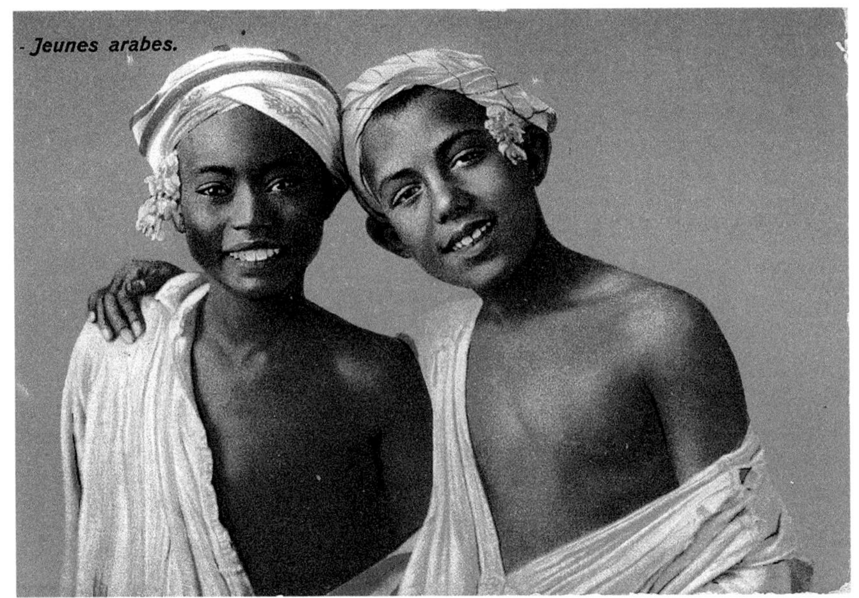

5.7. Rudolf Lehnert, *Jeunes Arabes, Tunis* (c. 1910). Colorized postcard. Courtesy of Dr. Joseph Allen Boone. Private collection. See also plate 5.

deemed backward and unmodern. While the subject in Bagheri's drawing *Untitled* (figure 5.5) lacks the jewelry of the young Egyptian boy of Délié and Béchard's photograph *Au Jardin de l'Esbekieh (Cairo)* (figure 5.6), the cherry earrings lay reference to this loss—a ghostly reminder of the köçek who remains only within the frame of Délié and Béchard's photograph but is now removed from public consciousness.

When relating Rudolf Lehnert's hand-painted photograph *Jeunes Arabes, Tunis* (1910; figure 5.7) to the men in Bagheri's *Untitled [II]* (figure 5.2) drawing, it becomes clear that kinship affiliation and embodiment becomes reimagined, as Bagheri insists on remembering and reinventing historical ways of being. This method allows for these archives to speak to one another in ways that uncover the very histories of colonialism and imperial power that led to their making. Unlike the young boys in Lehnert's photograph *Jeunes Arabes, Tunis* (figure 5.7), Bagheri's young men are more dominant and assertive in their pose. Taking up most of the picture frame in their composition, Bagheri's young men lack the passivity and docility of many Orientalist photographs, creating a different power dynamic between the subject and viewer. Drawing on the work of feminist film theorist Laura

Mulvey, it is in their traditional exhibitionist role that eroticized local young men are simultaneously looked at and displayed by European travelers and photographers. Like objectified women within the history of Western art, their appearance is coded for strong visual and erotic impact within Orientalist photography so that they can signify a desire "to-be-looked-at-ness."[45] The group of young men in Bagheri's drawing is noteworthy in the ways in which male homoerotic affective bonds were reimagined after homoeroticism and same-sex practices became marked as a sign of Iran's backwardness. Rejecting the heterosexualization of eros and sex that became a condition of achieving modernity,[46] Bagheri's drawing redefines the male same-sex intimacy that Europeans deemed a vice, and instead eroticism is once again depicted as a component of male bonding.

This analysis has used contemporary art in order to trace gender fluidity across much of North Africa and the changing scripts governing same-sex desire across multiple regions in the area. In this study, comparative analysis between time and place is essential in order to assess the movement of colonial powers and the changing beauty standards in Persia and the results of altered gender roles in the Ottoman Empire. In line with feminist theorist Gayatri Gopinath's use of the term "queer regions," this research displaces area studies through queer theory and applies a transtemporal exploration of the archive in order to better understand the current moment.[47]

Picturing Erasure within South-South Relationality

In examining Lehnert and Landrock's photograph *Young Boy with Headscarf* (figure 5.8) in relation to Bagheri's oeuvre, there is a parallel aesthetics of beauty with dancing boys and the handsome beardless youth who were hired at coffeehouses to serve patrons all across the Middle East and North Africa. As historian Khaled El-Rouayheb notes, the famous Damascene poet Ahmad al-'Inayati was said to have the habit of going every morning to the coffeehouses "with running water and handsome cup-bearer . . . and drink[ing] numerous cups of coffee."[48]

The archives I analyze in relation to Ebrin Bagheri's artwork are not only homoerotic, but they are also colonial and homocolonial archives of imperial encounter. Bagheri reimagines not just photographic subject matter, but

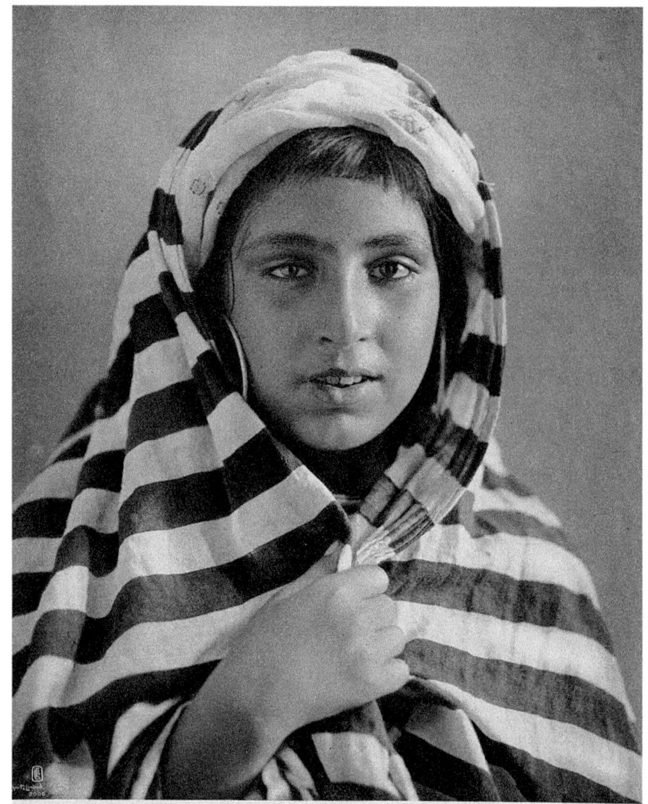

5.8. Rudolf Lehnert and Ernst Landrock, *Young Boy with Headscarf* (1910). Gelatin print. Courtesy of the Ken and Jenny Jacobson Orientalist Photography Collection, Getty Research Institute, Los Angeles.

through the process of drawing he uses his own hand to remove the colonial language imbued within the photographic development of the medium and within these archives. In this way he reinvents the original archival sources and, I argue, locates his own Iranian-ness within the once-Orientalized homoerotic photographs of young men taken by European travelers. He does so by inserting his local understandings of Iranian tradition that transcend geographic borders and share similar sexual discourses with the rest of the Middle East, North Africa, and West Asia. In an act of queering locally, Bagheri globalizes a regionally colonial history of desire and representation by using the language of the photographic archives in his contemporary drawing, thus blurring the lines between the photographic medium and the drawing technique. Bagheri's drawing is reminiscent of a premodern sexual script of the beardless amrad, the playfulness of the köçek, and the beautiful server boys working at the coffeehouses and bathhouses. By expanding local tradition to encompass much of the Ottoman Empire, Bagheri's drawing cites a specific moment in multiple geographic spheres and creates a network of interconnection between locales. These aesthetic and homosocial traditions are not necessarily solely Iranian but also speak widely to the conventions of beauty and sexual fluidity that were present across North Africa, the Middle East, and the entire Ottoman Empire.

The complication of temporal boundaries is important, as it is a valuable method for coping with the gaps within colonial archives. Archival records serve as primary documents within art history, but what happens when records from this period do not exist due to colonial encounter and imperialism? Often, the archives remaining in the Global South are the archives and objects that were left behind and deemed unworthy of looting by colonial powers, thus creating major gaps within archival records and surviving artifacts. What this analysis illustrates is that these archival gaps can also exist in other ways, the gaps themselves being seen within European representations of local populations. Due to the active erasure of local sexual scripts and same-sex desires that were imposed by European travelers, even the records that do remain will forever be clouded by an immense loss and absence. Imperial encounter and colonialism in and of itself has created this gap and changed the way local populations conceive of same-sex desire, including the ways in which it is pictured and visualized. It is because of this gap that I turn to contemporary artists who are actively reimagining these colonial archives, even those refiguring history at a subconscious or instinctive level, to create a counter-archive where homoerotic desire has not been silenced or removed. This complication of temporal boundaries, then, is a liberating complication of linear time and provides an empowered and anticolonial reading of history that accounts for the current moment and the diasporas experiencing these histories. In order for dynamics of power to always be at the fore of queer theoretical analysis, it is important to question how these sexual logics connect historic colonialism with the contemporary diaspora.

Diaspora Consciousness: A Practice of "Decolonial Aesthesis"

Through Bagheri's use of historic cultural tropes that are not only Iranian but are a part of many geocultural traditions across much of the Ottoman Empire, I excavate and uncover the trappings of colonial history that are embedded within the artist's diaspora consciousness.[49] The connections I make within this analysis are not links that the artist himself made. Archival research is not part of Bagheri's practice, and he has confirmed that he had not seen the archives within my study while producing his work. Therefore, I ask: What does it mean for Bagheri to produce drawings that visually echo photographs he has never seen?[50] How can this speak to the power of photography as a tool for excavation and locating colonial histories? What type of archival excavation can be accomplished by studying historical archives in tandem with contemporary art?[51] The ubiquity of photographs makes them perfectly suited to be something that "is not seen" but is somehow always present, especially at the core of identity formation and narratives of sexual desire.[52] This analysis contributes to demonstrating that artwork such as Bagheri's speaks to archival photography in ways that the archive may not be able to do alone. These colonial legacies are a part of his own identity as a queer Iranian man living in Canada and speak to the deeply entrenched homosocial practices and local traditions rooted in same-sex desire that have not fully been extinguished by colonialism, even within a multigenerational context.

Bagheri's own subject position informs his politics of artistic production and engagement in the ways that he becomes a bridge, or a link, between a premodern Iranian culture that he experiences, feels, and practices and the contemporary gay liberation politics he is entangled in as a diasporic queer subject in Canada. In the words of Walter Mignolo, "When you felt coloniality, you felt the colonial wound."[53] Bagheri depicts everyday forms of Islamicate same-sex desire with contemporary subjects mirroring traditional scenes that resemble scenes from the colonial archive, demonstrating they are not fully colonized because they inform Bagheri's conception of his own Iranian identity. I contend that his subject position and seemingly subconscious referencing of the visual tropes and aesthetic details that are present within the photographic archives show that these premodern sexual scripts are still alive and felt within the diaspora. From these archives, I argue that Bagheri, whether intentionally or not, does a queer reimagining of the photographic archives and produces drawings that are steeped in photographic history.

Diaspora consciousness again becomes a driving force in which to link contemporary art production and queer diasporic subjectivity. Within the case study explored in this chapter, diasporic consciousness stands in utopically as a figure for the imaginative completion of what Paul Gilroy identifies as a creative (and, by extension, theoretical) trajectory sometimes denied to minoritarian constituencies.[54] The historical record of desire and the aesthetics of intimacy are instrumental in locating contemporary notions of sexual discourse in the Middle East and the necessary cause-and-effect relationship sexuality discourses in the Middle East have on those currently living in the diaspora. This relationship is demonstrated in the artwork of contemporary artists currently living in the North American diaspora; in the artworks of Jamil Hellu, Ebrin Bagheri, and 2Fik (discussed in the following chapter) are in-depth case studies to provide an intellectual and methodological framework for these claims. In this way, the examples analyzed within this chapter illustrate how diaspora consciousness involves "a self-conscious transvaluation of diaspora [and] foregrounds the specular relationship of West and non-West; it thus brings to the fore issues of identity construction in cultural difference."[55]

This historical lens provides a necessary methodology for understanding human rights discourses around sexual tolerance and cultural specificity. Such exploration of diaspora consciousness as accounting for and being related to queer diasporic art production can be productive in shaping the dimensions of what Gilroy terms the "fatal junction of the concept of nationality with the concept of culture."[56] Thus, the study of historical visual culture concurrently with contemporary art is a productive method to illustrate how the history of same-sex desire in the Middle East is currently manifested and negotiated by artists transnationally in the queer diaspora. The diaspora, their "queer desires, bodies and subjectivities become dense sites of meaning in the production and reproduction of notions of 'culture,' 'tradition,' and communal belonging."[57] The link connecting diaspora consciousness and queer subjectivity in the diaspora is a large claim and one that I will continue to develop throughout this book. However, I examine these dense sites of meaning, as Gopinath puts it, in order to investigate the ways in which historical colonial trauma directly impacts meaning making for queer diasporic subjects in the West as a promising starting point.

The relationships outlined in this chapter between the diasporic artist and colonial trauma can be seen as being a part of a larger framework called *decolonial aestheSis*. Coined by Rolando Vazquez and Walter Mignolo, they define the term as follows:

> Decolonial aestheSis is a movement that is naming and articulating practices that challenge and subvert the hegemony of modern/colonial aestheSis. Decolonial aestheSis starts from the consciousness that the modern/colonial project has implied not only control of the economy, the political, and knowledge, but also control over the senses and perception. Modern aestheTics have played a key role in configuring a canon, a normativity that enabled the disdain and the rejection of other forms of aesthetic practices, or, more precisely, other forms of aestheSis, of sensing and perceiving. Decolonial aestheSis is an option that delivers a radical critique to modern, postmodern, and altermodern aestheTics and, simultaneously, contributes to making visible decolonial subjectivities at the confluence of popular practices of re-existence, artistic installations, theatrical and musical performances, literature and poetry, sculpture and other visual arts.[58]

To Vazquez and Mignolo, the shift from "aestheTics" to "aestheSis" is an important decolonial method, as aestheTics is "an aspect of the colonial matrix of power, of the imperial structure of control that began to be put in place in the sixteenth century with the emergence of the Atlantic commercial circuit and the colonization of the New World, and that was transformed and expanded through the eighteenth and nineteenth centuries, and up to this day."[59] Under their intellectual project of decolonizing aestheTics to become a decolonial aestheSis, my theories linking diaspora consciousness to the art production of the queer diaspora can contribute to naming practices that challenge and subvert the hegemony of modern and colonial norms.[60] Like decolonial aestheSis, my arguments, anchored on the queer diaspora reimagining colonial trauma within their artistic repertoire, are "an option that delivers a radical critique to modern, postmodern, and altermodern aestheTics and, simultaneously, contributes to making visible decolonial subjectivities at the confluence of popular practices of re-existence."[61] Studying historical colonialism through the vantage point of contemporary art helps to deliver such a radical critique of the modern for the ways it illustrates homophobia experienced by the diasporic subject today, offering a postcolonial understanding of queer contemporary art and aesthetics.

Conclusion: Drawing as Photography

What does it mean to locate photography within a drawing? To answer this question, I have turned to contemporary drawing as a method to study the use of colonial photography within the Middle East at the turn of the century. I used photography in order to analyze historical narratives of same-sex desire as the medium itself circulates, which helps create an imaginary of the Middle East that is then reified in culture and therefore trains us to see. While the photographs and drawings may be an unconventional pairing for analysis, it is my contention that to illustrate the colonial ramifications of photography that exist outside of the picture plane itself, it is important to look at how the living diaspora uses the language, tropes, composition, and stylistic elements that are particular to photography and examine how artists have developed this visuality into a decolonized representation of same-sex desire in other mediums.

In comparing the striking similarities in subject matter, composition, and monochromatic color between Bagheri's drawings and the photographs, it becomes clear that the photography of these images is inescapable. The language developed and cemented by photography to depict, sexualize, eroticize, and, in the case of these colonial archives, Orientalize is well embedded within the drawings of Ebrin Bagheri. It becomes unproductive to separate the photography from the drawing, and the drawings themselves not only reference a history of photography in the Middle East, but they also explore the language and tropes of local photography through a less mechanical medium. Elsewhere, I have explored contemporary Arab artists and their use of hand-painted photography to add subjectivity, inserting their "voice" to articulate their identity in a way that added a personal element of touch and manipulation to a photograph.[62] Here, we see something different; rather than further manipulate the photographs that hold the colonial knowledge of representation, the medium of photography itself is explored elsewhere, and Bagheri's drawing becomes inextricably tied to the photography that it references. The eroticized young men are pictured within the photograph; however, and more importantly, the reading of loss, of coloniality, and of local eroticization is located outside the frame of the photograph itself. It is for this reason that the turning to drawing as a way of understanding the colonial impacts of these photographs becomes less of a controversial decision and instead a necessary step in the analysis of visual culture that helps to understand the very study of colonial photography in the Middle East and the role photography played in the changing sexual politics that ensued from the nineteenth century and continue to develop today.

Bagheri's youthful subject marks a moment of decolonized sexual scripts that reflect Islamicate notions of beauty and desire, left to be interpreted and read in modern society with the language of modernized sexual scripts and under the purview of contemporary art. This interesting flux and flow of historicized sexual bodies and the contemporary artist brings premodern sexual discourses out of the archives and into the lived reality of queer diasporic subjects today. The shadow of homosociality and the erasure of alternative sexual codes and same-sex desire is seen in the longing gaze of Bagheri's youth, in that fleeting moment between being an object of desire to becoming an object of abjection. This work gestures to a compelling question about the im/possibilities of diasporic self-representation in relation to colonial frames and conventions of representation. This analysis questions the ways in which we can see ourselves outside the visualization regimes of the colonizing eye.

In this chapter I have examined photographs from several European travelers that are emblematic of a genre in order to historicize same-sex desire in the Middle East, West Asia, and across North Africa and the regions formerly a part of the Ottoman Empire to investigate diasporic contemporary art and its relationship to gender colonial discourses that had an impact on same-sex desire. The target analysis in this chapter and my overall research is contemporary diasporic art, and fully historicizing same-sex desire in the Ottoman Empire or a premodern Persianate society is beyond the scope of my research. Rather, as a method of building causal relationships between imperialism in Islamicate regions and the contemporary queer diaspora, I began by historicizing European and colonial encounters at the turn of the twentieth century. This was done by illustrating the effect Victorian sensibilities had on premodern homosociality and same-sex desire in Islamicate regions connected by language, culture, and empire. This history of changing sexual discourse was later illustrated through European colonial photographs in the Middle East that depict homoeroticism, specifically eroticized images of indigenous populations that were taken by Europeans. I focused on European travelers who photographed pictures of local young men (if my reading is correct), and I analyzed the aesthetics of these photographic archives in relation to contemporary drawings by Iranian artist Ebrin Bagheri as a way of investigating the modernist production of heterosexuality through the lens of gender and its reconceptualization as locally relevant and indigenous gender norms before increased contact with Europe in the sixteenth century. In exploring the visual art of a queer diasporic subject, I analyzed how Bagheri's contemporary drawings carry traces of premodern same-sex desire to elucidate that the colonial remnants of the colonized local sexual scripts are still alive and deeply embedded within diaspora consciousness.

As argued throughout this book, the double bind that the queer diasporic subject often faces can be linked to these aftereffects and tensions. To illustrate the Eurocentric canon of queer history that relegated Islamicate same-sex desire to the periphery, I used a multitemporal approach to show how premodern Islamicate sexual scripts were not fully colonized and still live on in the diaspora.[63] Weary of compartmentalized approaches of area studies that focus too heavily on nation-state epistemologies that are not adequately attuned to the interconnectedness of empire and culture, I propose a multitemporal approach that allows for a connection to be made visible between the gender logics of different locales existing within the lived experiences of the diaspora. This approach allows for tracing the ways in which diaspora consciousness holds facets of connected locales and colonial histories of gender and sexuality, thus better exploring how this impacts diasporic formation as queer subjects in the West through visual analysis of their artworks.

Importantly, this analysis is meant to challenge the Eurocentrism of dominant queer theory and gay scholarship by focusing on alternative sexual discourses that are not reducible to hegemonic Euro-American notions of gay identity. My examination of historical colonial encounter in relation to contemporary diasporic art becomes another logic used to challenge area studies scholarship, which remains centered on the nation-state. Focusing on local-to-local connections between different Islamicate regions in North Africa and the former Ottoman Empire allows for simultaneously challenging the homogeneity of "global gay identity" by addressing how colonial encounters have been transformed and negotiated in different local sites, and the similarities and differences between them. This chapter has illustrated that premodern Islamicate sexual scripts are not fully colonized and live on in multigenerational subjects of the diaspora. I have outlined the process of colonization and the immense struggle that Islamicate sexual discourses faced in the age of modernization. The study of visual culture (both archival and the contemporary art of living artists) shows how remnants of these sexual scripts are still alive and deeply entrenched within diaspora consciousness. The double bind that the queer diasporic subject often faces can be linked to these remnants and accompanying tensions, and the study of visual art and culture better illustrates the specific ways in which these sexual scripts are both manifested and negotiated by non-Western subjects in the West.

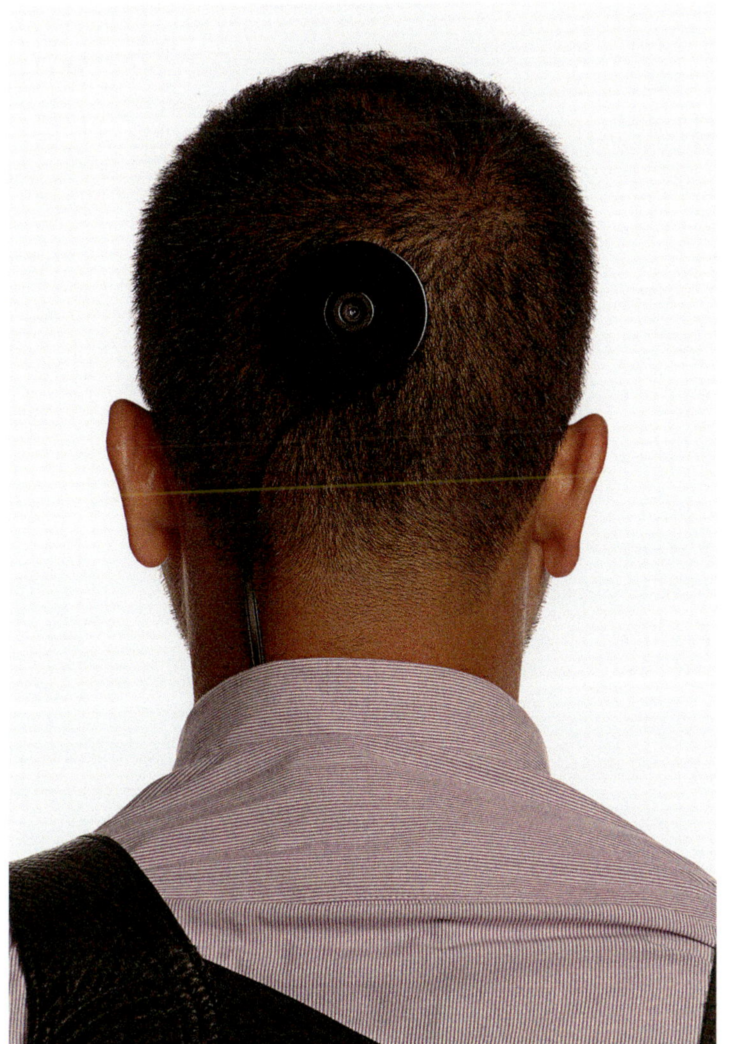

PLATE 1. Wafaa Bilal, *3rdi*. Surgically implanted camera (2010). Courtesy of the artist.

PLATE 2. Larissa Sansour, from *Nation Estate* photo series, *Olive Tree*, C-print, 75 × 150cm, (2012). Courtesy of the artist.

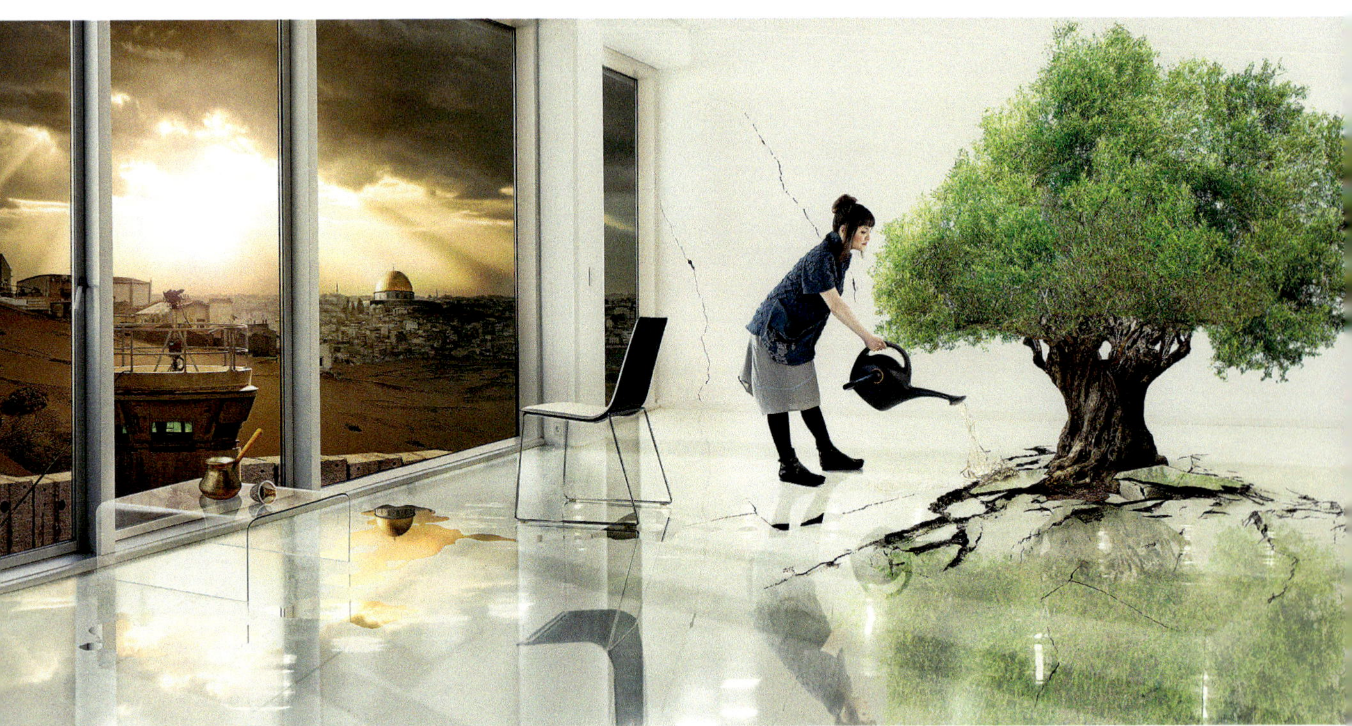

PLATE 3. Ebrin Bagheri, *Untitled*, from *Eastern Desires* series. Pencil crayon and ballpoint pen on paper. Courtesy of the artist. (2015)

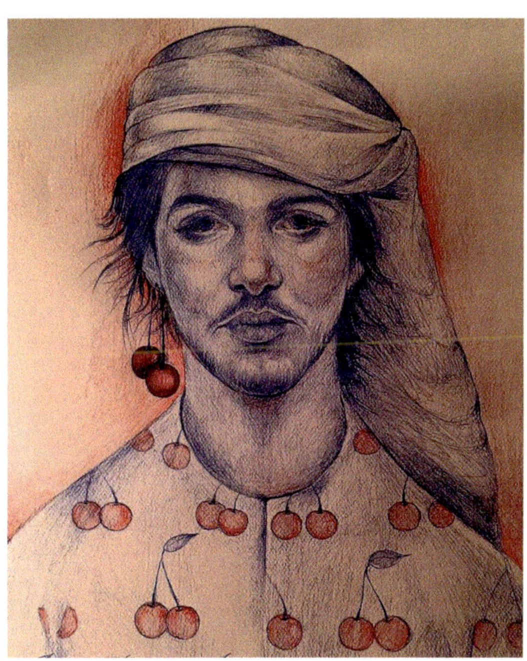

PLATE 4. Ebrin Bagheri, *Untitled [II]*, from *Someone Who Is Like No-One* series (2016). Watercolor paint and ballpoint pen on paper. Courtesy of the artist.

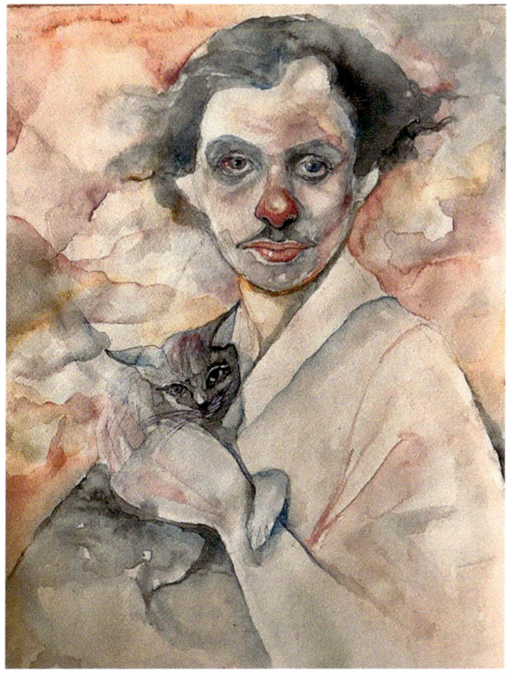

PLATE 5. Rudolf Lehnert, *Jeunes Arabes, Tunis* (c. 1910). Colorized postcard. Courtesy of Dr. Joseph Allen Boone. Private collection.

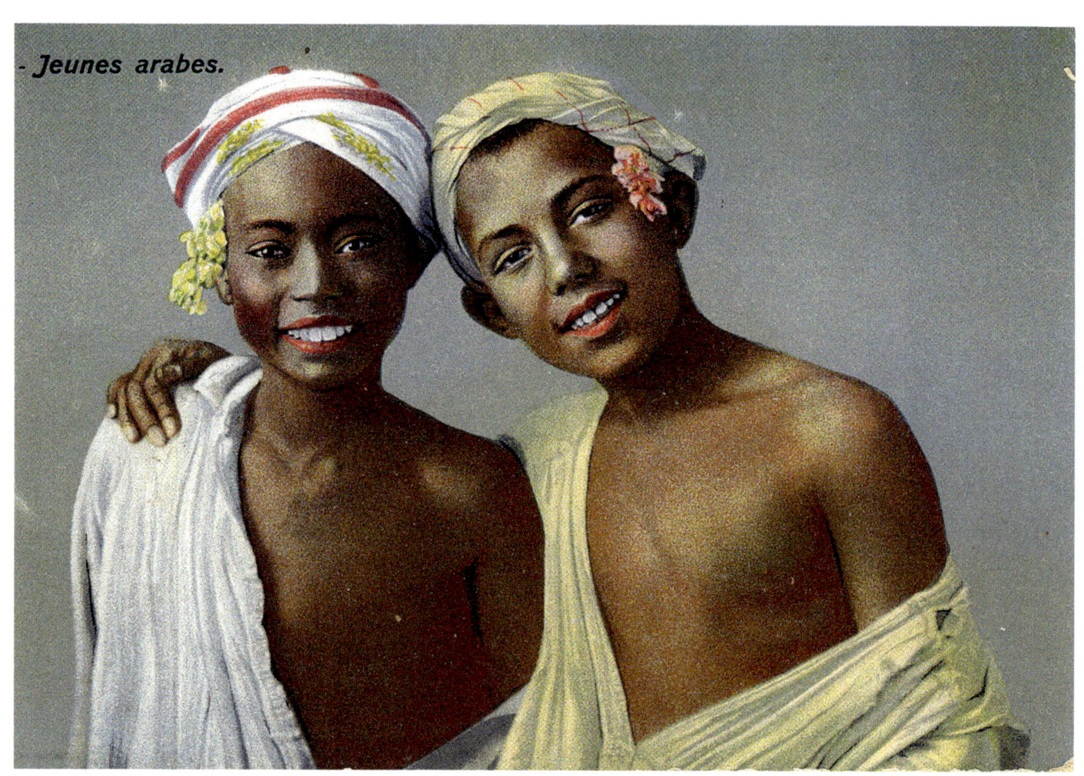

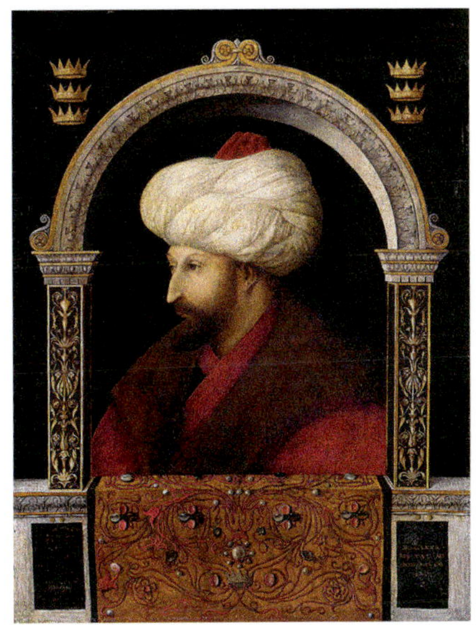

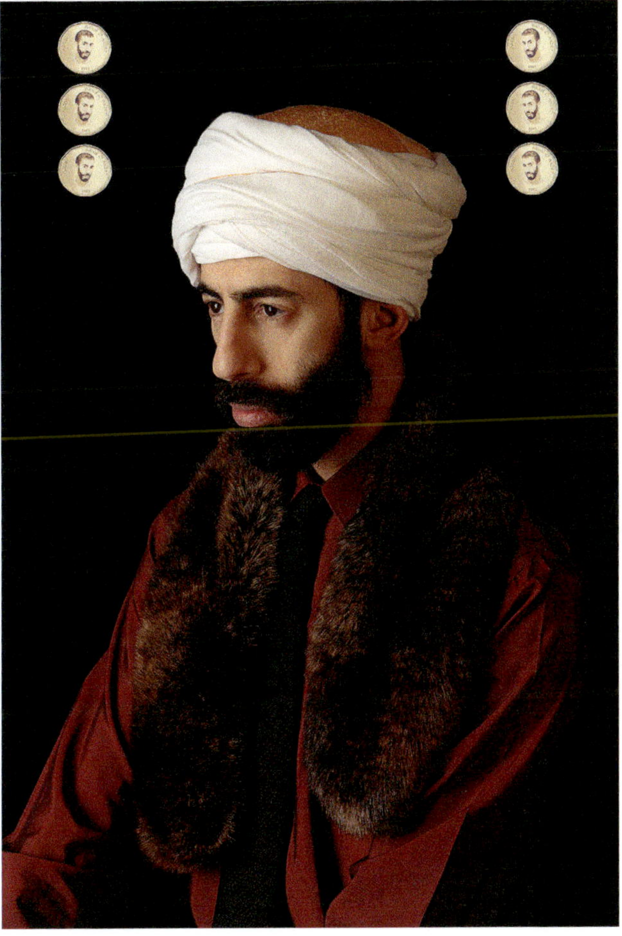

PLATE 6. *above*
Gentile Bellini,
The Sultan Mehmet II
(1480). Oil on canvas.
Courtesy of the
National Gallery of
London, UK.

PLATE 7. *right* 2Fik,
Le Sultan Abdel (2012).
Digital photograph.
Courtesy of the artist.

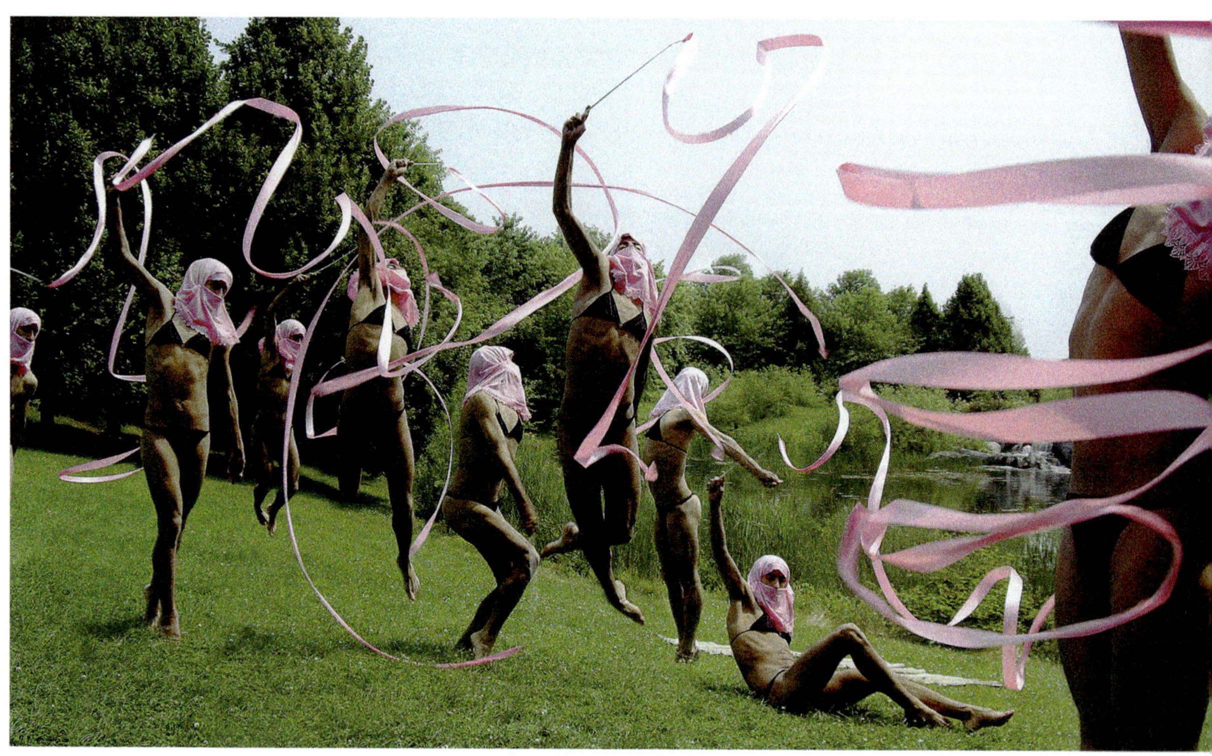

PLATE 8. 2Fik, *Arabesque* (2006). Digital collage and photograph. Courtesy of the artist.

PLATE 9. 2Fik, family portraits. Digital collage. Courtesy of the artist.

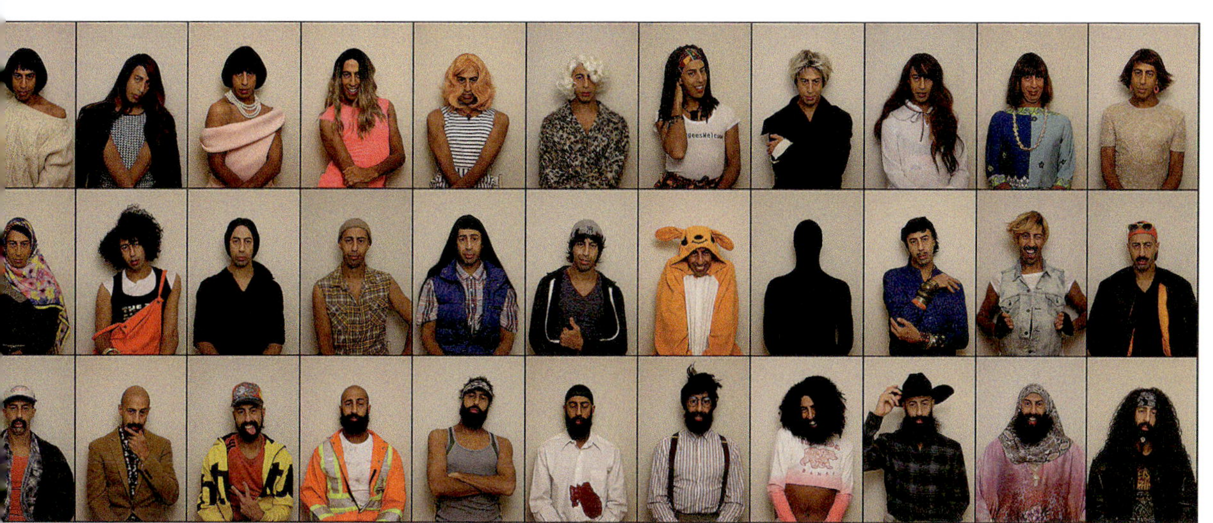

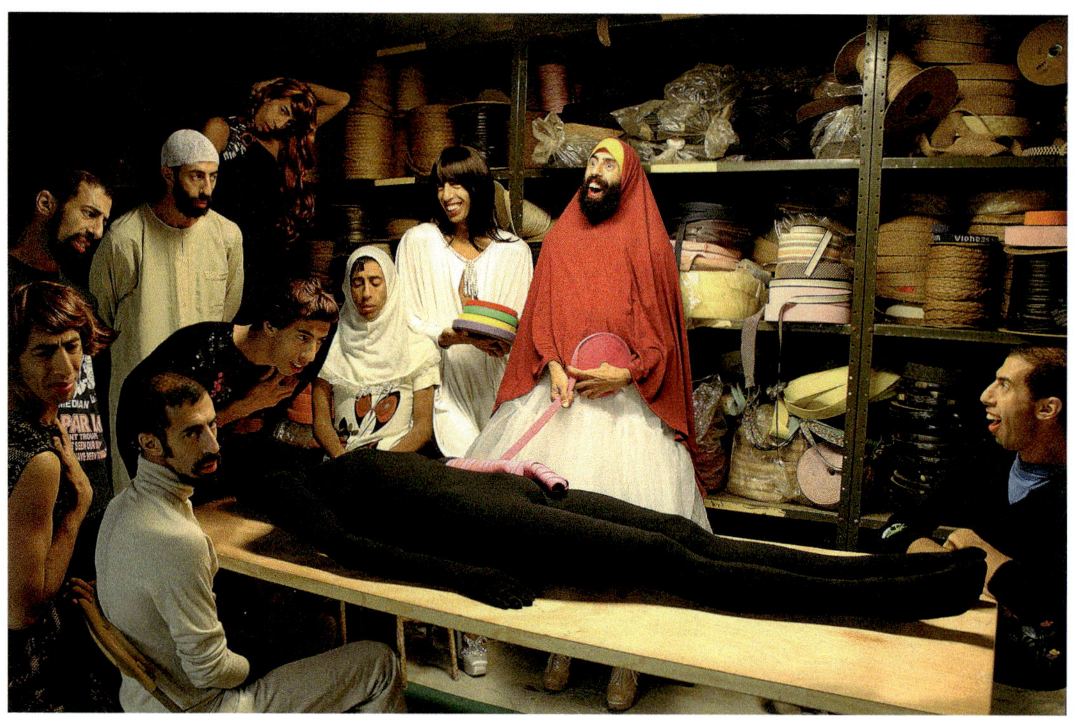

PLATE 10. 2Fik, *La leçon de folie de Ludmilla-Mary* (2012), based on Rembrandt van Rijn, *The Anatomy Lesson of Dr. Nicolaes Tulp* (1632). Digital photograph. Courtesy of the artist.

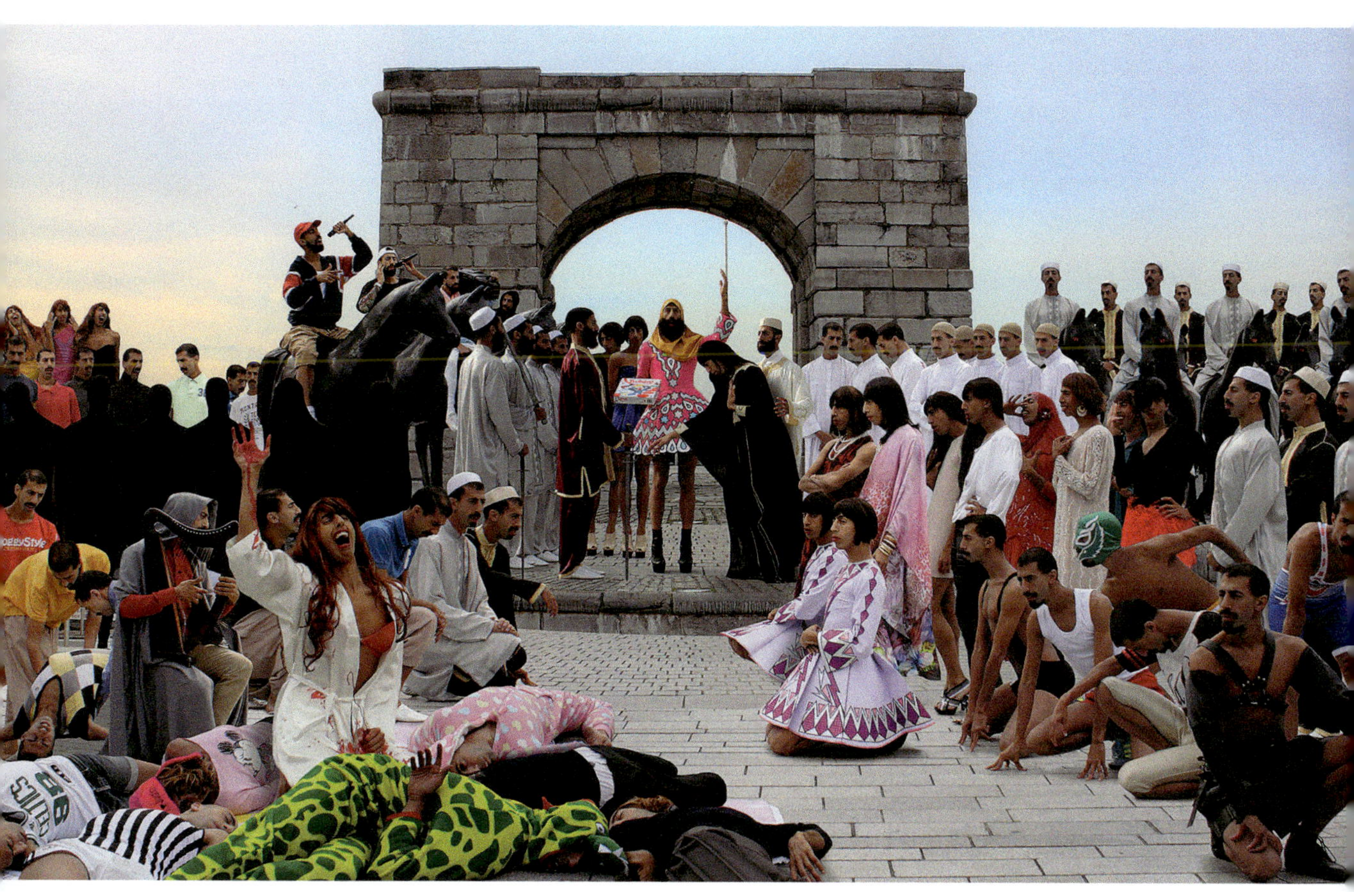

PLATE 11. 2Fik, *The Marriage of Abdel and Fatima* (2014), based on Daniel Maclise, *The Marriage of Strongbow and Aoife* (1854). Digital photograph. Courtesy of the artist.

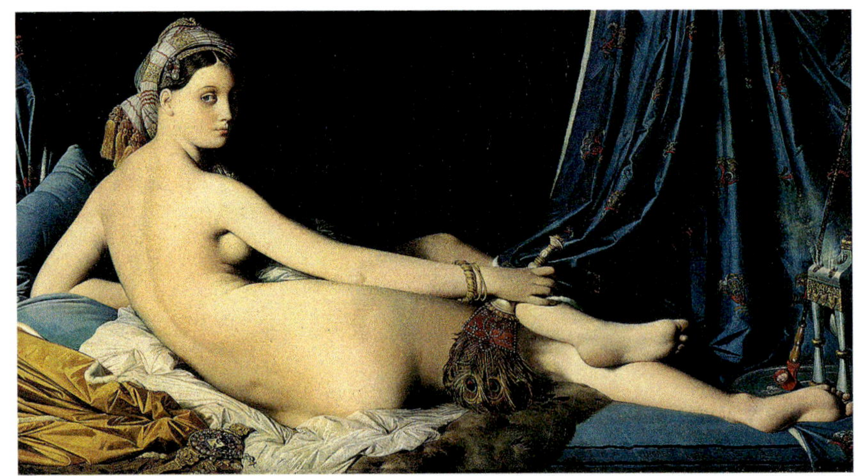

PLATE 12. *left*
Jean Auguste Dominique Ingres, *La Grande Odalisque* (1814). Oil on canvas. Courtesy of the Louvre Museum.

PLATE 13. *below*
2Fik, *La Grande Intendante* (2012), based on Ingres's *La Grande Odalisque*. Courtesy of the artist.

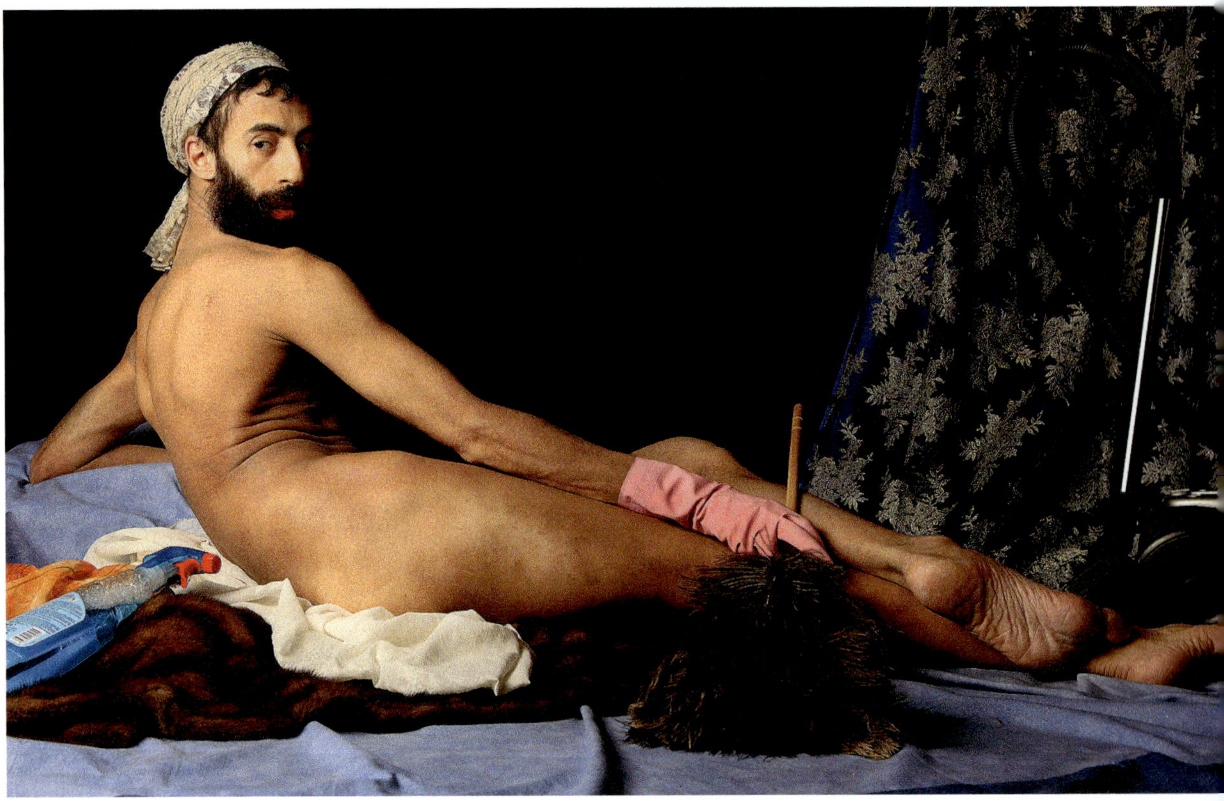

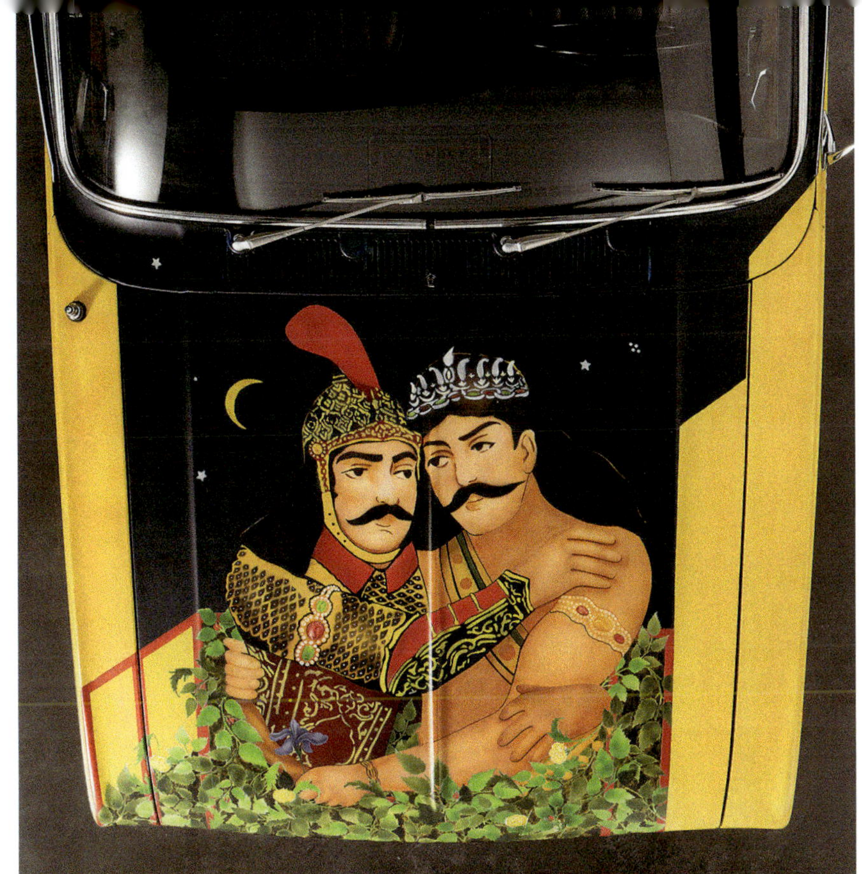

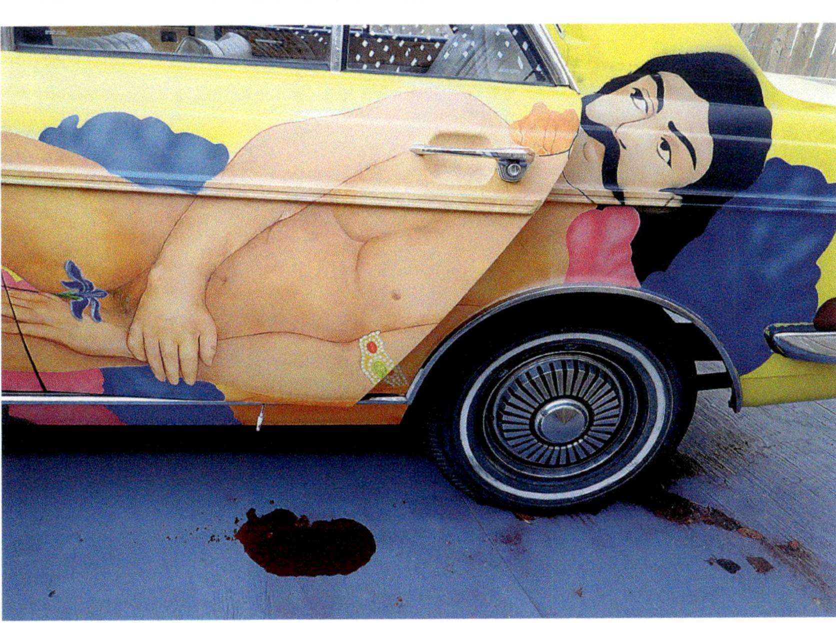

PLATE 14. *top*
Alireza Shojaian, *Sous le Ciel de Shiraz*, hood detail. Courtesy of the artist.

PLATE 15. *bottom*
Alireza Shojaian, *Sous le Ciel de Shiraz*, left side detail.

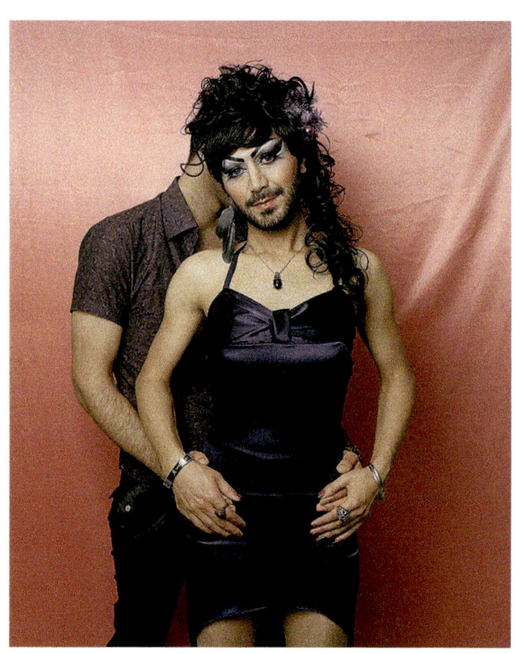

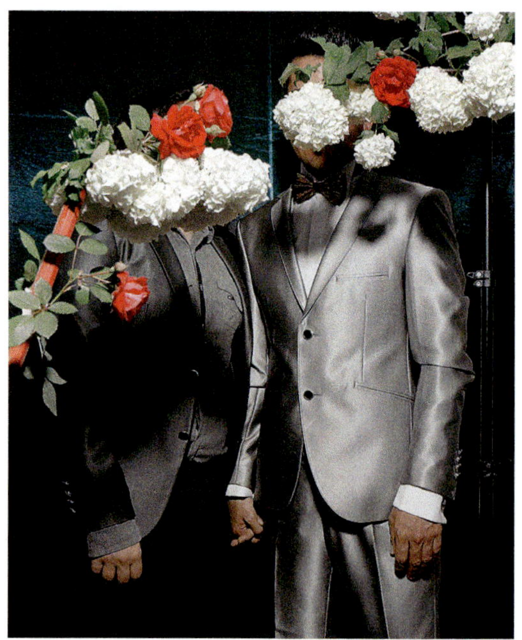

PLATES 16–17. Laurence Rasti, from *There Are No Homosexuals in Iran* series (2014). Inkjet print. Courtesy of the artist.

PLATES 18–19.
Laurence Rasti, from *There Are No Homosexuals in Iran* series (2014). Inkjet print. Courtesy of the artist.

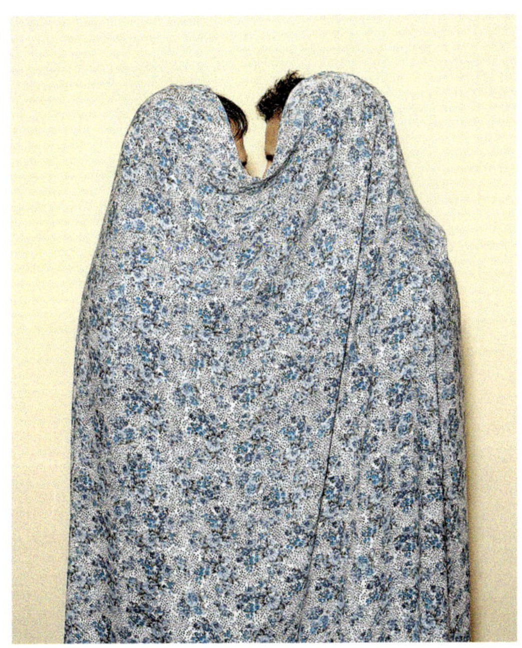

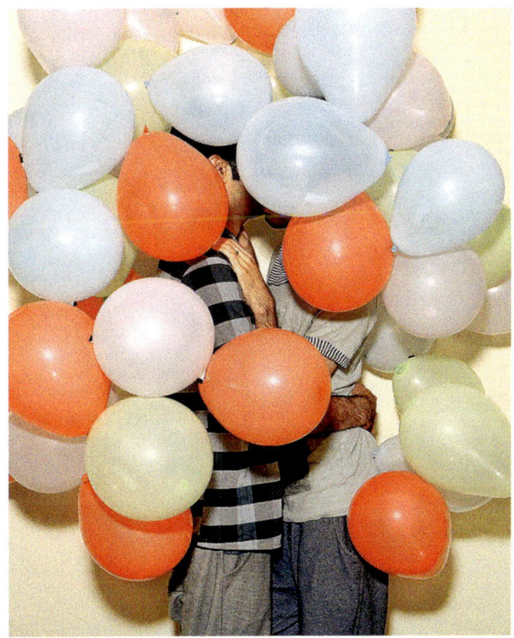

PLATE 20. *top* Rah Eleh, *Sham*, light drawing photography (2013). Courtesy of the artist.

PLATE 21. *bottom* Rah Eleh, *Oriental Drag*, film still (2013). Courtesy of the artist.

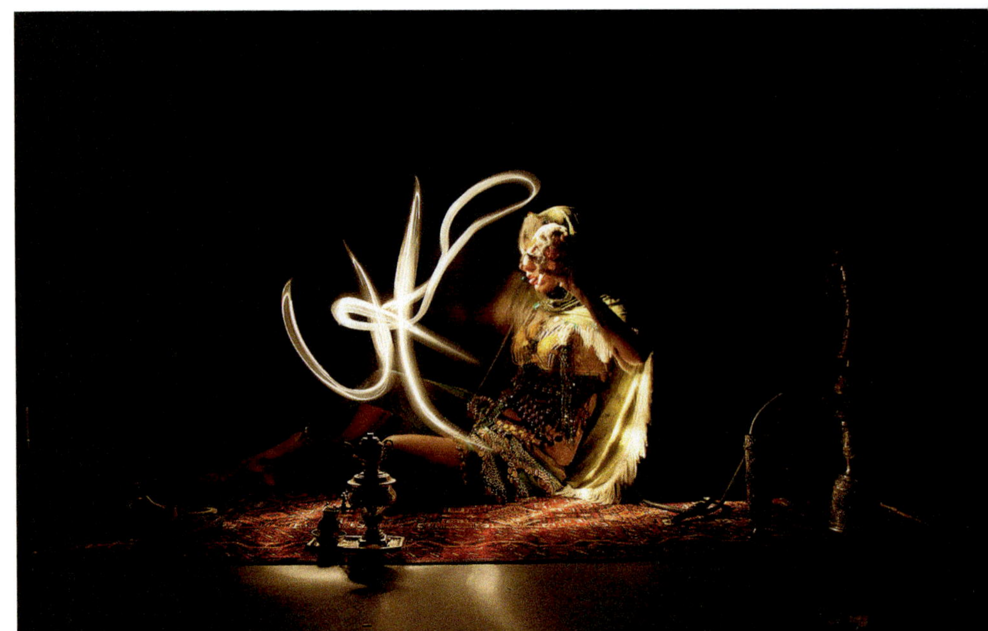

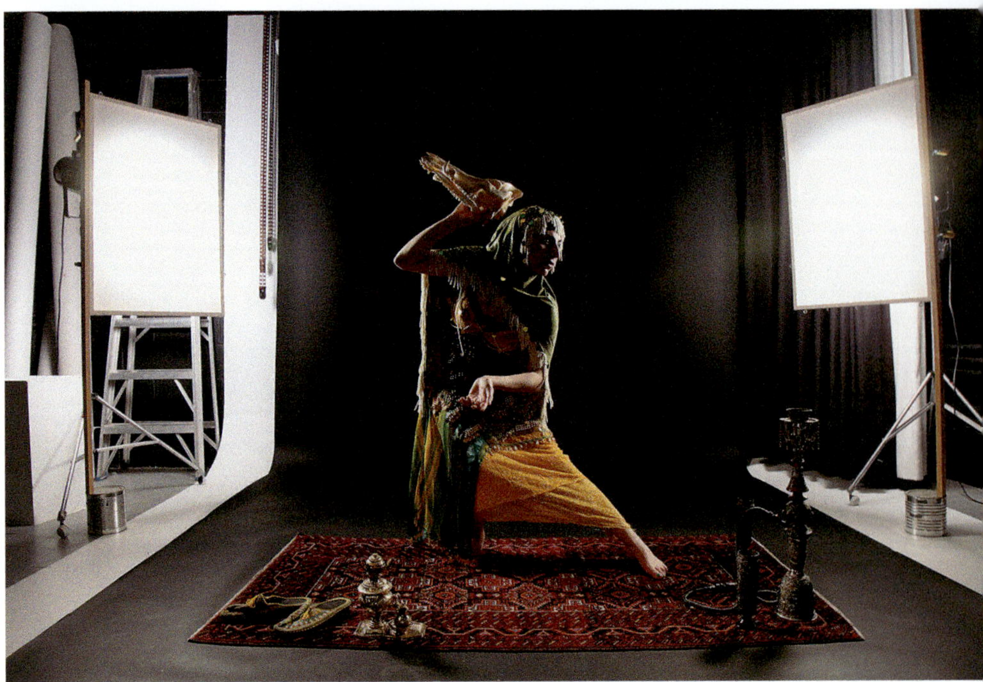

SIX

COMING OUT À L'ORIENTALE

DIASPORIC ART & COLONIAL WOUNDS

"The curves of my lips rewrite the history of Islam."
2FIK, quoted in Denis Provencher, *Queer Maghrebi French*

What does it mean to "come out *à l'orientale*"?[1] Coming out can be seen as an epistemology for gay individuals living open and free lives, and the concept is well theorized within Western queer theory.[2] But who is entitled to, and included within, the safety of living "out and proud"? The gatekeepers of Western modernity and Western gay identity regulate the parameters of what it means to live a "truly" gay life. For this reason, current literature engaging with Middle Eastern homosexuality focuses on issues of modernity, multiple modernities, and the West's claim to modernity. Traditionally, modernity as a time period signals social, political, and historic conditions at the end of the nineteenth century and the beginning of the twentieth century. However, numerous scholars now question this definition as an imperial structure of power that masks how modernity colonizes social and cultural practices in the name of Western advancement. For example, the postcolonial literature on Arab sexualities contends that the West created a discourse around sexuality that the Middle East never had, leading to the notion of homocolonialism or imperialist ideologies in the name of sexual tolerance. I use *homocolonialism* to mean the deployment of LGBTQI rights and visibility to stigmatize non-Western cultures, all the while reasserting supremacy of the Western nations' values, politics, and principles for a modern civilization.[3]

According to historian Khaled El-Rouayheb, the term *homosexualität* was coined in the late 1860s by the Austro-Hungarian writer Karl Maria Kertbeny, and the English equivalent first appeared in print some twenty years later.[4]

At the turn of the twentieth century, colonial governing bodies imposed Victorian and Euro-American sexual discourses on Middle Eastern cultures. As a push against colonial forces and imperialism, homosexuality was then made an illegal identity category in the Middle East, an identity category that many argue did not exist prior to increased contact with Western explorers and travelers. In an effort to appeal to these travelers and lay claim to modernity, Middle Eastern governing bodies self-regulated the sexuality of their citizens along heterosexual lines in keeping with Western modernity.[5] As El-Rouayheb notes, between the middle of the nineteenth century and the early decades of the twentieth, the prevalent tolerance of same-sex desire was declining, likely in part due to the adoption of European Victorian attitudes by the new, modern, educated, and Westernized elite.[6]

Queer theorist Momin Rahman argues that we must accept that the Muslim experience of sexual diversity politics is significantly different from the Western one and that this reality undermines any assumption that processes of Muslim modernization will inevitably lead to the same outcomes around sexuality as those experienced in the West. Middle Eastern homosexuality will never look the same as Western homosexuality.[7] Rahman posits that the queer Muslim, intersectional in identity, challenges the monolithic, monocultural versions of queer Western identity politics. Here, the sheer existence of queer diasporic Muslims destabilizes Western queer discourse.[8] This assertion of the Muslim queer subject lying outside of normative Western queer politics (and even the encouragement of being outside this Western queer politics) points to issues of genuine difference and incompatibility. As I have traced elsewhere,[9] these ideas are steeped in issues of colonialism and imperialism and are the remainders of precolonial sexual scripts that make the Islamicate queer subject an outlier.

Provincializing Modernity and Colonial Rule

What does it mean to provincialize Western modernity? What could identity narratives in the Middle East, and their sexual scripts, look like outside the purview of Western modernity? Taking a step backward in order to better evaluate the role of race and empire in premodern contexts, Italian artist Gentile Bellini's painting *The Sultan Mehmet II* (1480; figure 6.1), provides a rich source for artist 2Fik to explore themes of Islam, masculinity, and transnational encounter. The subject of the painting, Mehmet II (the Conqueror), brought an end to the Eastern Christian world of the Byzantine Empire in 1453 when he seized Constantinople. Mehmet marked the conquest by turning the greatest Byzantine church, Hagia Sophia, into a mosque. According to Tursun Beg, a historian of the fifteenth century, Mehmet built a great mosque, "which not only encompassed all the arts of Hagia Sophia, but modern features constituting a fresh new idiom unequalled in beauty."[10] At the time Bellini painted his work, the Turks posed a major threat to European powers, particularly in Italy. Poised at the threshold between East and West, Venice especially not only benefited financially from trade with Islamic leaders but also found itself facing incursions by ambitious Ottoman leaders. For sixteen years Venice was able to hold its own in a war with the Turks but ultimately was forced to conclude peace in 1479. As a part of this peace settlement, Bellini worked in Constantinople primarily for Mehmet II (r. 1444–1446; 1451–1481), painting the sultan's portrait and producing bronze medals bearing his likeness that made the image of the Ottoman ruler increasingly famous in Europe.[11] In fact, Bellini's portraiture of Sultan Mehmet II "has become emblematic of cultural exchange between Venice and the Ottomans,"[12] and a general argument can be made that Mehmet is painted as a representative of Islamic power. The sultan wears a deep red caftan and a luxurious brown fur mantle, donning a wrapped turban over a red *taj*, a headdress indicative of his rank as well as his identity as a Muslim. In a way, this portrait associates Mehmet the Conqueror and Islam with progress and power. This late medieval context of global imperialism, which will compound and lead to early Western modernity, shows the complex ways in which empire and colonization overlap, and for the diasporic experience it is noteworthy to evaluate how sexual discourses are a part of and often central to these entangled colonialisms.

2Fik's reimagining of *The Sultan Mehmet II* in his photograph *Le Sultan Abdel* (2012; figure 6.2) provides an interesting commentary on colonialism, power, and diasporic representation in the twenty-first century. In this work, 2Fik's culturally conservative and highly religious character and alter ego, Abdel, plays the role of Sultan Mehmet. Abdel sits in a conventional three-quarter portrait pose wearing a modern red dress shirt and black tie.

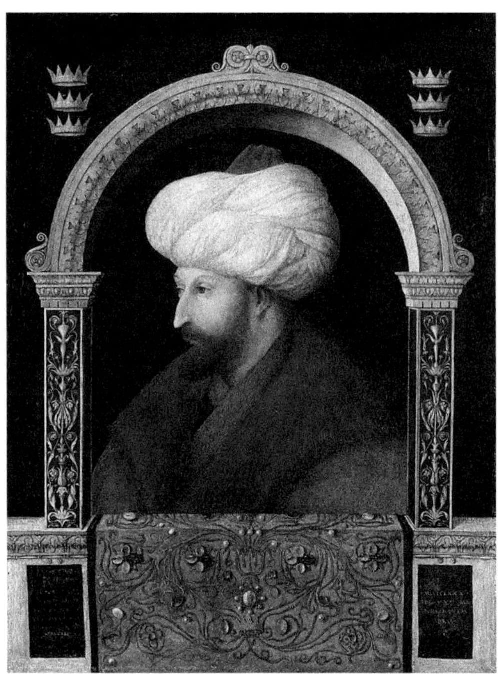

6.1. Gentile Bellini, *The Sultan Mehmet II* (1480). Oil on canvas. Courtesy of the National Gallery of London, UK. See also plate 6.

More traditionally, and as in the Bellini painting, Abdel also wears a brown fur mantle over his shoulders and a white turban on his head with a yellow prayer hat showing underneath. Playing the role of sultan, Abdel is a fully sovereign leader and has no dependence on a higher ruler. The title of "sultan" carries with it meanings restricted to Muslim countries and a religious significance, in contrast to the more secular "king," which is used in both Muslim and non-Muslim countries.

In this photograph, 2Fik reimagines himself as a sovereign ruler not governed by any colonial power and reimagines kinship relations as he queers his own family history. While Bellini painted six golden crowns hovering over Mehmet's head, 2Fik's photographic portrayal has six glowing portraits of his own face. The significance of the crowns in Bellini's portrait is unclear.[13] Art historians Paul Wood and Carol M. Richardson have suggested that they represent the six previous Ottoman sultans, "with Mehmet himself symbolized by the seventh crown made of pearls at the bottom centre of the jewelled textile at the front of the painting."[14] 2Fik's portrait, however, has little opulence, and no jeweled marker representing the subject's own importance. Instead, the viewer looks at the proud and prominent Abdel as he sits in solitude surrounded by the heads of his ancestors (or even current family members), each face looking down upon him. 2Fik uses his fictional characters as a way of queering kinship dynamics by reimagining familial relations across various diasporic imaginaries and by performing each character himself. He sits at the nucleus of this familial unit, depicting the religious and Islamic figure wearing modern Western clothing surrounded by the symbols of his cultural past. Here, the miniature portraits allow the viewer to move between both time and place, as the diasporic figure is linked not only to his cultural geography but also to temporal framings of modernity and tradition. In the vein of José Esteban

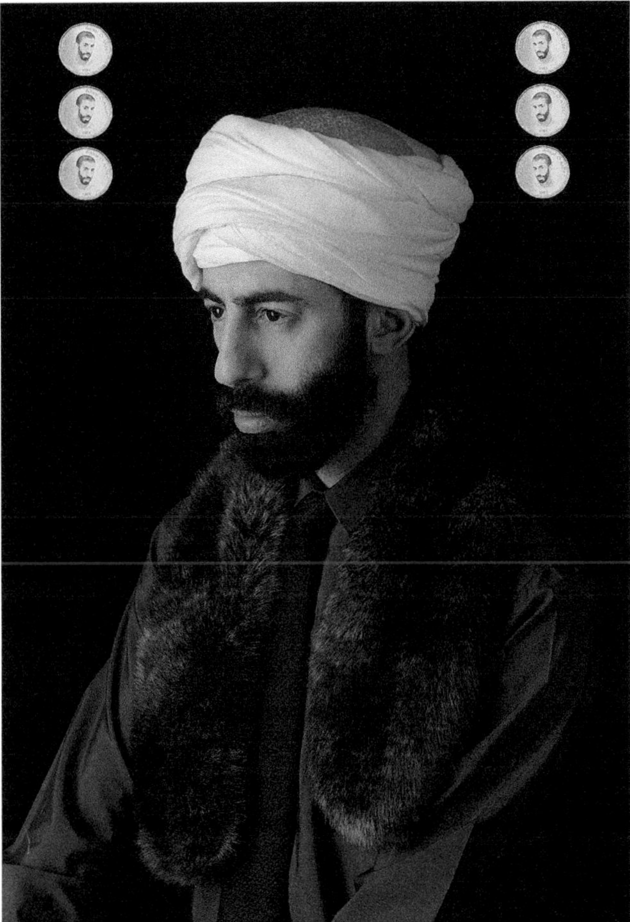

6.2. 2Fik, *Le Sultan Abdel* (2012). Digital photograph. Courtesy of the artist. See also plate 7.

Muñoz, this work provides a futurity for queer belonging, and I argue that 2Fik also rethinks a queer present. As Muñoz powerfully states, "The present is not enough. It is impoverished and toxic for queers and other people who do not feel the privilege of majoritarian belonging, normative tastes, and 'rational' expectations."[15]

In this way, the diasporic and culturally hybrid character of Abdel "is not enough." 2Fik queers and reimagines the present of one of his more culturally conservative family members by nostalgically locating him within a history of power and dominance, but he also reimagines and reinvents his own past as he shapes Abdel's own subject position. This rethinking of the present for queer diasporic subjects exposes the mythology of liberal tolerance for queer belonging in settler states. This visual strategy aims to push queer politics into a local imaginary that resonates with 2Fik's own experiences and beyond the privilege of heteronormative Western gay citizenship that is predicated on recognizing same-sex marriages, permitting legal adoption for queer citizens, and allowing gays to serve in the military. This work imagines a past and present fraught with colonial domination in order to contextualize the diasporic present. It is through the formation of the diasporic character Abdel, and 2Fik's own identity, that the artwork provides a reading of queer futurity, a queer present, and another way of reimagining identity formation in the Middle East.

This is related, in part, to how I conceptualize queer futurity. In *Cruising Utopia: The Then and There of Queer Futurity*, José Esteban Muñoz argues that we need to think outside of straight time. Straight time has a futurity promised out of reproductive majoritarian heterosexuality. The only possible futurity under these guidelines is homonormative capitalism, and queer time needs to step out of the linearity of such progress narratives and question the fundamental values of a queer utopian way of life. I contend that Muñoz's notion of "waiting" can also be seen as a progress narrative of modernity and the gay rights discourse in the Middle East.[16] Arab gays are in a state of waiting in white straight time. This notion of waiting is important for people of color because it lines their futurity as different from the future of white queer subjects. If we use the example of the Middle East as lacking modernity and being temporally outside the Western norm, the utopian future of progress would thus inherently be colonial; the future of a Middle East sexual discourse is already determined to align success and goals with Western sexual modernity narratives. How, then, can we reposition utopianisms with queer Middle Eastern futurity? 2Fik's artwork depicts a queer futurity by removing linear progress myths from his narrative and by reinventing a historical past in order to reimagine a different queer future for himself and his fictionalized family.

How, then, does 2Fik's reimagining of Western modernity speak to queering the past and, more importantly, the queering of Arab modernity? How does the portrayal and subversion of racialized subjects in colonial spaces, as in racist or Orientalist paintings, speak to sexual constructs at the time and modern understanding of sexuality as experienced by diasporic subjects today? To consider these queries, I draw on the ways in which Manu Vimalassery, Juliana Hu Pegues, and Alyosha Goldstein conceive of decolonization as a process of both becoming and unraveling beyond just moving past or healing historical violence. Decolonization has to move past the possibility of an endpoint, or a historical or finished process (whether achieved already or at some future date), to productively grapple with practice.[17] For example, thinking of anticolonial survival and resistance as a visual and artistic practice allows for the inclusion of the study of historic sexual discourses in the Middle East in relation to contemporary diasporic artists, which provides a way of bridging the disciplinary gap between queer theory and visual culture in order to more productively link a colonial past to a diasporic present.

Practicing Decolonial Aesthetics

Throughout this chapter, I argue that there exists a strong relationship between the historical construction of colonial sexualities and contemporary expressions of diasporic sexualities. I use the history of gender, sexuality, colonialism, and their triangulation in the Middle East as the foundation for outlining a cause-and-effect dynamic that reverberates to contemporary queer diasporic subjects. In order to link late nineteenth-century colonialism to the contemporary diaspora, I focus on contemporary art that uses these historic moments as the foundation for artistic inspiration. Here I investigate the performance art and photography of Montreal-based Moroccan artist 2Fik. A French-born Moroccan who migrated to the francophone province of Quebec, Canada, 2Fik uses his own diasporic identity as a subject in his work to explore the dichotomies of his Moroccan Canadian culture and his lived experience as a queer Arab.[18] Using performance and photography as primary modes of art production, 2Fik invents multifaceted characters that transform and translate the different aspects of his cultural and sexual identity, performing each character in complex narratives within his photography. Oftentimes language—Arabic, French, and English—works together with the visual in 2Fik's artwork to bring semiotic and etymological dimension to his visual art.[19] His performance art becomes an integral and inseparable part of his photography, for these characters provide a level of depth in investigating the process of cultural transformation that allows him to navigate geographic borders, geopolitics, and decolonial aesthetics.

I do not wish to speak ahistorically of settler colonial contexts, as homosexuality in the Global North was also criminalized in the past. What is important here, however, are the ways in which white settler puritanism has been used as a measuring stick to label the Other as backward and outside of modernity. This was true of the Middle East (and, it should be noted, of settler colonial contexts that labeled Indigenous peoples guilty of primitivism),[20] first for perceived gender fluidity and then, as sexual tolerance became the new marker of Western modernity, for the heterosexism the region had adopted in order to become modern. Thus, the gender and sexual discourses of the Middle East remain the reason the West's perception generally excludes the region as having achieved modernity. This vicious cycle of regulation by the West is inherently a colonial construct meant to control the very outcome it produces.

In this chapter, 2Fik's contemporary art is analyzed in an effort to illustrate the complexities of Islamicate sexualities within the diaspora. I use 2Fik's visual art as a case study to investigate the historical links between queer diasporic identities, modernity, and Western imperialism. To do so, I begin by outlining epistemologies of coming out as a way of illustrating transnational queer identity,[21] and in this case, coming out *à l'orientale*. Next, I turn to modern art to question how premodern Islamicate sexual scripts colonized by modernity might still exist within diasporic subjects today. Finally, I analyze the fictional characters that 2Fik has created in his artistic practice as a way of understanding the tensions between different dichotomies within his own diasporic identity—East versus West, traditional versus modern, and transnational versus hybrid. Throughout this discussion I draw links between settler colonialism and its intersection with the queer diaspora. Issues of modernity and progress in Canada (as well as the larger Euro-American context) are intrinsically tied to queer rights, liberal tolerance, and how these uphold whiteness and naturalize settler colonialism. This discussion illustrates how contemporary art can be used to queer kinship models and how queer identity can offer nuances of theories of transnationalism and diaspora, especially how sexuality is performed in transnational contexts.

I contend that queer contemporary Arab artists, not just 2Fik, can be seen as a necessary link bridging art history and modernity with contemporary queer identity.

What Is Coming Out *à L'Orientale*?

2Fik speaks about his self-discovery concerning his sexuality in terms of coming out à l'orientale, or, a Middle Eastern style of coming out. In an interview, 2Fik defined coming out à l'orientale as:

> [an] expression that makes reference to the use of eastern and Arab-Muslim cultural references in order to explain the disregard for social obligations related to heterosexuality (marriage, reproduction, etc.). The goal of this type of *coming out* is to take up the arguments of the culture of origin (Morocco) and not use those in the host culture (France) of the person in front of you (papa) hence reinforcing the thesis, encouraging comprehension of the message and avoiding any interpretation such as "victim-of-the-western-system-that-made-you-homosexual."[22]

Coming out à l'orientale calls upon local language and signifiers that 2Fik's father and any Moroccan listener can understand. It is a method of queer self-expression that provincializes global signifiers of gay identity, such as the rainbow flag or the pride parade, to center on a culturally local understanding of same-sex desire, kinship, and cultural practices.[23]

In the work titled *Arabesque* (2006) (figure 6.3), a gender-fluid subject wearing a black two-piece bikini and a pink hijab is digitally collaged to appear numerous times in the frame. The slender figure holds a baton with a pink ribbon tied to the end of it, mirroring the pink hijab that conceals the person's identity. In playful movements of dance and joie de vivre, the figure frolics in an open field twirling the baton so that the pink ribbon creates arabesque designs in the air. The movements of the pink ribbon resemble Arabic script, and the pink veil, its modesty juxtaposed with the black bikini, creates recognizable feminine signifiers as 2Fik situates himself within his own cultural context. As scholar Denis Provencher recounts, this image visually reinforces 2Fik's argument that any sort of communication with his parents has to occur *on* and *in* their own terms.[24] *Arabesque* then becomes a coming out of sorts, but the pink arabesque designs only *mimic* Arabic script. They create no real language and no real meaning, forming only a symbolic language that is visually recognizable but has no words. In expressing the inability of the rainbow flag to communicate his own coming out to his parents, 2Fik says, "You cannot communicate with people using your own lingo. Communication is a message that is sent and a message that comes back. You have to take into account your listener."[25] In this case, the global and arguably Western signifier of the rainbow flag becomes provincialized, and 2Fik insists on reverting back to a visual language that his parents can understand. Gender nonconformity is expressed through the juxtaposition of wearing a pink hijab while nearly nude and through the incongruity of masculinities and femininities being binary when 2Fik's *Arabesque* simultaneously evokes both in culturally specific ways. The gender fluidity, the culturally arabesque performance, and the religious signifiers of Islam present in this work all point to another method of expressing one's sexual identity in a local and culturally specific way.[26]

To illustrate what the incompatibilities between Western and non-Western signifiers looks like in a south-south comparison, queer theorist Martin Manalansan writes in his pivotal study on the queer Filipino diaspora that visibility and identity models based on individual proclamations of the self are historically and geographically specific to Western centers.[27] Reconceptualizing narratives such as "coming out" points to possibilities of negotiating and reconciling transnational diasporic sensibilities with transnational queer identification. For the *bakla*, the Tagalog term for a Filipino homosexual or effeminate person, undisclosed homosexuality is not synonymous with being "in hiding" or "inside the closet." Many Filipino gay men believe that silence is a part of the discourse of sexuality. This difference in identity formation relates to an individual identifying with a family unit and community in the Philippines versus the individualistic model of identity in North America. The process of coming out and the notion of the "closet" are not constituted for Filipino gay men in the same way as they are for the mainstream gay community in North America, where they are crucial to gay self-formation. Therefore, coming out does not translate to a meaningful category of identity

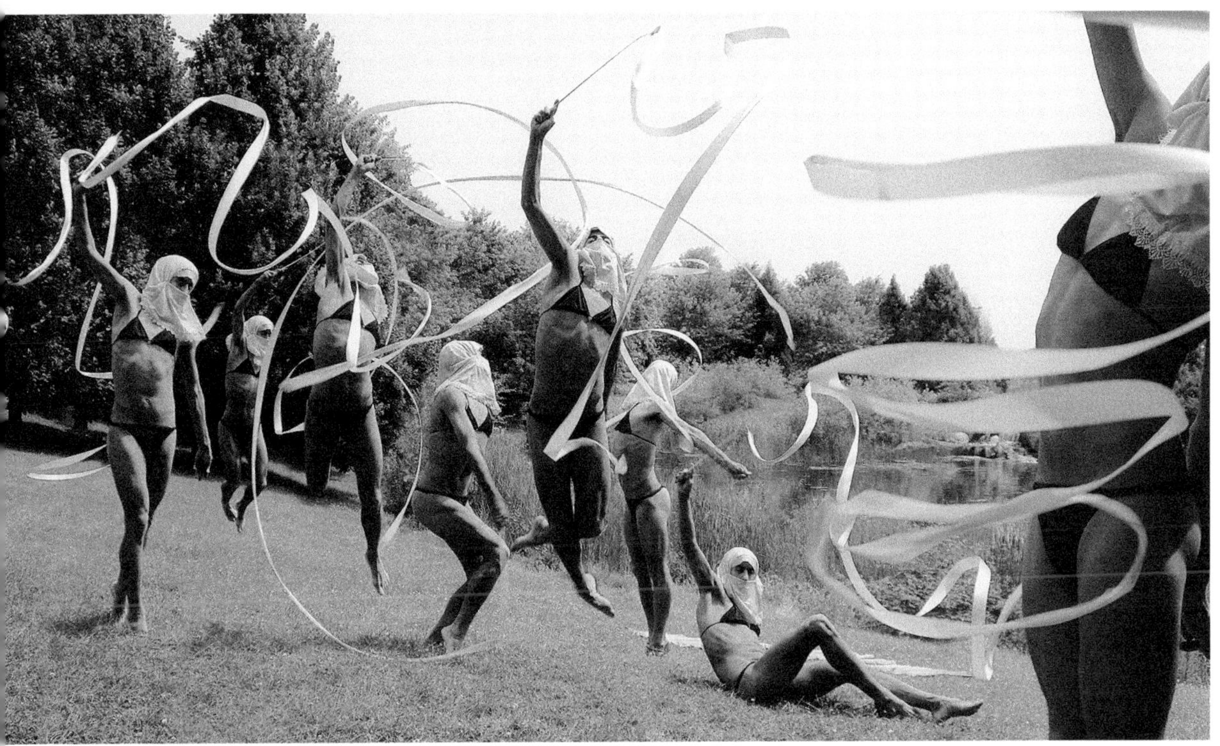

6.3. 2Fik, *Arabesque* (2006). Digital collage and photograph. Courtesy of the artist. See also plate 8.

formation for bakla, showing how queer identity is constructed differently outside the West.

2Fik's refashioning of queer subjectivity as coming out à l'orientale demonstrates the "queers' struggle towards finding, building, remembering, and settling into a home to create the sphere called diasporic intimacy."[28] This refashioning of what gay identity and coming out can mean for a racialized postcolonial queer shows the incompatibility between how a diasporic subject may be socialized as a queer subject in the West and the values and understandings of their own sexual desires from a cultural perspective. Within the context of the diaspora, it is important to question the truism of Canada as a gay-friendly nation, which tends to render invisible racist discourses within queer organizing and ignores past and ongoing processes of colonialism. The works of Indigenous, queer, feminist, and Two-Spirit activists and scholars demonstrate how gender and sexuality are centered in colonial processes.[29] Just as the bakla becomes both an identity and a linguistic tool, the non-Western sexuality scripts colonized by Western gay identity shape and transform how the diasporic subject *becomes* queer or learns to be a queer person of color.

The metaphor of "coming out" present in *Arabesque* poses certain incompatibilities with the Western notion of freeing oneself from the confines of the closet. The work represents the myriad ways Middle Eastern subjects in the diaspora express and live their sexual identities in meaningful ways. Psychologist Sekneh Hammoud-Beckett offers the notion of "letting in" as an alternative to normative models of "coming out."[30] This term refers to the conscious and selective invitation of people into one's "club of life." "Letting in" is a process that is highly relevant to the queer diaspora because it provides an alternative to the Western subject's imposition of visibility in order to be complete and thus alters perceptions of what it means to live a "truly" gay life. In its visual ambiguity and cultural specificity, 2Fik's *Arabesque* can be seen as a letting in and, I argue, a crucial part of what it means to come out à l'orientale. These methods and visual strategies link the experiences of gay subjects in the Middle East to those of members of the queer diaspora and complicate narratives of superiority and queer acceptance upheld in the Global North. Imperialist ideas that measure progress of a nation against their gay rights is destabilized when homophobia is discussed alongside the racism the queer diaspora experiences, even in the Global North. Rather than conceptualizing queer diasporic experiences only through the homogenous light of privilege and freedom in the Global North, this linking of queer diasporic subjectivity to local conceptions of queerness within the "host" country brings together the local and the global by a universalizing power of coloniality that affects both sets of subjects on the level of identification and subject formation.

The link between cultural differences and sexual discourses is important and is reiterated in the writing of diaspora scholar Nadine Naber. In her book *Arab America*, Naber argues that the diaspora can intensify its culture in North America, becoming even more culturally and religiously strict than the homeland. The result is a very complicated space for diasporic sexuality, because, while the judicial system may support queer subjects in the West, the cultural community and family unit can be the site of abuse, trauma, disownment, and danger.

The process of subjectification for the diasporic individual and the complexities of becoming a queer subject are in part related to the pressures that Western discourse puts on other cultures to reproduce a queer identity that is often hegemonic and incompatible with local settings. Theorist Joseph Massad's "Gay International" framework, discussed at length in previous chapters, explains this process as an incitement to discourse, creating a mission of homocolonialism and Western exceptionalism that seeks to export Western models of homosexuality to places where it did not previously exist, effectively erasing local sexual identity scripts.[31] The imposition of a seemingly universal "gay" identity that is inherently Western is, according to Massad, fundamentally linked to colonialism and colonizing discourses. Most non-Western civilizations, including Muslim and Arab civilizations, had not historically subscribed to binary categories of gender and sexuality, and their imposition produces harmful effects; neither did such binaries exist in the Indigenous Americas prior to colonization and slavery as reflected in gender-variant or two-spirited individuals within Indigenous cultures and ceremonies.[32] This incitement to discourse, I argue, is illustrated in 2Fik's own navigation of language and cultural specificity as a way of rejecting the colonial notion of homosexuality as existing in the Global North (and the white settler–state context of North America in particular) and instead creating an alternative existence based on his own lived experience, showing the ways in which diasporic subjects can exist outside of such rigid parameters of identity formation.

Identification Photography and Performing Diaspora

How does a diasporic subject perform Islamicate sexuality? What does the performance of sexuality say about the historical construction of race and its relationship to colonialism? To explore these questions, I analyze a series of photographs by 2Fik, all of which resemble passport or identification photographs, and ask how diasporic subjects construct and negotiate their individual identities within the inherited structures of modern sexuality. This section highlights several of 2Fik's performed characters (figure 6.4) that demonstrate his alternative kinship model of affiliation and belonging. To date, 2Fik has created thirty-three characters with biographies that comprise

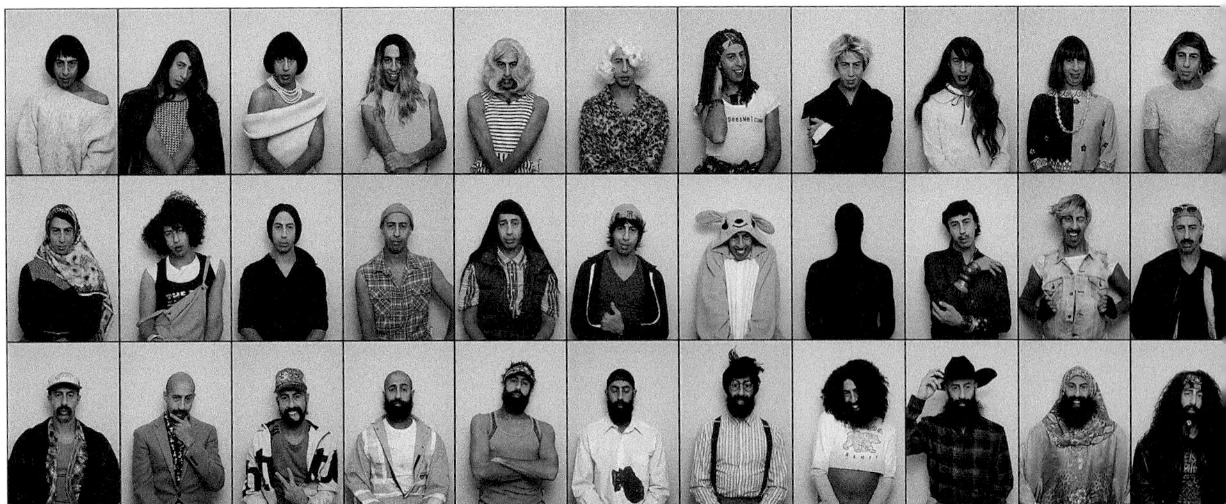

6.4. 2Fik, family portraits. Digital collage. Courtesy of the artist. See also plate 9.

his imagined family unit, and he performs and masquerades as each family member in his photographs. With backstories for each character, including migration or diasporic connections to either Morocco, France, or Canada, 2Fik's performative photography reimagines familial kinship and notions of national identity. Some characters illustrate tradition, strong ties to homeland, and strict cultural values. These characters are linked to modernity as a colonial and modernizing project in the Middle East. Other characters that evoke a notion of cultural hybridity are linked to the diaspora as a contemporary, Westernized subject. I analyze the characters and their headshots as photographic identities in their own right. These characters appear as subjects within every one of 2Fik's photographs, regardless of series, comprising the world he has created for himself in his art.[33] The interactions between the characters and their development in story lines is seen throughout the entirety of his photographic oeuvre and not within just one particular series.

Traditional characters like Abdel, a Moroccan-born man who is solely committed to his wife and following Islam, contrast with more liberal characters like Sofiane, Abdel's younger brother, who prides himself on rejecting religiosity as he works in the hip-hop scene in Tiohtià:ke (Montreal), Quebec. In Abdel's identification photograph (figure 6.5), which has the aesthetic and composition of a traditional passport photo, the subject sits up straight and is dressed simply but maturely in a red jacket over a plain white button-up shirt. He wears a serious expression, gazing directly at the viewer; a fully grown beard; and a black prayer cap sitting firmly atop his head. His younger brother, Sofiane, however, presents himself very differently (figure 6.6). Sofiane's body language is more casual in this youthful snapshot, as he sits with his shoulder and head tilted to one side, gives a half smile to the viewer, with his mouth open, and sticks out his tongue. Unlike the more honorable older brother, Sofiane is photographed with no markers of Islam or signs of religiosity. His beard is both trimmed down and heavily shaved on the sides in a trendy, youthful style rather than in the style of a cultural signifier of an observant Muslim. He wears a bright yellow T-shirt and a red sweatshirt, both embossed with the logo of his favorite soccer team, and a graffitied baseball cap, rather than a prayer cap, sits defiantly on his head. As both Abdel and Sofiane were born and raised in Casablanca, these identification photographs provide a glimpse of the ways in which culture and heritage are not heterogenous or reducible to geography. In this case, the brothers' shared birthplace and upbringing contrast with their nearly opposite personalities, and their own cultural and religious identities do not mirror each other despite their belonging to the same diasporic community and family.

Similar passport photographs provide background stories for all of 2Fik's

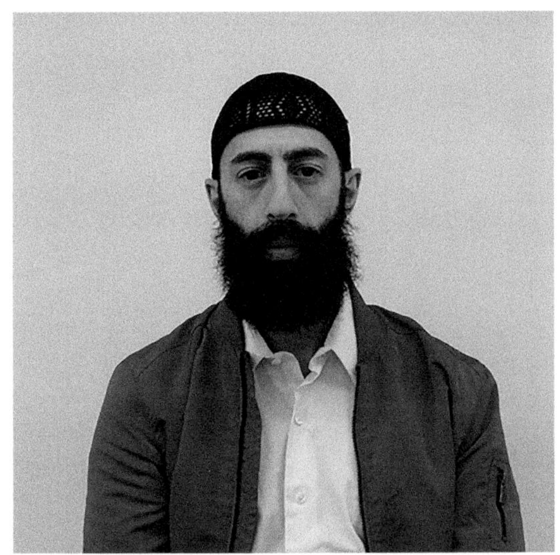

6.5. *left* 2Fik, identification photograph of Abdel.

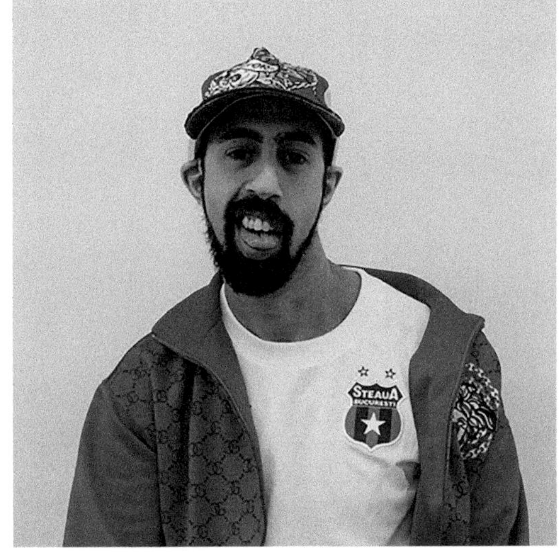

6.6. *right* 2Fik, identification photograph of Sofiane.

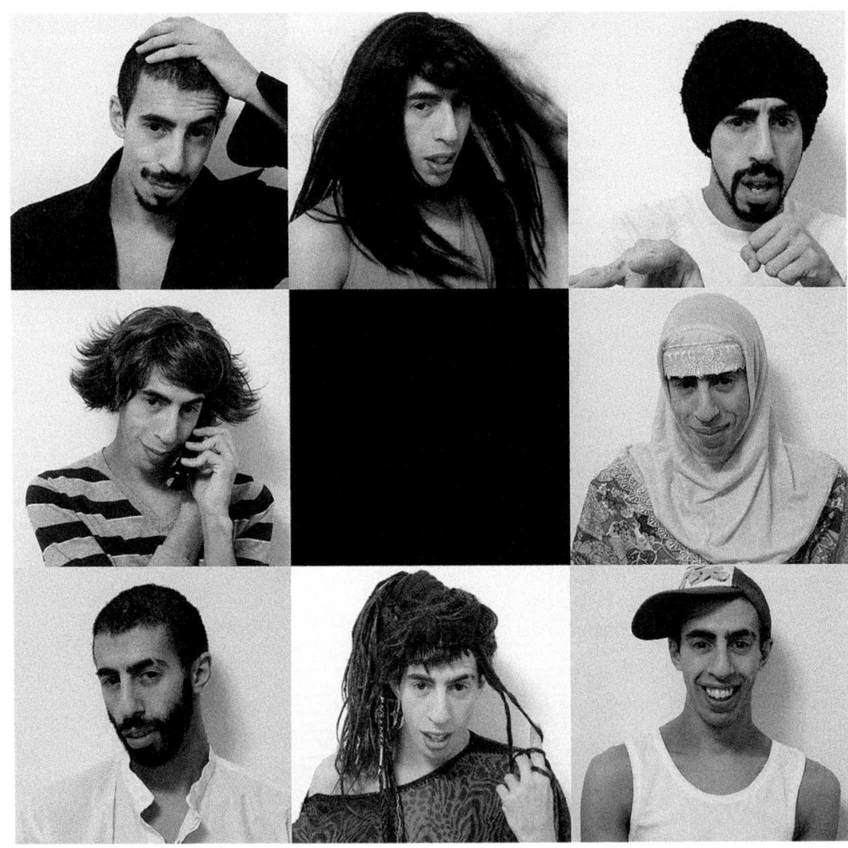

6.7. 2Fik, *Huit Facettes*. Digital collage and photograph. *Huit Facettes* portrays the characters in a way that highlights their national identity. In clockwise order starting in the top left-hand corner: In clockwise order starting in the top left-hand corner: Marco (Italian Moroccan), Alice (French Lebanese), Sofiane (Moroccan), Fatima (Moroccan), Benjamin (Arab-Quebecker), Manon (100% Québécoise), Abdel (Moroccan), Francine (Anglo-Canadian).

characters. 2Fik's solo exhibition, *2Fik: His and Other Stories*, taking place at Toronto's Koffler Gallery in spring 2017, provides a glimpse of how central these characters, family, and kinship are to 2Fik's art practice. Upon entering the exhibition of 2Fik's work, these photographs and biographies line the wall so that viewers can get to know his constructed family before viewing his other photographs.[34] The tensions between the two Moroccan-born brothers currently living in Montreal speak to ideas of tradition/modern and local/diaspora and how navigating cultural tradition within the parameters of Western modernity creates both isolation and seemingly incompatible values. While there is a universalism evoked in using passport photographs, this choice also connects different nations together through an implicit transnational movement provided by the passports; simultaneously, it references a settler-Canadian context of identification documents.

As a part of settler colonial rule in Canada, the Indian Act was instated in 1876 to subsume a number of colonial laws that aimed to eliminate First Nations culture in favor of forceful assimilation into Euro-Canadian society. An individual recognized by the federal government as being registered under the Indian Act is referred to as a Registered Indian, and the federal government has the sole authority, through the Indian Registrar, to determine who is entitled to be registered. Through this process of documentation, identification, surveillance, and, ultimately, over-policing, white settler identity was safeguarded in Canada through colonial laws that rely on the rigid definition of "us" and "them." In using the passport photos to greet visitors of his exhibition, 2Fik evokes an oppressive regime of surveillance and identification that was initiated to eradicate Indigenous culture and communities while simultaneously drawing on the dehumanizing processes of racialization that immigrants face in Canada. White settler colonialism was and still is intricately and intimately connected to the advance of gender binaries and imperial sexual discourses, and these logics further add to the complexities of a queered, racialized, and religious diaspora.

Visualizing Diasporic Sexuality

The ostensibly oppositional traits that are a constant tension between the two characters of Abdel and Sofiane are also seen in other members of the family.[35] Characters like Ludmilla-Mary (figure 6.8) complicate reductive readings of such binaries by embodying these contrasts and contradictions. Her passport photograph shows a fully bearded Muslim man wearing a woman's head covering and lists her origins as unknown. Her characteristic traits include "her big beard, her veil and her huge personality." While the artist uses female pronouns in her biography, the wide-eyed figure is sexually ambiguous, as her large black beard and brown skin are intensified by her white hijab and the white backdrop. The contrast between the veil and the large beard compromises her stable identity. Simultaneously presenting as both an observant Muslim man and a modest Muslim woman, Ludmilla-Mary directly addresses Islamophobia and homophobia through a complex portrayal of gender nonconformity and cultural hybridity. She embodies the fear and discomfort that the Brown-Middle-Eastern-Arab-Other instills,[36] manifesting these qualities visually.

Personifying the racialized Other, this gender-queer representation is absent of all identifying traits such as origin story, occupation, love status, ambitions, and personality—all aspects that are present for the majority of the other family members. This absence of identifying traits coupled with the undisclosed gender identity of this racialized character together reveals the very process of racial and sexual identity formation of diasporic subjects. Following Islamophobic rhetoric that marks her body as Other and illegible, perceived aggressive masculinity and subservient and victimized femininity are tested when combined in a nonbinary character whose sexual desire cannot be deciphered at first glance. As Provencher writes, "Creating these characters and taking pictures of them allows [2Fik] to critique stable identities and also to establish a critical distance from himself where he can conduct an analysis of himself and his family."[37] Furthermore, I argue, Ludmilla-Mary's visually unreadable gender and undetermined sexual identity are a part of the incompatibility between Arab-local and Western sexual desires that 2Fik alludes to in his photography, pointing to histories of conflict between Arab sexual discourses and modern Western notions of gay identity.

Between the hypermasculine Abdel and hyperfeminine characters like Kathryn (figure 6.9), gender-nonconforming characters like Ludmilla-Mary destabilize binaries that have become normalized within discussions of modernity and tradition. Some characters are immigrants from Morocco; others

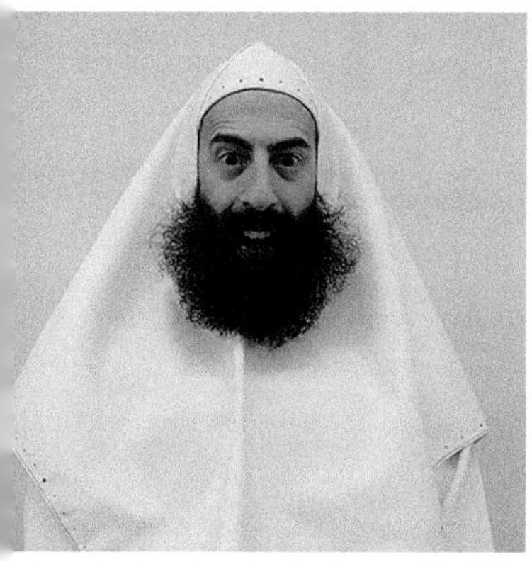

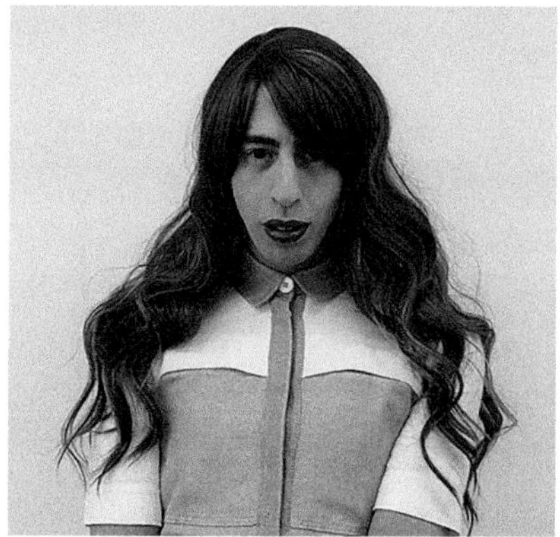

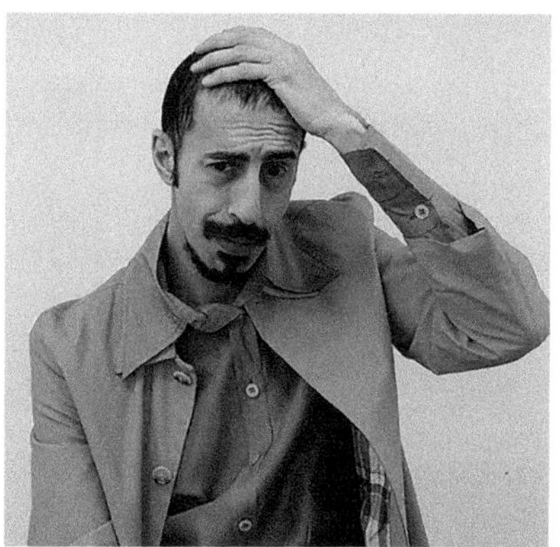

6.8. *left* 2Fik, identification photograph of Ludmilla-Mary.

6.9. *middle* 2Fik, identification photograph of Kathryn.

6.10. *right* 2Fik, identification photograph of Marco.

were born in Canada. The notions of cultural hybridity and authenticity are put to the test in characters like Marco (figure 6.10), who was born in Rome but spent several years in Marrakesh and lived in Paris before moving to Canada. As a "closeted gay man," Marco is quite macho and, according to the artist, is "straight-acting." His background in Rome and Paris creates inconsistencies with Western concepts of freedom and sexual liberation as he demonstrates a lack of freedom and openness despite living in "liberal" Europe. Being European, Maghrebi, and diasporic, he does not allow for questions of tradition versus modernity to be easily deduced from the experiences of his Brown body. Instead, this racialized figure holds the tensions of transnational sexual identity within his diasporic identity, tensions that resist any easy reduction of sexuality to a binary between queer progress in the West and the lack thereof in the Middle East.

Queering Modernity

2Fik also restages and recreates art historic paintings that often correspond to time periods of Western modernity in his practice in order to locate contemporary racialization and contemporary sexual identity. Links to a colonial past are present within his reinventions of art history and often modern art as he subverts the racialized subjectification of the diasporic body. His pastiche of canonical artworks includes *Le déjeuner sur l'herbe* (1862) by Édouard Manet (figure 6.11); *The Anatomy Lesson of Dr. Nicolaes Tulp* (1632) by Rembrandt

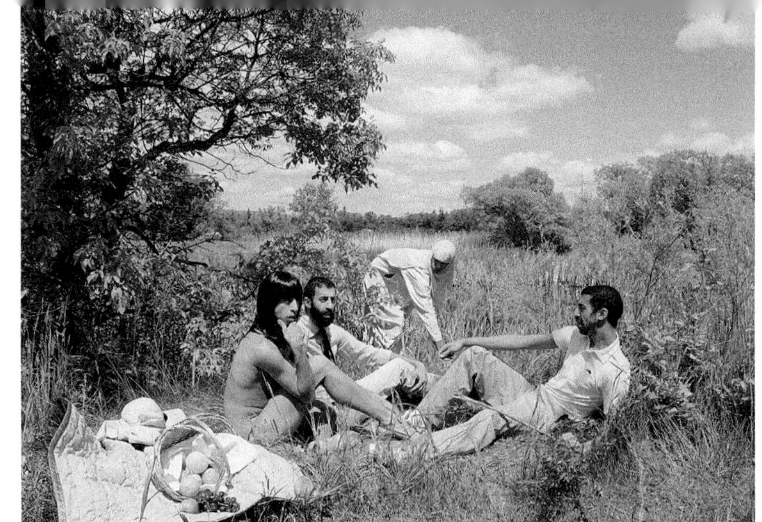

6.11. *top* 2Fik, *Le déjeuner sur l'herbe* (2010), based on Édouard Manet, *Le Déjeuner sur l'herbe* (1863).

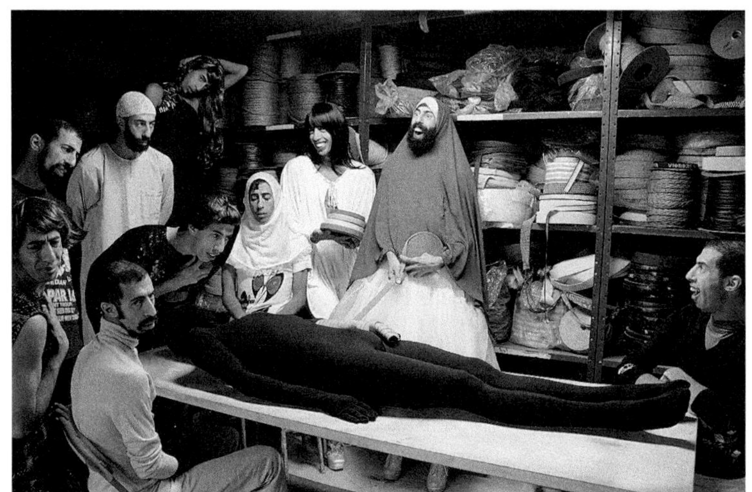

6.12. *middle* 2Fik, *La leçon de folie de Ludmilla-Mary* (2012), based on Rembrandt van Rijn, *The Anatomy Lesson of Dr. Nicolaes Tulp* (1632). See also plate 10.

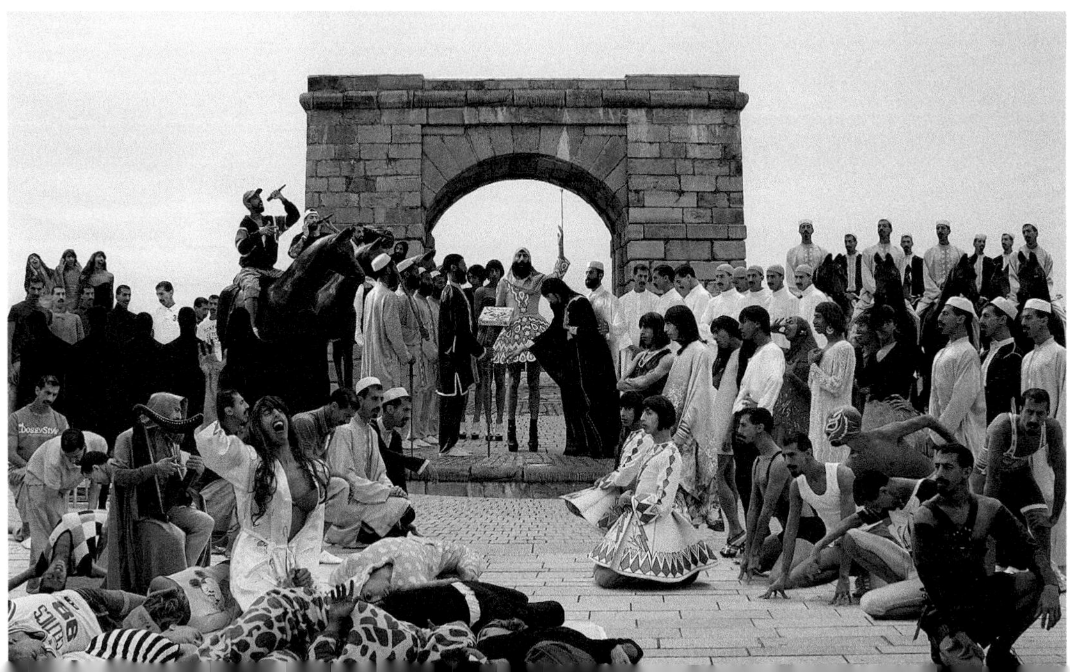

6.13. *bottom* 2Fik, *The Marriage of Abdel and Fatima* (2014), based on Daniel Maclise, *The Marriage of Strongbow and Aoife* (1854). See also plate 11.

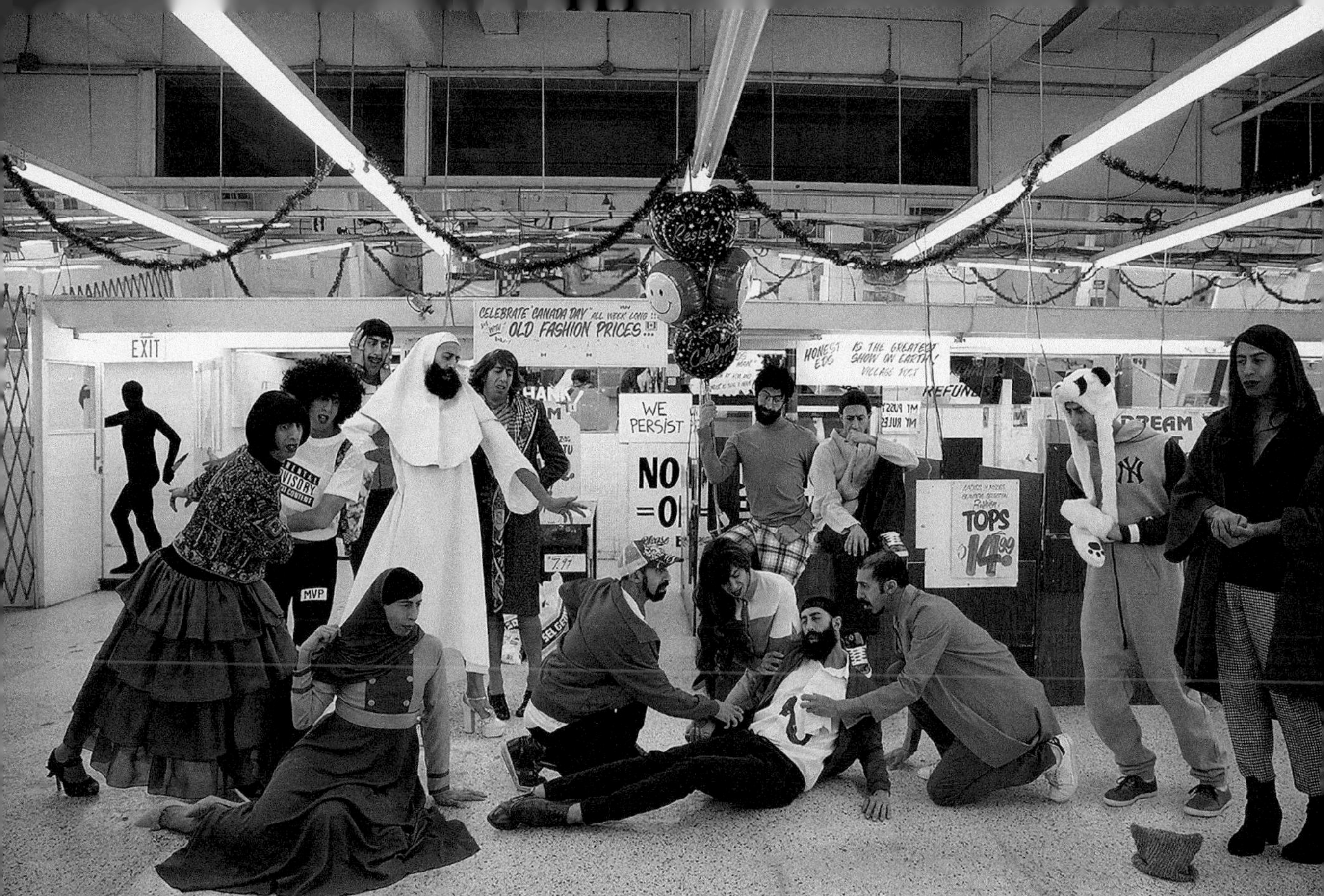

FIGURE 6.14. 2Fik, *The Death of Dishonest Abdel* (2017), based on Benjamin West, *The Death of General Wolfe* (1770). Courtesy of the artist.

van Rijn (figure 6.12); *Las Meninas* (1656) by Diego Velázquez; *The Marriage of Strongbow and Aoife* (1854) by Daniel Maclise (figure 6.13); and *The Death of General Wolfe* (1770) by Benjamin West (figure 6.14), among others.

French artist Jean Auguste Dominique Ingres painted *La Grande Odalisque* in 1814 (figure 6.15) at a time when France was expanding its colonial empire. This oil painting depicts an odalisque or concubine in a style heralded for its exotic romanticism. In this scene, a fair-skinned nude woman reclines with her back facing the viewer and her face slightly turned to meet our gaze. The Orientalism of this painting is inescapable; due to the setting of rich silk, jewels, and a hookah pipe, the viewer is meant to believe that this scene takes place in the "Near East." The fair-skinned woman is racialized by her attributes, and French viewers would have presumed her to be a sexual slave to an Arab man. Since odalisques were not actually courtesans or slaves, the woman depicted here is a French sexual myth that suited the colonial discourse of sexual deviance and Arab barbarism. In the mind of an early nineteenth-century French male viewer, the sort of person for whom this image was made, the odalisque would have conjured up not just a harem slave—itself a misconception—but a set of fears and desires linked to the long history of aggression between Christian Europe and Islamic Asia and North Africa.[38]

2Fik's photograph *La Grande Intendante* (2012; figure 6.16) provides a subversive intervention into Ingres's painting that confronts cultural privilege and links colonial history to diasporic identity. In this work, 2Fik's gender-nonbinary character Ludmilla-Mary poses as the odalisque, but her jewels and pearls have been replaced with window cleaning spray and rubber gloves. Though she is still adorned with a turban, many markers of the Orient are replaced with household cleaning supplies, like a vacuum cleaner and washrags. While this work can be read as a feminist critique of domestic labor and the misogyny that still exerts control over women's bodies,[39] it also speaks to modernity and diaspora. 2Fik has replaced the odalisque—a woman meant to satisfy the carnal pleasures of the sultan—with his own Brown, diasporic, and queer body. His large beard, traditionally associated with Islam,[40] is juxtaposed with the feminine pose of the odalisque, a pose historically saved for women in Western artistic tradition. His painted red lips add to the gender ambiguity, queering his sexual identity but also his role as concubine. Who is 2Fik in service to in this image?

Domestic labor is connected to migrant women who often come to Canada through temporary foreign worker programs such as the Live-In Caregiver Program.[41] The image therefore depicts a colonially gendered history of labor and enslavement that is tied to racialized migrant women, indentured labor, and enslaved women. Moreover, the settler colonial state historically used racialized bodies to maintain and support white settler domestic spaces, with immigrants inadvertently participating in active Indigenous elimination and erasure. As literary scholar Lisa Lowe explains, "These distinct yet connected racial logics constituted parts of what was in the nineteenth century an emergent Anglo-American settler imperial imaginary, which continues to be elaborated today."[42] The connection between labor and migration creates an undeniably diasporic reading of this image, as transnational migrant labor is often associated with a loss of homeland and separation of families.

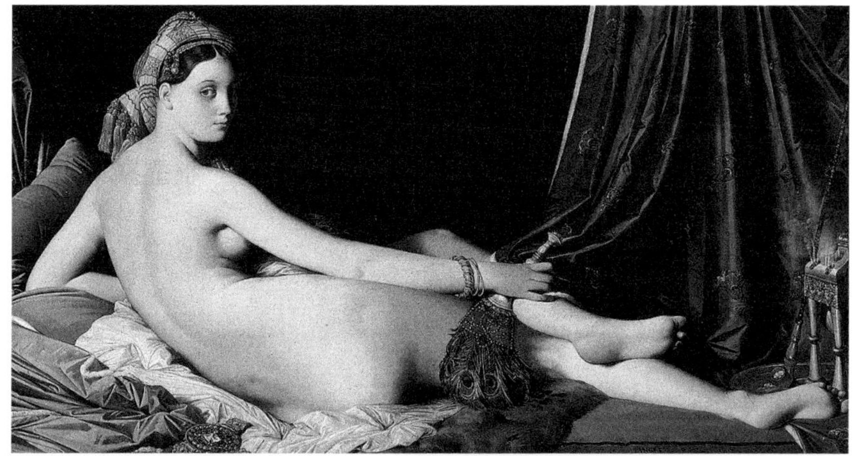

6.15. *left* Jean Auguste Dominique Ingres, *La Grande Odalisque* (1814). Oil on canvas. See also plate 12.

6.16. *below* 2Fik, *La Grande Intendante* (2012), based on Ingres's *La Grande Odalisque*. See also plate 13.

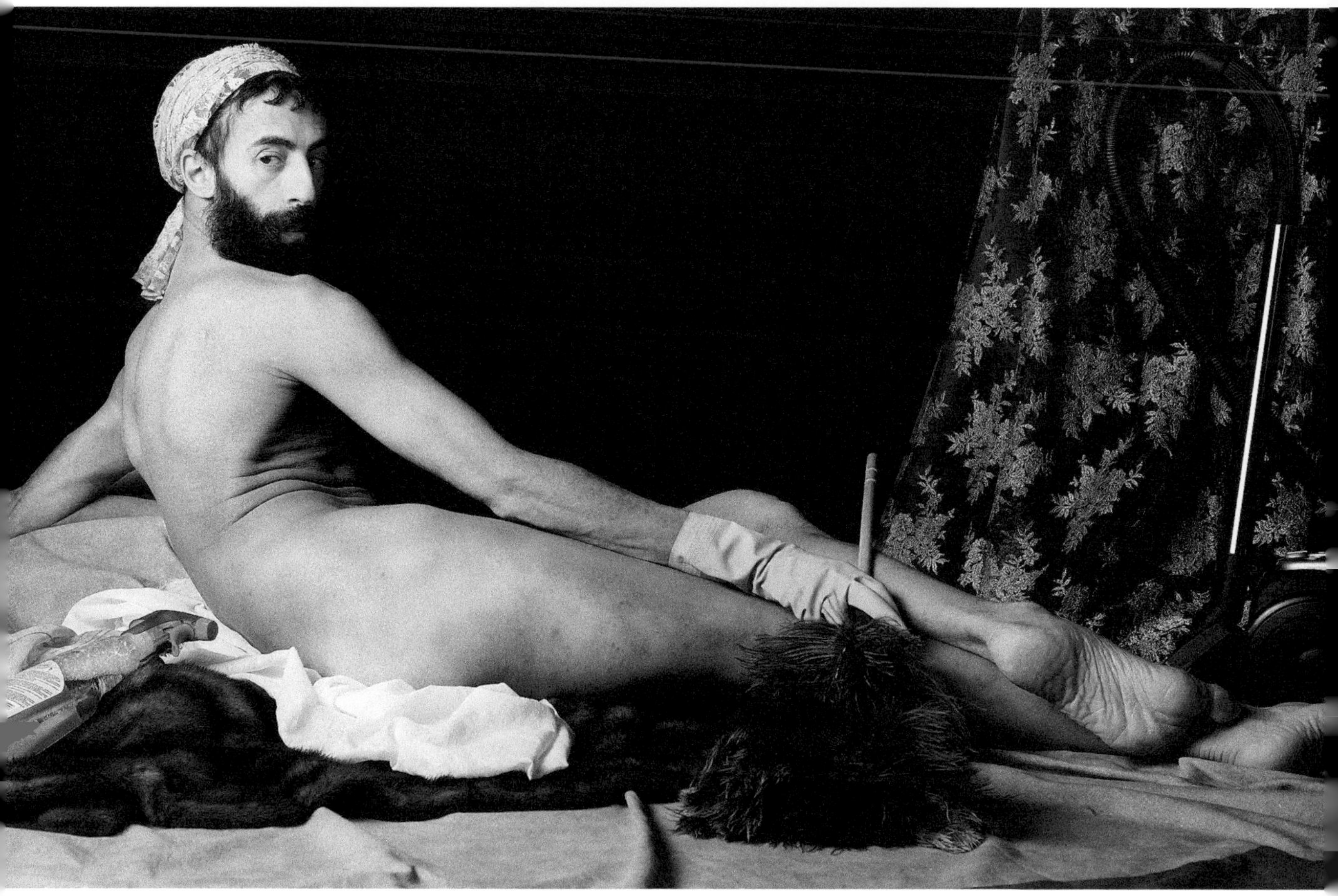

Given France's colonial empire in Morocco, Algeria, Tunisia, and much of North Africa when Ingres painted this image, Orientalism adds another dimension of coloniality that 2Fik reclaims from the scene. The original painting was in fact commissioned by Caroline Murat, Napoleon's sister and the queen of Naples, and it is clear that colonial politics played a role in the myth of the barbarian, a myth that served the French, who could then claim a moral imperative as they colonized and conquered Africa and the Near East. 2Fik's Brown, sexualized, but also ambiguously gendered body plays the role of the colonized body. Illustrating the absurdity of Orientalist traditions depicting the Middle East as backward and unmodern, 2Fik satirizes an aesthetic tradition that renders his own body as unmodern and deficient. With deficiency comes a lack, accounting for the incompatibility of Islam with homosexuality. This is unlike the West and its progressive, modern relationship to queer identity. Momin Rahman critiques the assumed mutual exclusivity between queerness and Middle Eastern or Asian cultures.[43] Rahman aims to illuminate the intersections and complexities of current binaries within Muslim communities and families, gay communities and culture, and wider Western political culture and discourses. His central argument is that the West has created a discourse of Islamic otherness that positions Islam against homosexuality, meaning that homosexuality is deployed as a marker of the superiority of Western modernity. In this way, a queer culture always existed in the Middle East, even if it was not termed as such, but the West attempted to criminalize it, confine it, and define it, which ultimately led to its suppression.

Even though homosexuality is far from universally accepted in the West, when sexual diversity arises in civilizational debates, it is cast as a defining feature of Western exceptionalism and superiority, thus drawing queerness into the core of definitions of Muslim incompatibility with modernity. Using queer subjectivity as a defining feature of modern nation-states is what feminist theorist Jasbir Puar calls homonationalism, "an analytic to apprehend state formation and a structure of modernity . . . an assemblage of geopolitical and historical forces, neoliberal interests in capitalist accumulation both cultural and material, biopolitical state practices of population control, and affective investments in discourses of freedom, liberation, and rights."[44] Building on the idea that homonationalism has become one of the key logics of modernity, postcolonial scholar Nishant Upadhyay argues that race must be seen as central to processes of homonationalism, because within the homonationalist project non-Indigenous queers of color who were historically colonized and marginalized can be included, over time, within the settler state by claiming heteronormative sexual citizenship.[45]

In 2Fik's *La Grande Intendante*, the viewer is meant to confront the absurdity not only of Orientalist depictions of the Other but also of the long history of sexuality and gender norms in Europe that contributed to the making of the original painting by Ingres. The red lips of the bearded Muslim subject in the photograph are not only gender-bending but also call on a long history of colonial tradition that created the very conception of homosexuality in the European settler colonial context (and throughout the Global North) and its assumed nonprogressive counterparts in the Global South. These East/West, modern/unmodern binaries are historically unstable and have always been reliant on one another. European visual tropes of Romantic Orientalism enabled Euro-American same-sex desire and provided a safe space for colonial Europeans to behave homosocially in the Middle East. For instance, historian Luke Gartlan examines the significance of outdoor photography in Cairo by Austro-Hungarian Orientalists as expressive of male bonding within the traveler-artist circle.[46] Gartlan argues for the importance of same-sex intimacy in the travels of Orientalist artists and photographers. The perceived tension between prudish Victorian sexual discourse and "sexually litigious" behaviors in the Middle East in the nineteenth century naturally allowed for European travelers to explore a greater range of acceptable codes of behavior. Thus, these generally male colonial tourists raise questions about a perceived Ottoman homosociality and a Euro-American heterosexuality—namely, why was there not a two-way exchange between colonial morality and colonial fantasy? In this artistic intervention by 2Fik, tradition and modernity are interrogated and the fixity of their binary construction is destabilized.[47]

Colonial Trauma and Contemporary Art

I would like to conclude with an analysis of 2Fik's own character (figure 6.17) created in his photographic body of work. In his passport photograph, the self-named black shell of a figure has absolutely no visual identity. Described

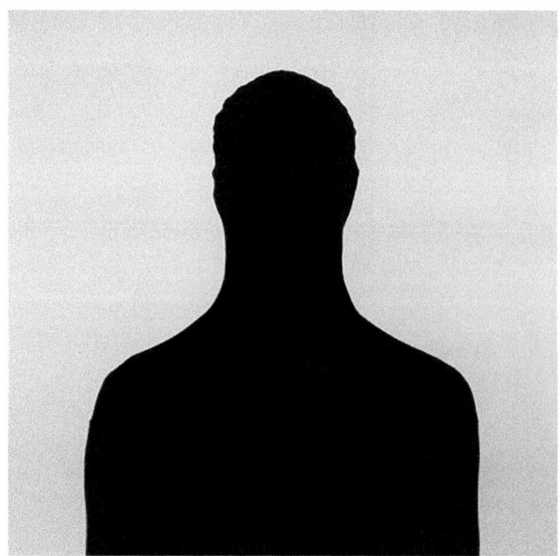

6.17. 2Fik, identification photograph of 2Fik.

as having no origins, his occupation is to play different characters and his ambition is to be a blank canvas that does its best to portray those characters. Under "personality traits," 2Fik's character is said to have none, and he exists only through the other characters he enacts. I argue that the absence of a visual identity, mirrored in the lack of identifying characteristics, represents what 2Fik nihilistically illustrates as his own queer diasporic identity.

As I have traced throughout this analysis, Islamicate sexualities in the diaspora are fraught with tensions of coloniality, visuality, and citizenship. I began by outlining how Western epistemologies of queerness are not always conducive to understanding queer, diasporic, and transnational sexual identities, and 2Fik's notion of coming out à l'orientale provides a reprieve from, and an alternative form of, sexual and artistic expression. From there, I analyzed 2Fik's passport photos as a way of zeroing in on diasporic subjectivity and the formation of diasporic identity. I then framed these sexual discourses historically, questioning the types of colonial relationships present within discourses of sexuality. Especially important are the imperial connections that have existed between the West and Islamicate regions, which have created a framework of difference that defines Arab sexualities as perpetually unmodern. Here, the colonial traumas that I identified at the start of this analysis are seen as repercussions of, and linked to, contemporary ways of being both diasporic and queer. That is, past colonial trauma is closely linked to the diasporic present and informs visual tropes like coming out à l'orientale in methods of artistic creation.

These methods involve queering kinship and imagining visual processes that require rewriting history in order to offer powerful reclamations of colonial domination and culturally impacted sexual discourses experienced in the Middle East. Diasporic artists such as 2Fik use performance, character creation, humor, pastiche, and satire productively and affirmatively as a way of laying bare colonial traumas that are often buried and rendered invisible through normative Western queer discourses and the civilizing missions of modernity, which always favor the West. The traumas that the diasporic subject carries are intrinsically tied to settler colonial histories, as immigration is a component of Western nations' national imaginary and can be used by the state to reproduce colonial amnesia through the active denial of present-day colonial projects.[48] Overall, in creating a visual description of colonial trauma, contemporary diasporic art exists outside of its own contemporaneity and is removed from a present moment of subjectivity. Instead, the queer diasporic individual both creates and develops methods to mediate their own relationships to the local and the global, the traditional and the modern, and, most importantly, the self and the other.

SEVEN

HISTORICIZING HOMOPHOBIA

CONTESTING THE DOUBLE BINDS OF HOMOCOLONIALISM AND HOMONATIONALISM

This chapter offers an analysis of Middle Eastern diasporic conditions through a focus on queer diasporic art and identity, especially under the auspices of migration. By engaging with the visual art of diasporic artists Alireza Shojaian, Laurence Rasti, and Nilbar Güreş, this chapter sheds light on the immense violence and trauma that queer and trans subjects face in the Middle East and the diaspora. These artists provide a rich platform to investigate the relationship between imperialism, trauma, and displacement within queer communities in North America and Europe, showing us that ideas of homeland complicate how sexual identity is realized within the diaspora. The artwork produced by and about the queer diaspora is helpful in discovering the ways clichés of sexual oppression in the Middle East versus the sexual acceptance in North America and Europe are being contested to show the racism present when we reduce human rights to these geographic terms. Instead, we should examine how imperialism, settler colonialism, and military interventions in the Middle East relate to the continued violence against queer communities in North America and in Europe. How are gay civil liberties imagined throughout the world, and who decides what these gay human rights look like everywhere in the world? While queer bodies can experience homophobia in Middle Eastern, African, and Asian contexts, Black and Brown bodies experience *racial* violence in Western countries like the United States, Canada, France, Germany, and Belgium. The queer diaspora is often the queer Black and Brown body, and the process of racialization, as well as sexualization, is the site where the queer diaspora is constituted. Because of this, the artists in this chapter show us the places where culture and sexuality meet transnationally and the ways they articulate their own experiences and identities that better inform this process.

This means we need to decolonize how we think about homosexual tolerance and queer liberation in the Middle East, Africa, and Asia in order to ensure that the specific needs of individual queer people are met. Throughout the years Western imperialism has created pressure in these regions to do away with the more fluid understandings of gender and sexuality that were once common in these regions. The irony is that as European countries, and later the United States, exported heterosexuality to their colonial outposts, they introduced laws that criminalize gay people in the Middle East, Africa, and Asia, because at the time, Europe and America had their own laws to criminalize gay people within their own borders. This means that laws against homosexuality in Middle Eastern, African, and Asian countries are often more recent than we first think, and they are directly influenced by the antigay legislation that was so popular in the West.[1] In fact, homosexuality was illegal in the West until very recently, with the United States decriminalizing gay marriage only in 2015.[2] To help frame this discussion, it is useful to think about how identities are formed and what queer world making can look like. As gay rights are championed in parts of the English-speaking world and so violently contested in others, we need to remember how queerness finds a way to dwell and remain in seemingly "inhospitable" places like the Middle East, Africa, and Asia. Studying the cultural production of the queer diaspora is fruitful in that it helps to rethink normative political categories around diaspora. I contend that these artistic expressions and compositions from a broadly defined "Islamicate queer diaspora" offer disruptive readings of both homocolonialism and homonationalism.

I explore these themes through the lens of visual art—in particular, through the works of three diasporic artists. Alireza Shojaian is an Iranian artist who began his career in Tehran and later moved to Beirut, where he explored queerness in his art with less censorship. He has been based in Paris since 2019. As an artist, he aims to challenge societal norms of gender and sexuality to make space for nonheteronormative masculine identities through reflecting upon the queer history of West Asia and putting it into contemporary context through his lived experience. Laurence Rasti is an Iranian Swiss visual artist who photographs queer Iranian refugees in Turkey; and Nilbar Güreş, a diasporic Turkish visual artist living and working in Vienna, sheds light on the immense violence and trauma that queer and trans subjects face both in the Middle East and the diaspora. It is through the visual analysis of these artists that I hope to contribute to better understanding the double binds of homocolonialism and homonationalism within queer world making.

Displacement in Diaspora: Censored Voices

In summer 2021, Iranian visual artist Alireza Shojaian turned an iconic Iranian-made car, the Paykan, into an art installation (figure 7.1). The first ever Iranian-made car, the Paykan was produced in Iran from 1967 to 2005 and represents a strong symbol of Iranian nationalism. The car was an icon of "Iranian Modernity, possibility and industrial capability."[3] Shojaian painted this beloved symbol of national pride with scenes inspired by the *Shahnameh*, the tenth-century Persian Book of Kings,[4] but in his version Persian folk heroes are reimagined in a homoerotic scene of same-sex desire. The PaykanArtCar Organization was created in 2021 and is a nonprofit, nonpartisan organization that bought the car and funded Alireza Shojaian's art installation. To paint one of these beloved national symbols was no easy task, and this Paykan in particular was a gift from the shah Mohammad Reza Pahlavi of Iran to the president of Romania, Nicolae Ceauşescu, in 1974. Remarkably, a car that was once owned by a dictator is now the canvas for a queer Iranian artist living in exile, providing a powerful critique on behalf of a suppressed minority living in a totalitarian regime. On October 4, 2021, the car was exhibited in Miami, and the press release confirmed plans for exhibiting the PaykanArtCar in Paris for the major art festival Asia NOW from October 21 to October 24 that same year. Unfortunately, as a subsequent press release from October 18 indicates, "Despite having approached and formally invited the artist, the Asia NOW organizers have revoked their invitation just days before the major art fair was set to start."[5] Their decision came after pressure from Tehran-based galleries that refused to exhibit alongside Alireza Shojaian's pro-LGBTQ+ artwork. In addition to the exclusion,

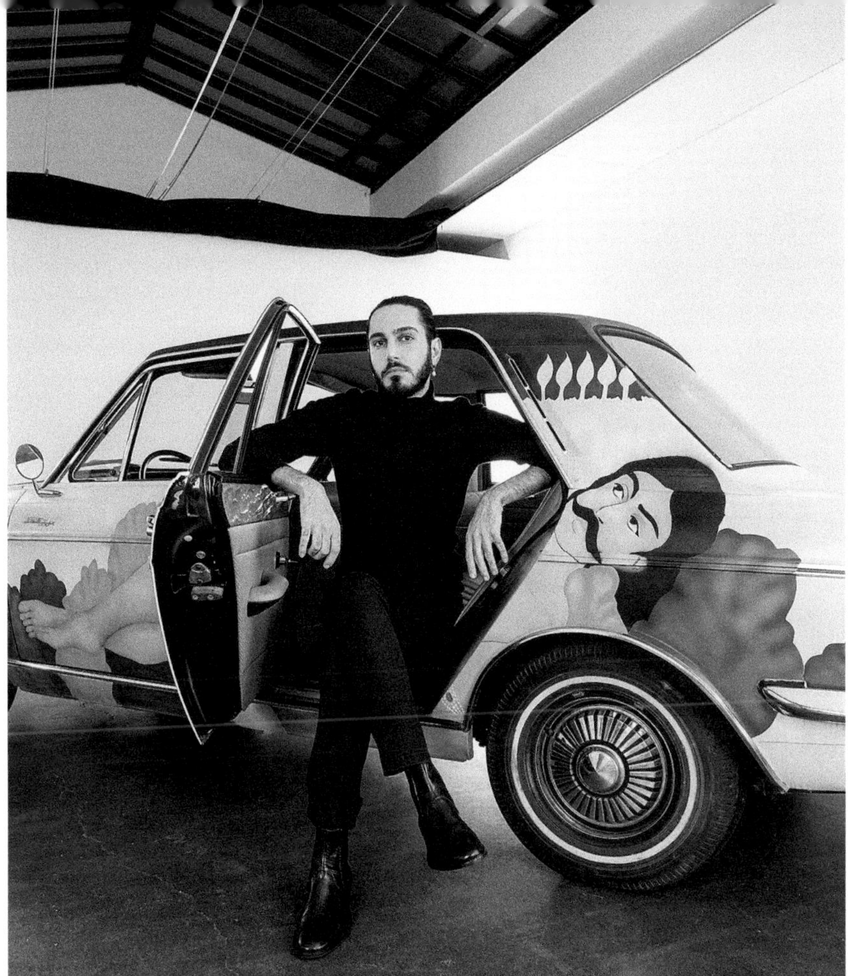

7.1. Alireza Shojaian, *Sous le Ciel de Shiraz*, PaykanArtCar (2021), taken at the artist's studio in Paris.

the organizers of the Asia NOW fair attempted to silence Alireza and his art through threats of legal actions. According to the artist, "At the request of art galleries supported by the Iranian government, as soon as these people heard about the PaykanArtCar and its symbol, they mobilized their agents to silence me."[6] After the artwork was censored by Asia NOW following threats by Iranian donors to remove their exhibiting artists from the show if the car was exhibited, Shojaian's car toured Canada in protest against Iran's antigay abuses and the censorship of the work in Paris.

This car is painted in the Ghahvehkhaneh, or coffeehouse style, characterized by bright dynamic colors, clear lines, and depictions of traditional stories from classic texts. These narrative depictions were often used as sites of learning and culture, and paintings made in this style were characteristically clear, with sharp colors and bold lines telling traditional and historically significant national stories. The two figures depicted on the car are inspired by the story of Rostam and Sohrab from the Persian book of *Shahnameh*, stories from which were often the subject of coffeehouse paintings. However, for his characters Alireza has borrowed the subjects of Sohrab and Shaban from the paintings of Hossein Qollar-Aghasi (1902–1966), titled *Sohrab and Shaban*, a spin-off created by Iranian folk storytellers referencing the *Shahnameh*. With this work, Shojaian subverts the image of Sohrab and Shaban, traditionally patriarchal symbols, into homosexual characters. He does this to narrate a contemporary story by turning the battle between these two national characters into a romantic moment (on the front of the car), which takes place in a Persian garden under the starry night of Shiraz. The two sides of the car depict scenes of their death as a result of their "forbidden" love. On the right side of the vehicle, the depiction of the tragic death scene of Sohrab can be read as referring to Article 234 of the penal code of the Islamic Republic of Iran, which states that same-sex relationships between men are possibly punishable by death. On the left side of the car, the painted figure of Shaban refers to the contemporary story of Alireza Fazeli-Monfared, a twenty-year-old gay man beheaded by his family in 2021 because of his sexuality,[7] and to the hundreds of similar murders caused by homophobia that are often unreported.[8] Embedded within artist Shojaian's retelling of this nationalistic, old folk tale through the painted car lies a modern story about how LGBTQ people suffer in Iran today.

Symbolism: Queer Visual Excavations

As will be made clear in this section, the art of the queer diaspora offers a rich vantage point from which the relationships of colonial trauma and displacement can be read. Furthermore, these artworks complicate notions of homeland by exposing and alluding to the experiences of living with and through a transnational sexual identity. The cultural production of the queer diaspora and diasporic sexuality can help complicate and disturb the metanarrative that characterizes Middle Eastern cultures as sexually oppressive and intolerant on the one hand and reductively assumes Western cultures as sexually liberated and accepting on the other.

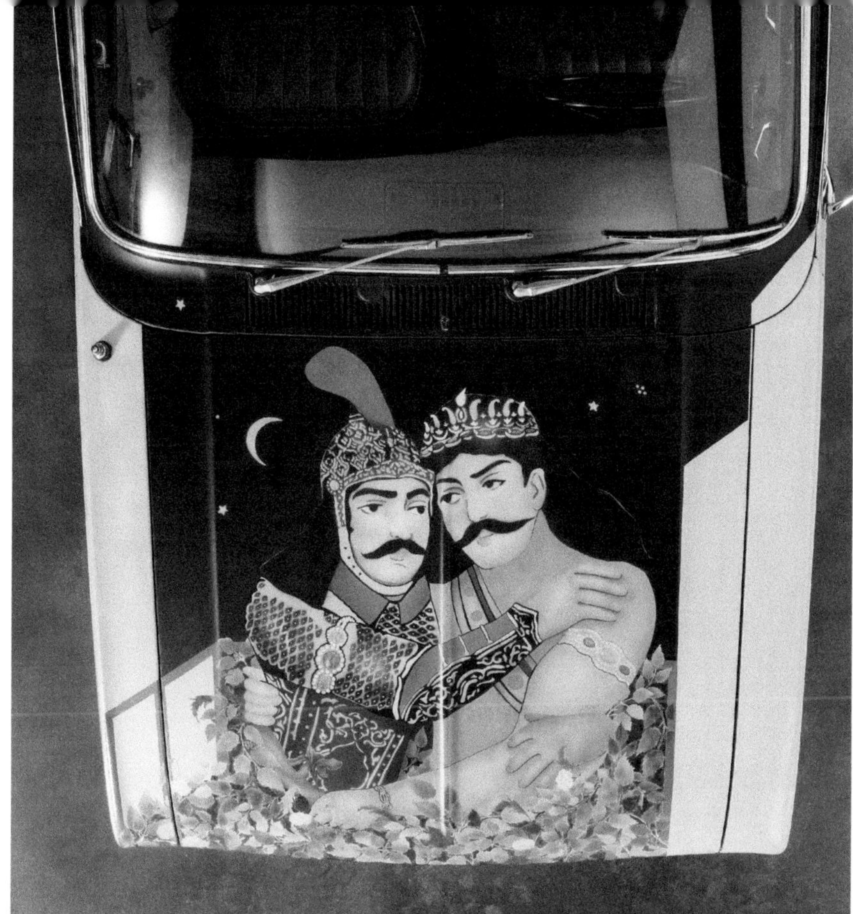

7.2. Alireza Shojaian, *Sous le Ciel de Shiraz*, hood detail. Courtesy of the artist. See also plate 14.

On the hood of the brightly painted yellow car, two men embrace (figure 7.2). Sohrab is shirtless, with a jeweled armband around his left bicep, a bracelet around his wrist, and a bloody slash spreading from his left shoulder to underneath his right arm. His right arm is extended across his body to reach his lover, Shaban, and he holds a blue and purple iris flower in his hand. These two men are sitting in an embrace, and the viewer can see Sohrab's left arm wrapped around and across Shaban's back. Shaban is clothed in gold and red, mirroring the gold armor on his arm and chest. Shaban's arm is extended, and he tenderly embraces Sohrab with his hand on his shoulder. In a display of harmony and balance between the two figures, both men wear jeweled armbands: Sohrab's has a yellow stone, adorned with red jewels on each side, and Shaban's has a red stone in the middle, adorned with green stones on either side.

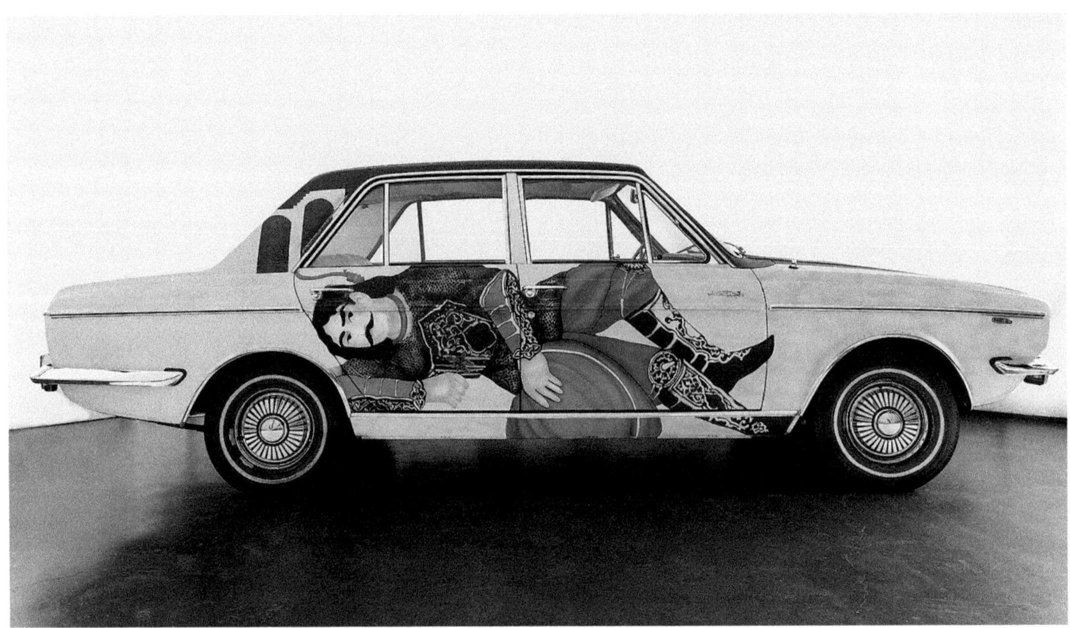

7.3. Alireza Shojaian, *Sous le Ciel de Shiraz*, right side. Courtesy of the artist.

The viewer sees only the men's torsos; everything below their waist is covered in green leaves from a vine-like plant growing below. There are small red buds on the vine, not yet in flower, and yellow flowers that are open appear in blossom. These two figures are lying together under the dark blue night sky with a crescent moon and stars visible. They are painted to be looking at each other, with a loving quality to their gazes, and the gestures of their embrace further add to the romantic and tender image.

Shaban is painted in armor and wearing a helmet with a large red feather sticking out of the top, accentuating the dark hair flowing down. His helmet is adorned with gold on the top, with a red and yellow border around his face. Sohrab, who appears on the right, is adorned with a silver jeweled helmet, with a border of red and green, mirroring the colored jewels on his lover's arm. This painting on the hood of the car is incredibly similar to the inspiration piece by modernist Iranian painter Hossein Qollar-Aghasi (1902–1966) titled *Sohrab and Shaban*. This painting depicts the same story artist Shojaian is taking up from the *Shahnameh* as inspiration for the PaykanArtCar. In Qollar-Aghasi's version, we see the same outfits for both men, but instead of embracing, the figure in armor is reaching for something on the other's belt.

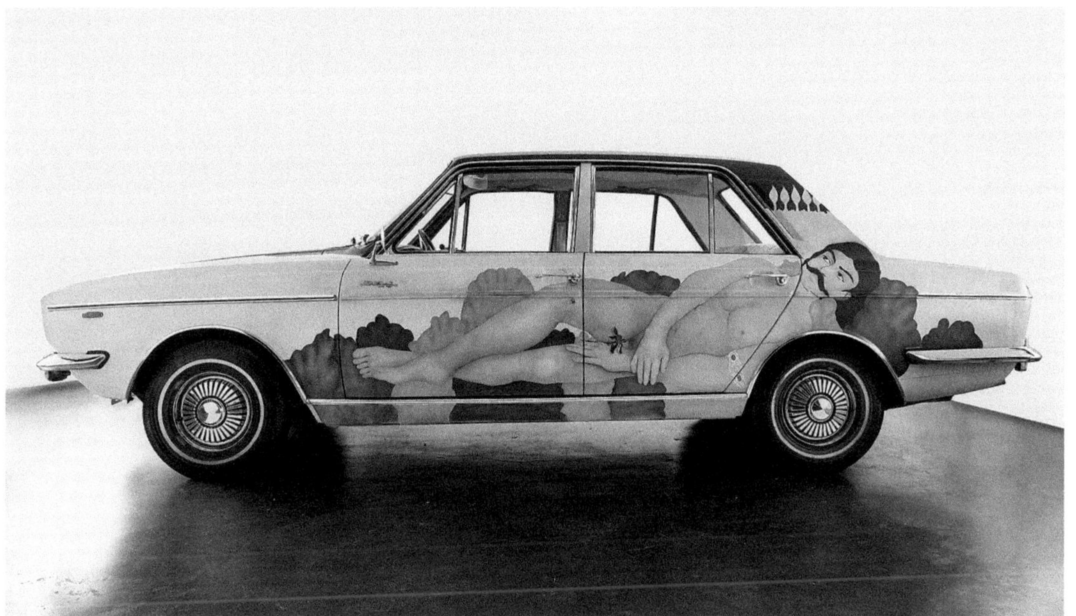

7.4. Alireza Shojaian, *Sous le Ciel de Shiraz*, left side. Courtesy of the artist.

Shojaian has painted a love and affection between the characters forcefully into the composition, and additional allegorical details can be seen in his painting that were not present in the original.

On the right side of the PaykanArtCar (figure 7.3), Shaban lies almost dead. The viewer can see the same gold and red uniform, but Shaban lies sprawled on his side, his helmet removed. Amid his shoulder-length black hair a red noose hangs around his neck. Clutched in his right hand is an iris, the same flower his lover Sohrab was holding on the hood of the car while affectionately embracing one another. Shaban's eyes are still open, and they appear to be looking upward, perhaps toward the night sky, as he lies vulnerable.

On the left side of the car (figure 7.4), Sohrab is painted reclining fully nude. His feet are crossed, as are his hands covering his groin, in a pose referencing a reclining nude popular in Western paintings like Édouard Manet's depiction of Olympia. Sohrab also holds an iris in this scene, a recurring motif between the two men referencing the painting on the hood of the vehicle. The use of the iris is deliberate, for it is a visual reference to the flower named after the goddess Iris, who, according to mythology, created

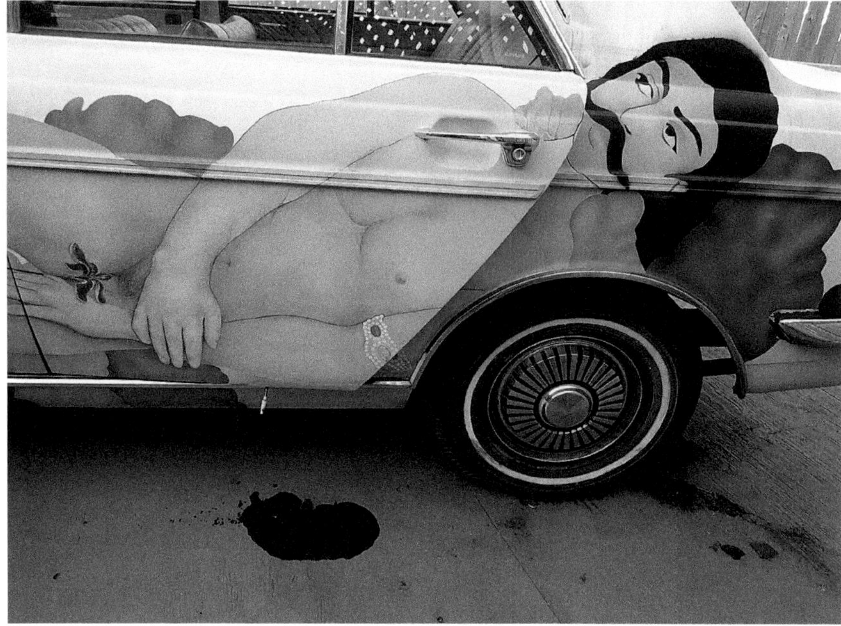

7.5. Alireza Shojaian, *Sous le Ciel de Shiraz*, left side detail. See also plate 15.

the rainbow, a relevant symbol for gay pride. Choosing not to overtly use the Western symbol of the rainbow flag for LGBTQ+ rights, artist Alireza Shojaian narrates how homosexuality is not a Western import but has been part of Iran since the time of the Book of Kings in the eleventh century.[9] Unlike the door painting on the other side of the car depicting Shaban, there is no noose around Sohrab's neck, but the way he is lying means that when the rear door is opened, it appears as if he has been decapitated. The composition of the reclining nude Sohrab makes decapitation inevitable each time the rear car door is opened, and the seam of the car door visually creates an invisible noose that mimics the red noose painted on Sohrab's lover, Shaban, on the other side of the car. Nude and in a vulnerable position, Sohrab's head is positioned directly above the rear wheel well so that when the rear door is opened, it violently cuts him directly across the neck and chest. Given that the PaykanArtCar is a multimedia art installation, in addition to the painted surfaces there is a trail of blood coming from this particular wheel well, slowly dripping from underneath Sohrab's neck and pooling on the floor (figure 7.5). The blood dripping down from the open door and the bloody knife painted on the trunk of the car suggest the horrific "honor" killing by decapitation that Alireza Fazeli-Monfared suffered at the hands of his family in 2021. Inside the car, a speaker plays audio notes sent by Alireza Fazeli-Monfared to his boyfriend (who had fled to Turkey days before his boyfriend's murder)[10] speaking about the threats he was facing from his father, and this chilling postmortem recording plays along with other recordings of numerous news channels announcing Alireza Fazeli-Monfared's death.[11]

The brutal murder of Alireza Fazeli-Monfared committed by his half brother and two cousins is rooted in homophobia and bigotry and becomes an important element of the PaykanArtCar, but one that received the least amount of public attention when the car was exhibited. The incredibly colorful paintings that cover the surface of the car are more noticeable than the audio track playing within the vehicle, and the details of the blood dripping out of the wheel well become overshadowed by the wonderfully flamboyant paintings. However, it is these details that relate to the "honor" killing of Alireza Fazeli-Monfared that I would like to focus on, for his inclusion within the artwork adds an important transtemporal and transhistoric approach to understanding queer diasporic subjectivities, especially through the lens of the artist's own lived experiences. Before his murder, twenty-year-old Alireza Fazeli-Monfared had hoped to escape the country where he felt stifled by the Iranian regime's restrictions on homosexuality. He had dreams of modeling or becoming a make-up artist, his partner Aghil Abiat told CNN. In long phone calls and video messages with his boyfriend Abiat—who is an asylum-seeking refugee in Turkey after being outed in Iran—Alireza Fazeli-Monfared would describe the experiences he longed to have and the life he wanted to build.[12] Always seething in the background, however, was the building family pressure and Iran's laws against homosexuality that make same-sex relations a potential capital offense. "He was always stressed. He bit his nails so there were never any left," his boyfriend Abiat recalled.[13]

Iran is one of sixty-eight countries where same-sex relations between consenting adults is criminalized, according to Human Rights Watch reports.[14] Researcher for Human Rights Watch, Tara Sepehri Far, says, "There are no statistics or records of the number of anti-LGBTQ 'honor killings'—which are perpetrated by relatives who feel the LGBTQ person has brought 'dishonor' to the family—that happen in Iran or other countries that criminalize homosexuality."[15] In another interview she goes on to say that "the LGBTQ community is one of the most marginalized in Iran, they face various levels of discrimination and hate. The most obvious one is by law but there is also a lot of homophobia in society depending on where you are and which demographic you belong to. . . . The family can sometimes be the most dangerous place."[16] The last time Alireza Fazeli-Monfared and Abiat spoke before he was killed, on May 2, 2021, Fazeli-Monfared said he would go to a store to switch his phone. Then he planned to buy a train ticket from Ahvaz, his hometown in southwest Iran's Khuzestan Province, to the capital, Tehran, to get a COVID-19 test for travel to Turkey and join his boyfriend Abiat. Abiat, who is also Iranian and left the country three years ago after a former partner outed him to his family, was still in a transit zone as a refugee waiting for resettlement in Turkey.

Narrating this brutal killing through the medium of painting a car is noteworthy, for it is not just any car but a 1974 Paykan. As Iran's only domestically made car from 1967 until it was discontinued in 2005, the Paykan holds nostalgic significance for Iranians. Artist Shojaian aimed to capture the attention of his diasporic audiences, and "it's a symbol of masculinity, toxic masculinity," he explained in an interview. "Having the expectation of masculinity that comes with this car and then using it to narrate the story of LGBTQ people in Iran . . . this is shocking for some people."[17] Artist Alireza Shojaian narrates the diaspora in this piece through an interesting vantage point. He experienced censorship of his art while attending university in Tehran, and because of this, he obtained only his bachelor's degree in fine arts and painting from the Islamic Azad University in 2014. He was not allowed to complete his master's degree, because he chose queer art as the subject of his thesis and final project. Shojaian kept his work hidden throughout his university years and did not exhibit in Iran.

The sanctions against Iran prevented Shojaian from moving to the United States and Europe, but he met a Lebanese patron in Iran who encouraged him to move to Beirut. Shojaian settled in the more liberal Beirut in February 2017, where he was able to develop his artwork and held two solo exhibitions in 2017 and 2018. He was invited by the French embassy in Lebanon to participate in a project for the Académie des Beaux-Arts, leading him to move to Paris, and in 2019, after three years in exile, he was granted asylum in France. Through his experience, Shojaian speaks from both within and outside of the nation and activates a diasporic imaginary from a unique vantage point. The personal story of transnational migration in search of queer liberation makes the decision by the organizers of the Asia NOW exhibition to revoke their invitation to Shojaian to exhibit in the Paris show even more egregious. Shojaian, an asylum seeker in exile in Paris from the homophobia he experienced in Iran, could no longer exhibit the Paykan car in the Paris exhibition after Tehran-based galleries refused to exhibit next to this pro-LGBTQ work, and the organizers once more censored his voice and caved to the homophobic demands to disinvite Shojaian. "I'm shocked that the Iranian regime has now found another way to silence him and his pro-LGBTQ art in France, supposedly a bastion of free speech and liberalism," said executive director and cofounder of PaykanArtCar, Dr. Hiva Feizi, in a press release.[18]

Queering Diaspora Transnationally

Queer diasporic art often cites the links between and critiques of the colonial past and the present, creating powerful points of relationality between visual culture and diasporic consciousness. In a similar vein, I argue that an interplay of sameness and difference underpins the queer Arab diaspora's search for belonging. Since the late nineteenth and early twentieth centuries, same-sex desires have been marked by derision in the modern Middle East, eventually leading to the open hostility toward queer identity we find today. Homophobia in the Middle East has often been explained as a legacy of colonialism and symptomatic of postcolonial nation-building projects. The resultant assumption of Middle Eastern homophobia can be felt in diasporic settings like North America and Europe, where there is a heightened sense of difference between "us" and "them"—that is, the assimilationist process that marks "good" immigrants from "bad." Sherene Razack describes a common trope in Middle Eastern and Muslim immigrant experiences that she explains as "the story of the unassimilable, fatally pre-modern Muslim community encountering an advanced [Western] civilization."[19] Within this logic, the gay or queer Muslim or Middle Eastern subject must be unproblematically "homonormative" in the West and live in awe of the liberal values that grant them the "right" to be gay. This Orientalizing trope enforces a strict binary between same-sex desire and being Muslim, a dichotomy felt in both the Middle East and the diaspora.

Nadine Naber interrogates the dichotomies that ensnare Arab communities as they clamor for a sense of safety and belonging in the United States. She argues that "conventional nationalisms rely on a patrilinear heteronormative reproductive logic that maintains community boundaries through the ideal of heterosexual marriage and reproduction."[20] In their edited collection, *Arab and Arab American Feminisms*, Rebab Abdulhadi, Evelyn Alsultany, and Nadine Naber argue that when articulating Arabness in the United States, the diaspora has been shaped by an assemblage of different visions of how Arabs survive in North America: "Historical and contextual factors related to the imperialist relationship between the United States and the Arab world have produced distinct forms of racism against and criminalization of individuals and communities perceived to be Arab or Muslim, especially in the aftermath of September 11, 2001."[21]

This means that the racism and cultural differences Arab families often experience in the West can lead to an intensification of nationalism and a reification of some sort of authentic cultural heritage. For diasporic subjects, this means that difference and dichotomies are heightened, and notions of what it means to be Arab in North America and Europe are radically different from being Arab in the Middle East. Importantly, Naber argues that for the Middle Eastern diaspora in the United States, gender and sexuality are among the most powerful symbols consolidating an imagined difference between Arabs and Americans. This has, more often than not, cast out queer Arabs and Middle Easterners from what it means to be an integrated part of the diaspora. As Naber reflects, "I learned that many of the Arabs I knew in the [San Francisco] Bay Area had more socially conservative understandings of Arab concepts of religion, family, gender, and sexuality than their counterparts in Jordan."[22]

The Islamicate queer subject becomes disruptive not only to ideas of authenticating diasporic cultural projects of survival but also equally to a larger set of imperialist dynamics whereby Islamicate queer subjects in the diaspora are used as part of a Western homocolonial project. Momin Rahman argues against the erroneously assumed mutual exclusivity between queer and Middle Eastern or Asian cultures and aims to illuminate the intersections and complexities of current binaries between and within Muslim communities and families, gay communities and culture, and wider Western political culture and discourses. Most importantly, Rahman argues that we must accept that the Muslim experience of sexual diversity politics is significantly different from the Western experience and that this reality undermines any assumption that the processes of "Muslim modernization" will inevitably lead to the same outcomes around sexuality as those experienced in the West. Thus, Middle Eastern homosexuality, including in the diaspora, will never look the same as Western homosexuality. Rahman goes on to define homocolonialism as "the deployment of LGBTIQ [*sic*] rights and visibility to stigmatize non-Western cultures and conversely reassert the supremacy of the Western nations and civilization." Specifically, Rahman characterizes "Western exceptionalism as the primary political idea that is triangulated through the process of homocolonialism."[23] Rahman posits that the queer Muslim subject is intersectional in the spaces they take up in society, and they naturally challenge the monolithic, monocultural versions of queer Western identity politics and the positioning of queer politics both in the Middle East and the diaspora. Here, the sheer existence of queer diasporic Muslims destabilizes Western queer discourse and the ways in which queer subjectivity is "knowable."

Articulations of Arabness, then, are grounded in Arab traditions and sensibilities about family, selfhood, and ways of being in the world, but they are also hybrid and historically contingent. Benedict Anderson has argued that nation, nationality, and nationalism have all proven notoriously difficult to define, let alone to analyze. He argues that "nationality," "nation-ness," and "nationalism" are cultural artifacts that require interrogation, especially their coming into being and the ways their meanings have changed over time.[24] Therefore, I propose to study the art of diasporic queer Middle Eastern subjects as artifacts of postcolonial nation-ness. This is all the more necessary given that a queer Middle Eastern diaspora has traditionally been excluded or written out of what it means to be Arab, Middle Eastern, or Muslim. Thus, in turning to them, new ways of imagining and reading postcolonial subjectivity in the diaspora can be afforded. Visual culture often provides another language to better articulate these complex identities and subjectivities. Therefore, I explore the potential that visual art of the queer diaspora has to disrupt authentic notions of Arabness and to expose a Western, neo-imperial, homogenous gay identity that remains a site of violence for the queer diaspora.

Queer Migration in the Art of Laurence Rasti

To illustrate the complexities of becoming a queer subject for the diasporic individual and how these experiences intersect with queer discourses in the Middle East, I turn to Laurence Rasti's photographic series *There Are No Homosexuals in Iran* (2017). Rasti was born to Iranian parents in Geneva, Switzerland. Using both Swiss and Iranian cultural codes, Rasti's photographs explore gender, identity, and migration. In *There Are No Homosexuals in Iran*, Rasti focuses on Iranian president Mahmoud Ahmadinejad's 2007 speech at Columbia University, where he proclaimed, "In Iran, we do not have homosexuals like in your country" (Rasti, preface). Coupled with interviews that voice the personal experiences of anonymous migrants, Rasti photographs asylum seekers in Denizili, Turkey, where hundreds of gay Iranian refugees are stuck in a transit zone. "Set in this state of limbo, where anonymity is the best protection," Rasti's photographs juxtapose and reimagine the facelessness these migrants experience in the transit zone with Ahmadinejad's attempts to erase their sexual identity from Iranian public consciousness. In one image in the series (figure 7.6), two women obscure each other by gently cupping their hands to each other's faces. This interplay of visibility and self-preservation is important within refugee and migrant experiences but also to queer experiences in both the Middle East and the diaspora. It is important to dispel the myth of a utopian gay liberation for the queer Middle Eastern diaspora in the Global North, for racial and community violence can be the source of physical and emotional pain as homophobic logics become entwined with articulating Arabness outside of the Middle East. As the historical-colonial heterosexualization of the Middle East inevitably led to criminalizing same-sex desires, so too does a heterosexualization take place in the diaspora as Middle Eastern cultures are forced into strongly held binaries based on anti-Muslim and anti-Brown racism in the Global North. The queer diaspora is, unfortunately, one of the casualties of the racist and homophobic forces that come from both host and home cultures.

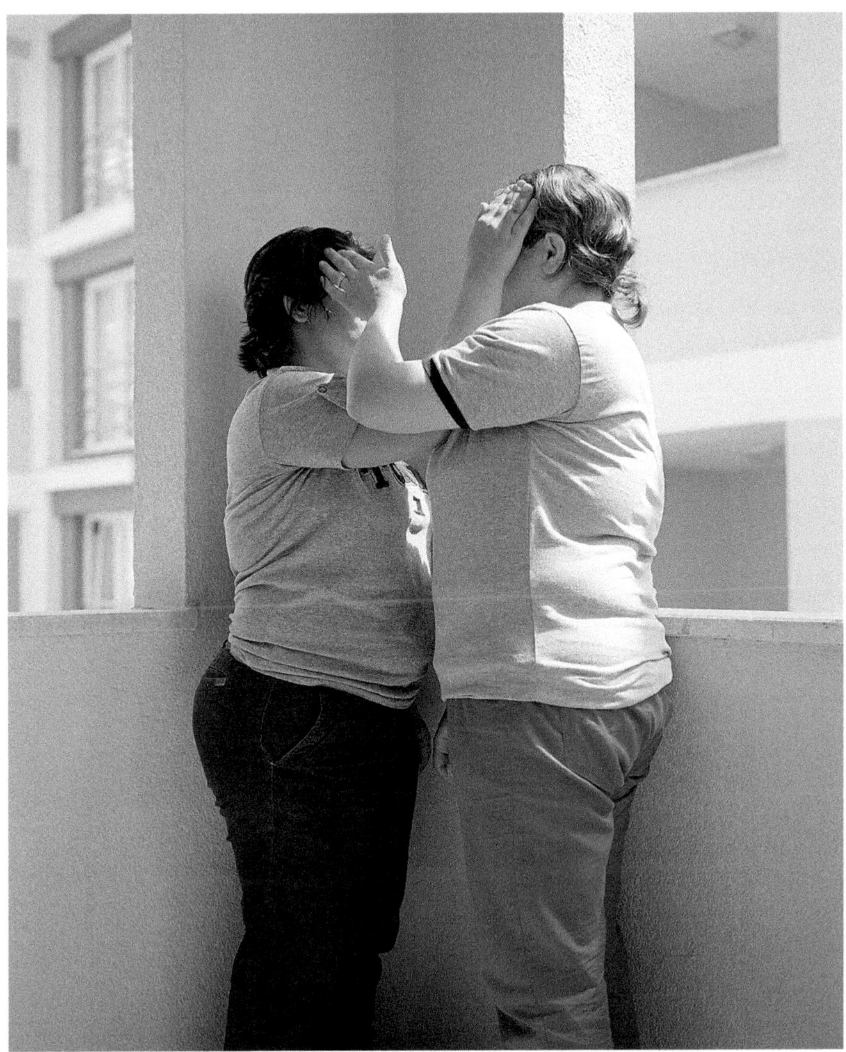

FIGURE 7.6. Laurence Rasti, photograph of two women from *There Are No Homosexuals in Iran* series (2014). Inkjet print. Courtesy of the artist.

For the two women in figure 7.6, their Iranian identity is in direct (and manufactured) conflict with their Iranian-ness and their queerness. The ways their Iranian nationality should somehow make them immune to feeling same-sex desire and the attitude that gay love can exist only in the West are both signs of sexual exceptionalism. Sexual exceptionalism occurs through stagings of a U.S. nationalism, for instance, that works in tandem with sexual othering, one that exceptionalizes the identities of U.S. citizens, often in contrast to Orientalist constructions of perverse "Muslim sexuality,"[25] Sexual exceptionalism is understood here as the possession of a feature, such as the West's ostensible championing gay rights or Iran's condemning homosexuality, that gives a unique mission to a state or a polity and is seen as an anchor to its national identity. This means that sexual exceptionalism, an example of which can be seen in Ahmadinejad's 2007 assertion that "in Iran, we do not have homosexuals like in your country," puts Iranian racial identities in direct opposition to a singular, and reductive, queer identity that corresponds to and comes out

7.7. *left* Laurence Rasti, photograph of two men from *There Are No Homosexuals in Iran* series (2014). Inkjet print. Courtesy of the artist.

7.8. *right* Laurence Rasti, from *There Are No Homosexuals in Iran* series (2014). Inkjet print. Courtesy of the artist. See also plate 16.

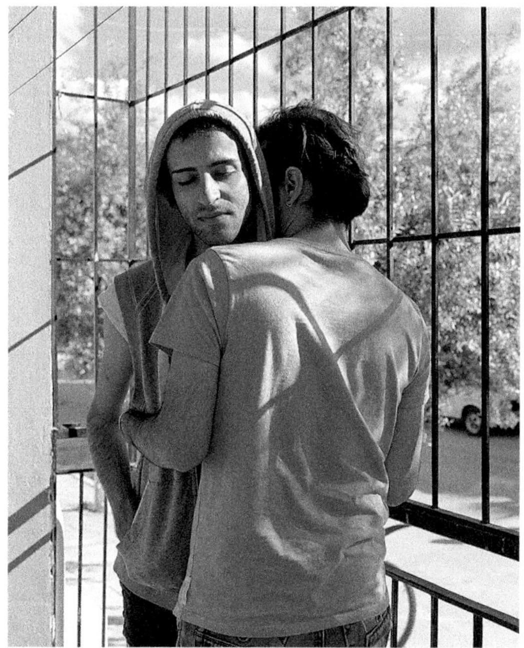

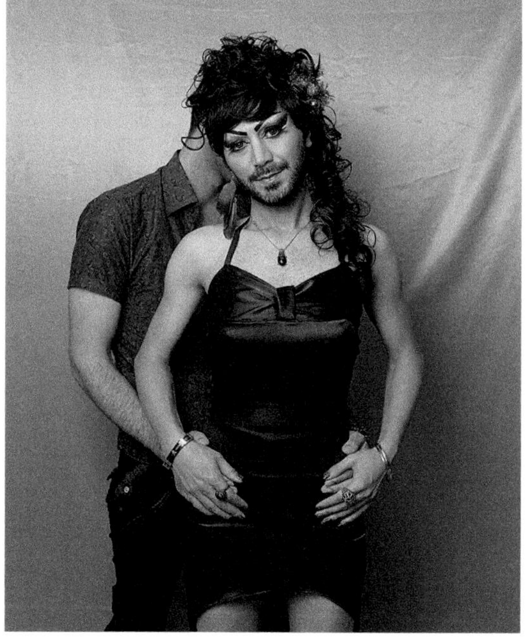

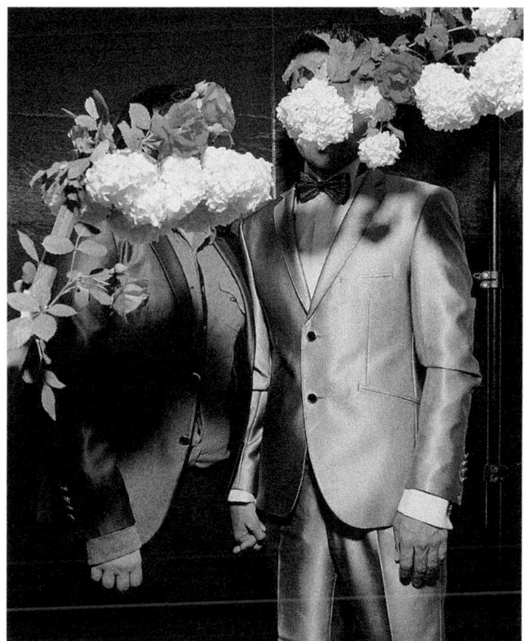

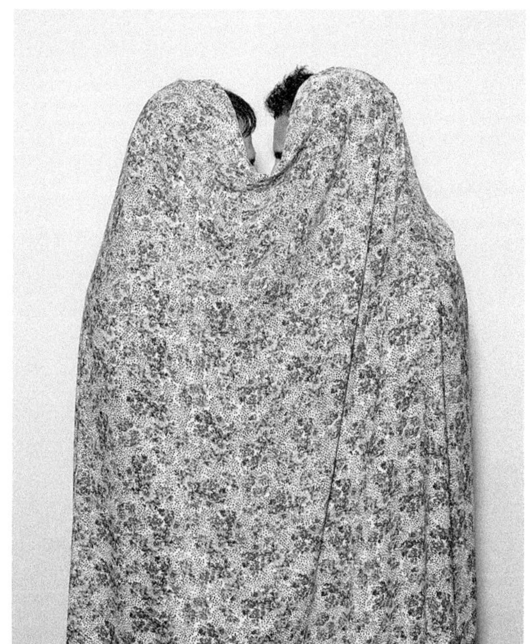

7.9. *left* Laurence Rasti, from *There Are No Homosexuals in Iran* series (2014). Inkjet print. Courtesy of the artist. See also plate 17.

7.10. *right* Laurence Rasti, from *There Are No Homosexuals in Iran* series (2014). Inkjet print. Courtesy of the artist. See also plate 18.

of the exceptionalism of the American empire's sexual freedoms. This dualism and "national homosexuality" is part of what Puar terms "homonationalism" and is a significant part of queer diasporic migrant experiences.[26]

The antagonistic dualism created when one's sexual identity seemingly contradicts their cultural identity is a tension that aims to define a normative script for both homosexuality and nationalism, placing aspects of racialized queer subjectivity in assumed conflict with one another. Not all subjects in Rasti's photographs are anonymous; some reveal their faces in these scenes of intimacy. Figure 7.7 shows two men standing outside, one embracing the other with his face nuzzled behind his companion's neck. The man being hugged, however, is fully visible to the viewer, closing his eyes in a peaceful embrace. Figure 7.8 similarly portrays two individuals embracing one another, this time with a man holding his partner's hips from behind as he shields his face. His partner, with long, curly hair and wearing a purple silk dress, however, has bold makeup and painted nails. The gender-fluid figure in the forefront makes

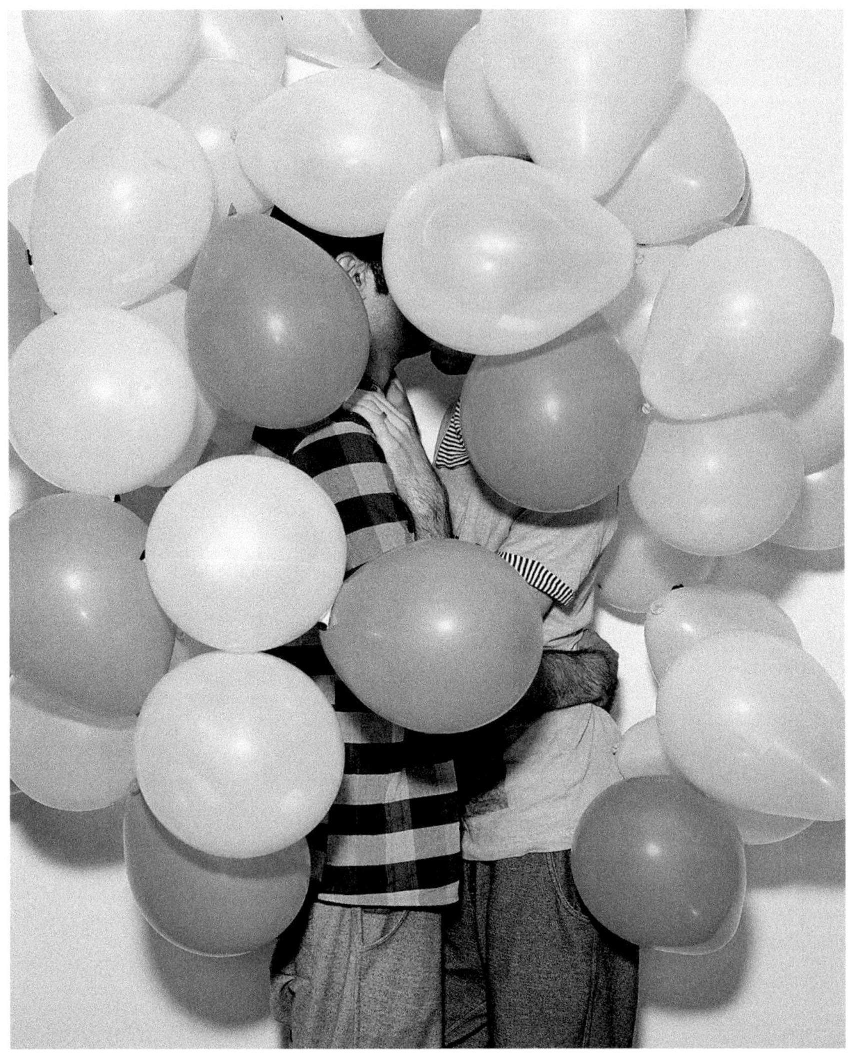

7.11. Laurence Rasti, from *There Are No Homosexuals in Iran* series (2014). Inkjet print. Courtesy of the artist. See also plate 19.

eye contact with the viewer, ensuring that the heavy eyeliner, pink lips, and unshaven beard do not go unnoticed. In this scene, both gender conventions and norms of beauty are questioned, revealing the very dualism that at once makes homosexuality punishable by death in Iran and racially stigmatized outside of the Middle East. This brand of homosexuality that the Middle East deems too American and America deems exceptional, as Puar argues, "operates as a regulatory script not only for normative gayness, queerness, or homosexuality, but also of the racial and national norms that reinforce these sexual subjects."[27] What does this tell us about the sociological and political landscape of the queer diaspora? As Gayatri Gopinath suggests, to understand queerness as diasporic and diaspora as queer is to recuperate "desires, practices, and subjectivities that are rendered impossible or unimaginable within conventional diasporic or nationalist imaginaries."[28] Such a critical framework of a "specifically queer diaspora . . . may begin to unsettle the ways in which the diaspora shores up the gender and sexual ideologies of dominant nationalism on the one hand, and processes of globalisation on the other."[29]

Visualizing Homocolonialism, Homonationalism, and Human Rights

It is important to contextualize decolonization as it pertains to homosexual tolerance and liberation in the Middle East. The arguments thus far presented take issue with the historical upset of Middle Eastern sexualities by an intolerant Western colonialism and more recently what Joseph Massad terms the "Gay International." These imperialist projects have in turn shaped local sexual discourses in the Middle East, which were more fluid and community-oriented and not identity-based, forcing a Western binary gender-identity model of heteronormativity onto the so-called Other in the Middle East. At the height of these colonial projects from the nineteenth and twentieth centuries, homosexuality was also illegal in the legal systems of the colonizers; consequently, the prohibition of homosexuality in the Middle East was a measure taken as part of a broader formula of mimicking Western modernity.[30] The legacies of Western imperialism on local sexual discourses were a catalyst for homophobic attitudes that more recently have sought to identify "primitive" sexual discourses in the Middle East and contrast these to the liberal sexual exceptionalism of the United States.

This dilemma is precisely where homocolonialism and homonationalism intersect. As a critique of lesbian and gay liberal rights discourses, homonationalism attends to how such discourses produce narratives of progress and modernity that continue to advance civilizational discourses in some contexts and limit the progression of the "backward" Other.[31] As Euro-American homocolonialism sought an erasure of same-sex desires in the Middle East, Euro-American homonationalism now champions the same-sex desires they once crushed in an effort to align gay liberation with modernity. Jasbir Puar argues that for the queer subject, national recognition and inclusion "is contingent upon the segregation and disqualifications of racial and sexual others from the national imaginary."[32] While homosexuality is currently restricted and criminalized in Middle Eastern societies but is relatively protected in certain Western cultures, contemporary discourses of sexual liberation need to be attentive to these histories of imperial violence at the risk of replicating the same coloniality that led to gay criminalization in the first place.[33] Homosexuality is illegal in ten of the eighteen Arab countries in Northern Africa and Western Asia (regions considered as Arab countries include Bahrain, Egypt, Iraq, Jordan, Kuwait, Lebanon, Libya, Mauritania, Morocco, Oman, Palestine, Qatar, Saudi Arabia, Sudan, the Syrian Arab Republic, Tunisia, the United Arab Emirates [UAE] and Yemen).[34] Muslim-majority countries like Tunisia and Algeria are not always included in the commonly accepted list of Arab countries because of their distinct location in the Maghrib, or Northwest Africa. Homosexuality is punishable by death in six of these eighteen countries. All sexual orientations are legal in Bahrain, Cyprus, Lebanon, Jordan, Turkey, and the settler state of Israel. Female homosexual activity is legal in Palestine and Kuwait; however, female homosexuality in Egypt is sporadically policed. Even though female homosexuality is less consistently punished when compared to men having sex with men, few of these countries recognize legal rights and provisions for gay individuals. Male homosexual activity is illegal and punishable by imprisonment in Kuwait, Egypt, Oman, Qatar, and Syria. It is punishable by death in Iran, Iraq, Saudi Arabia, Qatar, and the UAE. In Yemen and Palestine the punishment might differ between death and imprisonment depending on the act committed.[35]

In the Egyptian context, British occupation of formerly Ottoman territory in 1882 generated a political nationalism that was profoundly gendered in its rhetorical and material plans for liberating the nation.[36] This Victorian reordering of gender relations in Egypt, an example of homocolonialism, meant documenting and categorizing sexual "perversions," which are deviations from the expected Victorian norm of asexual femininity, "sexually passive women and heterosexually oriented men and women."[37] The British used domestic norms, marital customs, gender presentation, and codes of Egyptian masculinities and femininities to classify non-Western subjects as Other, and to justify and shape colonial policy for ruling Egypt.[38] Upon the British invasion and subsequent occupation of Egypt in 1882, British officials used these homocolonial logics to legitimize an expensive and seemingly unwanted extension of their overseas rule, claiming that Egyptians had to be reformed before they could have self-governance. The only way to correct these historical-colonial dynamics that caused irreparable damage for sexual discourses in the Middle East is a human rights advocacy that does not focus on protecting people's sexuality today in a monolithic version of queerness that is manufactured in and exported from the Global North.[39] Echoing Massad's claims, this suggests that human rights discourses that seek to replicate Western queer models of identity will only reproduce imperial control over sexual discourses in the Middle East.

So what does decolonization refer to as it pertains to homosexual tolerance and liberation in the Middle East? Queer theory literature on the region takes issues with the historical upset of Middle Eastern sexualities by an intolerant Western colonialism and, more recently, what Joseph Massad terms the "Gay International."[40] Arab cultures, he explains, have always expressed same-sex desires, but he warns that these homosocial and homoerotic histories should not be read through the taxonomy of homosexuality. Instead, this imperialist pressure imposed predefined sexual identities in the Middle East that impacted gender fluidity and sexual desires that were not identity-based, forcing a Western binary gender-identity model of heteronormativity in the Middle East, Africa, and Asia.[41] At the time of this colonial contact, homosexuality was also illegal in the judicial systems of the Western colonizers, and the laws instated all over the Middle East to criminalize homosexuality, including Egypt, were imports from British and French homophobic legislation. Therefore, homosexuality as taboo and prohibited in the Middle East was a relatively more recent measure taken to replicate the formula of Western modernity after increased contact with Western travelers and imperialists in the region.

Dangers of Heterosexualization through the Art of Nilbar Güreş

These sexual codes of conduct have lasting effects on the Middle Eastern diaspora, both in the queerness of diasporic subjects, illustrated through Shojaian's artwork, and on an exilic formation of people who flee the region to escape persecution, as seen in the subjects of Rasti's photographic series.[42] The heterosexualization of a Middle Eastern culture that actively denies the existence of same-sex desires has very real consequences. The violence inflicted on queer bodies can be seen in the photo-video installation *Torn* (2018) by diasporic artist Nilbar Güreş, a Turkish artist who lives and works in Vienna (figure 7.12). Güreş's artwork explores female identity, the relationships between women and domestic/public spaces, as well as intersectional, transnational, and transcultural queer identity. Güreş uses video and photography to tell the story of her friend Didem, a transgender woman who was continually discriminated against and aggressively harassed for being queer in Turkey. In the installation, a one-channel video shows Didem standing defiantly in the center of the frame, arms crossed as she stares into the camera, meeting the viewer's gaze. Behind her is a rectangular textile with deep orange and red patterns that frames her head like a halo. The video slowly zooms in on Didem while a low guttural sound reverberates through the speakers. She stands still throughout the video, making each scene reminiscent of a photograph capturing a moment in time. It is only in moments when the wind gently blows through her hair or with fluttering blinks of her eyelashes that the audience realizes that Didem is actively present and standing witness by looking back at the viewer. The video ends with Didem walking away from the frame and revealing the full textile that was partially hidden behind her. Hanging on the rooftop balcony in Didem's hometown of Izmir, the viewer sees a large tear in the textile, once concealed by Didem's presence in the frame. This slash tells the tragic story of when Didem was brutally dragged into a car in Istanbul, robbed, and almost murdered when attackers slit her throat. In the textile, Güreş uses scissors to cut a large, elongated hole in the shape of the scar on Didem's neck. According to Güreş, the cut in the cloth "references the violent emptiness of a society that tries to cover itself up through its victims. LGBTQAI [Lesbian, Gay, Bisexual, Trans, Queer, Asexual, Intersex] people are the victims of hate crimes."[43]

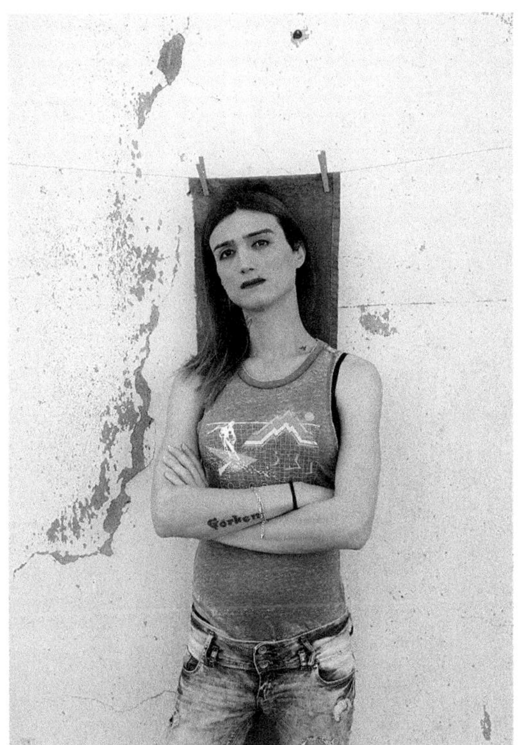

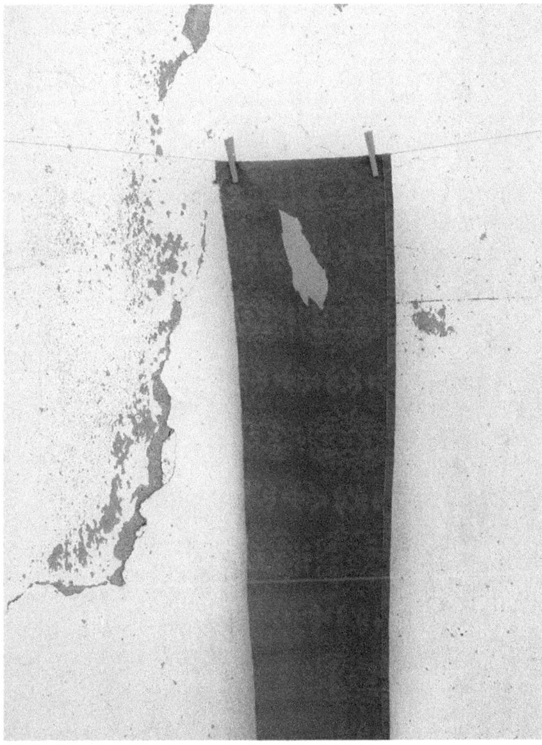

FIGURE 7.12. Nilbar Güreş, still image from video *Torn* (2018). HD video, color, sound, 6:00 min. Courtesy of the artist and Martin Janda Gallery, Vienna.

Considering Güreş's artwork in relation to Shojaian's and Rasti's visual art brings interesting connections and frictions to the notion of queer diaspora. In *Torn*, Nilbar Güreş is creating art from the diaspora about the trauma and violence her queer loved ones experience in her homeland of Turkey. Laurence Rasti is creating art from the diaspora about queer migration and the struggle for queer refugees from Iran patiently waiting for asylum from their transit zones in Turkey. Alireza Shojaian produces visual art from the diaspora about the history of colonial violence and sexual imperialism relating to his Iranian heritage and the violence suffered by queer subjects in Iran. These examples provide a rich site to interrogate: What makes an artwork queer? What makes an artwork diasporic? If "diasporic art" as a didactic and visual category demands that the art itself be produced in the diaspora, this signals that an artist's diasporic identity is the driving force in determining the diasporic nature and content of the art.

When asking what makes an artwork queer, similar slippages happen to the logic that governs our understanding of complex formations of race, sexuality, and visuality. Does the queerness of an artwork lie in the queer content of the artwork or in the queerness of the artist? One then has to question the reductive nature to categorize and delimit certain visual practices as belonging to "gay art" or "minority art" and instead see the full potential of queer diasporic formations. When freed from the disciplinary and academic distinctions between discursive categories such as "queer" or "diasporic," queer diasporic visual practices that foreground the personal can "create deeply affective counter-archives of regional (un)belonging" regardless of place.[44] Gayatri Gopinath's newest study on the aesthetic practices of the queer diaspora teaches us that asking these questions and creating these disciplinary ruptures within our logics illuminate the unexpected convergences between seemingly disparate sites of analysis. In particular, part of the rubric for the "aesthetic practices of the queer diaspora" that Gopinath puts forth is the unexpected convergences between "the interrogation of the visual field and the limits of a politics of visibility and representation, on the one hand, and on the other hand queerness as an optic and reading practice that brings alternative modes of affiliation and relationality into focus."[45]

Diasporic Bodies and Queer World Making

To better situate these artistic expressions and literature within ideas of a queer diaspora, it is useful to think of identity formation in relation to queer world making. This means reassessing the gatekeeping mechanisms that have dictated some bodies as queer, diasporic, or both, and, depending on the transnational context, neither. As this analysis of contemporary visual art illustrates, queerness finds a way to dwell and remain in seemingly "inhospitable" places like the Middle East, Africa, and Asia. It begs the question: Who defines queer hospitality? The answer, of course, is Western queerness and its unquestionable authenticity. The frictions and tensions that queer bodies can have within the Middle East might be lessened in other locales, but these places can be sites in which diasporic bodies are the source of racial tensions and violence. The queer diaspora is often the queer Black and Brown body, and the process of racialization, as well as sexualization, is where the queer diaspora is constituted. To demystify the fallacy that it is contradictory to be both Brown and queer, it is vital to challenge the concept of stable or fixed identities that foreclose other ways of being. Postcolonial theorist Homi Bhabha argues that cultural hybridity results from various forms of colonization and leads to cultural collisions and interchanges. In the attempt to assert colonial power and create civilized subjects, "the trace of what is disavowed is not repressed but repeated as something different—a mutation, a hybrid."[46] This hybrid subject, or the contemporary queer diaspora, contradicts both the attempt to fix and control indigenous cultures and the illusion of cultural authenticity or purity. Here, the notion of the in-between is relevant, for the queer diasporic is then left with opposing views of Western and non-Western sexual practices, a tense historical framing of Arab-sexual discourses, all the while being measured by Western narratives of modernity, progress, and enlightened (Euro-American) sexual identity. In these performances and failures, belongings and exclusions, recognitions and disidentifications, the postcolonial queer subject articulates nation-ness in complex ways, a process that is better informed by the visual art they produce.

CONCLUSION
QUEER WORLD MAKING, DIASPORA CONSCIOUSNESS, AND FUTURITY

I have explored the ways in which diasporic articulation of culture is integral to understanding how Middle Eastern sexuality narratives can function globally and are internalized/reconceptualized by diasporic sexualities in North America and within Europe. Rather than articulating Arabness outside of imperial history and under the purview of Orientalist stigma, reconceptualizing Arabness from different diasporic perspectives helps delineate historic narratives of migration and cultural identity. As argued throughout this book, highlighting the visual art of the diasporic individual has the potential to complicate the absurdity of Orientalist discourse, allowing for a sociological understanding of how community and belonging are made across the diaspora. By correlating racial identity with gender performativity, herein lies the possibility of decolonizing and rearticulating Arabness beyond Orientalism and historically racist representations. My hope is that the visual analyses, theoretical engagements, and critiques that this research offers mark an instance of that possibility.

In this book, I conducted deep readings of visual art as case studies to investigate Middle Eastern diasporic artists in North America and Europe who are creating political art surrounding queer identity. These artists' art production, read together, provides methodology and analytic approaches to better explore colonial contact zones as a way of expanding upon and contributing to the growing scholarship on Middle Eastern contemporary art and cultural studies. By incorporating different sociological strategies in the analysis of contemporary art, this research developed as a way to make self-identification categories less dichotomous and more expansive. Through visual analysis and multitemporal comparative studies, I have theorized the various mechanisms of resistance that allow artworks of Arab artists in the diaspora to illustrate queer identities that are different from the global-to-local homocolonialism of Western gay identity, and to provide examples of how local networks of identity are transmitted through visual language and how alternative sexuality scripts are written within transnational contexts.

In examining the artworks of diasporic contemporary artists Jamil Hellu, Ebrin Bagheri, 2Fik, Alireza Shojaian, Laurence Rasti, and Nilbar Güreş, I have focused on the concept of multiple modernisms and their relationship to displacement, trauma, and Arab sexualities/masculinities/femininities within a postcolonial and anti-imperialist framework. Global art histories and transnational queer theory are pillars of my theoretical framework, and a postcolonial approach is instrumental in locating contemporary notions of sexual discourse in the Middle East.[1] Such a postcolonial framework illuminated the necessary cause-and-effect relationship that historic sexuality discourses have had on contemporary understandings of sexuality and how this history affects those currently living in the diaspora. Histories of multiple modernisms are evidence of modernity as a period of industrialized and economic growth happening outside the Global North, and this concept is a critical approach to queer theory and art history in its capacity to decenter European humanist thought that has universalized Western progress as the only mode of cultural advancement. This discussion is part of a decolonial inquiry that works to reframe Islamicate homosexualities in terms of desire and alternative masculinities/femininities rather than through Western notions of visibility and coming out; narratives that are not conducive to understanding how queer Arabs living in the West experience their sexuality.

As demonstrated by the visual art analyzed within this study, diaspora consciousness is a major proponent to keeping alive the link between the precolonial past and a contemporary diasporic present. It is interesting to note how diaspora consciousness manifests itself in varying ways and the psychological processes that shape both belonging and subject formation for the queer diaspora. In the case of Jamil Hellu, diaspora consciousness is a powerful tool that connects his lived experiences and personal understandings of what it means to be a queer man with Syrian heritage. Associating his trauma with the Victorian-era homocolonialism that wreaked havoc on local ways of being, Hellu's diaspora consciousness holds an imperial violence that shapes the way he understands his own identity in relation to his culture.

This utterance of pain and loss is manifested differently for Ebrin Bagheri, because his diaspora consciousness was the driving force behind the unintentional imagery of his artistic creations. Unaware of the specific archives to which his artwork bears similarities, the power of diaspora consciousness to shape subjectivity is seen on a deeply hidden level within his oeuvre. Bagheri's drawings, which are based on his imagination, are so woven within narratives of Persian history and cultural identity that the ways of understanding his own contemporary sexuality are inseparable from these mechanics. The subconscious or involuntary referencing of historical ways of being and the deep history of Orientalism and objectification inflicted onto local young men in Islamicate regions bear great weight on how he sees this historic past as being related to his current identity. For Bagheri, diaspora consciousness becomes a driving force that informs his visual art production and the indexical meaning that is associated with the imagery he creates.

In contrast to Bagheri, 2Fik uses historical remembering as a visual strategy to depict how fragile and vulnerable subjectivity is formed. 2Fik's artworks are indicative of an art practice that directly connects diaspora consciousness to a queer futurity in its capacity to visualize trauma and culture transtemporally, and kinship is reimagined in complex ways through the characters he develops. Weaving historical trauma with diasporic futurity and queer contemporaneity, then, is vital to understanding the ways in which art production can be a valuable site for understanding the formation of diaspora consciousness on a deeply personal level. As demonstrated throughout this study, diaspora consciousness is an integral component to embedding colonial histories, trauma, and loss within diasporic experiences today, intertwining culturally traditional ways of understanding gender, sexuality, and the self with contemporary ways of being. In other words, the very ways in which queer diasporic artists articulate diaspora consciousness—by having components of former, colonized, historic ways of understanding gender and sexual identity—is indeed noteworthy.

For Alireza Shojaian, his PaykanArtCar created impact from several different sites. Initially working from within Iran, Shojaian's queer art was censored; when planning to exhibit the PaykanArtCar in Paris, his art was once again censored. His experiences break apart the fallacy of Europe being a safe haven for queers, and the assumed open-mindedness that is stereotypically associated with European nations is shattered when coupled with the racism and homophobia Shojaian experienced in Paris. Shojaian centers his work on the brutal murder of Alireza Fazeli-Monfared that took place in Iran days before his attempted escape to Turkey, where he was going to reunite with his boyfriend, Aghil Bayat, who was seeking asylum while in a refugee camp. This heartbreaking individual story nonetheless is linked to countless others with similar experiences in Laurence Rasti's photographic series *There Are No Homosexuals in Iran*, photographing queer Iranian refugees seeking asylum in Turkey. With Rasti demonstrating the real perils of homonationalism when queerness is used as a marker of the state, Shojaian illustrates the impact homocolonialism has had on local gender and sexual discourses in Iran by using the eleventh-century Book of Kings as his source material. Likewise, the experiences of Didem and the transphobic violence they experienced in Nilbar Güreş's video is the unfortunate outcome of homonationalism and homocolonialism creating the vulnerabilities and threats to safety that queer subjects experience.

Ultimately, the study of diaspora means having to contend with the colonial moment, and I shift my methodological approach to investigate the history of colonialism through the photographic archive. I believe this methodological shift from studying a history of sexuality to investigating a history of colonial encounter provides a more productive way of exploring queer identity in the diaspora and its relationship to local ways of being. This book has done a queer diasporic reading of both contemporary art and the colonial archives in order to have them resonate with the themes of trauma, displacement, and unbelonging that echo from queer diasporic identity.

In my linking of diasporic contemporary art with historical archives of both visual culture and queer theory, this scholarship is a part of an intellectual effort that by default discusses the recent past and the present condition for the queer Middle Eastern diaspora. Even through the purview of the historical archive, the case studies and frameworks offered in this analysis show that it is through both the visual analysis and the focus on contemporary artists that histories of colonial violence and imperial logics must be better linked to the current experiences of queer desire in the Middle East and in the diaspora.

The conditions of immigration and a family's settlement experience could lay the groundwork for examining a subject's internalization of historical traumas. The dominant narrative around coming out is that it is a vital part of self-actualization and fulfilment as a queer individual. This narrative is connected to liberation, freedom, relief, an immediate reduction in stress and isolation, and, ultimately, a promise of having a weight lifted off your shoulders. Within this narrative, it is only after coming out that a person truly experiences pride. For the queer diaspora, however, the challenges are particularly unique for a lot of LGBTQ Middle Eastern subjects living in North America or Europe, and the benefits of coming out don't always outweigh the challenges. The biggest of these challenges includes fear and rejection—not just from family but also from one's faith and from one's community. Within a cultural setting, if a queer racialized subject has been socialized to think about a system in the world that punishes them for their sins, and they come to understand themselves as sinful, then that can be a major difficulty to overcome or to work through.[2] Aside from the religious and cultural value judgments that are associated with a particular gay identity that is understood differently around the world, there is also the challenge of visibility within the normative coming out narrative in the West. Often for the queer diaspora, a paramount concern if one comes out is how will that affect their family or their community? And in terms of self-preservation techniques that the queer diaspora employs, does their sudden visibility, whether it is on social media or at a queer event, make it harder for them to compartmentalize their life when compartmentalization might actually be a very necessary form of protection for them?

In their article "The Whiteness of 'Coming Out': Culture and Identity in the Disclosure Narrative," Asiel Adan Sanchez, who identifies as Latino and nonbinary, talks about how coming out might erase the nuances of their cultural identity. In their Latin American culture, the concept of pride is seen as sinful and indulgent, so the idea of celebrating pride goes against a community value of humility. They describe having their partner come visit them at home to have dinner with their family and that their family, by and large, accepts their partner. However, they can appreciate that if they asked for explicit conversation and acceptance from their parents, or for the other person to be named as their boyfriend, then their parents would be less receptive. They suggest that seeking explicit acceptance in this very particular way is actually a Western construct and that if they try to do that, it erases the ways that their family has already come to accept them and undermines their cultural identity, where acceptance looks different.[3] It is important to understand that for the queer diaspora, such dichotomous thinking about needing to choose between coming out or their family, between their sexuality and their community, is a false dichotomy based on a Western coming out narrative. The underlying problem here is that dominant culture teaches us that queerness is rooted in whiteness, and in this way, internal identity conflict, anticipation of loss, and opposing communities of belonging are rooted in white supremacy.[4]

As previously mentioned in this book, narrative psychologist Sekneh Hammoud-Beckett coined the term "letting-in" as a way to negotiate and alter Western narratives of coming out. This is a process that she describes as the conscious and selective invitation of people into one's "club of life" as she puts it.[5] Here, letting-in is a process that is highly relevant to the diaspora, as it is a way to alter perceptions of what it means to live a truly gay life, and falsifies the Western need to become more visible in order to be complete. Likewise, social worker Rahim Thawer writes about a similar paradigm that is helpful for the queer diaspora, and that is the concept of "coming in"—that is, coming into one's identity and sharing that identity intentionally with people they trust. To him, "One's place in the world needs to be neither destabilized by nor contingent upon the big coming out experience—it can be done selectively, following some simple cost-benefit calculations."[6] What both of these ideas demonstrate is that the factor that still needs thorough attention is the dichotomous thinking imposed on racialized queer subjects: that we must choose between sexuality and culture/religion, as this logic incites so much dissonance, conflict, and loss. In this book I have attempted to historicize homophobia globally in an effort to denaturalize these dichotomies between sexuality and culture/religion. These dichotomies create violence, trauma, and severe non-belonging that continue to have lasting effects on the queer diaspora. These dichotomies likewise create violence, trauma, and a safety risk for queer subjects in the region, and I have aimed to historicize the Orientalism that blindly marks Middle Eastern societies as homophobic and unproblematically labels Western societies as progressive. In demonstrating the falsity of these logics and historicizing why homophobia shapes queer experiences in the region and in the diaspora, I hope there becomes a greater postcolonial and antiracist understanding of human rights discourses that truly liberate, protect, and advocate for queer subjects transnationally.

There is something to be said for isolation and how isolation can be weaponized and used against the queer diaspora by their families and communities. The fear of coming out is often the fear of losing one's family and being completely alone. If a person does come out or is outed to their family or community, there might also be an imposed isolation to distance the family or community from the queer subject. It is this moment of isolation that I would like to reflect on. In this event comes feelings of abandonment and the confusion of why this feeling of non-belonging seems to be imposed from external forces. Once in this isolated space, there are a few things that happen to the queer diaspora, as their culture becomes difficult to access and perform. Take, for instance, the issue of language: When a queer racialized subject is isolated from their community of native-language speakers, where will they continue to practice their language and continue speaking their mother tongue? When members of the queer diaspora are isolated from their families and communities, how do they learn to cook the traditional food and recipes they grew up with? When phoning your mother for her tips and suggestions on cooking your favorite dish becomes an impossibility, how do you still foster connection with your cultural roots? After being disowned when it becomes impossible to access family photo albums, your baby pictures, or stories from your family history and past, how else do you find closeness to your heritage when isolation can create a rupture of sorts?

This isolation is more than physical; it is psychological and has ramifications beyond the abandonment of family and not feeling the unconditional love that parents should give their children. Instead, there is a cultural abandonment at play here as well. For when the queer diasporic subject is isolated in this way, their culture becomes a bargaining chip that is also taken away from them by the family and community who are closely related to culture and heritage. For the queer diaspora facing isolation, these seemingly minor

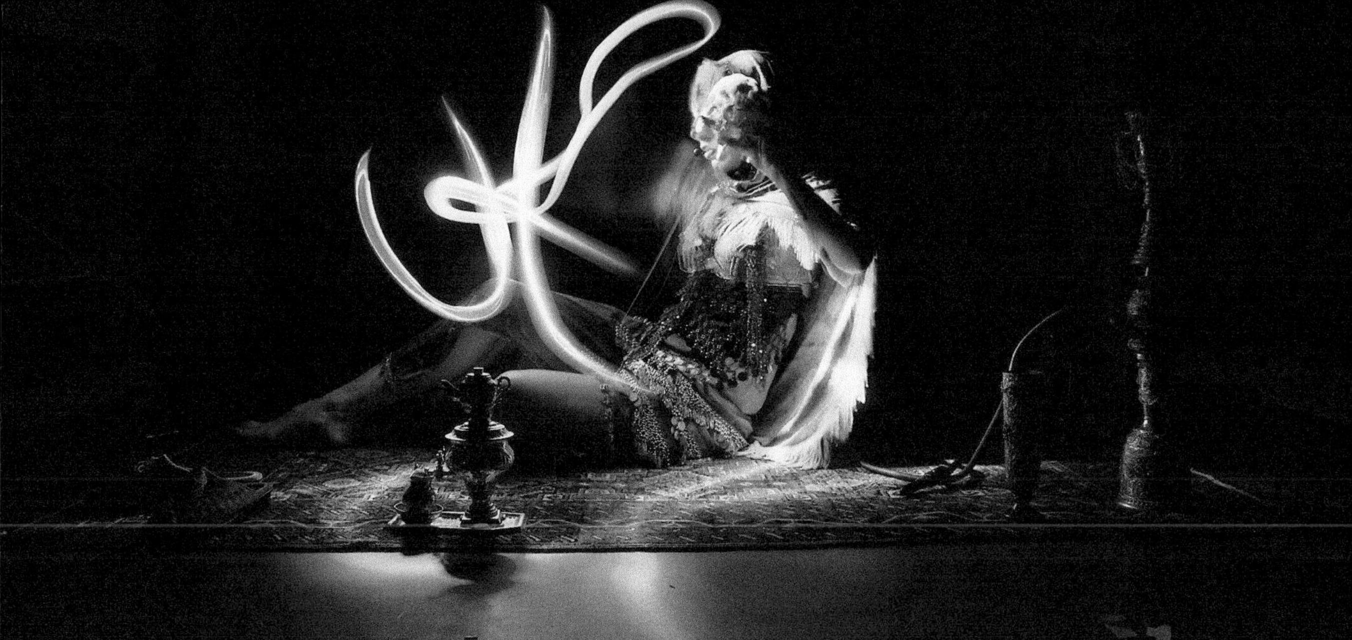

8.1. Rah Eleh, *Sham*, light drawing photography (2013). Courtesy of the artist. See also plate 20.

details—like speaking your native language less and less, or not being able to easily have access to eating your traditional food—become a major source of loss. It is then that an isolated queer diaspora has to forge new connections to their heritage and establish new roots in the culture they now have a hard time feeling connected to. Some strategies I have found noteworthy are abandoning the desire for "mom's recipe" and instead learning the traditional way to make cultural dishes; in my case, gradually learning how to cook Egyptian meals gave me a sense of power. Not only did it feel powerful to take control of the cultural isolation that was imposed on me, but each time I cooked these meals I felt connected to my culture, my heritage, and my ancestors.

On the topic of language within the diaspora, I would like to introduce the artwork of Iranian Canadian artist Rah Eleh, currently based in Toronto. In this 2013 photograph titled *Sham* (figure 8.1), Rah uses light drawing to try to write her own name in Farsi. *Light painting, painting with light, light drawing*, and *light art performance photography* are terms that describe photographic techniques of moving a light source while taking a long-exposure photograph, often to shine light at the camera to "draw" or by moving the camera itself during exposure of light sources. Light drawing is ephemeral, and Rah repeats the action over and over again to try to reproduce her name in a language she does not read or write due to her experiences as a diasporic woman in Canada. Often an overlooked symptom of diaspora, language is commonly lost through the assimilation process that we call immigration, and many first- and second-generation people in the diaspora slowly lose their language, or their immigrant parents purposely do not teach them their mother tongue, in order to fit in better within Canadian and North American contexts. Cultural exclusion and cultural authenticity are tensions within this artwork, as seen in different Orientalist tropes found throughout the scene,

FIGURE 8.2. Rah Eleh, *Oriental Drag*, film still (2013). Courtesy of the artist. See also plate 21.

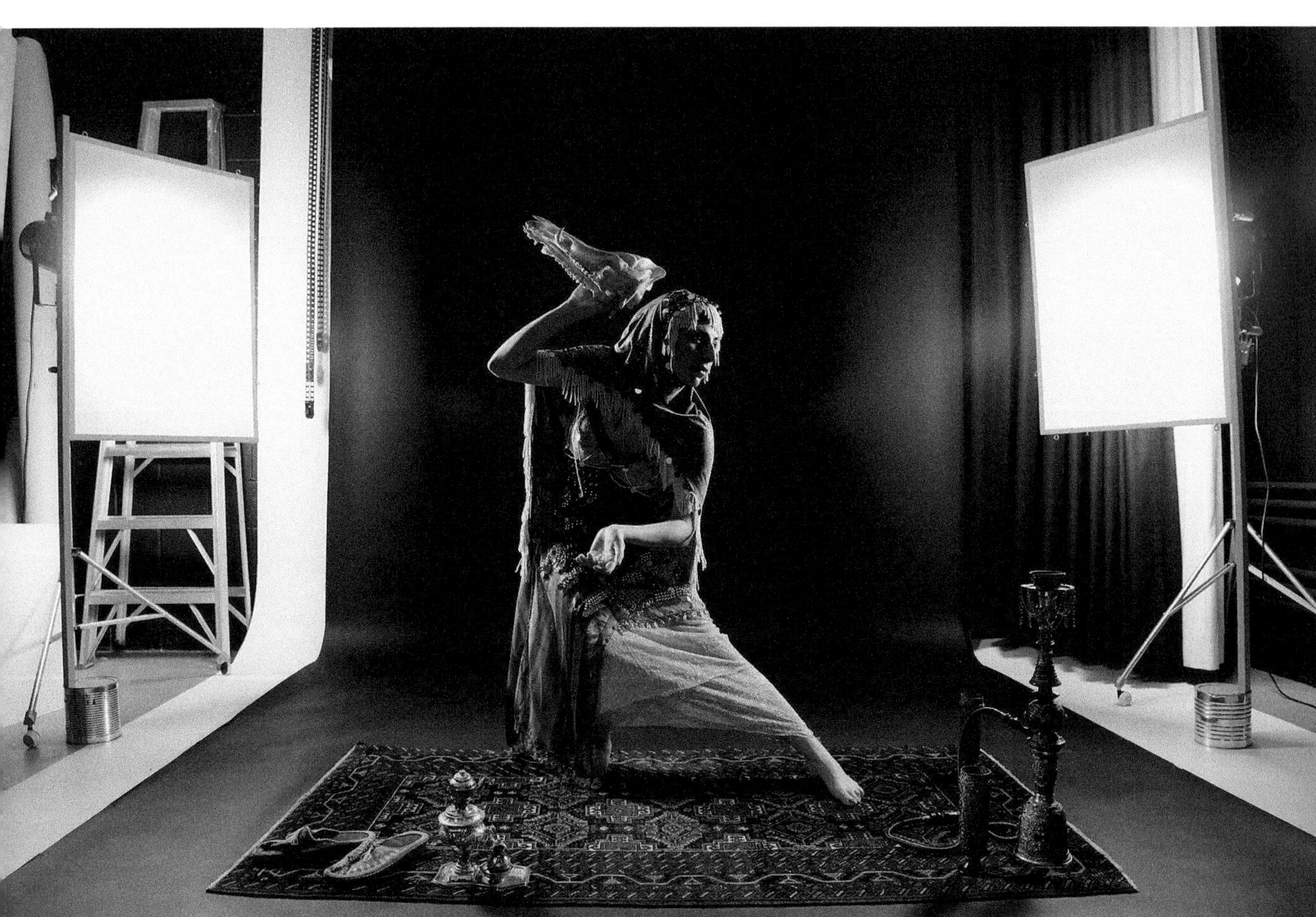

to highlight the unique plight of diasporic individuals in Canada as they navigate migrant identities.

Like many in the diaspora, Rah speaks the Farsi she learned talking with her family growing up, but the need to learn how to write or read Farsi was not as valued during the immigration process and growing up in Canada after arriving as a young child. This is a very common pattern repeated in many immigrant households, where a mother tongue is learned for family conversations but English-language learning is prioritized over learning how to read and write the parents' native language. In addition to creating a linguistic, cultural, and ideological divide between immigrant and refugee parents and the diasporic children growing up between two worlds, these issues of language are often used as measures of cultural authenticity. Diasporic individuals can be seen as outsiders within their own cultural communities because of these differences in language, even mocked for not speaking their native language well enough. When this is coupled with the isolation felt being in the queer diaspora, these issues of language and searches for cultural authenticity become lifelong searches for belonging and acceptance.

These features of diasporic identity can often be issues of hybridity and cultural translation. I would like to close this book by reflecting on this point through more of Rah Eleh's visual art. In figure 8.2, we see a film still from Rah's video work *Oriental Drag*. This video was made using a stop-motion technique that consists of one thousand photographs edited together to make a video. The poses in each image are inspired by hip-hop, vogue, and traditional Iranian dancing, and the mélange of fragmented poses and dance styles creates a new hybrid dance that is neither Western nor Persian. Aesthetically, the first thing that is noticeable to the viewer is likely how constructed the image looks, taking place in what seems to be a photo studio. The artist makes no effort to conceal the mechanics of taking these images, instead showing the audience all of the ways she constructed this scene, making visible the camera studio, lighting, and camera equipment. It is this construction of the image that I want to explore. In the work, Rah seems to be dancing on what looks like a Persian rug, embroidered slippers off to the side, and flanking the carpet is an incense burner and a hookah pipe. In the still images, it looks as though Rah herself is dressed in traditional Persian garments and is dancing a traditional Persian dance. Knowing the hybrid forms that Rah is using to combine dance, clothing, and objects from different cultures, showing the viewer how the image is manufactured and created becomes an important point. The process involved in making this artwork is as important as the image itself. For Rah to show us the constructed, artificial, and highly curated scene, she is questioning notions of cultural authenticity and forces the viewer to consider what cultural purity even means. As a racialized woman in the diaspora, ideas of being authentically Iranian or authentically Canadian seem to contradict, and Rah here wants us to see and visualize this contradiction.

As I have traced throughout this book, Middle Eastern contemporary art by the queer diaspora is fraught with tensions of hybridity, coloniality, transnationalism, and citizenship. Through these various artists, we see how colonial traumas are repercussions of, and linked to, contemporary ways of being both diasporic and queer. Queer diasporic artists in North America and Europe use tropes such as performance, visibility, historical reimagining, character creation, humor, pastiche, and satire as a way of laying bare colonial traumas within Middle Eastern contemporary art. The traumas that the diasporic subject carries are tied to settler colonial histories in both home countries, with the Western imperial forces often at work in the Middle East, and even in host countries, as immigration is often an important factor in multicultural nationalism, like that found in Canada. In creating a visual description of colonial trauma that links an imperially traumatic past to a complicated homophobic and racist present day, contemporary Middle Eastern diasporic artists in North America and Europe reenvision their relationships between homeland/host-land to complicate the relationship between the local and the global, the traditional and the modern, and, most importantly, the self and the nation.

Prologue

1. "Subaltern" refers to the social group that is socially, politically, and geographically outside of the hegemonic power structure. Largely informed by Michel Foucault, Gayatri Spivak has been instrumental in writing about the voice and resistance of the subaltern. For more, see Chakravorty, *In Other Worlds*; Spivak, *A Critique of Postcolonial Reason*. I also acknowledge my privilege in having the opportunity and platform to develop these ideas as a first-generation Egyptian Canadian growing up in a suburb of Toronto, and my voice is informed by this subject position.

2. Fournier, *Autotheory as Feminist Practice in Art, Writing, and Criticism*, 7.

3. Fournier, *Autotheory as Feminist Practice in Art, Writing, and Criticism*, 2.

Introduction

1. I define the "Middle East" loosely as the geopolitical designation of western Asia and Northeast Africa that includes the nations on the Arabian Peninsula, Egypt, Iran, Iraq, Jordan, Lebanon, Palestine, Syria, and Turkey. Even though some of these regions, like Iran and Turkey, are not technically a part of the Middle East, a historiographical emphasis makes it integral to include regions that were connected by empire, culture, and language. It is worth noting that "Arab" is an ethnolinguistic category, identifying people who speak the Arabic language as their mother tongue. Arabs trace their national roots to the twenty-two member states of the League of Arab States: Egypt, Sudan, Jordan, Syria, Lebanon, Iraq, Saudi Arabia, Kuwait, Bahrain, Qatar, United Arab Emirates, Oman, Yemen, Djibouti, Somalia, Eritrea, Libya, Tunisia, Algeria, Comoros, Morocco, and Mauritania. Religiously, they include Muslims (Sunnis, Shiites, Alawites, and Ismailis), Christians (Protestants, Catholics, Greek Orthodox, Coptic Orthodox, Caldeans, Assyrians, and Maronites), and Jews. Unlike Arabs, Middle Eastern people come from countries of the Arabian Peninsula.

2. Rahman, *Homosexualities, Muslim Cultures, and Modernity*, 7.

3. Rahman, *Homosexualities, Muslim Cultures, and Modernity*, 118.

4. Massad, "Re-Orienting Desire," 362.

5. See El-Rouayheb, *Before Homosexuality in the Arab-Islamic World, 1500–1800*; Ze'evi, *Producing Desire*; Massad, "Re-Orienting Desire"; Najmabadi, *Women with Mustaches and Men without Beards*; Boone, *The Homoerotics of Orientalism*.

6. Ze'evi, *Producing Desire*, 150. For a partial description of this travel literature, see Findley, "An Ottoman Occidentalist in Europe," 15.

7. In 1974 Marshall G. S. Hodgson published *The Venture of Islam: Conscience and History in a World Civilization* and coined the term *Islamicate* as a way of opening up the borders posed by modern scholarship. Hodgson identifies the issue in using the terms *Islam* and *Islamic* in unspecific ways, outlining that when one speaks of "Islamic literature or art," one is speaking less about Islam as a faith. To make this distinction,

Islamicate is used to refer not directly to the religion of Islam itself but to the social and cultural complexities historically associated with Islam, Muslims, and inclusive of non-Muslims living within the same region. This reading of the Islamicate can foster new meanings not only to "Islamic art" but can also include art from other regions of the world that share colonial histories and are linked in various ways.

8. See Marshall G. S. Hodgson, *Venture of Islam*, 57, 59.

9. I use *transnationalism* in my research in a way that is conscious of the tension inherent within the term *trans-national*. This tension exists on a methodological level wherein the nation-state is the primary foil in which to situate cultural paradigms within the global. In an effort to locate transnationalism within a paradigm that stressed complex connections and slippages between the local and the global, I use *transnational* in my study as synonymous to *trans-local* and *trans-regional*. For more on the study of transnationalism, see Freitag and von Oppen, *Translocality*.

10. Understanding the queer diaspora, both as a terminology and as a subject position, requires the simultaneous consideration of cultural production by the Arab diaspora in North America as well as a contestation of the gender and sexual politics of the nation in the diasporic context.

11. According to Gregor Jansen and Robert Klanten, political art has had a significant place in art history ever since the French Revolution and Romanticism. The political emphasis of the Age of Enlightenment extended to the aesthetic sphere, and from the beginning of postmodernism in the 1960s, art's political aspect has challenged the basic regulation of all areas of social life. Building on this, Bruno Latour conceptualized "the political" in terms of artistic representational strategies, while Jansen and Klanten define "political art" as being related to Aristotle's *res republic*. Within this definition, political art is relevant to the wider public; it is always "context art" that relates to a certain set of circumstances, and it is a result of artistic research into public affairs. See Jansen and Klanten, *Art and Agenda*.

12. In *Culture and Imperialism* (1994), Edward Said introduced a contrapuntal mode of analysis that takes into account intertwined histories and perspectives. Specifically, contrapuntal analysis is used in interpreting colonial texts to consider the perspectives of both the colonizer and the colonized. This approach is not only helpful but also necessary in making important connections within colonial and imperial narratives. Reading contrapuntally is interpreting different perspectives simultaneously and seeing how the text interacts with itself and with historical contexts. It is reading with "awareness both of the metropolitan history that is narrated and of those other histories against which (and together with which) the dominating discourse acts" (51). Joseph Boone demonstrates this type of research in *The Homoerotics of Orientalism* (2014), where he uses contrapuntal readings between modern and contemporary, and Oriental and Occidental archives and texts to imagine the interpretive possibilities that exist between the lines on the micro level of narrative in order to make visible the important role that a homo-Orientalist discourse has played in constructing the West's

history of sexuality (xxiv). Mary Louise Pratt coined the evocative term "contact zone" to designate cross-cultural exchanges in those liminal spaces where self and other (colonizer and colonized) meet "in terms of copresence, interlocking understandings and practices" that reshape the subjectivities and desires of colonizer and colonized alike. Pratt, "Arts of the Contact Zone."

13. Diaspora studies has been a growing field over the past two decades. The inaugural issue of the journal *Diaspora* in 1991 arguably marked the start of institutionalized diaspora studies, as it is where William Safran wrote his seminal text in an attempt to define diaspora consciousness. In this text, Safran concluded that the main features of the diaspora include "a history of dispersal, myths/memories of the homeland, alienation in the host country, desire for eventual return, ongoing support of the homeland, and a collective identity importantly defined by this relationship." See Safran, "Diasporas in Modern Societies."

14. Unpacking the rigid guidelines William Safran created in an attempt to define the diaspora, James Clifford encourages a multilocal definition of diasporic identity, stressing that transnational connections linking diasporas need not be articulated primarily through a real or symbolic homeland. See Clifford, "Diasporas."

15. Rather than *transnationalism* meaning all forms of contemporary migration, by questioning the distinctness of geographic areas within a comparative framework (while still respecting historical and cultural specificities), the transnational in relation to world art studies enables new insights into the workings of gender and patriarchy across various borders rather than only within the parameters of the state or nation.

16. In this case, I use "diasporic" as being a part of "non-Western" identity in order to center people of color and the experiences of marginalized identities from a critical race perspective.

17. Gopinath, *Impossible Desires*, 4.

18. Gopinath, *Impossible Desires*, 11. See also Manalansan, "In the Shadow of Stonewall," for an important interrogation of contemporary gay transnational politics.

19. The *Islamicate* does not refer directly to the religion of Islam itself but to the social and cultural complexities historically associated with Islam. It is also inclusive of non-Muslims living within the same regions. Geographically, it also opens up the limits of studying only places such as the "Middle East" and encompasses other geographic regions where Islam is dominant both religiously and culturally, such as Iran and parts of Asia. Hodgson, *Venture of Islam* (1974), 57–59.

20. The diasporic subject in this instance is also the non-Western subject, and this conflation needs discussion. According to Samir Dayal, diasporic double consciousness shows us how the racialized Other is simultaneously Orientalized as being any culture that is not Western, all the while being expected to demonstrate a modernity that is only in keeping with Western culture. See Dayal, "Diaspora and Double Consciousness."

21. The Arabic word for sex, *jins*, appeared sometime in the early twentieth century, carrying with it not only its new meanings of biological sex and national origin but

also its old meanings of type, kind, and ethnolinguistic origin, among others. The word in the sense of type and kind has existed in Arabic since time immemorial and is derived from the Greek word "genus." As late as 1870, its connotation of sex had not yet come into usage. An unspecific word for sexuality, *jinsiyyah*—which also means nationality and citizenship—was coined in the 1950s by translators of the works of Freud. See Massad, "Re-Orienting Desire," 372.

22. More recently Mutaʿ al-Safadi, translator of Michel Foucault's *History of Sexuality*, has introduced the more specific term, *jinsaniyyah*. Important here is the legacy this linguistic coloniality has on the current Middle Eastern discourse of sexuality. European expressions of sexual deviance were adopted in Arabic in the mid-1950s, translating it literally as *al-shudhudh al-jinsi*; this became a coinage now commonly used in the media and in polite company to refer to the Western concept of homosexuality. See Mutaʿ al-Safadi, trans., *Iradat al-ma'rifah, al-juz 'al-awwal min tarikh al-jinsaniyya* [*The History of Sexuality*, vol 1: *The Will to Knowledge*], by Michel Foucault (Beirut: Markaz al-Inma' al-Qawmi, 1990). Abridged in Massad, "Re-Orienting Desire," 372.

23. Bhabha, *Location of Culture*, 111.

24. See Babayan and Najmabadi, *Islamicate Sexualities*, 39; Jacob, "Middle East"; Georgis, *Better Story*; Habib, *Female Homosexuality in the Middle East*; Massad, *Desiring Arabs*; Rahman, *Homosexualities, Muslim Cultures, and Modernity.* Modernity is not to be confused with modernism, which points to the cultural trends that respond to the conditions of modernity in a myriad of ways, such as modern art.

25. It should be noted that in 1991 Bruno Latour argued in his book *We Have Never Been Modern* that we fundamentally misunderstand the condition in which we live. The age of modernity, which is characterized by careful distinctions between nature and society, human and thing, fact and value, is in reality defined by an overarching hybridity, a defiance of clear delineation, and an undermining of the essence of modernization. See Mignolo, *Darker Side of Western Modernity*; Mignolo, *Local Histories/Global Designs*; Silverblatt, *Modern Inquisitions*; Saldívar-Hull, *Feminism on the Border.*

26. Mignolo, *Darker Side of Western Modernity.*

27. "Coloniality" is a term that Mignolo uses in his writing that signals modernity's elaborate façade of "civilizing" as its necessary foundation in the terror-logic of imperial rule. See Mignolo, *Darker Side of Western Modernity*, x, 3.

28. The evidence suggests that a stable homosexual identity did not exist in premodern Arab-Islamic civilizations, and instead same-sex desire was simply a non-categorized facet of everyday life that was legally condemned but otherwise tolerated.

29. Joseph Massad accuses the Gay International of an "incitement to discourse" of homosexuals in the Arab world. This incitement to discourse looks like a strong reaction to the universalizing gay agenda of the Gay International, pushing many to declare it a sin and fueling laws that criminalize homosexuality in an effort to avoid Westernization.

30. For example, Dror Ze'evi's study *Producing Desire* maps out the progress of Western sexuality colonizing the local traditions of homosocial desire in the Ottoman Middle East.

31. Traub, "The Past Is a Foreign Country?"; Rahman, *Homosexualities, Muslim Cultures and Modernity*.

32. An example of why these historical colonial moments matter would be language and the terminology that the Middle Eastern diaspora inherited and uses within contemporary queer identification. For more on the formation of the Arabic term for sexuality, *jinsiyyah*, see Massad, "Re-Orienting Desire," 372.

33. I would like to note the differences among some of the critics cited. Both Joseph Boone and Joseph Massad, for example, are cited affirmatively in this book because each theorist contributes a new dimension to the study. But Massad has harshly criticized Boone in a review of his book despite the fact that Massad had previously assessed an essay by Boone published in *PMLA*—"Vacation Cruises," an essay that would be incorporated into the book—in a very positive way. Likewise, I find the engagement of both Jasbir Puar and Massad's theories productive, whereas many other critics have played Puar against Massad. I find theories of homonationalism, homocolonialism, and the Gay International not existing in silos but working together to offer a fuller picture of the sexual and racial dynamics at play.

34. Habib, *Islam and Homosexuality*, vol. 1.

35. Babayan and Najmabadi, *Islamicate Sexualities*, xxiii.

36. Babayan and Najmabadi, *Islamicate Sexualities*, xxii.

37. Human rights lawyer Lydia Lin also makes these arguments in relation to gay marriage and international human rights law. See Weber and Lin, "Freedom of Conscience and New 'LGBT Rights' in International Human Rights Law"; and Henneberg, *LGBT Rights*, 88–93.

38. Ghaziani and Brim, *Imagining Queer Methods*, 14.

39. Habib, "Introduction: Islam and Homosexuality," in *Islam and Homosexuality*, 1:xvii.

40. Habib, "Introduction," in *Islam and Homosexuality*, 1:xviii.

41. While North America and Europe have held major claims to championing gay liberation, the decriminalization of homosexuality still pertains to very recent history. For example, in the United States, sexual activity between consenting adults of the same sex became legal in 2003, pursuant to the U.S. Supreme Court ruling in *Lawrence v. Texas*. In Canada, same-sex sexual activity between consenting adults was decriminalized in 1969 as a result of legislation introduced in 1967. Until 1971, homosexuality was punishable in Austria, and until 2002 there were still minimum age limits for homosexual relationships in the Austrian penal code (different from heterosexual relationships). For more on gay liberation, see Gilreath, *End of Straight Supremacy*.

42. As Jasbir Puar notes, sexual exceptionalism occurs through stagings of U.S.

nationalism, for instance, that work in tandem with a sexual othering. This sexual othering exceptionalizes the identities of U.S. citizens often in contrast to Orientalist constructions of perverse "Muslim sexuality." Puar, *Terrorist Assemblages*, 4. As a critique of lesbian and gay liberal rights discourses, homonationalism attends to how such discourses produce narratives of progress and modernity that continue to advance civilizational discourses in some contexts, and limit the progression of the "backward" Other. See Dryden and Lenon, *Disrupting Queer Inclusion*.

43. Patel, *Productive Failure*, 7.

44. Gopinath, *Impossible Desires*, 7.

45. Conrad, *What Is Global History?*, 234.

46. Lionnet and Shih, *Minor Transnationalism*, 8.

47. Lionnet and Shih, *Minor Transnationalism*, 8.

48. Conrad, *What Is Global History?*, 132.

49. Conrad, *What Is Global History?*, 234.

50. Gopinath, "Queer Visual Excavations," 327.

51. This is not a form of comparative analysis per se, as the different geographic regions are not used to measuring distinctions and differences between the two. Rather, the different geographic regions are used collectively within her analysis to argue a central query, ensuring that nation-state borders do not hinder two regions speaking to each other productively within academic inquiry.

52. Gopinath, *Unruly Visions*, 25–26.

53. Cathy Hannabach, "Imagine Otherwise: Gayatri Gopinath on Queer Diasporic Aesthetics," *Ideas on Fire*, August 15, 2018. https://ideasonfire.net/69-gayatri-gopinath.

54. Chen, *Asia as Method*. Françoise Lionnet and Shu-mei Shih coined the term "Minor Transnationalism" in order to move beyond the limitations of postcolonialism, globalization theory, ethnic studies, and transnationalism for the study of minority communities. Within this idea they argued that transnational studies and its related fields emphasize the interactions and relationships between the minor culture and mainstream society. Importantly, they criticize that by exclusively analyzing these vertical connections, "we forget to look sideways to lateral networks that are not readily apparent." Lionnet and Shih, "Introduction: Thinking through the Minor, Transnationally," in *Minor Transnationalism*, 1–23.

55. The term "queer regions" is used by Gopinath as a way of studying various historical formations under a different lens. An example Gopinath gives is the Southern states of the United States of America. While the American South is a subnational region, it is also the archetypal example of American nationalism. The American South, then, is a queer region in that national idealism is put onto the region at the subnational level, meaning the region's relationship to gender, race, and sexuality becomes even more intertwined with the national imaginary.

56. Gopinath, *Unruly Visions*, 10.

57. Moussawi, *Disruptive Situations*, 2.

58. Moussawi, *Disruptive Situations*, 3.

59. Moussawi, *Disruptive Situations*, 8.

60. Moussawi, *Disruptive Situations*, 9.

61. Moussawi, *Disruptive Situations*, 7.

62. Patil, *Webbed Connectivities*, 7.

63. Appadurai, *Modernity at Large*, 18.

64. For instance, in her seminal book, *Impossible Desires* (2005), queer theorist Gayatri Gopinath examines film and literary texts, what she calls a public culture, to dissect the ways in which discourses of sexuality are inseparable from histories of colonialism, nationalism, racism, and migration. In examining cultural texts that are produced by the South Asian diaspora, Gopinath extends the power of this cultural production as even influencing the homeland. Here, cultural texts going back and forth between homeland and diaspora contribute to and create a shaping of both sets of cultures, falsifying the notion of diaspora being oriented toward and dependent only on homeland. Gopinath, *Impossible Desires*.

65. Abdulhadi, Alsultany, and Naber, *Arab and Arab American Feminisms*, 234.

66. Naber, *Arab America*. See also Abdulhadi, Alsultany, and Naber, *Arab and Arab American Feminisms*.

67. To help situate this discussion in terms of nationalism and diaspora in the post 9/11 context, see Jamal and Naber, *Race and Arab Americans Before and After 9/11*.

68. Semati, "Islamophobia," 257.

69. Bacchetta, Campt, Grewal, Kaplan, Moallem, and Terry, "Transnational Feminist Practices against War," 305.

70. Razack, *Casting Out*, 5.

71. Anderson, *Imagined Communities*.

72. Anderson defines the nation as an imagined political community, imagined as both inherently limited and sovereign. The nation is *imagined* because members of even the smallest nation will never know most of their fellow members, yet in their minds they are all connected. The nation is imagined as *limited* because even the largest nation has finite boundaries, beyond which are other nations. The nation is imagined as *sovereign* because the concept of nation was born at a time when Enlightenment and Revolution were destroying the legitimacy of religious ruling, and nationalism became an emblem of freedom (even freedom under a deity).

73. Bhabha, *Location of Culture*.

74. Aly, *Becoming Arab in London*, 181.

75. Rahman, *Homosexualities, Muslim Cultures, and Modernity*.

76. Savcı, *Queer in Translation*, 3.

77. Bacchetta, Maira, and Winant, *Global Raciality*, 11.

78. Saffari, Akhbari, Abdolmaleki, and Hamdon, *Unsettling Colonial Modernity in Islamicate Contexts*.

79. The terms *sociology* and *sociological* are used in the broadest sense within my

research. With sociology being a social science that studies society and human behavior, the study of art history with a focus on the human impacts of gender, sexuality, and, in turn, artistic production contributes to a refining of the theoretical understanding of social processes. With my research focusing on the visual and cultural turns from modernity to contemporary moments, this art historical project has a crossover with social research.

80. Luke Gartland, Ali Behdad, Joseph Boone, Christopher Pinny, and other scholars outline how the region was the principal training grounds for early photography.

81. Patil, *Webbed Connectivities*, 94.

82. Including El-Rouayheb, *Before Homosexuality in the Arab-Islamic World*; Ze'evi, *Producing Desire*; Massad, "Re-Orienting Desire"; Najmabadi, "Mapping Transformations of Sex, Gender, and Sexuality in Modern Iran"; Gartlan, "Dandies on the Pyramids"; Boone, *The Homoerotics of Orientalism*; Babayan, *Islamicate Sexualities*; Rowson and Wright, *Homoeroticism in Classical Arabic Literature*; Habib, *Islam and Homosexuality*.

83. Chimamanda Ngozi Adichie argues that single stories often originate from simple misunderstandings or one's lack of knowledge of others but that these stories can also have a malicious intent to suppress other groups of people due to prejudice. Adichie contends that when there's only a single story about a group of people, it robs them of their dignity. The single story reduces people, rendering them incomplete, flat, one-dimensional. As a result, it becomes difficult to recognize equal humanity in the characters of a single story. Relevant to our discussion here on visual representation, Adichie asserts that media and literature available to the public often only tell one story, which causes people to generalize and make assumptions about groups of people. See Chimamanda Ngozi Adichie's "The Danger of a Single Story," TED Talk from July 2009, YouTube, https://www.youtube.com/watch?v=D9Ihs241zeg.

84. *Futurity* is defined as being the concept of subjugated citizens dreaming the possibilities of a future that is different from their present. This idea of dreaming of a better future holds power not only in its capacity to voice current social injustices and current oppressive conditions but also in the liberation of imagining what futures look like outside of the repressive present condition. Influenced by José Esteban Muñoz's book *Cruising Utopia*, I borrow from the concept that the political LGBTQI agenda has been stifled by a narrow-minded focus on the present, which can be short-sighted and assimilationist. Muñoz contends that queerness is instead a futurity-bound phenomenon, a "not yet here" that critically engages pragmatic presentism. Powerfully, Muñoz argues that the present is not enough. It is impoverished and toxic for queers and other people who do not feel the privilege of majoritarian belonging, normative tastes, and "rational" expectations (27). See Muñoz, *Cruising Utopia*.

ONE Thinking Decolonially

1. Belting, Buddensieg, and Weibel, *Global Contemporary and the Rise of New Art Worlds.*

2. Mignolo and Walsh, *On Decoloniality*, 116.

3. According to the *Stanford Encyclopedia of Philosophy*: "Colonialism is a practice of domination, which involves the subjugation of one people to another. One of the difficulties in defining colonialism is that it is hard to distinguish it from imperialism. Frequently the two concepts are treated as synonyms. Like colonialism, imperialism also involves political and economic control over a dependent territory. The etymology of the two terms, however, provides some clues about how they differ. The term colony comes from the Latin word *colonus*, meaning farmer. This root reminds us that the practice of colonialism usually involved the transfer of population to a new territory, where the arrivals lived as permanent settlers while maintaining political allegiance to their country of origin. Imperialism, on the other hand, comes from the Latin term *imperium*, meaning to command. Thus, the term imperialism draws attention to the way that one country exercises power over another, whether through settlement, sovereignty, or indirect mechanisms of control." See Margaret Kohn and Kavita Reddy, "Colonialism," *Stanford Encyclopedia of Philosophy* (Fall 2017 edition), ed. Edward N. Zalta. https://plato.stanford.edu/cgi-bin/encyclopedia/archinfo.cgi?entry=colonialism.

4. Mignolo and Walsh, *On Decoloniality*, 116.

5. Historians date the beginning of British imperialism in the Middle East to 1798, the year Napoleon invaded Egypt. Concerned that France would block British access to the eastern Mediterranean and thereby threaten critical trade routes to India, the British navy collaborated with Ottoman authorities to evict French troops from Egypt. From this episode until decolonization in the mid-twentieth century, British policies in the region reflected the interplay of Great Power rivalries and the balancing of strategic and economic interests. "British Colonialism, Middle East," Encyclopedia of Western Colonialism since 1450, *Encyclopedia.com*, April 14, 2019. https://www.encyclopedia.com/history/encyclopedias-almanacs-transcripts-and-maps/british-colonialism-middle-east.

6. Heavily colonized countries in North Africa include Egypt, Sudan, Tunisia, Algeria, Morocco, and Libya. Egypt was most recently a British colony as of 1882 and became a British protectorate in 1914; the last British troops departed from the Suez Canal Zone in 1956. Sudan from 1899 onward was under British control as part of an Egyptian-Sudanese colony, independent only after 1956. Tunisia was a French colony from 1881 and regained independence in 1956. The French conquest of Algeria began in 1830, and Algeria won the war of independence from France in 1962. Morocco was a French protectorate imposed in 1912, becoming independent in 1956. Libya was an Italian colony from 1911, and when Italy lost in World War II, Libya ceased being under

Italian rule. Colonized countries from the Fertile Crescent that were initially a part of the Ottoman Empire before the first World War include Syria, Iraq, Jordan, and Lebanon. Syria was colonized by France in 1918 and became independent in 1946. Iraq was occupied by Britain in World War I and became nominally independent after 1932. Jordan was a British Mandate territory after 1918 and achieved independence in 1946. Palestine was a British Mandate territory after 1918 and has endured ongoing colonial occupation from Israel starting from 1948 to 1967. Lebanon was a French Mandate territory after 1918 and achieved independence in 1943. For more regarding histories of the Cold War and the Middle East, see the writings of historian Lisa Reynolds Wolfe.

7. Tuck and Yang, "Decolonization Is Not a Metaphor," 2.

8. For scholarly texts on colonialism in the Middle East, see Cole and Kandiyoti, introduction to "Nationalism and the Colonial Legacy in the Middle East and Central Asia."

9. Patil, *Webbed Connectivities*, 2.

10. Chen, *Asia as Method*, 3.

11. Lionnet and Shih, *Minor Transnationalism*, 2.

12. Brzyski, *Partisan Canons*, 2.

13. "Periphery" in this context refers to secondary histories that are generally associated with the Global South. Periphery histories reference the unbalanced power dynamics within historical discourse and the increased importance placed on primary histories that are located in the center of this paradigm, enforcing Eurocentrism and a focus on the Global North.

14. Chen, *Asia as Method*.

15. See also Iskin, *Re-envisioning the Contemporary Art Canon*.

16. This is reflected in the deep art historical research that is being produced about art from the Middle East and the general-knowledge textbooks being published highlighting the region. While too numerous to list here, such books include the following: Mouasher and Jamdagni, *Modern and Contemporary Arab Art from the Levant*; Rogers and van der Vlist, *Arab Art Histories*; Muller, Moore, Demos, and Cotter, *Contemporary Art in the Middle East*; Amirsadeghi, Mikdadi, and Shabout, *New Vision*; Boullata and Berger, *Palestinian Art, 1850–2005*.

17. Karnouk, *Modern Egyptian Art*; Kholeif and Stobbs, *Imperfect Chronology*; Shabout, *Modern Arab Art*.

18. Peggy Levitt, "Move Over Mona Lisa: Just How Global Is Art History?" (lecture presented at the 107th annual meeting of the College Art Association, Los Angeles, February 2018).

19. Peggy Levitt, "Move Over Mona Lisa."

20. Aruna D'Souza, introduction to Casid and D'Souza, *Art History in the Wake of the Global Turn*, xviii.

21. Lionnet and Shih, *Minor Transnationalism*, 7.

22. Hall, "The West and the Rest: Discourse and Power."

23. Mukhtar subscribed to the *Nahda* ideal of an Egyptian cultural and national renaissance. The discovery of the tomb of Tutankhamen in 1922 occurred just as Egypt was granted a form of political independence and fed the Pharaonist iconography that was important in the nationalist movement. For further reading, see Sam Bardaouil, "Between the Palace and the Street: Mahmoud Mukhtar and the Fate of Egyptian Art Today," *Huffington Post*, March 29, 2011. https://www.huffpost.com/entry/between-the-palace-and-th_b_840302.

24. Shabout, *Modern Arab Art*, 18.

25. For recent scholarship, see Lenssen, Rogers, and Shabout. *Modern Art in the Arab World*; and Bardaouil and Fellrath, *Art et Liberté*.

26. Eigner and Hadid, *Art of the Middle East*; Shabout, *Modern Arab Art*.

27. Lionnet and Shih, *Minor Transnationalism*, 8.

28. Chen, *Asia as Method*, 226.

29. There are many difficulties posed when trying to map "power" methodologically as a framework. Since power itself can be manifested colonially (imperial power leading to colonial violence) and ideologically (the power that heterosexuality exerts to subjugate and criminalize homosexuality), I turn to queer theory for a methodology that can be combined to read power productively in different contexts. Following Amin Ghaziani and Matt Brim's provocations from their book *Imagining Queer Methods*, a distinctively queer methodology must: (1) reject unchanging categories in both language and identity (i.e., homosexual and heterosexual), (2) reject impermeable categories that nuance binary assumptions about identity and difference, and (3) reject dualism that has helped power operate and oppress through conceptual binaries.

30. Patil, *Webbed Connectivities*, 122.

31. Piotrowski, "Toward a Horizontal History of the European Avant-Garde," 51.

32. Piotrowski, "Toward a Horizontal History of the European Avant-Garde," 54.

33. My use of the term *provincialize* in this sense borrows from Dipesh Chakravarty's influential monograph *Provincializing Europe*. For more specific reading on art historians engaging in this line of study, see works by Dadi, "The Middle East and South Asia: Aesthetic Mobilities"; Tiampo, *Gutai: Decentering Modernism*; Brzyski, *Partisan Canons*; Belting, *Florence and Baghdad*; Cheah, *What Is a World?;* Khullar, *Worldly Affiliations;* Mignolo and Walsh, *On Decoloniality;* Onians, "World Art Studies and the Need for a New Natural History of Art"; Tomii, *Radicalism in the Wilderness;* and Zijlmans and van Damme, *World Art Studies*.

34. In *The Creolization of Theory*, Lionnet and Shih define *creolization* as a theoretical and analytical rubric that describes the development of a reciprocal, relational, and intersectional critical approach attentive to the legacies of colonialism.

35. See Lord and Meyer, *Art and Queer Culture*; Jones and Silver, *Otherwise: Imagining Queer Feminist Art Histories*; and J. Doyle, *Sex Objects: Art and the Dialectics of Desire*.

36. Lord and Meyer, *Art and Queer Culture*.

37. I use *transnationalism* in my research in a way that is conscious of tension inherent within the term *transnational*. This tension exists on a methodological level wherein the nation-state is the primary foil in which to situate cultural paradigms within the global. In an effort to locate transnationalism within a paradigm that stressed complex connections and slippages between the local and the global, I use *transnational* in my study as being synonymous with *translocal* and *transregional*. For more on the study of transnationalism, see Freitag and von Oppen, *Translocality*.

38. Within art history, this follows the recent trend of world art studies. As Kitty Zijlmans and Wilfried van Damme argue in *World Art Studies*, through its combined global and multidisciplinary approach, world art studies is creating a new framework in the study of art. Within the mapping of world art studies, postcolonial studies can be seen as an approach that is particularly concerned with the impact of colonialism and its aftermath on art and culture.

39. According to scholars Bert Hoffmann and Andreas Mehler, area studies is the multidisciplinary social research focusing on specific geographic regions or culturally defined areas. Area studies as it exists today can be seen as having its origins in the colonial expansion of European powers during the eighteenth century and the accompanying academic efforts to better understand the languages, cultures, and social organizations of colonized peoples. In that sense, area studies emerged as a "child of empire," often driven by commercial and political interests or the perceived civilizing mission of the colonial powers. The nineteenth century saw the establishment of colonial studies in European universities. In the United States, interdisciplinary centers for area studies first emerged after World War I and received a strong impulse after World War II, corresponding to the rise of the United States as a global power. A better understanding of societies in Asia, Africa, the Middle East, and Latin America was seen as urgent in the context of the Cold War rivalry between competing superpowers looking for local clients and supporters, particularly in the developing world. Arguably, a similar security-driven incentive to promote the study of foreign cultures was again seen after the attacks of September 11, 2001. Andreas Mehler and Bert Hoffmann, "Area Studies," *Encyclopedia Britannica*, February 4, 2015. https://www.britannica.com/topic/area-studies.

TWO Trauma and the Single Narrative

1. Archive of the photographs captured within the project can be found on the *3rdi* website: http://www.3rdi.me.

2. Wafaa Bilal, *3rdi*. http://wafaabilal.com/thirdi.

3. Wafaa Bilal, *Shoot an Iraqi*. http://wafaabilal.com/shoot-an-iraqi.

4. Historians of photography have generally assigned only marginal importance to the Middle East in the works of the many European photographers in the nineteenth

century and even less importance to the various traditions of indigenous photography that emerged in the region soon after the introduction of the daguerreotype in 1839. Behdad and Gartlan, *Photography's Orientalism*, 1.

5. Notable European photographers that dominate the history of Middle Eastern photography include Le Gray, Du Camp, Salzmann, Tancrède Dumas, Francis Frith, Felice Beato, Emile Béchard, Hippolyte Arnoux, and Alexandre Leroux, as well as Maison Bonfils, Maison Lehnert & Landrock, Maison Garrigues, Photoglob Zurich, and Underwood and Underwood.

6. Behdad and Gartlan, *Photography's Orientalism*.

7. After Louis-Jacques-Mandé Daguerre introduced his invention to the Chambre des députés in France, politician, mathematician, and physicist Dominique François Arago commented on "the extraordinary advantages that could have been derived from so exact and rapid a means of reproduction during the expedition to Egypt" and recommended that the Institut d'Egypte be equipped immediately with the new visual technology. D. F. Arago, "Report of the Commission of the Chamber of Deputies," in A. Trachtenberg, *Classic Essays on Photography*, 17. This intrinsic link between photography and the Middle East is also seen in Daguerre's British counterpart, William Henry Fox Talbot, who in 1846 published a pamphlet titled "The Talbotype Applied to Hieroglyphics," which was distributed among archeologists and Orientalists. N. Perez, *Focus East*, 15.

8. Behdad and Gartlan, *Photography's Orientalism*, 1.

9. Nassar, Sheehi, and Tamari, *Camera Palaestina*, 4.

10. I use Jasbir Puar's conception of U.S. exceptionalism in that "exceptionalism gestures to narratives of excellence, excellent nationalism, a process whereby a national population comes to believe in its own superiority and its own singularity." Puar, *Terrorist Assemblages*, 5.

11. To be clear, local photographers in the Middle East certainly existed. However, until recently the focus and canon within the history of photography on the region has focused on Western photographers visiting the Middle East. For more resources on Arab photographers working in the Middle East, see Sheehi, *Arab Imago*; and Ritter and Scheiwiller, *Indigenous Lens*.

12. Azoulay, *Civil Contract of Photography*, 13.

13. Some milestones contributing to this shift include the launching of major art fairs like Art Dubai in 2007, the establishment of Mathaf: Arab Museum of Modern Art in Doha in 2010, Arab pavilions at the Venice Biennale, and the announcement that major Western museums, such as the Louvre and the Guggenheim, are planned to open locations on Saadiyat Island in Abu Dhabi. Notable patrons in the Middle East have contributed to more institutional attention being given to art from the region, and a strong focus has been given to rewriting dominant art historical narratives that traditionally exclude Arab art. Such patronage has led to the founding of art institutions,

including the Jordan National Gallery of Fine Arts, established in 1979; the Sultan Gallery in Kuwait, established in 1969; the establishing of Al Mansouria Foundation in 1988 to support Arab and Saudi artists; the Dar Al Fan in Beirut in 1967; the Green Art Gallery in Dubai in 1995; and the Atassi Foundation in Syria to support Syrian modern and contemporary art.

14. Myrna Ayad, "Why There Is More to Middle Eastern Art Than Women and War," *CNN*. http://www.cnn.com/2017/03/15/arts/dubai-art-week-op-ed/index.html/. As mentioned in chapter 1, Shirin Neshat was the only Arab artist to have been included in encyclopedic editions of art history textbooks, and her work famously foregrounds the veil.

15. Sontag, *Regarding the Pain of Others*.

16. Kaplan, "Global Trauma and Public Feelings."

17. Azoulay, *Civil Contract of Photography*, 10.

18. Sontag, *Regarding the Pain of Others*.

19. Mikdadi and Shabout, introduction to *New Vision*, 10.

20. Downey, *Uncommon Grounds*, 17.

21. Downey, *Uncommon Grounds*, 17.

22. Larissa Sansour, public lecture, Art Creates Change Speaker Series, OCAD University, Toronto, Canada, September 21, 2016.

23. Shabout, "Contemporaneity Art in the Arab World," 46.

24. Vasari, *Lives of the Most Excellent Painters, Sculptors, and Architects*.

25. For feminist interventions within art history, see Nochlin, "Why Are There No Great Women Artists?"; Pollock, "Women, Art and Ideology; Parker and Pollock, *Old Mistresses*.

26. Muller, "Contemporary Art in the Middle East."

27. Muller, "Contemporary Art in the Middle East," 17.

28. Ramadan, "Aesthetics of the Modern."

29. It should be noted that I am not arguing for "art for art's sake," which was a concept criticized by scholars in the 1970s who proposed a social history of art. Quite the contrary, I believe that the social histories of art are so important that it is necessary to remove colonial and imperial epistemologies that are shaped by Orientalism and racism.

30. Kaplan, "Global Trauma and Public Feelings," 4.

31. Al-Bahloly, Saleem. "Art History Outside the History of Art."

32. Hoffman, *Empathy and Moral Development*, 30.

33. Kaplan, "Global Trauma and Public Feelings," 9.

34. Kaplan, "Global Trauma and Public Feelings," 9.

35. Likewise, in the tradition of literature and art in China, Korea, and Japan, the identity of author, whether scholar or professional, was considered to be a determining factor in evaluating their art.

36. Buali, "Digital, Aesthetic, Ephemeral."

37. Such exhibitions are numerous and can be seen on macro levels within institutions as well as on smaller levels, thus impacting the general types of attention that are devoted to the region. Exhibitions in North America seem particularly keen to use such narratives, such as the 2016 *Aftermath: The Fallout of War—America and the Middle East*, organized by the Harn Museum of Art in Florida. Another instance of the singular story of trauma and war can be seen in the 2014 exhibition *War from Victims' Perspective* comprised of sixty black-and-white highly aestheticized photographs by Swiss photographer Jean Mohr in Boston, Massachusetts.

38. Theorist Gayatri Gopinath conceives aesthetics and aesthetic practices following Jacques Rancière's formulation of "the aesthetics regime of art" as being that which intervenes in "the very distribution of the sensible that delimits the horizons of the sayable and determines the relationship between seeing, hearing, doing, making, and thinking." (See Gopinath, *Unruly Visions*, 177n30.) However, I find Alpesh Patel's usage of art historian Jill Bennett's definition of "practical aesthetics" to be better suited for evaluating imagery within the contexts of violence, trauma, and Orientalism. Bennett writes that practical aesthetics is defined by an orientation to real-world experience and provides a means of inhabiting and moving through events. By "aesthetics" Bennett is specifically invoking the more recent use of the term as a "general theory of sensori-emotional experience" that brings together art, psychology, and the social rather than being concerned with judgment and highly fraught notions of beauty and taste. (See Patel, *Productive Failure*, 189; and Bennett, *Practical Aesthetics*, 36.)

39. This does not mean that national identity in itself is something essentially negative, but rather the negativity stems from the racism and Orientalism associated with certain national identities. The concerns mentioned in this analysis are not against nationalism per se but are against the racism associated with cultures located outside the Global North.

40. The Whitney Biennial is an exhibition of contemporary American art on display at the Whitney Museum of American Art in New York City.

41. I am not contradicting my previous criticism on the artist's subjectivity, but I find that asking these questions is productive and helps to shed light on the issues surrounding race and representation.

42. Piotrowski, "Toward a Horizontal History," 50.

43. Piotrowski, "Toward a Horizontal History," 54.

44. Siegrist, "Comparative History of Cultures and Societies," 379.

45. Siegrist, "Comparative History of Cultures and Societies," 380.

46. Gopinath, *Unruly Visions*, 10–11.

47. Gopinath, *Unruly Visions*, 26.

THREE Islamicate as Method

1. The groundwork for this chapter was inspired by a collaborative project with Dr. Victoria Nolte and a panel we chaired for the College Art Association (CAA). At the 106th CAA annual conference, which took place in Los Angeles in 2018, we prepared a panel focusing on diaspora and global art history. Working through these complex issues of globalization with scholars of world art, global art studies, and diasporic art stimulated the way I theorize global narratives and diaspora studies in my own work.

2. Hans Belting explains that the term *world art* was initially coined as a colonial notion that was in use for collecting the art of "the others" as a different kind of art, an art that was evaluated by anthropologists rather than art critics. Between the two terms, Belting clarifies that "*world art* and *global art* today have very different meanings, ever since the notion *global art* came up around twenty years ago. *World art* is an old idea complementary to modernism. . . . It continues to signify art from all ages, the heritage of mankind. In fact, world art included art of every possible provenance while at the same time excluding it from Western mainstream art—a colonial distinction between art museums and ethnographic museums. *World art* is officially codified in international laws for the protection of cultural heritage and monuments. *Global art*, on the other hand, is recognized as the sudden and worldwide production of art that did not exist or did not garner attention until the late 1980s. By its own definition global art is contemporary and in spirit postcolonial; thus it is guided by the intention to replace the center and periphery scheme of a hegemonic modernity, and also claims freedom from the privilege of history." See Belting, Buddensieg, and Weibel, *Global Contemporary and the Rise of New Art Worlds*.

3. Scholars such as Terry Smith, Paul Wood, Elaine O'Brien, Anna Brzyski, James Elkins, and Ming Tiampo aim to complicate the narratives of global art histories and determine a historical narrative that does not "other" non-Western art as periphery and derivative of the European canon.

4. Tiampo, "Transversal Articulations."

5. Brzyski, *Partisan Canons*, 1.

6. Brzyski, *Partisan Canons*, 5.

7. Zijlmans and van Damme, *World Art Studies*.

8. Onians, "World Art Studies and the Need for a New Natural History of Art," 206–9.

9. As I situate my research within the broader disciplinary literature, I do not ignore that this discussion has already been taking place among Islamic art scholars. The limits of the term "Islamic art" and the questioning of its effectiveness as an artistic category or cultural signifier has been debated within the field. Instead, my research is aligned with scholarship on global art histories and studies on colonial/multiple modernities. I do this purposefully, as I find it important to have these methodological

debates within the wider discipline and not only between scholars of Islamic art. I position myself with these theories in order to shift the discussion to instead focus on colonial borders, nation-state identities, and the maintenance of colonial boundaries. This is a way of bringing critical race theory into productive dialogue with art history as a discipline, advancing questions and theorization of Islamic art to account for wider methodological concerns, and to avoid being confined within the study of Arab, Islamic, or Middle Eastern art.

10. Dr. Ming Tiampo first introduced me to this term in a public lecture, where she presented a paper exploring new ways of implementing and developing world art histories. The concept of "worlding" is also inspired by the work of Heidegger, Pheng Cheah's work on world literature and cosmopolitanism, and Sonal Khullar's research on worldly affiliations within Indian artistic practices. See Cheah, *What Is a World?*; and Khullar, *Worldly Affiliations*.

11. The goal is not to replace one grand narrative with another, nor is it to introduce a stable definition or guideline for what constitutes the Islamicate. I do not believe in neatly demarcating the parameters of what constitutes and does not constitute Islamic art or what cultures and nation-state identities should be a part of the Islamicate. Such guidelines, I feel, foreclose the very possibilities that a framework like the Islamicate can offer, and these restrictions can lead to reproducing the very disciplinary limitations I aim to combat. Instead, I wish to open up the linguistic and methodological frameworks within art history in order to offer an alternative approach to discuss art histories within a global turn. It is more important that this framework allow for the incorporation of diasporic identities that do not fit neatly in nation-state identities and complicate the borders that define these identities.

12. Hodgson, *Venture of Islam*, 57.

13. Instances of these generalities can be seen in exhibitions like the permanent collection display titled *Arts of the Islamic World* at the Smithsonian Museum in Washington, DC.

14. Hodgson, *Venture of Islam*, 58–59n12 (emphasis in original).

15. It should be noted that since 1974 the term *Islamicate* has been widely used within other disciplines such as history, philosophy, and cultural theory. However, museums and art history have not adopted this language and method of cultural organization as readily, resulting in the issues outlined in this chapter. The "Islamicate" may prove more useful for future research, and this is reflected in new titles adopting this more flexible language, such as Sussan Babaie and Melanie Gibson's edited volume, *The Mercantile Effect: Art and Exchange in the Islamicate World during the 17th and 18th Centuries*.

16. Hodgson, *Venture of Islam*, 59.

17. Walcott, "Caribbean Pop Culture in Canada," 128.

18. The curatorial program at the Aga Khan Museum of Islamic Art in Toronto,

Canada, is starting to move in this direction. With their permanent collection of historic Islamic art spanning the Muslim presence in Spain, Turkey, and Hindustan (the north and west of the Indian subcontinent), Islamic history is being reconceived and retold in ways that illustrate colonial borders and encounters productively. While the word "Islamicate" does not appear anywhere in the galleries of the permanent collection, the value of reconceptualizing the ways histories and cultures are organized and grouped in museums, and the narrative histories these exhibition groupings permit becomes clear.

19. James Adams, "Taking a Look into the Arab Art World," *Globe and Mail*, November 8, 2015. https://www.theglobeandmail.com/arts/art-and-architecture/taking-a-look-into-the-arab-art-world/article27156762.

20. At a public lecture in Toronto, I had the opportunity to ask Sheikha Hoor Al-Qasimi about the very concerns raised within this chapter. See Sheikha Hoor Al-Qasimi, "Art and Culture in the Gulf," lecture given at the 10th Annual Eva Holtby Lecture on Contemporary Culture, Royal Ontario Museum, November 10, 2015.

21. Shabout, 'Contemporaneity Art in the Arab World," 16.

22. At the University of Toronto art history symposium, which took place on March 9, 2018, art historian Iftikhar Dadi cautioned against throwing away old terminology that we deem insufficient; instead, he finds it more productive to push current language to hold new meanings. I would like to stress that the *Islamicate* is not meant to provide a new word or definition. Rather, I push the terminology that was already coined by Hodgson in 1974 to better encompass the complexity of Islamic art and test the limits of current disciplinary language and its effect on knowledge production within museums in order to better theorize the incompatibilities that rigid geography-based methodologies pose in studying diasporic and transnational identities.

23. Zijlmans and van Damme, *World Art Studies*.

24. S. Nelson, "Conversation without Borders," 85.

25. One example is the Asian Art department at the Victoria and Albert Museum. As in other institutions, "The collections of the Asian Department are very broad in terms of chronology, geography and media. They cover a period of more than 5000 years, from 3,500 BC to the present day, and a huge region that encompasses China, Korea and Japan, South-East Asia, from Burma to Indonesia, Pakistan, India and the other countries of South Asia, Central Asia, from Tibet to the Caspian Sea and the Middle East." "Asian Department," http://www.vam.ac.uk/content/articles/a/asian-department.

26. Van Damme, "Introducing World Art Studies," in Zijlmans and van Damme, *World Art Studies*, 55.

27. Conceptually, I connect the Islamicate to notions of transnationalism and diaspora in how it offers a new way of envisioning a more complex understanding of cultural circulation, heritage formation, and community outside of colonial nation-state definitions that ignore imperial histories.

28. S. Nelson, "Conversation without Borders."

29. S. Nelson, "Conversation without Borders," 85.

30. Tomii, *Radicalism in the Wilderness*, 12.

31. Dewan and Zotova, *Embellished Reality*. This catalogue accompanies an exhibition of the same title, *Embellished Reality: Indian Painted Photographs*, held at the ROM from June 4, 2011, to June 17, 2012. The cited text appears on the dust jacket of the catalogue. The catalogue itself is more specific and is comprised of two coherent essays, one dealing with the history and development of the painted photograph in India and the other with the study of the use of color in the manipulation of these images.

32. Dewan and Zotova, *Embellished Reality*.

33. Behdad and Gartlan, *Photography's Orientalism*, 1.

34. Gayatri Spivak, "Rethinking Comparativism," in Spivak, *Aesthetic Education in the Era of Globalization*, 475.

35. In 1988 Gayatri Spivak published her influential essay "Can the Subaltern Speak?" The term "subaltern" designates the populations that are socially, politically, and geographically outside of dominant and hegemonic power structures. The essay contends that Western academic thinking is produced in order to support Western economic interests. Spivak holds that knowledge is never innocent and that it expresses the interests of its producers. For Spivak, knowledge is like any other commodity that holds imbalanced power dynamics between the Global South and Global North. Spivak, "Can the Subaltern Speak?"

36. Shih, "Comparison as Relation."

37. Van Damme, "Introducing World Art Studies," in Zijlmans and van Damme, *World Art Studies*, 27–29n11.

38. Mignolo, "On Comparison," 6.

39. Mignolo, "On Comparison," 1.

40. Conrad, *What Is Global History?*, 64–65.

41. See the research of Kobena Mercer, *Cosmopolitan Modernisms*; Steven Nelson, *Conversation without Borders*; Parul Dave-Mukherji, *Art History and its Discontents in Global Times*; Aruna D'Souza, *Whitewalling: Art, Race & Protest in 3 Acts*, and others within the volume *Art History in the Wake of the Global Turn*, edited by Casid and D'Souza.

42. D'Souza, introduction to Casid and D'Souza, *Art History in the Wake of the Global Turn*, xv.

FOUR An Alternative History of Sexuality

1. Foucault, *History of Sexuality: An Introduction*, 69.

2. Patil, *Webbed Connectivities*, 2.

3. Stoler, *Race and the Education of Desire*. Also see Lavrin, *Sexuality and Marriage*

in Colonial Latin America; Pratt, *Imperial Eyes*, esp. chapter 5; and Rafael, *Contracting Colonialism*, which deals specifically with sexuality and confession in the Philippines under Spanish rule.

4. Stoler, *Race and the Education of Desire*, 5.

5. Stoler, *Race and the Education of Desire*, 5.

6. Patil, *Webbed Connectivities*, 3.

7. Colonial fantasies were very strong contributors to the binaries between a sexually salacious East and the more puritanical West, reinforcing these binaries. While European tourists shamed the Middle East for shameful display of same-sex intimacy, Romantic Orientalist European paintings, such as portraits of English poet Lord Byron (1788–1824) in fancy Oriental dress, expressed a European fascination with non-European homoeroticism and can be read as clearly flamboyant. Lord Byron himself echoed these very tensions with his love of colorful Eastern dress that began as early as the age of fourteen, when he attended a masquerade dressed as a Turkish boy. As an adult he traveled through the Ottoman Empire, and it is clear from his correspondence that one of his main motives in setting out on extended travels in 1809–1810 was a hope for a homosexual experience. Eustathius Georgiou, a volatile Greek boy with "ambrosial curls," carried a parasol to protect his complexion from the sun, which made Byron's valet cringe. The Franco-Greek Nicolo Giraud, with his limpid eyes, taught Byron Italian in Athens, taking a whole day to conjugate the verb "to embrace." By the end of Byron's stay in Greece, he was boasting to his Methodist friends that he had achieved more than 200 "pl and opt Cs," their code for unlimited sexual intercourse taken from Petronius's *Satyricon*—"*coitum plenum et optabilem*." Later in life Byron joined the Greek War of Independence against the Ottoman Empire, for which Greeks revere him as a national hero. When Byron arrived back in England in the summer 1811, prejudice against homosexuals was on the rise, and he was exiled due to sodomy, a crime bearing the death sentence in homophobic nineteenth-century England. See Fiona MacCarthy's biography of Lord Byron, *Byron: Life and Legend*.

8. Mignolo, *Darker Side of Western Modernity*.

9. "Coloniality" is a term that Walter Mignolo uses in his writing, and signals modernity's elaborate façade of "civilizing" as its necessary foundation in the terror logic of imperial rule. See Mignolo, *Darker Side of Western Modernity*, x, 3.

10. Dr. Robert Aldrich's study *Colonialism and Homosexuality* is an example of this scholarship. However, his book lies outside of the dominant academic canon. Aldrich's study primarily focuses on micro histories of male intimacy in imperial settings, examining a broad range of colonial empires. While Aldrich's book is a necessary study that breaks new ground in surveying the relationship between homosexuality and imperialism, his thesis does not account for coloniality and the ways in which imperialism changed local sexual discourses within the colonies. Rather, colonial outposts are written about as being spaces of sexual liberation for European men who did not fit

the metropole's heterosexual social norms. While this may be true, the decolonization of histories of sexualities lies in naming the crucial power imperialism had in erasing local sexual discourses and either leaving a void or replacing them with a heterosexualized version mirroring that of Western modernity. The denial or disregard of this relationship between imperialism and changing sexual discourses, then, does not account for coloniality and, I argue, is not adequately contributing to antiracist, deimperialist, and decolonial scholarship on sexuality.

11. This quote was taken from the back cover of Stephen O. Murray and Will Roscoe's *Islamic Homosexualities*. The quote was a review given by the *American Anthropologist* and pays testament to the homocolonial discourse this wave of scholarship on Arab sexualities relies on, as well as its constant relation of Arab sexualities with Western notions of sexualities.

12. Joseph Massad critiques Schmitt and Sofer's Orientalist study for their use of the seventh-century Qur'an to study Muslims of the twentieth century, creating ahistoricism and universalized Western "gay" concepts as the vehicle of inquiry. See Massad, *Desiring Arabs*, 166; Schmitt and Sofer, *Sexuality and Eroticism among Males in Moslem Societies*.

13. Status-differentiated homosexual relations include all sexual relations between males where one partner is of a higher status than the other. This hierarchical model of sexuality was based on a distinction between the man with the higher status doing the inserting and the man of lower status penetrated. Roscoe cites Boswell and his terms of the "penetration code." Murray and Roscoe, *Islamic Homosexualities*, 56. Age-differentiated homosexual relations include the practice of pederasty, which is the relationship between an adult male mentor and their younger sexual partner. This flourished in Athens and ancient Greece and is historically prevalent throughout Islamicate societies.

14. Murray and Roscoe, *Islamic Homosexualities*, 41.

15. The concept of *homosociality* describes and defines social bonds between persons of the same sex. It is, for example, frequently used in studies on men and masculinities and defined as a mechanism and social dynamic that explains the maintenance of hegemonic masculinity. Hammarén and Johansson, *Homosociality: In Between Power and Intimacy*. More precisely for our purposes here, Afsenah Najmabadi identifies *homosociality* as spaces of male socialization, such as old-style coffeehouses and *zurkhanah* (male sports clubs in Iran), and they often act as spaces of seduction and illicit sex. Najmabadi, *Men with Mustaches and Women with Beards*, 19.

16. Murray, and Roscoe, *Islamic Homosexualities*, 62.

17. Momin Rahman defines homocolonialism as "the deployment of LGBTIQ rights and visibility to stigmatize non-Western cultures and conversely reassert the supremacy of the Western nations and civilization." Rahman, *Homosexualities, Muslim Cultures, and Modernity*, 7. Specifically, Rahman characterizes "Western exceptionalism

as the primary political idea that is triangulated through the process of 'homocolonialism' that institutes the opposition of Muslim cultures and sexuality politics by deploying LGBTIQ rights and visibility to punish non-Western cultures, and conversely reassert the supremacy of the 'home' Western nations and civilization." Rahman, *Homosexualities, Muslim Cultures, and Modernity*, 118.

18. Joseph Massad defines the Gay International as the missionary universalization of Western gay rights with an "orientalist impulse, borrowed from predominant representations of the Arab and Muslim worlds in the United States and Europe, [that] continues to guide all branches of the human rights community." Massad critiques the book *Islamic Sexualities* to point out that *Islamic* is an adjective referring to the religion of Islam, while *Muslim* refers to people who adhere to it; Massad points out that it is unclear how Islam, the religion, can have a homosexuality. Massad, Re-Orienting Desire," 362, 370.

19. Massad, "Re-Orienting Desire," 371.

20. El-Rouayheb, *Before Homosexuality in the Arab-Islamic World*, 1.

21. El-Rouayheb outlines very detailed descriptions of how *liwāt* (was handled in Islamic law, specifically in the four acknowledged schools of law in the Ottoman Empire: *Hanaf'i, Shafi'i, Hanbali, Maliki*. El-Rouayheb, *Before Homosexuality in the Arab-Islamic World*, 119–21.

22. El-Rouayheb, *Before Homosexuality in the Arab-Islamic World*, 136.

23. Ze'evi, *Producing Desire*, 168–69.

24. Foucault, *History of Sexuality: An Introduction*, 3.

25. El-Rouayheb, *Before Homosexuality in the Arab-Islamic World*, 160.

26. El-Rouayheb, *Before Homosexuality in the Arab-Islamic World*, 158.

27. Ze'evi, *Producing Desire*, 165.

28. Massad, "Re-Orienting Desire," 372.

29. See al-Safadi, *Iradat al-ma'rifah, al-juz 'al-awwal min tarikh al-jinsaniyya*, 372.

30. Massad, "Re-Orienting Desire," 372.

31. Foucault, *History of Sexuality: An Introduction*, 6.

32. Patil, *Webbed Connectivities*, 120.

33. Foucault, *History of Sexuality: An Introduction*, 57.

34. Joseph Massad critiques Schmitt and Sofer for the same Eurocentricism, quoting their use of "us" in the text to only refer to Western gay audiences, relegating Muslims as subjects to be observed but never active agents in scholarship. See Massad, *Desiring Arabs*, 166; Schmitt, and Sofer, *Sexuality and Eroticism among Males in Moslem Societies*, 20.

35. Foucault, *History of Sexuality: An Introduction*, 58.

36. Foucault, *History of Sexuality: An Introduction*, 68.

37. Foucault, *History of Sexuality: An Introduction*, 70.

38. Najmabadi, *Women with Mustaches and Men without Beards*, 19.

39. Focusing more on visual culture, Joseph Boone's book *Homoerotics of Orientalism* anthologizes many of the themes discussed by the aforementioned scholars by fluctuating between contemporaneity and historiography as a way to avoid dichotomizing cultures. More so than other sources, Boone links this historicized Orientalism with current global issues and the political reverberations that modernity and its projects had on sexual discourses in the Middle East.

40. Boone, *Homoerotics of Orientalism*, 49.

41. Boone, *Homoerotics of Orientalism*, xxiii.

42. Traub, *Thinking Sex with the Early Moderns*, 17.

43. Boone, *Homoerotics of Orientalism*, xxx.

44. Boone, *Homoerotics of Orientalism*, 35.

45. Najmabadi, *Women with Mustaches and Men without Beards*, 19.

46. Ze'evi, *Producing Desire*, 8. See also Oberhelman, "Hierarchies of Gender, Ideology, and Power in Ancient and Medieval Greek and Arabic Dream Literature."

47. This pattern of locating histories of sexualities that show resonances and have patterns in multiple places in Islamicate regions is the reason why micro studies focusing on one region often do not account for transregionalism within these histories. Edited by Kathryn Babayan and Afsaneh Najmabadi, the volume *Islamicate Sexualities* (2008) focuses on a wide cross-section of Muslim cultures ranging from Iberia in the mid-sixteenth century to Arab literatures in Egypt from the late medieval times. Supported by a variety of historical literary studies, the anthology takes the task of naming language and translation as a primary dilemma within their arguments, avoiding falling into the pitfalls of Massad's Gay International and the risk of perpetuating a homocolonial discourse. Conscious of this postcolonial and antiracist trajectory, the editors chose Marshall G. S. Hodgson's coinage, *Islamicate*, which was intended to highlight a complex of attitudes and practices that pertain to cultures and societies that live by various versions of the religion of Islam. This is important as it provides a language and framework to address issues of sexuality in places that are different but nonetheless related, like Southeast Asia and the Middle East while providing academic and theoretical grounding for this work.

48. Foucault, *History of Sexuality: An Introduction*, 58.

49. For a partial description of this travel literature, see Findley, "Ottoman Occidentalist in Europe," 15.

50. Ze'evi, *Producing Desire*, 150.

51. The guiding principles of Ze'evi's ideas use the notion of "scripts" put forward by John Gagnon and applied by Jeffery Weeks. In their 1984 essay "Sexual Scripts," John Gagnon and William Simon define scripts as being a metaphor for conceptualizing the production of behavior within social life. It has been a highly influential study on the sociological aspects of sexuality, the social constructionist approach, and the foundational text to view sexuality as scripted. John Gagnon suggests that "scripts, like

blueprints, the whos, whats, whens, wheres, and whys for given types of activity . . . [are] like a blueprint or roadmap or recipe, giving directions." See Gagnon, *Human Sexualities*, 6.

52. Ze'evi also examines the period of modernity and the changes within the nineteenth century as the foremost comparison with all premodern examples of homosocial desire. Colonialism, and in this case homocolonialism, is at the forefront of his argument. This provides valuable insight to the shaping of European ideas about sexuality and the profound impact this had on the Ottoman Middle East. This temporal and geographic parallel—between Eastern sexual discourses and that of Western ideals, both pre- and postmodernity—is precisely the claim that El-Rouayheb does not engage with.

53. Najmabadi, *Women with Mustaches and Men without Beards*, 137.

54. Najmabadi, *Women with Mustaches and Men without Beards*, 240.

55. Foucault, *History of Sexuality: An Introduction*, 57.

56. To explain why these historic attitudes about gender and sexuality persisted in the diaspora and not in the host country, I turn to the scholarship of Nadine Naber once more. In Naber's view on articulating Arabness in the United States, the diaspora has been shaped by an assemblage of different visions of how Arabs survive in North America. This means that the racism and cultural differences Arab families experience in the West can often lead to an intensification of nationalism and a reification of some sort of "authentic" cultural heritage. For diasporic subjects, this means that differences and dichotomies are heightened, and notions of what it means to be Arab in North America are radically different from being Arab in the Middle East. This often is related to the ways in which nationalism, nationhood, and essentialist versions of Arabness become stuck in time and oriented toward past memories for families of migration who have settled in a new land. While nations in the Middle East are fundamentally changing and developing over time, the diasporic experience of nationhood could mean holding on to an unchanged version of what national identity looks like and an unmoving conception of what it means to be Arab. Naber, *Arab America*. See also Abdulhadi, Alsultany, and Naber, *Arab and Arab American Feminisms*.

57. Homo-Orientalism follows the same pattern of reductive stereotypes and essentializing features of traditional Orientalist depictions but highlight the sexually perverse nature of Arab men. This can be done by oversexualizing the Arab men, making them promiscuous, and a level of homoeroticism adds to a visual narrative of sexual deviance. Puar, *Terrorist Assemblages*.

58. For contemporary gay Middle East studies, see Merabet, *Queer Beirut*; Georgis, *The Better Story*; Rahman, "Queer as Intersectionality"; Aly, *Becoming Arab in London*; Kugle, *Living Out Islam*; Kugle, *Homosexuality in Islam*

59. The accounts of revision and erasure of homosociality happened over time but not very long ago. Many of these shifts were still seen in my parents' generation in

Egypt (1950s), when many of these linguistic changes (for example) were taking place. This reverberates to people of that generation's own understanding of homosexuality, a rejection of homosocial relations, and indoctrination in vehement anti-homosociality rhetoric pushed as measures of modernizing the nation and themselves.

60. According to Robin Cohen, diasporas exhibit several of the following features: "(1) dispersal from an original homeland, often traumatically; (2) alternatively, the expansion from a homeland in search of work, in pursuit of trade or to further colonial ambitions; (3) a collective memory and myth about the homeland; (4) an idealization of the supposed ancestral home; (5) a return movement; (6) a strong ethnic group consciousness sustained over a long time; (7) a troubled relationship with host societies; (8) a sense of solidarity with co-ethnic members in other countries; and (9) the possibility of a distinctive creative, enriching life in tolerant host countries." Cohen, *Global Diasporas*, 180.

61. On diaspora consciousness, see: Cohen, *Global Diasporas*, 184–87; Gilroy, "Diaspora and the Detours of Identity," 318; Clifford, *Routes*, 256.

62. Cohen, *Global Diasporas*, 184–87.

63. Gilroy, "Diaspora and the Detours of Identity," 318.

64. Gilroy, "Diaspora and the Detours of Identity,' 318.

65. Razack, *Casting Out*, 117.

66. Clifford, *Routes*, 256–57.

67. Rafael Soldi, "Q&A with Jamil Hellu," *Strange Fire Collective*. http://www.strangefirecollective.com/qa-jamil-hellu.

68. The artist states that they use the Victorian-era layout of domestic spaces and furniture as a metaphor for the cultural history of sexual repression. It should be noted that the furniture design within the installation is emblematic of the work of Thomas Chippendale, an eighteenth-century Georgian furniture maker who popularized Rococo and Neoclassical furniture in Britain and the United States.

69. Tensions between what it means to be a Western queer subject while still maintaining culturally relevant ideologies of gender and sexuality is something queer theorist Martin Manalansan addresses in his book *Global Divas: Filipino Gay Men in the Diaspora*.

70. El-Rouayheb, *Before Homosexuality in the Arab-Islamic World*; Najmabadi, *Women with Mustaches and Men without Beards*; Ze'evi, *Producing Desire*; Boone, *Homoerotics of Orientalism*.

71. As Jasbir Puar notes, sexual exceptionalism occurs through stagings of U.S. nationalisms that work in tandem with a sexual othering, one that exceptionalizes the identities of U.S. citizens, often in contrast to Orientalist constructions of perverse "Muslim sexuality" Puar, *Terrorist Assemblages*, 4. As a critique of lesbian and gay liberal rights discourses, homonationalism attends to how such discourses produce narratives of progress and modernity that continue to advance civilizational discourses in

some contexts and limit the progression of the "backward" Other. Dryden and Lenon, *Disrupting Queer Inclusion*.

72. H. Pérez, *Taste for Brown Bodies*, 3.

73. This is reflected in the literature of Momin Rahman's discussions of exclusion in "Queer as Intersectionality," Martin Mansalan's writing on difference and incompatibility in *Global Divas*, and why Sekneh Hammoud-Beckett proposes alternative models of coming out for Arab and Muslim queer-identifying subjects in "Azima Ila Hayati: An Invitation in to My Life: Narrative Conversations about Sexual Identity."

74. For example, "bears" comprise a subculture of gay men who valorize the larger, hairy body. BDSM is a variety of often erotic practices or roleplaying involving bondage, discipline, dominance and submission, sadomasochism, and other related power dynamics. For critical writing on gay subcultures, see Hennen, "Bear Bodies, Bear Masculinity."

75. This point is supported by Ramy Aly's argument that fashions and aesthetic orientation in the Arab world and the Arab diaspora seem to flow in opposite directions. See Aly, *Becoming Arab in London*.

76. Naber, *Arab America*, 9.

77. Rahman, *Homosexualities, Muslim Cultures, and Modernity*.

78. Muñoz, *Cruising Utopia*, 1.

79. Muñoz, *Cruising Utopia*, 182.

FIVE Queering Archives of Photography

1. I refer to the subconscious less in the psychoanalytic sense and more as a component of diaspora consciousness. In the context of diaspora consciousness, a generational distance is arguably necessary when processing and representing traumatic memory. As Cathy Caruth has expressed on remembering trauma, "The pathology consists, rather, solely in the *structure of its experience* or reception: the event is not assimilated or experienced fully at the time, but only belatedly, in its repeated *possession* of the one who experiences it." To this effect, traumatic memory is not experienced during the event itself, but it is the later coping of the traumatic event that creates such difficult memories. Here, it is clear that the distancing of the traumatic event either through time or in this case generationally can result in a better understanding of the traumatic event itself, leading to a more effective managing of the traumatic memory. See Caruth, preface (xii–ix, 1–12) and introduction (4) to Caruth, *Trauma*.

2. Massad, "Re-Orienting Desire," 365.

3. Massad, *Desiring Arabs*.

4. Examples of antiquated human rights arguments can be found in Brian Whitaker's book *Unspeakable Love*. While outlining key issues in Middle Eastern sexuality studies through interviews and firsthand accounts, Whitaker takes a human rights

stance that dichotomizes sexuality discourses into Western categories of identification—namely, a Euro-American universalism and that of the Other. This othering of the sexual discourses that do not resemble that of Western homosexuality is one of the pitfalls this universalist human rights methodology creates.

5. Foucault, *History of Sexuality: An Introduction.*

6. For instance, in Khaled El-Rouayheb's study *Before Homosexuality in the Arab-Islamic World*, he outlines the overwhelming numbers of biographic accounts, poetic anthologies, and belletristic writings that are openly dedicated to same-sex relations, such as poems of a man's passion for a teenage boy. El-Rouayheb, however, criticizes modern historians for presuming these instances to be manifestations of "homosexuality" and urges more temporally and locally specific readings of these same-sex relations.

7. There is a site of productive tension in questioning the use and nonuse of "queerness" as a marker of non-Western centric desire. A main issue surrounding this contention is that scholars of Islamicate same-sex desires have proposed that a stable gay identity did not exist prior to the modern period and that this is in fact a Western concept of subjectivity. To use the term "queer" in an analysis of historical desire in the Global South would then be inaccurate. While scholars like Joseph Massad contend that contemporary queer identification in the Middle East stems from colonialism, scholars like Samar Habib deny Massad's protest against the view that there is an authentic form of homosexual identity indigenous to the Arab world. Habib rejects Massad's assertion that coming out and visibility strategies are Western imports that are colonial impositions, labeling this as oppressive to Arab individuals who do in fact identify as gay and still live in the Middle East. As the terminology of "queer" becomes contentious in postcolonial contexts, the productive tension I wish to draw upon lies in the contrapuntal study of historic and contemporary art—that is, questioning how queer is identified in one context and disidentified in another, all while analyzing premodern same-sex desire in relation to a contemporary queer artist. The conceptual discussion I would then like to have is about pushing back against a hegemonic gay Western identity in the usage of the term "queer" and instead imagining other ways of discussing same-sex and homoerotic desire. See Habib, "Introduction: Islam and Homosexuality," in *Islam and Homosexuality*, xvii.

8. Informed by Sharon Holland and her book *The Erotic Life of Racism*, my use of the term "erotic" does not anchor itself in the psychoanalytic but rather fluctuates between dictionary definitions of the words "desire" and "erotic." The homoeroticism I study is located between the object relations inherent in "desire"—a wish for something—and the desired subject as object, demonstrating the way in which sexuality is inextricable from the erotic itself. It is also important to think of "colonial homoeroticism" in relation to and distinct from "diasporic homoeroticism," for the power dynamics that govern the sexual body change within the two conceptions of eroticization. See Holland, *Erotic Life of Racism.*

9. See Ali Behdad, "The Powerful Art of Qajar Photography: Orientalism and (Self)-Orientalizing in Nineteenth-Century Iran"; Behdad and Gartlan, *Photography's Orientalism*.

10. Behdad, "Powerful Art of Qajar Photography," 143.

11. Behdad, "Powerful Art of Qajar Photography," 149.

12. Behdad, "Powerful Art of Qajar Photography," 148.

13. Behdad and Gartlan, *Photography's Orientalism*, 1.

14. Dominique François Arago, "Report of the Commission of the Chamber of Deputies," in Trachtenberg, *Classic Essays on Photography*, 17.

15. Behdad and Gartlan, *Photography's Orientalism*, 1.

16. N. Perez, *Focus East*, 15.

17. Behdad and Gartlan, *Photography's Orientalism*, 1.

18. For scholars trying to fill this gap and correct the oversight of indigenous photographers in the Middle East, see Ritter and Scheiwiller, *Indigenous Lens*.

19. In the most recent study by Issam Nassar, Stephen Sheehi, and Salīm Tamārī, *Camera Palaestina*, they say that within a short period after its "invention" in 1839, the Ottoman court adopted photography and it is said to have been practiced by Sultans Abdülmacid and Abdülaziz. The Abdullah Frères and Pascal Sébah (and eventually his son Jean) would become the Ottoman Middle East's most renowned photographers, far surpassing any European photographer in prestige and output, if not quality. Less well known is that, in 1861, Muhammad Said Pasha, the Wali of Egypt, sent the first photographer and cartographer, Muhammad Sadiq Bey, to Medina. Sadiq Bey would be the first to photograph Mecca some years later. By the turn of the century, Armenian and Arab photographers became established in Palestine (4). For more on this history, see Nassar, Sheehi, and Tamārī, *Camera Palaestina*.

20. Sheehi, *Arab Imago*, xxi.

21. Orientalism is defined as the West's patronizing representations of "The East" and the overall exoticization of the societies and peoples who inhabit countries in Asia, North Africa, and the Middle East. According to Edward Said, Orientalism is inextricably tied to the imperialist societies who produced it, which makes much Orientalist work inherently political and central to power. Said, *Orientalism*.

22. This summary of photography in the Middle East is expanded on as a case study in Gayed and Angus, "Visual Pedagogies."

23. Modernity as a time period signals social, political, and historic conditions (typically urbanization, mass production, democratization, etc.) at the end of the nineteenth century and early twentieth century. This is not to be confused with modernism, which points to the cultural trends that respond to the conditions of modernity in a myriad of ways, such as modern art.

24. Najmabadi, *Women with Mustaches and Men without Beards*, 3.

25. See El-Rouayheb, *Before Homosexuality in the Arab-Islamic World*; and Ze'evi, *Producing Desire*.

26. Najmabadi, *Women with Mustaches and Men without Beards*, 4.

27. Foucault, *History of Sexuality: An Introduction*, 3.

28. Ze'evi, *Producing Desire*, 165.

29. Wright and Rowson, *Homoeroticism in Classical Arabic Literature*; Babayan and Najmabadi, *Islamicate Sexualities*; Boone, *Homoerotics of Orientalism*; Ze'evi, *Producing Desire*; El-Rouayheb, *Before Homosexuality in the Arab-Islamic World*; Najmabadi, "Mapping Transformations of Sex, Gender, and Sexuality in Modern Iran."

30. Najmabadi, *Women with Mustaches and Men without Beards*, 15.

31. As Najmabadi points out, this term was linked to *ʿubnah*, which in medical discourse is considered an illness. Socially, the male love desire was acceptable before this point, and decrees against shaving one's beard showed the cultural fear that young men may want to remain an object of desire rather than over time (and age) becoming the desiring man. The same disapproval was true if an older man was no longer beardless but they remained interested in other older men. See Najmabadi, *Women with Mustaches and Men without Beards*, 16, 23.

32. Najmabadi, *Women with Mustaches and Men without Beards*, 15.

33. Najmabadi, *Women with Mustaches and Men without Beards*, 16.

34. Najmabadi, *Women with Mustaches and Men without Beards*, 138.

35. Najmabadi, *Women with Mustaches and Men without Beards*, 15.

36. Najmabadi, *Women with Mustaches and Men without Beards*, 93.

37. See Boone, *Homoerotics of Orientalism* (106) as well as the homoerotic photographs studied and shown in Behdad and Gartlan, *Photography's Orientalism*.

38. In 1888 Henri Béchard published a set of photogravures titled *L'Égypte et la Nubie*.

39. They had the photographic concession at the Cairo antiquities museum and produced the photo book *Album du Musée Boulaq: Photographie par Délié et Béchard, avec texte explicatif par Auguste Marriette Bey (Cairo, 1872)*.

40. The timing of their partnership is unclear, but it is certain that both worked separately at various times. This is known because cartes-de-visite and cabinet cards exist with both single logos for each photographer as well as with a joint logo. See Hannavy, *Encyclopedia of Nineteenth-Century Photography*.

41. Boone, *Homoerotics of Orientalism*, 104.

42. Ouseley, *Travels in Various Countries of the East*, 405.

43. Patil, *Webbed Connectivities*, 117.

44. Boone, *Homoerotics of Orientalism*, 106.

45. Mulvey, "Visual Pleasure and Narrative Cinema."

46. Najmabadi, *Women with Mustaches and Men without Beards*, 147.

47. Gopinath, "Who's Your Daddy?," 274.

48. El-Rouayheb, *Before Homosexuality in the Arab-Islamic World*, 43.

49. The term *geocultural* is from the discipline of cultural geography, which is the study of the many cultural aspects found throughout the world and how they relate to

the spaces and places where they originate and then travel as people continually move across various areas.

50. This question can be answered in part by the discussion in chapter 2, "Trauma and the Single Narrative," bringing the phantom image in dialogue with diasporic consciousness. This connection indicated that the phantom image relates heavily to the subconscious production of visual art and is linked to colonial trauma and imperial archives in powerful ways.

51. While this case study deals with one artist, and this is accompanied by additional artists elsewhere in the book, this broader claim is built through cumulative research and future studies. As this research develops, more artists will be added to the corpus of queer diasporic art production, furthering the connection between colonial archives and contemporary art.

52. Within my analysis, "identity" is not a stable commodity; instead, I am pushing for a different conception of subjectivity that is not fully anchored in linear/stable/hegemonic "identity" per se. For instance, we can think of "erotic" as not solely being called into existence through "identity," but the "erotic" can be that which helps constitute various forms of identification and disidentification in different contexts. In this analysis, identity involves how a queer person of color is perceived by transnational social orders and how they "disidentify" with essentialist Eurocentric markers of identity. In this way, subject formation falls outside the boundaries of nation-state and normative citizenship and identifications.

53. Mignolo, "Foreword: Decolonial Body-Geo-Politics at Large," vii.

54. Gilroy, *Black Atlantic*, 132–33.

55. Dayal, "Diaspora and Double Consciousness," 51.

56. Gilroy, *Black Atlantic*, 2.

57. Gopinath, *Impossible Desires*, 2.

58. Mignolo and Vazquez, "Decolonial AestheSis: Colonial Wounds/Decolonial Healings," *Social Text*, July 15, 2013, 4. https://socialtextjournal.org/periscope_article/decolonial-aesthesis-colonial-woundsdecolonial-healings.

59. Mignolo and Vazquez, "Decolonial AestheSis: Colonial Wounds/Decolonial Healings," *Social Text*, July 15, 2013, 6. https://socialtextjournal.org/periscope_article/decolonial-aesthesis-colonial-woundsdecolonial-healings.

60. As Gayatri Gopinath suggests in *Impossible Desires*, to understand queerness as diasporic and diaspora as queer is to recuperate "desires, practices, and subjectivities that are rendered impossible or unimaginable within conventional diasporic or nationalist imaginaries" (11). Such a critical framework of a "specifically queer diaspora . . . may begin to unsettle the ways in which the diaspora shores up the gender and sexual ideologies of dominant nationalism on the one hand, and processes of globalization on the other" (10).

61. Mignolo and Vazquez, "Decolonial AestheSis: Colonial Wounds/Decolonial

Healings," *Social Text*, July 15, 2013, 5. https://socialtextjournal.org/periscope_article/decolonial-aesthesis-colonial-woundsdecolonial-healings/5.

62. For analysis of hand-painted photography, see Gayed, "Exilic Aesthetic: Articulations of Patriotism by the Expatriate." See also Gayed, "Nationalism, Migration and Exile: The Photographs of Youssef Nabil." MA diss., Carleton University, Ottawa, Ontario, April 2016.

63. I conceptualize "the premodern" as being a time period before the turn of the century and prior to the period of modernity as defined by the West. Premodern histories in the Global South signal a period before one that has been characterized by Western modernity as being the pinnacle of the advancement of modern industrial societies and social progress. Conceptually, I anchor this term in relation to an Islamicate premodern history that is not geographically specific but connected in surprising and productive ways through gender and sexual discourses. In bringing the contemporary diaspora in relation to Islamicate premodern histories, I see this story as divested from anachronistic Western conceptions of progress and authentic gay identity. In this regard, I conceptualize my analysis as remediating understandings of temporality (and spatiality), and the transtemporal queer gaze is in reference to a contemporary diasporic identity formation that is in constant relation to a homocolonial history.

SIX Coming Out *à l'Orientale*

1. 2Fik came up with the notion of a "coming out *à l'orientale*" in an interview with Denis Provencher. This interview, quoted on page 71 (chapter 1) in his book *Queer Maghrebi French* (2017), was conducted in French, yet the expression "coming out" was left in in English in the original. This work on the difficulty of culturally translating the Anglo-American notion of coming out into French follows work in Provencher's first book on this question. 2Fik coined the expression in conversation with Provencher. I would also like to acknowledge the important work done by queer Maghrebianists to the fields impacted by this book.

2. See Sedgwick, *Epistemology of the Closet*; Somerville, "Feminism, Queer Theory, and the Racial Closet"; Jack Halberstam, *In a Queer Time and Place*; Eribon and Lucey, *Insult and the Making of the Gay Self*; Edelman, *No Future: Queer Theory and the Death Drive*; and Bersani, *Is the Rectum a Grave? and Other Essays*.

3. In Momin Rahman's core argument, he explains homocolonialism as being an actor in the specific understandings of modernity that underpins the sources of oppression between Muslim cultures and sexual diversity. See Rahman, *Homosexualities, Muslim Cultures, and Modernity*.

4. El-Rouayheb, *Before Homosexuality in the Arab-Islamic World*, 5.

5. As seen in the previous chapters, premodern same-sex desire is well documented in the Middle East. El-Rouayheb outlines numerous biographic accounts, poetic

anthologies, and belletristic writings openly dedicated to same-sex relations, such as poems about a man's passion for a teenage boy. See *Before Homosexuality in the Arab-Islamic World*, 1–42. Historians also cite the travel journals of Europeans who visited various regions of the Ottoman Empire, noting their astonishment and disgust with same-sex tradition and local men openly flaunting their relations with other men and adolescent boys. It should be noted that these travel journals were often translated into Arabic and local languages in order to be circulated to cause shame and embarrassment, thus making them a part of irreparable acts of repression and sexual imperialism. See Ze'evi, *Producing Desire*; and Boone, *Homoerotics of Orientalism*.

6. El-Rouayheb, *Before Homosexuality in the Arab-Islamic World*, 156.

7. Rahman, *Homosexualities, Muslim Cultures, and Modernity*.

8. Intersectionality is a framework designed to explore the dynamic between coexisting identities (e.g., woman, Black) and connected systems of oppression (e.g., patriarchy, white supremacy). The term was coined by Black feminist legal scholar Kimberlé Crenshaw to challenge the assumption that continues to undermine the feminist movement that women are a homogeneous group, equally positioned by structures of power. In a feminist context, it allows for a fully developed understanding of how factors such as race and class shape women's lived experiences, how they interact with gender. See Crenshaw, "Mapping the Margins."

9. See Gayed, "Queering Middle Eastern Contemporary Art and Its Diaspora," 140–55; Gayed, "Islamicate Sexualities."

10. Beg, *History of Mehmed the Conqueror*; Jonathan Jones, "The Sultan Mehmet II, Attributed to Gentile Bellini (1480)," April 25, 2003, *The Guardian*, https://www.theguardian.com/culture/2003/apr/26/art.

11. "The Sultan Mehmet II," 2017, Annenberg Learner, Art through Time: A Global View. https://www.learner.org/series/art-through-time-a-global-view/converging-cultures/the-sultan-mehmet-ii.

12. Gatward, "Bellini, Bronze, and Bombards."

13. The crowns also appear in a banner depicted in the *Saint Ursula* cycle of paintings by Carpaccio. Historian Mary L. Pixley writes, "The series of three crowns refers to the three kingdoms of Asia, Greece and Trebizond which were controlled by the Ottoman Turkish empire." Pixley, "Islamic Artifacts and Cultural Currents in the Art of Carpaccio," 9. Art historian Paul Wood has also noted, "On the reverse of Bellini's portrait medal there are three of them, usually taken to refer to the three components of the Ottoman Empire: the original territories in Asia, Greece (including Constantinople), and Trebizond (the Black Sea port and gateway to the Silk Route into central Asia, captured by Mehmet from Venetian control within a decade of the end of Byzantium, in 1461)." Carol M. Richardson and Paul Wood, "Art in Renaissance Venice: A Portrait," OpenLearn Course at the Open University. https://www.open.edu/openlearn/history-the-arts/culture/visual-art/art-renaissance-venice/content-section-1.4.

14. Pedani Fabris, cited by S. Bagci in "Art in Renaissance Venice," 434. Richardson and Wood, "Art in Renaissance Venice: A Portrait." https://www.open.edu/openlearn/history-the-arts/culture/visual-art/art-renaissance-venice/content-section-1.4.

15. Muñoz, *Cruising Utopia*, 27.

16. Muñoz, *Cruising Utopia*, 182.

17. Vimalassery, Hu Pegues, and Goldstein, "On Colonial Unknowing."

18. It should be noted that in his interviews with Denis Provencher, 2Fik used the term "Arab" to refer to his own cultural experience and to identify his own performative characters. Provencher, *Queer Maghrebi French*.

19. For an in-depth analysis of the languages used by queer Maghrebi French artists, writers, and filmmakers, see Provencher, *Queer Maghrebi French*.

20. Historian Partha Mitter argues that the discipline of art history has yet to change in any substantive manner the implicit evaluation of non-Western modernism as derivative and devoid of originality. Mitter examines the way Picasso is applauded for using African masks, or primitive art, within his cubist modernist paintings but then goes on to show that this is not the way art historians treat non-Western artists who do the same. In fact, when the artist is a racialized subject who responds to an intellectual product of the "dominant" European culture, these non-Western artists who make art using Western motifs or styles are then labeled as derivative, copying, unoriginal, and lacking authentic vision. At worst, their works are labeled as not being good art or even art at all. For this reason, Mitter argues that this underlying assumption about the lack of originality of non-Western modernisms continues to be symptomatic of a widespread bias. This is precisely the complex discourse of power, authority, and hierarchy involved in the study of non-Western avant-garde artists that Partha Mitter calls the Picasso manqué syndrome. See Mitter, "Interventions–Decentering Modernism," 531.

21. I use the term *transnational queer identity* to speak of a non-Western way of being a queer subject, most often referring to sexual norms of the Global South. A transnational queer identity is necessarily diasporic and involves different global, local, and multinational negotiations in order to form queer subjectivity in the diaspora.

22. Provencher, *Queer Maghrebi French*, 57.

23. Dipesh Chakrabarty's *Provincializing Europe* points to Eurocentrism within the study of historical modernity and the centrality that Europe takes in histories of civilization, industrialization, and progress. Chakrabarty begins with outlining how conventional theoretical models have been based on European history, with key themes like the development of capitalism and modernity being central to these narratives. He argues that Europe is a template of modernity, a body of scholarship that defines how academics view the world, and not just a geographic region. Provincializing Europe entails returning Europe to its rightful place as *one* world region among many, decentered as a way of thinking through the experiences of political modernity in non-Western nations.

24. Provencher, *Queer Maghrebi French*, 81.

25. Provencher, *Queer Maghrebi French*, 80.

26. Islamicate gender fluidity is seen in surviving Middle Eastern and later Islamic literature from the fourth to the thirteenth centuries, which narrates examples of homosocial relations and gay desire but not "gay" as a stable identity. For instance, homoerotic relationships between the Mamluk elite in late-medieval Egypt and Syria show that the public expression of homoeroticism (especially in poetry) was fully permitted by Islamic societies both before and during the thirteenth and fourteenth centuries. See Rowson, "Two Homoerotic Narratives from Mamluk Literature." Likewise, premodern Arab-Islamic texts speak frequently of the androgynous beauty of beardless boys, and poetry and other texts are explicit about anal intercourse and fellatio. Traub, *Thinking Sex with the Early Moderns*, 24.

27. Manalansan, *Global Divas*.

28. Manalansan, *Global Divas*, 91.

29. See, for example, Smith, *Conquest: Sexual Violence and American Indian Genocide*; Smith, "Queer Theory and Native Studies"; Morgensen, "Settler Homonationalism"; Morgensen, "Queer Settler Colonialism in Canada and Israel."

30. Hammoud-Beckett, "Azima Ila Hayati: An Invitation in to My Life," 29–39.

31. Massad, *Desiring Arabs*, 188.

32. For scholarship on queer settler colonialism see Morgensen, "The Biopolitics of Settler Colonialism"; Morgensen, "Settler Homonationalism" Smith, "Queer Theory and Native Studies"; Greensmith and Giwa, "Challenging Settler Colonialism in Contemporary Queer Politics."

33. As in *The Marriage of Abdel and Fatima* (figure 6.13).

34. See exhibition shot: Mona Filip, "2Fik: His and Other Stories," Koffler Centre of the Arts, Toronto, Canada, 2017. https://kofflerarts.org/Exhibitions/Gallery/Online-Publications/2Fik-His-and-Other-Stories.

35. 2Fik's character Alice (French Lebanese), for example, could act as a bridge between his characters Fatima (Moroccan) and Manon (born in Quebec). According to the artist, Alice stands in as a sort of transition from the East to the West on all levels: religious, cultural, social, educational, etc. Provencher, *Queer Maghrebi French*, 63.

36. This term of the Brown-Middle-Eastern-Arab-Other is inspired by the work of critical race theorist Sherene Razack, who cites the term "Muslim-looking" as part of a resurgence of old Orientalism that "provides the scaffold for the making of an empire dominated by the United States and the white nations who are its allies." Razack, *Casting Out*, 5. Furthermore, this hyphenated term is part of what Razack identifies as "race thinking," which she defines as the denial of a common bond of humanity between people of European descent and those who are not. Race thinking is the belief that there are two levels of humanity and two corresponding legal regimes. It is a structure of thought that divides the world between the deserving and the undeserving according to descent, developing into racism through its use as a political weapon (6, 8, 179).

37. Provencher, *Queer Maghrebi French*, 66.

38. Beth Harris and Steven Zucker, "Painting Colonial Culture: Ingres's La Grande Odalisque," Khan Academy. https://www.khanacademy.org/humanities/ap-art-history/later-europe-and-americas/enlightenment-revolution/v/ingres-la-grande-odalisque-1814.

39. Mona Filip, "2Fik: His and Other Stories," Koffler Centre of the Arts, Toronto, Canada, 2017. https://kofflerarts.org/Exhibitions/Gallery/Online-Publications/2Fik-His-and-Other-Stories.

40. Muslims learn about the prophet's views on facial hair not from the Qur'an but through hadith or sayings attributed to Muhammad. One such hadith, in a collection compiled centuries ago by Muslim scholar Muhammad al-Bukhari, stipulates, "Cut the moustaches short and leave the beard." The prophet Muhammad is believed to have had a beard, and those who insist that devout Muslims grow beards argue that they are doing no more than asking the faithful to emulate the prophet's actions. There are schools of Islamic law—Hanafi, Maliki, Hanbali, and Shafi'i—that, among many other things, hold strong positions on beard length and the act of shaving. For more, see Farmanfarmaian, "Fear of the Beard"; Delaney, "Untangling the Meanings of Hair in Turkish Society"; and BBC News, "Are Beards Obligatory for Devout Muslim Men?," June 27, 2010, https://www.bbc.com/news/10369726. Shaving one's beard could thus be a sign of modernity. Feminist theorist Afsenah Najmabadi outlines the importance of facial hair in her book *Women with Mustaches and Men without Beards*.

41. The Live-In Caregiver program (LCP) was established in order to support middle- and upper-class families in Canada as adults balance work and care for family members, including children and elderly parents. The LCP makes available the opportunity for nannies and domestic workers to become permanent residents and citizens of Canada and facilitates the immigration of spouses and children and the reconsolidation of families in the diaspora. See Diaz, Largo, and Pino, *Diasporic Intimacies*, 15. For more on nonnormative and queer intimacies in transnational feminist writing about gender and labor within the LCP, see Catungal, "Toward Queer(er) Futures."

42. Lowe, *Intimacies of Four Continents*, 8.

43. Rahman, *Homosexualities, Muslim Cultures, and Modernity*.

44. Puar, *Terrorist Assemblages*, 337.

45. Nishant Upadhyay argues that homonationalism has become one of the key logics of modernity, whereby certain queer bodies are reconstituted as worthy of recognition and protection by nation-states. These queer subjects become indispensable to the maintenance and continuance of the nation-state while others are excluded through logics of white supremacy, racism, Islamophobia, heteropatriarchy, neoliberalism, and settler colonialism. See Jackman and Upadhyay, "Pinkwashing Israel, Whitewashing Canada," 201.

46. For Gartlan's study, see Behdad and Gartlan, *Photography's Orientalism*.

47. Colonial fantasies often lie at the crux of these binaries. While European tourists shamed the Middle East for their display of same-sex intimacy, Romantic Orientalist European paintings, such as portraits of poet Lord Byron (1788–1824) in fancy Oriental dress, expressed a homoeroticism and can be read as clearly flamboyant.

48. Jackman and Upadhyay, "Pinkwashing Israel, Whitewashing Canada," 201.

SEVEN Historicizing Homophobia

1. In 1967 the Sexual Offences Act, an Act of Parliament in the United Kingdom, was passed that decriminalized private homosexual acts between men over twenty-one while at the same time imposing heavier penalties on street offenses of homosexuality. The law was not changed for Scotland until 1980 nor for Northern Ireland until 1982. Legislation to allow same-sex marriage in England and Wales was eventually passed by the Parliament of the United Kingdom in July 2013 and took effect on March 13, 2014.

2. Within the United States, in 1961, beginning with Illinois, states began to decriminalize same-sex sexual activity, and in 2003, through *Lawrence v. Texas*, all remaining laws against same-sex sexual activity were invalidated. In 2004, beginning with Massachusetts, states began to offer same-sex marriage, and in 2015, through *Obergefell v. Hodges*, all states were required to offer it; 2015 marks the year gay marriage was hence decriminalized in America. Canada was more progressive on this front, and in a landmark decision in 1995, *Egan v. Canada*, the Supreme Court of Canada held that sexual orientation is constitutionally protected under the equality clause of the Canadian Charter of Rights and Freedoms. In 2005, Canada was the fourth country in the world, and the first in the Americas, to legalize same-sex marriage nationwide.

3. From the PaykanArtCar website. https://paykanartcar.com/paykanartcar/#statement.

4. The *Shahnameh*, or "The Book of Kings," consists of some fifty thousand couplets (two-line verses) and is one of the world's longest epic poems. It was written by the Persian poet Ferdowsi between c. 977 and 1010 CE and is the national epic of Greater Iran. It tells mainly the mythical, and to some extent the historical, past of the Persian Empire from the creation of the world until the Muslim conquest in the seventh century.

5. Nazanine Nouri, '"Asia Now' Fair in Paris Cancels Display of Paykan Art Car, Project Supporting Iran's LGBTQs," *KAYHAN LIFE* (blog), October 19, 2021. https://kayhanlife.com/authors/paykan-car-becomes-artwork-to-support-irans-lgbtq-community.

6. Nazanine Nouri, '"Asia Now' Fair in Paris Cancels Display of Paykan Art Car, Project Supporting Iran's LGBTQs," *KAYHAN LIFE* (blog), October 19, 2021. https://kayhanlife.com/authors/paykan-car-becomes-artwork-to-support-irans-lgbtq-community.

7. May Rude, "A Dictator's Car Is Transformed into Symbol for LGBTQ+ Iranians," October 22, 2021. https://www.out.com/news/2021/10/15/dictators-car-transformed-symbol-lgbtq-iranians.

8. Zachary Jarrell, "The PaykanArtCar Is Putting LGBTQ+ Rights for Iranians on the Map," *Los Angeles Blade: LGBTQ News, Rights, Politics, Entertainment* (blog), January 3, 2022. https://www.losangelesblade.com/2022/01/02/the-paykanartcar-is-putting-lgbtq-rights-for-iranians-on-the-map.

9. PaykanArtCar, "Artist Statement." https://paykanartcar.com/paykanartcar/#statement.

10. Brett Berk, "To Protest Iran's Anti-Gay Abuses, an Artist Painted a Dictator's Car," *New York Times*, November 1, 2021, sec. Business. https://www.nytimes.com/2021/11/01/business/art-car-iran.html.

11. *ARTnews* press release, November 16, 2021. "PaykanArtCar: A Driving Force against Human Rights Abuses Tours Canada."

12. Gul Tuysuz, "A Card Exempted a Gay Man from Serving in Iran's Military. It May Have Cost Him His Life," CNN, May 15, 2021. https://www.cnn.com/2021/05/15/middleeast/alireza-fazeli-monfared-iran-death-intl/index.html.

13. Gul Tuysuz, "A Card Exempted a Gay Man from Serving in Iran's Military. It May Have Cost Him His Life," CNN, May 15, 2021. https://www.cnn.com/2021/05/15/middleeast/alireza-fazeli-monfared-iran-death-intl/index.html.

14. #Outlawed. "The Love That Dare Not Speak Its Name," Human Rights Watch. http://internap.hrw.org/features/features/lgbt_laws/index-june15.html#type-of-laws.

15. Jo Yurcaba, "Gay Iranian Man Dead in Alleged 'Honor Killing,' Rights Group Says," NBC News, May 11, 2021. https://www.nbcnews.com/feature/nbc-out/gay-iranian-man-dead-alleged-honor-killing-rights-group-says-n1266995.

16. Gul Tuysuz, "A Card Exempted a Gay Man from Serving in Iran's Military. It May Have Cost Him His Life," CNN, May 15, 2021. https://www.cnn.com/2021/05/15/middleeast/alireza-fazeli-monfared-iran-death-intl/index.html.

17. Daphne Gordon, "Alireza Shojaian's Art Painted on a Vintage Iranian Paykan Car Challenges Middle Eastern Ideals of What It Means to Be a Man," *Toronto Star*, December 10, 2021. https://www.thestar.com/entertainment/visualarts/2021/12/10/alireza-shojaians-art-painted-on-a-vintage-iranian-paykan-car-challenges-middle-eastern-ideals-of-what-it-means-to-be-a-man.html.

18. "PaykanArtCar: A Driving Force against Human Rights Abuses Tours Canada," *ARTnews*, November 16, 2021. https://www.artnews.com/art-news/sponsored-content/paykanartcar-tours-canada-1234609646.

19. Razack, *Casting Out*, 117.

20. Naber, *Arab America*, 234.

21. Abdulhadi, Alsultany, and Naber, *Arab and Arab American Feminisms*, xxii.

22. Naber, *Arab America*, 4.

23. Rahman, *Homosexualities, Muslim Cultures, and Modernity*, 7, 118.

24. Anderson, *Imagined Communities*.

25. Puar, *Terrorist Assemblages*, 4.

26. Puar, *Terrorist Assemblages*, 2.

27. Puar, *Terrorist Assemblages*, 2.

28. Gopinath, *Impossible Desires*, 11.

29. Gopinath, *Impossible Desires*, 10.

30. In *Before Homosexuality in the Arab-Islamic World*, El-Rouayheb provides detailed descriptions of how *liwāt* (sodomy) was criminalized and handled in Islamic law, specifically in the four acknowledged schools of law in the Ottoman Empire: *Hanaf'i*, *Shafi'i*, *Hanbali*, and *Maliki* (119–21). Historian Dror Ze'evi, in *Producing Desire*, also argues that, historically, major conflicts about the permissibility of same-sex relations simply did not exist. Though legally frowned upon, same-sex desires were taken to be part of life and their illegality was usually ignored until modernization (and Westernization) led a previously invisible part of life to suddenly become an object for observation and comparison with Victorian cultural norms (168–69).

31. See Dryden and Lenon, *Disrupting Queer Inclusion*.

32. Puar, *Terrorist Assemblages*, 2.

33. Language is one of the sites that conditions sexual experiences in the Global South. Tarik Bereket and Barry Adam's research on gay identities in Turkey contends that the contemporary concept of "gay" is a particularly generational and classed identity category dependent on a certain social status and education level. Bereket and Adam, "The Emergence of Gay Identities in Contemporary Turkey." However, in MSM (men who have sex with men) relations, for instance, terms such as "active" and "passive" dictate how the individual performs their masculinity and are more socially relevant categories at the local level. These ideas of masculinity scripts are relatively in line with Judith Butler's (2011) notion of performativity, reiterating a type of masculinity that serves to define an individual's identity as being either active or passive; the passive subject refuses to take on the active image of the hypermasculinized, as it conflicts with his identity script as passive. Butler, *Bodies That Matter*.

34. It is worth noting that "Arab" is an ethnolinguistic category, identifying people who speak the Arabic language as their mother tongue. Arabs trace their national roots to the twenty-two member states of the League of Arab States: Egypt, Sudan, Jordan, Syria, Lebanon, Iraq, Saudi Arabia, Kuwait, Bahrain, Qatar, United Arab Emirates, Oman, Yemen, Djibouti, Somalia, Eritrea, Libya, Tunisia, Algeria, Comoros, Morocco, and Mauritania. Religiously, they include Muslims (Sunnis, Shiites, Alawites, and Imailis), Christians (Protestants, Catholics, Greek Orthodox, Coptic Orthodox, Caldeans, Assyrians, and Maronites), and Jews. Unlike Arabs, Middle Eastern people are defined to come from countries of the Arabian Peninsula: Iraq, Syria, Lebanon, Jordan, Palestine, Israel, Kuwait, Turkey, Egypt, and Iran.

35. According to the Immigrant and Refugee Board of Canada, Gaza and the West

Bank follow two different sets of laws. They state that "in the Gaza Strip, British Mandate laws remain in force; in the West Bank, Jordanian penal codes remain in effect. While each set of these laws deals with the question of sexual minorities differently, the end result is a matter of interpretation, often leading to condemnation driven by largely negative attitudes toward sexual minorities." See section on treatment of sexual minorities in the Gaza Strip, Immigration and Refugee Board of Canada. https://irb-cisr.gc.ca/en/country-information/rir/Pages/index.aspx?doc=457658&pls=1/. For more detailed information, see "Audacity in Adversity: LGBT Activism in the Middle East and North Africa," Human Rights Watch, April 16, 2018. https://www.hrw.org/report/2018/04/16/audacity-adversity/lgbt-activism-middle-east-and-north-africa.

36. Egypt was one of many heavily colonized countries in North Africa. Egypt was most recently a British colony as of 1882 and a British protectorate in 1914; the last British troops departed from the Suez Canal Zone in 1956. Pollard, *Nurturing the Nation*, 73–99. See also Pollard, chapter 3, abridged in Wilson Chacko Jacob, *Working Out Egypt*, 17.

37. Rahman and Jackson, *Gender and Sexuality*, 22.

38. On Victorian family ideals, see Davidoff and Hall, *Family Fortunes*.

39. In "The Homosexuals Have Arrived," Rinaldo Walcott states that "Canada is deeply involved in exporting its homosexual rights agenda elsewhere, and even within its borders, its homosexual rights agenda differentiates across race, sexual practices, and place of 'origin'" (xiii). An example of this is the inauguration of Pride House as part of the 2010 Winter Olympic Games, which were held in Vancouver and Whistler, to position Canada as a gay haven. Imagining itself as a safe space where sexual minorities (both athletes and their allies) from around the world were welcome, "Pride House showcased Canadian (sexual) exceptionalism on a world stage." Dryden and Lenon, *Disrupting Queer Inclusion*, p. 3.

40. Joseph Massad defines the Gay International as the missionary universalization of Western gay rights with an "orientalist impulse, borrowed from predominant representations of the Arab and Muslim worlds in the United States and Europe, [that] continues to guide all branches of the human rights community." "Re-Orienting Desire," 362.

41. The impositions of European ideas on non-Western cultures are well discussed in Said, *Culture and Imperialism*; and Pratt, *Imperial Eyes*.

42. I would like to note the complexity of both reading images queerly and producing queer images. Artist Laurence Rasti herself is not queer but uses her art to create queer visual documentation for stateless and voiceless refugees who are on a journey of queer migration. In Rasti's own words: "As someone who has worked in photojournalism, documentary photography and the fine arts, I don't know where the line is when giving visibility to a subject and weighing the benefit and risk within that work. I learned to use images as a means of communication, and my concerns were about the violation of human rights when I produced this series. However, in the last few years,

the question of my subject position and the legitimacy of the artist in relation to their work started to make its way into my mind. Today, I don't know if I should have done this series, and I know I would not produce the same series again today. Concerned by the problematic idea of a straight artist taking space within queer narratives, I am conscious that another voice would have brought another vision, and their unique subject position would make the work even truer to their experience. I only know what benefit the work could bring to some of the queer subjects photographed within the series, and maybe for these individuals the benefits they felt from having their identifies validated, their stories heard and their love made visible, maybe for them this was enough. But maybe not. I'm not aware of the invisibility or pain this series may have brought to others because of my own limited world view. The best thing for an artist to do is reconsider everything, try to listen, collaborate with others and include their subjects as co-authors of the artwork to remove power imbalances and potential objectification. Therefore, I consider myself more of an art worker to bring questions or convey a message. In order to minimize the potential harm or objectification of those people within my work, today I have moved forward by paying professional fees and starting agreements of co-authorship with the protagonist/subject of my new works. As a non-queer artist who has garnered success and notoriety from this series that importantly represents gaps in international human rights, I employ these methods now to try and avoid future ethical problems and work with increased care as we navigate our different subject positions within the art production."

43. Cornell, Schmutz, and Eiblmayr, *Nilbar Güreş: Overhead*, 78.

44. Gopinath, *Unruly Visions*, 11.

45. Gopinath, *Unruly Visions*, 10.

46. Bhabha, *Location of Culture*, 111.

Conclusion

1. In this book, transnational queer theory as a concept has been conceptualized in tandem with queer of color critique and queer diasporic critique in order to provide important theoretical and political contributions and interventions within the study of race, gender, sexuality, nation, and diaspora. Within a Canadian context, scholars like Robert Diaz, Richard Fung, and Amar Wahab have taken diasporic and transnational approaches in tracing the cultural politics of racialized sexual minorities.

2. Rahim Thawer is a Toronto-based social worker who writes about issues of queer mental health for a Muslim population in the diaspora. For more, see Rahim Thawer, "How to Be Culturally Competent When Supporting LGBTQ+ Muslims," *Medium*, January 12, 2022. https://medium.com/@rahimthawer/how-to-be-culturally-competent-when-supporting-lgbtq-muslims-7f7686a0563c.

3. Asiel Adan Sanchez, "The Whiteness of 'Coming Out': Culture and Identity in

the Disclosure Narrative," *Archer*, July 7, 2017. http://archermagazine.com.au/2017/07/culture-coming-out.

4. In his article "How to Be Culturally Competent When Supporting LGBTQ+ Muslims," social worker Rahim Thawer makes this point and writes, "As a racialized queer Muslim, I never would have imagined the many actual possibilities for acceptance in my own community, and that isn't for lack of imagination. I think it's because the world around me taught me to think in a way that's characterized by dichotomous thinking and polarization." *Medium*, January 12, 2022. https://medium.com/@rahimthawer/how-to-be-culturally-competent-when-supporting-lgbtq-muslims-7f7686a0563c.

5. Hammoud-Beckett, "Azima Ila Hayati."

6. Rahim Thawer, "How to Be Culturally Competent When Supporting LGBTQ+ Muslims," *Medium*, January 12, 2022. https://medium.com/@rahimthawer/how-to-be-culturally-competent-when-supporting-lgbtq-muslims-7f7686a0563c.

BIBLIOGRAPHY

Abdulhadi, Rabab, Evelyn Alsultany, and Nadine Naber. *Arab and Arab American Feminisms: Gender, Violence, and Belonging*. Syracuse, NY: Syracuse University Press, 2011.

Ahmed, Leila. *A Border Passage: From Cairo to America—A Woman's Journey*. New York: Penguin Books, 2000.

al-Azzawi, Dia. *Art in Iraq Today*. Milan, Italy: Skira, 2012.

Al-Bahloly, Saleem. "Art History Outside the History of Art." In *Arab Art Histories: The Khalid Shoman Collection*, edited by Sarah A. Rogers and Eline Van Der Vlist, 255–65. Amman, Jordan: Khalid Shoman Foundation, 2014.

Aldrich, Robert. *Colonialism and Homosexuality*. London: Routledge, 2003.

Al-Kassim, Dina. "Psychoanalysis and the Postcolonial Genealogy of Queer Theory." *International Journal of Middle East Studies* 45, no. 2 (2013): 343–46.

al-Safadi, Mutaʿ, trans. *Iradat al-ma'rifah, al-juz 'al-awwal min tarikh al-jinsaniyya* [*The Will to Know*, Vol. 1: *The History of Sexuality*], by Michel Foucault. Beirut: Markaz al-Inma' al-Qawmi, 1990. Abridged in Massad, "Re-Orienting Desire."

Aly, Ramy M. K. *Becoming Arab in London: Performativity and the Undoing of Identity*. London: Pluto Press, 2015.

Amirsadeighi, Hossein, Salwa Mikdadi, and Nada Shabout. *New Vision: Arab Contemporary Art in the 21st Century*. London: Thames and Hudson, 2009.

Anderson, Benedict. *Imagined Communities: Reflections on the Origin and Spread of Nationalism*. Revised ed. New York: Verso, 2006.

Appadurai, Arjun. *Modernity at Large: Cultural Dimensions of Globalization*. Minneapolis: University of Minnesota Press, 1996.

Awwad, Julian. "The Postcolonial Predicament of Gay Rights in the Queen Boat Affair." *Communication and Critical Cultural Studies* 7, no. 3 (2010): 318–36.

Azoulay, Ariella. *The Civil Contract of Photography*. Brooklyn, NY: Zone Books, 2008.

Azoulay, Ariella Aïsha. *Potential History: Unlearning Imperialism*. New York: Verso, 2019.

Babaie, Sussan, and Melanie Gibson, eds. *The Mercantile Effect: Art and Exchange in the Islamicate World during the 17th and 18th Centuries*. Chicago: University of Chicago Press, 2019.

Babayan, Kathryn, and Afsaneh Najmabadi. *Islamicate Sexualities: Translations across Temporal Geographies of Desire*. Harvard Middle Eastern Monographs 39. Cambridge, MA: Center for Middle Eastern Studies of Harvard University, 2008.

Bacchetta, Paola, Tina Campt, Inderpal Grewal, Caren Kaplan, Minoo Moallem, and Jennifer Terry. "Transnational Feminist Practices against War." *Meridians* 2, no. 2 (2002): 302–8.

Bacchetta, Paola, Sunaina Maira, and Howard Winant. *Global Raciality: Empire, PostColoniality, DeColoniality*. New York: Routledge, 2019.

Bakshi, Sandeep, Suhraiya Jivraj, and Silvia Posocco. *Decolonizing Sexualities*. Oxford, UK: Counterpress, 2016.

Bardaouil, Sam, and Till Fellrath, eds. *Art et Liberté: Rupture, War, and Surrealism in Egypt (1938–1948)*. [Milan, Italy]: Skira, 2016.

———. *Told Untold Retold: 23 Stories of Journeys through Time and Space*. Milan, Italy: Skira, 2010.

Barthes, Roland. *Camera Lucida: Reflections on Photography*. Trans. Richard Howard. Reprint, New York: Hill and Wang, 2010.

Béchard, Émile. *Album du Musée Boulaq: Photographie par Délié et Béchard, avec texte explicatif par Auguste Marriette-Bey*. (Cairo: Mourès & Cie, 1872.

Beg, Tursun. *The History of Mehmed the Conqueror*. Trans. Halil İnalcık. Minneapolis: Bibliotheca Islamica, 1978.

Behdad, Ali. *Camera Orientalis: Reflections on Photography of the Middle East*. Chicago: University of Chicago Press, 2016.

———. "The Powerful Art of Qajar Photography: Orientalism and (Self)-Orientalizing in Nineteenth-Century Iran." *Iranian Studies* 34, no. 1–4 (2001): 141–51.

Behdad, Ali, and Luke Gartlan, eds. *Photography's Orientalism: New Essays on Colonial Representation*. Los Angeles: Getty Research Institute, 2013.

Belting, Hans. *Florence and Baghdad: Renaissance Art and Arab Science*. Trans. Deborah Lucas Schneider. Cambridge, MA: Harvard University Press, 2011.

Belting, Hans, Andrea Buddensieg, and Peter Weibel. *The Global Contemporary and the Rise of New Art Worlds*. Karlsruhe, Germany: ZKM Center for Art and Media, 2013.

Bennett, Jill. *Practical Aesthetic Events, Affects, and Art after 9/11*. London: I. B. Tauris, 2012.

Bereket, Tarik, and Barry D. Adam. "The Emergence of Gay Identities in Contemporary Turkey." *Sexualities* 9, no. 2 (2006): 131–51.

Bersani, Leo. *Is the Rectum a Grave? and Other Essays*. Chicago: University of Chicago Press, 2010.

Bhabha, Homi K. *The Location of Culture*. Special Indian ed. New York: Routledge, 2004.

Boone, Joseph Allen. *The Homoerotics of Orientalism*. New York: Columbia University Press, 2014.

Boullata, Kamal, and John Berger. *Palestinian Art, 1850–2005*. London: Saqi, 2009.

Brzyski, Anna, ed. *Partisan Canons*. Durham, NC: Duke University Press, 2007.

Buali, Sheyma. "Digital, Aesthetic, Ephemeral: A Brief Look at Image and Narrative." In *Uncommon Grounds: New Media and Critical Practice in the Middle East and North Africa*, edited by Anthony Downey, 169–83. London: I. B. Tauris, 2014.

Butler, Judith. *Bodies That Matter: On the Discursive Limits of Sex*. New York: Routledge, 2011.

Caruth, Cathy, ed. *Trauma: Explorations in Memory*. Baltimore: Johns Hopkins University Press, 1995.

Casid, Jill H., and Aruna D'Souza. *Art History in the Wake of the Global Turn*. Williamstown, MA: Sterling and Francine Clark Art Institute, 2014.

Catungal, John Paul. "Toward Queer(er) Futures: Proliferating the 'Sexual' in Filipinx Canadian Sexuality Studies." In Diaz, Largo, and Pino, *Diasporic Intimacies*, 23–40.

Chakrabarty, Dipesh. *Provincializing Europe: Postcolonial Thought and Historical Difference*. Princeton, NJ: Princeton University Press, 2012.

Chakravorty, Gayatri. *In Other Worlds: Essays in Cultural Politics*. New York: Routledge, 1988.

Cheah, Pheng. *What Is a World?: On Postcolonial Literature as World Literature*. Durham, NC: Duke University Press, 2016.

Chen, Kuan-Hsing. *Asia as Method: Toward Deimperialization*. Durham, NC: Duke University Press, 2010.

Clifford, James. "Diasporas." *CUAN Cultural Anthropology* 9, no. 3 (1994): 302–38.

———. *Routes: Travel and Translation in the Late Twentieth Century*. London: Harvard University Press, 1999.

Cohen, Robin. *Global Diasporas: An Introduction*. London: UCL Press, 1997.

Cole, Juan R. I., and Deniz Kandiyoti. Introduction to "Nationalism and the Colonial Legacy in the Middle East and Central Asia." Special issue, *International Journal of Middle East Studies* 34, no. 2 (May 2002): 189–203.

Conrad, Sebastian. *What Is Global History?* Princeton, NJ: Princeton University Press, 2017.

Cornell, Lauren, Hemma Schmutz, and Silvia Eiblmayr. *Nilbar Güreş: Overhead*. Exhibition Catalogue. Linz, Austria: Lentos Kunstmuseum Linz. 2018.

Crenshaw, Kimberlé. "Mapping the Margins: Intersectionality, Identity, and Violence against Women of Color." *Stanford Law Review* 43, no. 6 (1991): 1241–300.

Dadi, Iftikhar. "The Middle East and South Asia: Aesthetic Mobilities." In *Imperfect Chronology: Arab Art from the Modern to the Contemporary Works from the Barjeel Art Foundation*, edited by Omar Kholeif, 81–91. New York: Prestel, 2015.

Dave-Mukherji, Parul. "Art History and Its Discontents in Global Times." In Casid and D'Souza, *Art History in the Wake of the Global Turn*, 87-106.

Davidoff, Leonore, and Catherine Hall. *Family Fortunes: Men and Women of the English Middle Class, 1780–1850*. Chicago: University of Chicago Press, 1987.

Dayal, Samir. "Diaspora and Double Consciousness." *Journal of the Midwest Modern Language Association* 29, no. 1 (1996): 46–62.

Delaney, Carol. "Untangling the Meanings of Hair in Turkish Society." *Anthropological Quarterly* 67, no. 4 (1994): 159–72.

Demos, T. J. "Desire in Diaspora." In *Contemporary Art in the Middle East*, 42–50. London: Black Dog, 2009.

De Sondy, Amanullah. *The Crisis of Islamic Masculinities*. London: Bloomsbury Academic Press, 2014.

Dewan, Deepali, and Olga Zotova. *Embellished Reality: Indian Painted Photographs.* Toronto: Royal Ontario Museum Press, 2011.

Diaz, Robert, Marissa Largo, and Fritz Pino, eds. *Diasporic Intimacies: Queer Filipinos and Canadian Imaginaries.* Evanston, IL: Northwestern University Press, 2018.

Dobson, Kit, and Aine McGlynn. *Transnationalism, Activism, Art.* Toronto: University of Toronto Press, 2013.

Downey, Anthony. *Dissonant Archives: Contemporary Visual Culture and Contested Narratives in the Middle East.* London: I. B. Tauris, 2015.

———. *Uncommon Grounds: New Media and Critical Practice in the Middle East and North Africa.* London: I. B. Tauris, 2014.

Doyle, Jennifer. *Sex Objects: Art and the Dialectics of Desire.* Minneapolis: University of Minnesota Press 2006.

Dryden, OmiSoore H., and Suzanne Lenon. *Disrupting Queer Inclusion: Canadian Homonationalisms and the Politics of Belonging.* Vancouver: UBC Press, 2016.

Edelman, Lee. *No Future Queer Theory and the Death Drive.* Durham, NC: Duke University Press, 2007.

Eigner, Saeb, and Zaha Hadid. *Art of the Middle East: Modern and Contemporary Art of the Arab World and Iran.* London: Merrell, 2010.

Elkins, James, ed. *Is Art History Global?* Art Seminar; v. 3. New York: Routledge, 2007.

El-Rouayheb, Khaled. *Before Homosexuality in the Arab-Islamic World, 1500–1800.* Chicago: University of Chicago Press, 2005.

Eribon, Didier, and Michael Lucey. *Insult and the Making of the Gay Self.* Durham, NC: Duke University Press, 2004.

Farmanfarmaian, Abouali. "Fear of the Beard." *Transition* 67 (1995): 48–69.

Findley, Carter Vaughn. "An Ottoman Occidentalist in Europe: Ahmed Midhat Meets Madam Gülnar." *American Historical Review* 103, no. 1 (February 1998): 15-50.

Foucault, Michel. *The History of Sexuality: An Introduction.* Reissue edition. New York: Vintage, 1990.

———. *The History of Sexuality*, Vol. 2: *The Use of Pleasure.* Reissue edition. New York: Vintage, 1990.

———. *The History of Sexuality*, Vol. 3: *The Care of the Self.* REP edition. Vintage, 1988.

Fournier, Lauren. *Autotheory as Feminist Practice in Art, Writing, and Criticism.* Cambridge: MIT Press, 2021.

———. "Sick Women, Sad Girls, and Selfie Theory: Autotheory as Contemporary Feminist Practice." *A/b: Auto/Biography Studies* 33, no. 3 (2018): 641–42.

Freitag, Ulrike, and Achim von Oppen. *Translocality: The Study of Globalising Processes from a Southern Perspective.* Leiden, The Netherlands: Brill, 2010.

Gagnon, John H. *Human Sexualities.* Glenview, IL: Scott Foresman, 1997.

Gagnon, John H., and William Simon. "Sexual Scripts." *Sexual Conduct: The Social Sources of Human Sexuality.* London: Aldine Publishers, 1973.

Gartlan, Luke. “Dandies on the Pyramids: Photography and German-Speaking Artists in Cairo.” In Behdad and Gartlan, *Photography's Orientalism*, 129–52.

Gatward, Cevizli A. “Bellini, Bronze, and Bombards: Sultan Mehmed II's Requests Reconsidered.” *Renaissance Studies* 28, no. 5 (2014): 748–65.

Gayed, Andrew. “The Exilic Aesthetic: Articulations of Patriotism by the Expatriate.” *Persona Journal, the Department of Theatre and Film Arts at the Superior School of Art in Portugal*. Experiments and Displacements, Vol. 2, no. 1 (2014): 37–54.

———. “Islamicate Sexualities: The Artworks of Ebrin Bagheri.” *Esse Arts + Opinions*, Special Issue, *LGBTQIA* 91 (2017): 16–25.

———. “Nationalism, Migration, and Exile: The Photographs of Youssef Nabil.” MA Diss., Carleton University, Ottawa, Ontario, April 2016.

———. “Queering Middle Eastern Contemporary Art and Its Diaspora.” In *Unsettling Colonial Modernity: Islamicate Contexts in Focus*, edited by Siavash Saffari, Roxana Akhbari, Kara Abdolmaleki, Evelyn Hamdon, 140–55. London: Cambridge Scholars Publishing, 2017.

Gayed, Andrew, and Siobhan Angus. “Visual Pedagogies: Decolonizing and Decentering the History of Photography.” *Studies in Art Education* 59, no. 3 (2018): 228–42.

Georgis, Dina. *The Better Story: Queer Affects from the Middle East*. Albany: State University of New York Press, 2013.

Ghaziani, Amin, and Matt Brim. *Imagining Queer Methods*. New York: New York University Press, 2019.

Gilreath, Shannon. *The End of Straight Supremacy*. Cambridge, UK: Cambridge University Press, 2011.

Gilroy, Paul. *The Black Atlantic: Modernity and Double Consciousness*. Cambridge, MA: Harvard University Press, 1993.

———. “Diaspora and the Detours of Identity.” In *Identity and Difference*, edited by Kathryn Woodward. London: Sage, 1999.

Gopinath, Gayatri. *Impossible Desires: Queer Diasporas and South Asian Public Cultures*. Durham, NC: Duke University Press, 2005.

———. “Queer Visual Excavations: Akram Zaatari, Hashem El Madani, and the Reframing of History in Lebanon.” *Journal of Middle East Women's Studies* 13, no. 2 (2017): 326–36.

———. *Unruly Visions: The Aesthetic Practices of Queer Diaspora*. Durham, NC: Duke University Press, 2018.

———. “Who's Your Daddy?: Queer Diasporic Framings of the Region.” In *The Sun Never Sets: South Asian Migrants in an Age of U.S. Power*, edited by Vivek Bald, Miabi Chatterji, Sujani Reddy, and Vijay Prashad. New York: New York University Press, 2013.

Greensmith, Cameron, and Sulaimon Giwa. “Challenging Settler Colonialism in Contemporary Queer Politics: Settler Homonationalism, Pride Toronto, and Two-Spirit

Subjectivities." *American Indian Culture and Research Journal* 37, no. 2 (2013): 129–48.

Habib, Samar. *Female Homosexuality in the Middle East: Histories and Representations*. New York: Routledge, 2009.

———. *Islam and Homosexuality*. 2 vols. Santa Barbara, CA: Praeger, 2010.

Hadeed, Khalid. "Homosexuality and Epistemic Closure in Modern Arabic Literature." *International Journal of Middle East Studies* 45, no. 2 (2013): 271–91.

Halberstam, Jack. *In a Queer Time and Place: Transgender Bodies, Subcultural Lives*. New York: New York University Press, 2005.

Hall, Stuart. "The West and the Rest: Discourse and Power." In *Modernity: An Introduction to Modern Societies*, edited by Stuart Hall, David Held, Don Hubert, and Kenneth Thompson, 184-227. Oxford, UK: Blackwell Publishers, 1996.

Hammarén, Nils, and Thomas Johansson. "Homosociality: In Between Power and Intimacy." *SAGE Open* 4, no. 1 (2014): 1–11.

Hammoud-Beckett, Sekneh. "Azima Ila Hayati: An Invitation in to My Life: Narrative Conversations about Sexual Identity." *International Journal of Narrative Therapy and Community Work* 2007, no. 1 (2007): 29–39.

Hannavy, John. *Encyclopedia of Nineteenth-Century Photography*. New York: Routledge, 2008.

Henneberg, Susan. *LGBT Rights*. New York: Greenhaven, 2016.

Hennen, Peter. "Bear Bodies, Bear Masculinity: Recuperation, Resistance, or Retreat?" *Gender and Society* 19, no. 1 (2005): 25–43.

Hodgson, Marshall G. S. *The Venture of Islam: Conscience and History in a World Civilization*. Chicago: University of Chicago Press, 1974.

———. *The Venture of Islam*. Vol. 1: *The Classical Age of Islam*. Chicago: University of Chicago Press, 1977.

———. *The Venture of Islam*. Vol. 2: *The Expansion of Islam in the Middle Periods*. Chicago: University of Chicago Press, 1977.

———. *The Venture of Islam*. Vol. 3: *The Gunpowder Empires and Modern Times*. Chicago: University of Chicago Press, 1977.

Hoffman, Martin. *Empathy and Moral Development: Implications for Caring and Justice*. New York: Cambridge University Press, 2000.

Holland, Sharon Patricia. *The Erotic Life of Racism*. Durham, NC: Duke University Press, 2012.

Human Rights Watch. *In a Time of Torture: The Assault on Justice in Egypt's Crackdown on Homosexual Conduct*. New York: Human Rights Watch, 2004.

Iskin, R. E. *Re-envisioning the Contemporary Art Canon: Perspectives in a Global World*. London: Routledge, 2017.

Jackman, Michael Connors, and Nishant Upadhyay. "Pinkwashing Israel, Whitewashing Canada: Queer (Settler) Politics and Indigenous Colonization in Canada." *WSQ: Women's Studies Quarterly* 42, no. 3–4 (2014): 195–210.

Jacob, Wilson Chacko. "The Middle East: Global, Postcolonial, Regional, and Queer." *International Journal of Middle East Studies* 45, no. 2 (2013): 347–49.

———. *Working Out Egypt: Effendi Masculinity and Subject Formation in Colonial Modernity, 1870–1940*. Durham, NC: Duke University Press, 2011.

Jamal, Amaney A., and Nadine Christine Naber. *Race and Arab Americans Before and After 9/11: From Invisible Citizens to Visible Subjects*. Syracuse, NY: Syracuse University Press, 2008.

Jansen, Gregor and Robert Klanten. *Art and Agenda: Political Art and Activism*. Berlin: Gestalten, 2012.

Jones, Amelia, and Erin Silver. *Otherwise: Imagining Queer Feminist Art Histories*. Manchester, UK: Manchester University Press, 2016.

Kapadia, Ronak K. *Insurgent Aesthetics. Security and the Queer Life of the Forever War*. Durham, NC: Duke University Press, 2019.

Kaplan E. Ann. "Global Trauma and Public Feelings: Viewing Images of Catastrophe." *Consumption Markets & Culture* 11, no. 1 (2008): 3–24.

Karnouk, Liliane. *Modern Egyptian Art: 1910–2003*. Cairo, Egypt: The American University in Cairo Press, 2005.

Khalaf, Samir, and John H. Gagnon. *Sexuality in the Arab World*. London: Saqi, 2006.

Kholeif, Omar, and Candy Stobbs. *Imperfect Chronology: Arab Art from the Modern to the Contemporary: Works from the Barjeel Art Foundation*. New York: Prestel, 2015.

Khullar, Sonal. *Worldly Affiliations: Artistic Practice, National Identity, and Modernism in India, 1930–1990*. Oakland: University of California Press, 2015.

Kugle, Scott. *Homosexuality in Islam: Critical Reflection on Gay, Lesbian, and Transgender Muslims*. Oxford, UK: Oneworld, 2010.

———. *Living Out Islam: Voices of Gay, Lesbian, and Transgender Muslims*. New York: New York University Press, 2014.

Lavrin, Asuncion, ed., *Sexuality and Marriage in Colonial Latin America*. Lincoln: University of Nebraska Press, 1989.

Lensson, Anneka, Sarah A. Rogers, and Nada M. Shabout. *Modern Art in the Arab World: Primary Documents*. New York: Museum of Modern Art, 2018.

Levitt, Peggy, and Markella Rutherford. "Move Over Mona Lisa: Just How Global Is Art History?" Lecture presented at the 107th annual meeting of the College Art Association, Los Angeles, February 2018

Lionnet, Françoise, and Shu-mei Shih, eds. *The Creolization of Theory*. Durham, NC: Duke University Press, 2011.

———. *Minor Transnationalism*. Durham, NC: Duke University Press, 2005.

Lord, Catherine, and Richard Meyer. *Art and Queer Culture*. London: Phaidon, 2013.

Lowe, Lisa. *The Intimacies of Four Continents*. Durham, NC: Duke University Press, 2015.

MacCarthy, Fiona. *Byron: Life and Legend*. London: John Murray Publishers, 2002.

Manalansan, Martin F. *Global Divas: Filipino Gay Men in the Diaspora*. Durham, NC: Duke University Press, 2003.

Manalansan, Martin. "In the Shadow of Stonewall: Examining Gay Transnational Politics and the Diasporic Dilemma." *GLQ* 2, no. 4 (1995): 425–38.

Massad, Joseph Andoni. *Desiring Arabs*. Chicago: University of Chicago Press, 2007.

———. "Re-Orienting Desire: The Gay International and the Arab World." *Public Culture* 14 (2002): 361–85.

McCormack, Donna. *Queer Postcolonial Narratives and the Ethics of Witnessing*. New York: Bloomsbury Academic, 2014.

McCormick, Jared. "Hairy Chest, Will Travel: Tourism, Identity, and Sexuality in the Levant." *Journal of Middle East Women's Studies* 7, no. 3 (2011): 71–97.

Merabet, Sofian. *Queer Beirut*. Reprint ed. Austin: University of Texas Press, 2015.

Mercer, Kobena. *Cosmopolitan Modernisms*. Cambridge: MIT Press, 2005.

Mignolo, Walter. *The Darker Side of Western Modernity: Global Futures, Decolonial Options*. Durham, NC: Duke University Press, 2011.

———. "Foreword: Decolonial Body-Geo-Politics at Large." In *Decolonizing Sexualities: Transnational Perspectives, Critical Interventions*, edited by Sandeep Bakshi, Suhraiya Jivraj, and Silvia Posocco. Oxford, UK: Counterpress, 2016.

———. *Local Histories/Global Designs: Coloniality Subaltern Knowledges and Border Thinking*. Princeton, NJ: Princeton University Press 2012.

———. "On Comparison: Who Is Comparing What and Why?" In *Comparison: Theories, Approaches, Uses*, edited by Rita Felski and Susan Friedman. Baltimore: Johns Hopkins University Press, 2013.

Mignolo, Walter D., and Catherine E. Walsh. *On Decoloniality: Concepts, Analytics, Praxis*. Durham, NC: Duke University Press, 2018.

Mikdadi, Salwa, and Nada M. Shabout. Introduction to *New Vision: Arab Contemporary Art in the 21st Century*, 8–14. London: TransGlobe Publishing, 2011.

Mikdashi, Maya. "Queering Citizenship, Queering Middle East Studies." *International Journal of Middle East Studies* 45 (2013): 350–52.

Mitter, Partha. "Interventions–Decentering Modernism: Art History and Avant-Garde Art from the Periphery." *Art Bulletin* 90, no. 4 (2008): 531.

Morgensen, Scott Lauria. "The Biopolitics of Settler Colonialism: Right Here, Right Now." *Settler Colonial Studies* 1, no. 1 (2011): 52–76.

———. "Queer Settler Colonialism in Canada and Israel: Articulating Two-Spirit and Palestinian Queer Critiques." *Settler Colonial Studies* 2, no. 2 (2012): 167–90.

———. "Settler Homonationalism: Theorizing Settler Colonialism and Queer Modernities." *GLQ: Journal of Lesbian and Gay Studies* 1–2 (2010): 105–32.

Mouasher, Majida, and Kumar Jamdagni. *Modern and Contemporary Arab Art from the Levant*. Amsterdam: Schilt Publishing, 2016.

Moussawi, Ghassan. *Disruptive Situations: Fractal Orientalism and Queer Strategies in Beirut*. Philadelphia: Temple University Press, 2020.

Muller, Nat. "Contemporary Art in the Middle East." In Muller et al., *Contemporary Art in the Middle East*.

Muller, Nat, Lindsay Moore, T. J. Demos, and Suzanne Cotter. *Contemporary Art in the Middle East*. London: Black Dog, 2009.

Mulvey, Laura. "Visual Pleasure and Narrative Cinema." *Screen* 16, no. 3 (1975): 6–18.

Muñoz, José Esteban. *Cruising Utopia: The Then and There of Queer Futurity*. Sexual Cultures. New York: New York University Press, 2009.

———. *Disidentifications: Queers of Color and the Performance of Politics*. Cultural Studies of the Americas 2. Minneapolis: University of Minnesota Press, 1999.

Murray, Stephen O., and Will Roscoe. *Islamic Homosexualities: Culture, History, and Literature*. New York: New York University Press, 1997.

Naber, Nadine. "Decolonizing Culture: Beyond Orientalist and Anti-Orientalist Feminisms." In Abdulhadi, Alsultany, and Naber, *Arab and Arab American Feminisms*, 78–90.

Naber, Nadine Christine. *Arab America: Gender, Cultural Politics, and Activism*. New York: New York University Press, 2012.

Najmabadi, Afsaneh. "Mapping Transformations of Sex, Gender, and Sexuality in Modern Iran." *Social Analysis* 49 (2005): 52–76.

———. *Women with Mustaches and Men without Beards: Gender and Sexual Anxieties of Iranian Modernity*. Berkeley: University of California Press, 2005.

Nassar, Issam, Stephen Sheehi, and Salīm Tamārī. *Camera Palaestina: Photography and Displaced Histories of Palestine*. Oakland: University of California Press, 2022.

Nelson, Steven. "Conversation without Borders." In Casid and D'Souza, *Art History in the Wake of the Global Turn*, 79–87.

Nochlin, Linda. "The Imaginary Orient." *Art in America*. (1983): 119–31.

———. "Why Are There No Great Women Artists?" *Aesthetics* (1998): 314–23.

Oberhelman, Steven M. "Hierarchies of Gender, Ideology, and Power in Ancient and Medieval Greek and Arabic Dream Literature." In Wright and Rowson, *Homoeroticism in Classical Arabic Literature*, 55–93.

Onians, John. "World Art Studies and the Need for a New Natural History of Art." *Art Bulletin* 78, no. 2 (1996): 206–9.

Ouseley, William. *Travels in Various Countries of the East; More Particularly, Persia*. 3 Vols. London: Rodwell and Martin, 1823.

Parker, Rozsika, and Griselda Pollock. *Old Mistresses: Women, Art and Ideology*. London: I. B. Tauris, 2013.

Patel, Alpesh Kantilal. *Productive Failure: Writing Queer Transnational South Asian Art Histories*. Manchester, UK: Manchester University Press, 2017.

Patil, Vrushali. *Webbed Connectivities: The Imperial Sociology of Sex, Gender, and Sexuality*. Minneapolis: University of Minnesota Press, 2022.

Pérez, Hiram. *A Taste for Brown Bodies: Gay Modernity and Cosmopolitan Desire*. New York: New York University Press, 2015.

Perez, Nissan N. *Focus East: Early Photography in the Near East 1839–1885*. New York: Harry N. Abrams, 1988.

Piotrowski, Piotr. "On the Spatial Turn, or Horizontal Art History." *Umění / Art* 56, no. 5 (2008): 378–83.

Piotrowski, Piotr. "Toward a Horizontal History of the European Avant-Garde." In *Europa! Europa? The Avant-Garde, Modernism, and the Fate of a Continent*, edited by Sascha Bru, Jan Baetens, Benedikt Hjartarson, Peter Nicholls, Tania Ørum, and Hubert van den Berg, 49–58. European Avant-Garde and Modernism Studies, Vol 1. Berlin: Walter de Gruyter, 2009.

———. "Towards Horizontal Art History." *Crossing Cultures*. Ed. Jaynie Anderson. *Comité International d'Histoire de l'Art, CIHA*. (2009): 82–85.

Pixley, Mary L. "Islamic Artifacts and Cultural Currents in the Art of Carpaccio." *Apollo* 158, no. 501 (November 2003): 9–18.

Pollard, Lisa. *Nurturing the Nation: The Family Politics of Modernizing, Colonizing and Liberating Egypt 1805/1923*. Berkeley: University of California Press, 2005.

Pollock, Griselda. "Women, Art, and Ideology: Questions for Feminist Art Historians." *Woman's Art Journal* (1983): 39–47.

Pratt, Mary L. "Arts of the Contact Zone." *Profession* (1991): 33–40.

Pratt, Mary Louise. *Imperial Eyes: Travel Writing and Transculturation*. London: Routledge, 1992.

Provencher, Denis M. *Queer Maghrebi French: Language, Temporalities, Transfiliations*. Oxford, UK: Liverpool University Press, 2017.

Puar, Jasbir. "Rethinking Homonationalism." *International Journal of Middle East Studies* 45 (2013): 336–39.

———. *Terrorist Assemblages: Homonationalism in Queer Times*. Durham, NC: Duke University Press, 2007.

Rafael, Vincente. *Contracting Colonialism*. Ithaca, NY: Cornell University Press, 1988.

Rahman, Momin. *Homosexualities, Muslim Cultures, and Modernity*. Basingstoke: Palgrave Macmillan, 2014.

———. "Queer as Intersectionality: Theorizing Gay Muslim Identities." *Sociology* 44 (2010): 944–61.

Rahman, Momin, and Stevi Jackson. *Gender and Sexuality: Sociological Approaches*. Cambridge, UK: Polity Press, 2010.

Ramadan, Dina. "The Aesthetics of the Modern: Art, Education, and Taste in Egypt 1903–1952." PhD diss. Columbia University, Graduate School of Arts and Sciences, 2013.

Rasti, Laurence. *There Are No Homosexuals in Iran*. Zürich: Edition Patrick Frey, 2017.

Razack, Sherene. *Casting Out: The Eviction of Muslims from Western Law and Politics*. Toronto: University of Toronto Press, 2008.

Ritchie, Jason. "How Do You Say 'Come Out of the Closet' in Arabic? Queer Activism and the Politics of Visibility in Israel-Palestine." *GLQ* 16, no. 4 (2010): 557–75.

Ritter, Markus, and Staci Gem Scheiwiller, eds. *The Indigenous Lens: Early Photography in the Near and Middle East*. Berlin: Walter De Gruyter, 2017.

Rogers, Sarah. "Imagined Geographies: Diaspora and Contemporary Arab Art." In *New Vision: Arab Contemporary Art in the 21st Century*, 36–46. London: Trans-Globe Publishing, 2011.

Rogers, Sarah A., and Eline van der Vlist, eds. *Arab Art Histories: The Khalid Shoman Collection*. Amman, Jordan: Khalid Shoman Foundation, 2013.

Rowson, Everett K. "Two Homoerotic Narratives from Mamluk Literature: Al-Safadi's Law at al-shaki and Ibn Daniyal's al-Mutayyam." In Rowson and Wright, *Homoeroticism in Classical Arabic Literature*, 158–91.

Rowson, Everett, and J. W. Wright. *Homoeroticism in Classical Arabic Literature*. New York: Columbia University Press, 1997.

Saffari, Siavash, Roxana Akhbari, Kara Abdolmaleki, and Evelyn L. Hamdon. *Unsettling Colonial Modernity in Islamicate Contexts*. Newcastle, UK: Cambridge Scholars Publishing, 2017.

Safran, William. "Diasporas in Modern Societies: Myths of Homeland and Return." *Diaspora: A Journal of Transnational Studies* 1, no. 1 (1991): 83–99.

Said, Edward W. *Culture and Imperialism*. New York: Vintage, 1994.

———. *Orientalism*. New York: Vintage, 1979.

Saldívar-Hull, Sonia. *Feminism on the Border: Chicana Gender Politics and Literature*. Berkeley: University of California Press, 2000.

Savci, Evren. *Queer in Translation: Sexual Politics under Neoliberal Islam*. Durham, NC: Duke University Press, 2021.

Scheiwiller, Staci Gem. *Liminalities of Gender and Sexuality in Nineteenth-Century Iranian Photography: Desirous Bodies*. New York: Routledge, 2016.

Schmitt, Arno, and Jehoeda Sofer. *Sexuality and Eroticism among Males in Moslem Societies*. Binghamton, NY: Routledge, 1992.

Sedgwick, Eve. *Epistemology of the Closet*. Berkeley: University of California Press, 2008.

Semati, Mehdi. "Islamophobia, Culture, and Race in the Age of Empire." *Cultural Studies* 24, no. 2 (2010): 256–75.

Shabout, Nada M. "Contemporaneity Art in the Arab World." In Mikdadi and Shabout, *New Vision: Arab Contemporary Art in the 21st Century*.

———. *Modern Arab Art: Formation of Arab Aesthetics*. Gainesville: University Press of Florida, 2015.

Sheehi, Stephen. *The Arab Imago: A Social History of Portrait Photography, 1860–1910*. Princeton, NJ: Princeton University Press, 2016.

Shih, Shu-mei. "Comparison as Relation." In *Comparison: Theories, Approaches, Uses*, edited by Rita Felski and Susan Stanford Friedman, 79–98. Baltimore: Johns Hopkins University Press, 2013.

Siegrist, Hannes. "Comparative History of Cultures and Societies: From Cross-Societal Analysis to the Study of Intercultural Interdependencies." *Comparative Education* 42, no. 3 (2006): 377–404.

Silverblatt, Irene Marsha. *Modern Inquisitions: Peru and the Colonial Origins of the Civilized World*. Duke University Press 2004.

Smith, Andrea. *Conquest: Sexual Violence and American Indian Genocide*. Cambridge, MA: South End Press, 2005.

———. "Queer Theory and Native Studies: The Heteronormativity of Settler Colonialism." In *Queer Indigenous Studies: Critical Interventions in Theory, Politics, and Literature*, edited by Qwo-Li Driskill, Chris Finley, Brian Joseph Gilley, and Scott Lauria Morgensen, 43–65. Tucson: University of Arizona Press, 2011.

Somerville, Siobhan. "Feminism, Queer Theory, and the Racial Closet." *Criticism* 52, no. 2 (2010): 191–200.

Sontag, Susan. *Regarding the Pain of Others*. New York: Picador, 2004.

Spivak, Gayatri. "Can the Subaltern Speak?" In *Marxism and the Interpretation of Culture*, edited by Cary Nelson and Lawrence Grossberg. Urbana: University of Illinois Press, 1988.

———. *A Critique of Postcolonial Reason: Toward a History of the Vanishing Present*. Cambridge, MA: Harvard University Press, 1999.

Spivak, Gayatri Chakravorty. *An Aesthetic Education in the Era of Globalization*. Reprint ed. Cambridge, MA: Harvard University Press, 2013.

Stoler, Ann Laura. *Race and the Education of Desire: Foucault's History of Sexuality and the Colonial Order of Things*. Durham, NC: Duke University Press, 1995.

Tarik, Bereket, and Adam Barryd. "The Emergence of Gay Identities in Contemporary Turkey." *Sexualities* 9, no. 2 (2006): 131–51.

Tiampo, Ming. *Gutai: Decentering Modernism*. Chicago: University of Chicago Press, 2011.

———. "Transversal Articulations: Decolonial Modernism and the Slade School of Fine Art." In *Postwar–A Global Art History, ca. 1945-1965*, edited by Atreyee Gupta and Okwui Enwezor. Durham, NC: Duke University Press, Forthcoming 2023.

Tomii, Reiko. *Radicalism in the Wilderness: International Contemporaneity and 1960s Art in Japan*. Cambridge: MIT Press, 2016,

Trachtenberg, Alan, ed. *Classic Essays on Photography*. New Haven, CT: Leete's Island Books, 1980.

Traub, Valerie. "The Past Is a Foreign Country? The Times and Spaces of Islamicate Sexuality Studies." In Babayan and Najmabadi, *Islamicate Sexualities*, 1–40.

———. *Thinking Sex with the Early Moderns*. Philadelphia: University of Pennsylvania Press, 2016.

Tuck, Eve, and K. Wayne Yang. "Decolonization Is Not a Metaphor." *Decolonization: Indigeneity, Education, and Society* 1, no. 1 (2012): 1–40.

Vanj, Hamzić. "The Case of 'Queer Muslims': Sexual Orientation and Gender Identity in International Human Rights Law and Muslim Legal and Social Ethos." *Human Rights Law Review* 11 (2011): 237–74.

Vasari, Giorgio. *The Lives of the Most Excellent Painters, Sculptors, and Architects.* Trans. Gaston du C. de Vere. Ed. Philip Jacks. New York: Modern Library, 2005.

Vimalassery, Manu, Juliana Hu Pegues, and Alyosha Goldstein, "On Colonial Unknowing." *Theory and Event* 19, no. 4 (2016).

Walcott, Rinaldo. "Caribbean Pop Culture in Canada: Or, the Impossibility of Belonging to the Nation." *Small Axe* 5, no. 1 (2001): 123–39.

———. "The Homosexuals Have Arrived!" Foreword to Dryden and Lenon, *Disrupting Queer Inclusion.*

———. *Queer Returns: Essays on Multiculturalism, Diaspora and Black Studies.* London, Ont., Canada: Insomniac Press, 2016.

Watriss, Wendy, Karin Adrian von Roques, Samer Mohdad, Claude W. Sui, and Mona Khazindar. *View from Inside: Contemporary Arab Photography, Video and Mixed Media Art.* Houston: FotoFest, 2014.

Weber, Travis, and L. Lin. "Freedom of Conscience and New 'LGBT Rights' in International Human Rights Law." *Public Discourse: The Journal of the Witherspoon Institute*, March 31, 2016.

Whitaker, Brian. *Unspeakable Love: Gay and Lesbian Life in the Middle East.* Los Angeles: University of California Press, 2006.

Wright, J. W., and Everett K. Rowson, eds. *Homoeroticism in Classical Arabic Literature.* New York: Columbia University Press, 1997.

Ze'evi, Dror. *Producing Desire: Changing Sexual Discourse in the Ottoman Middle East, 1500–1900.* Berkeley: University of California Press, 2006.

Zijlmans, Kitty, and Wilfred van Damme. *World Art Studies: Exploring Concepts and Approaches.* Amsterdam: Valiz, 2008.

INDEX

Page numbers in *italics* refer to illustrations